Praise

"It's malpractice to not study this and Mark's book is the gold standard."

—John Romano, past president of the Florida Justice Association and editor of *Anatomy of a Personal Injury Lawsuit*

"Lawyers often—and wrongly—think of the federal rules as restraints. They are wrong to do so. When understood and prudently applied, the rules provide flexible, economical, and effective ways to marshal the facts and bring the law to bear on a contested case. A hard-litigated case is a real fight, but it's a structured fight. The rules provide the structure. Mark Kosieradzki shows you how Rule 30(b)(6) cuts through corporate or governmental fog. He teaches the steps you need to get to the facts and the people who know them. His book provides lawyers with powerful tools to build and win their cases."

—Judge James Rosenbaum, United States District Judge (Ret.), former Chief Judge of the District of Minnesota

"Mark Kosieradzki has taken the rather mundane 30(b)(6) corporate representative deposition and created one of the most important books for plaintiffs' lawyers in the last twenty years. Using Mark's techniques will bring you a treasure trove of information that the generic 30(b)(6) deposition and requests for production would never get."

—Paul Scoptur, author of *Advanced Depositions Strategy and Practice*, member of the American Society of Trial Consultants

"Mark Kosieradzki's book covers the law and strategy for dealing with every possible question about 30(b)(6) depositions. No matter how obstructive the opposition, this book gives you the path and the strategy to prevail."

—Phillip Miller, author of *Advanced Depositions Strategy and Practice*

"Mark Kosieradzki, an outstanding trial lawyer, wrote this book with his almost four decades of experience. This comprehensive and easily readable book combines illustrations, examples, and summaries; legal analysis of the nuances involved in the rule; and is supported by detailed authority."

—Mike Steenson, director of law review; Larry and Christine Bell Distinguished Professorship, Mitchell Hamline School of Law

"Mark Kosieradzki's new book not only reveals how to spell his last name, but also walks you through the entirety of 30(b)(6) depositions. He focuses on the technical basics and purposes of these essential depositions, and guides you to using them skillfully. If you're new at it, Mark's thorough book takes you from zero to sixty with extraordinary clarity. If you think you know all about 30(b)(6)s, Mark's book will still fill in gaps you don't even know you have. This is not just another strategy book; it is an essential primer of the technical skills that will help you maximize the benefits of a well-executed 30(b)(6)."

—David Ball, author of *David Ball on Damages*

"Tired of corporate defendants giving you the runaround and producing nothing useful in discovery? Mark Kosieradzki's book is the key to unlocking the vault where defendants hide the secret documents you need to win your case. This book is an invaluable resource you will use every time you do a 30(b)(6) deposition."

—Randi McGinn, author of *Changing Laws, Saving Lives* and president of the Inner Circle of Advocates

"This book allows every plaintiffs' lawyer in any state or jurisdiction to become an expert on taking corporate representatives' depositions. Stop the wild hunt for the right witness."

—Sach Oliver, member of the Arkansas Trial Lawyers Association

"Long before a presidential candidate told us, 'Corporations are people too,' the Federal Rules of Civil Procedure required corporations to testify through a single human voice. This rule blocks corporations from putting up a thicket of know-nothing witnesses who hide the corporation's knowledge behind 'not me.' The great weapon that is 30(b)(6) finally has a great explainer and brilliant teacher in Mark Kosieradzki. All advocates for people up against big entities owe heartfelt thanks to Mark for opening his toolbox to the rest of us."

—Patrick Malone, member of Inner Circle of Advocates, coauthor of *Rules of the Road*, and author of *The Fearless Cross-Examiner*

"When a party is an institution, discovering facts is often laced with obstruction, evasion, and frustration. Rule 30(b)(6) offers real assistance but only if well understood. Mark Kosieradzki's book provides an engaging, accessible, and thorough exploration of the rule and explains essential steps for using it. Mark's book will likely be seen as intended for plaintiffs' lawyers, but it offers insight for defense attorneys and would be a good read for law students too."

—David Walker, emeritus professor of law, former dean of Drake Law School

"For years, I have followed Mark Kosieradzki around the country to attend his presentations on 30(b)(6), eagerly awaiting the release of this book. His writing and teaching style are content-rich but accessible to even a novice attorney. A well-planned and well-executed 30(b)(6) can win a case, and the techniques I learned from Mark allowed me to take 30(b)(6) depositions at a skill level far beyond my years of practice and win my first civil jury trial. You could spend decades trying to harness the power of 30(b)(6) on your own, or you could read this book."

—Amanda Francis, board member of the Colorado Trial Lawyers Association, member of the Colorado Bar Association's Litigation Committee

"If your case involves a party with a name ending in 'Inc.,' 'Corp.,' 'PA,' 'LLC,' 'Partnership,' 'Trust,' 'Dept. of,' 'Gov't. of,' or if knowledge from any of these bears on your case, (virtually any case being litigated today), this book is pure gold. Kosieradzki's *30(b)(6)* is not only plainly written with straightforward advice, examples, and supporting case law, but a delight to read. I wish he had written it twenty-five years ago."

—Carl Bettinger, author of *Twelve Heroes, One Voice*

"Deposing a corporate representative is one of the most powerful tools available to a trial lawyer. Mark Kosieradzki's book is the owner's manual that shows you the correct way to use it. WARNING: Failure to Follow the Manual May Result in Serious Damage to Your Case!"

—Bob Pottroff, former president of the Kansas Association for Justice and former chair of the American Association for Justice Railroad Litigation Group

"Mark's book is an absolute must-read for every lawyer, whether a beginning trial lawyer or a seasoned practitioner who is undertaking a 30(b)(6) deposition. A brilliant work with something of value on virtually every page. A road map to success."

—Jim Bartimus, fellow of the International Academy of Trial Lawyers

"Far too many lawyers practice law using folklore. This book helps those of us who want to read and understand the rules. There aren't many silver bullets, but this book is one."

—John Taussig, co-chair of the Colorado Trial Lawyers Association Bad Faith seminar, graduate of the Spence Trial Lawyer's College

"Mark has spent twenty years developing a 30(b)(6) roadmap to make it easier and more efficient to use these depositions as part of our discovery. Anyone who deposes corporations, organizations, or the government should read this book."

—Steve Langer, past president of the Indiana Trial Lawyers Association

"Mark has taught me how to get documents that the defense would never produce. By speaking directly to the source, I have found boxes of unproduced documents and neutralized objections before the defense can utter them. They are helpless. I use these tools with every commercial defendant and have generated incredible results for my clients. I am forever indebted to Mark for teaching me how to be a 'Rebel with a Kos.'"

—Render Freeman, faculty member for the American Association for Justice and graduate of the Spence Trial Lawyer's College

"In over forty years of law practice, I've never read a better practice manual. Mark Kosieradzki has distilled decades of hard work and experience in this single volume. Build off Mark's experience and improve your results when litigating with corporate or governmental entities that want to play 'hide the ball.'"

—Ken Connor, trial lawyer with verdicts totaling over $200 million and has tried cases from Florida to California

"In *30(b)(6)*, Mark Kosieradzki provides a unique approach and a roadmap for truly fact-finding corporate and government depositions. Over more than thirty years, Mark has refined the art of the 30(b)(6) corporate representative deposition. His well-honed techniques will make you a better advocate for your clients. I have been eagerly waiting for this book."

—Julie Braman Kane, president of the American Association for Justice, past chair of the National College of Advocates

"Thorough, detailed, and comprehensively researched, this book reminds every lawyer that 30(b)(6) depositions are the overlooked and misunderstood gem of discovery. Kosieradzki opens his briefcase, hands you his notes, and then explains in detail exactly how to use them to defeat the enemy. Don't reinvent the wheel: Kosieradzki's wheel is better and already battle tested."

—Zoe Littlepage, member of the Inner Circle of Advocates and recipient of the American Association for Justice's Pursuit of Justice Award, 2015

"Canadians, don't be fooled by the title. American and Canadian discovery rules are the same. The computer systems that store documents in America are the same as those in Canada. I have been using Mark's techniques in Canada for years to get information I would never otherwise have uncovered."

—Robyn Wishart, practices across Canada specializing in spine and brain injury

"Practitioners have long recognized the power of a 30(b)(6) deposition. Even if the opposing party comes empty-handed, a well-taken 30(b)(6) deposition can lead to the discovery of dispositive facts. Mark Kosieradzki's work offers practical advice for ensuring that your 30(b)(6) deposition lives up to its potential."

—Andrew M. Pardieck, associate professor of law, Southern Illinois University School of Law

"In truck crash litigation, the 30(b)(6) deposition is one of the most potentially powerful weapons in the plaintiff lawyer's arsenal—but only if you issue notices, prepare for them, and take them properly. Mark has been the go-to authority on 30(b)(6) depositions for years and with this book he shares his innovative work with us all. Look out world."

—Joe Fried, founder of the Academy of Truck Accident Attorneys and faculty member of the Spence Trial Lawyer's College

"I've worked with Mark and seen first-hand the power of his techniques to force corporate defendants to answer questions they don't want to answer. This book is an excellent step-by-step guide so that you, too, can cut through the evasiveness of corporate wrongdoers. You need this book. Your clients need you to have this book."

—Deborah Nelson, past president of the Washington State Association for Justice

30(b)(6)
Deposing Corporations, Organizations, and the Government

Mark Kosieradzki

Trial Guides, LLC

30(b)(6): Deposing Corporations, Organizations, and the Government

Trial Guides, LLC, Portland, Oregon 97210

Copyright © 2016 by Mark Kosieradzki. All rights reserved.

TRIAL GUIDES and logo are registered trademarks of Trial Guides, LLC.

ISBN: 978-1-941007-54-9

Library of Congress Control Number: 2015956167

These materials, or any parts or portions thereof, may not be reproduced in any form, written or mechanical, or be programmed into any electronic storage or retrieval system without the express written permission of Trial Guides, LLC unless such copying is expressly permitted by federal copyright law. Please direct inquiries to:

Trial Guides, LLC
Attn: Permissions
2350 NW York Street
Portland, OR 97210
(800) 309-6845
www.trialguides.com

Editor: Tina Ricks
Production Editor: Travis Kremer
Interior Template Designer: Laura Lind Design
Interior Designer: Melissa Gifford
Cover Designer: Michael Fofrich
Copyeditor: Patricia Esposito
Proofreader: Molly K.B. Hunt
Indexer: Lucie Haskins

Printed and bound in the United States of America.
Printed on acid-free paper.

To my father, Henry, who taught us that, with initiative, all problems can be solved.

To my mother, Danuta, who taught us to be passionate about every moment of our lives.

Sto Lat!

Contents

Acknowledgments..................................... xxii
Publisher's Note xix
Introduction..1

1. Deposing Organizations........................5
   Introduction 7
   Learning about 30(b)(6) 8
   Deposing Organizations in State Courts 10
   The Steps of Rule 30(b)(6).....................11
   Summary..14

2. Building a Record.............................17
   Introduction 19
   Set Up the Legal Framework 19
   Lock Down Facts................................20
   Establish Standards of Conduct.................22
   Establish Motive 24
   Neutralize Defenses 25
   Summary 27

3. Details of Rule 30(b)(6): Deposing
   Organizations by Issue Designation 29
   Introduction 31
   Rule 30(b)(6) by Issue Designation 31
   Depose Nonparties with Rule 30(b)(6) 37
   Subpoenas Are Issued by the Presiding Court ...41
   Location of a Nonparty 30(b)(6) Deposition.....42
   Objections to Nonparty Subpoenas 45
   You Can Depose Noncorporate
     Organizations with 30(b)(6)..................48
   Depose Government Entities with 30(b)(6).......54

  Depose Foreign Organizations with 30(b)(6). 55
  Summary. 55

4.   RULE 30(b)(6) LOGISTICS: LOCATION,
 DURATION, AND NUMBER OF DEPOSITIONS. 57
  Introduction 59
  Sequence of Depositions 59
  Location of a Party Deposition 61
  Location of a Nonparty Deposition 64
  Multiple Witnesses for a Single 30(b)(6) Notice. 65
  Multiple 30(b)(6) Notices 68
  Designee v. Individual Depositions 72
  Video Depositions. 76
  Summary. 79

5.   DEPOSING OFFICERS, DIRECTORS, AND MANAGING
 AGENTS: 30(b)(1) DEPOSITIONS 81
  Introduction 83
  A Managing Agent's Word
   Binds an Organization 84
  Where Do Depositions Take Place? 87
  Is Your Witness a Managing Agent? 88
  Former Officers, Directors,
   and Managing Agents. 93
  Deposing Executives 101
  Who Establishes that This
   Deposition Is Necessary?. 104
  30(b)(6): An Alternative to
   Deposing the Executive. .110
  Summary. 111

6.   DEPOSING LOW-LEVEL EMPLOYEES 113
  Introduction 115
  Informal Communication Employees 116
  Former Employees. 123
  Responsibilities During the Investigation. 126

Involuntary Representation .130
Summary. 134

7. CRAFTING THE 30(b)(6) NOTICE:
   THE REQUESTING PARTY'S DUTIES 135
   Introduction 137
   Reasonable Particularity
   and Painstaking Specificity 137
   Qualifiers. 142
   What Can You Ask in the
   Matters of Examination?. .145
   You Decide the Method of Discovery. 156
   Summary. 160

8. RULE 30(b)(6), RULE 30(b)(2), AND
   RULE 34 DOCUMENT DEPOSITIONS. 161
   Introduction 163
   Problems with Rule 34 Document Requests 163
   Combining Rules 30(b)(2), 30(b)(6),
   and 34 to Get Complete Responses
   to Document Requests 165
   Objections to Document Requests. 166
   What Is Possession, Custody, and Control? 172
   Produced Documents
   Must Be Organized. 174
   The Solution: Rule 30(b)(6), Rule 30(b)(2),
   and Rule 34 Document Deposition 175
   Rule 30(b)(2): Producing Documents on Time 180
   Rule 30(b)(6). 181
   Foundation Concerning the Document Search 184
   Preempt Improper Objections 202
   Duty to Supplement 203
   Summary. 204

9. ELECTRONIC DISCOVERY 207
   Introduction 209

  Technological Framework .210
  Understanding the Interplay of
   Discovery Rules for Tailoring Requests 212
  Overcoming Objections with
   Rule 30(b)(6) Depositions 221
  Email 30(b)(6) Testimony 227
  Overburdensome by Design .235
  Identifying Incomplete
   E-Discovery Using 30(b)(6) 236
  Requiring Witnesses to Interpret
   Data Dumps through 30(b)(6) 238
  Internal Database Report Capabilities 240
  Using 30(b)(6) to Prove Spoliation of ESI 241
  Summary. 243

10. DUTY TO ATTEND 245
  Introduction 247
  Duty to Appear 247
  Summary. 261

11. DUTY TO PREPARE. 263
  Introduction 265
  Duty to Designate 266
  Duty to Prepare. 272
  Privilege Waiver. 284
  Duty to Substitute a New Witness. 287
  Summary. 290

12. SCOPE OF INQUIRY. 291
  Introduction 293
  Limiting the Scope Is Not Allowed 293
  Scope of Inquiry Objections 298
  Instructions Not to Answer .299
  Summary. 300

13. Deposition Obstruction........................301
    Introduction 303
    Obstructive Deposition
       Tactics Are Prohibited....................305
    Conferring with Witnesses
       during Depositions 309
    Objections..................................314
    Sanctions...................................329
    Conclusion 334
    Summary....................................335
14. Motions to Compel and Sanctions..............337
    Introduction 339
    Motion to Compel Facts 339
    Motion to Exclude Different Testimony..........339
    Failure to Provide a Witness 340
    Delay Tactics 342
    Appearance with Inadequate
       or Unprepared Testimony 343
    Duty to Confer 347
    Expenses for Compelled Depositions............349
    Failure to Comply with an Order for
       Disclosure: Subsequent Sanctions..........352
    Summary....................................355
15. Binding Effect..............................357
    Introduction 359
    The Witness Does Not Have Information 363
    Summary....................................370
16. Changing the Testimony 373
    Introduction 375
    Sham Affidavit Rule 375
    Deposition Errata Sheet Changes 376
    Three Schools of Permissible Change...........380

  Inquiring into the Basis for
    the Errata Sheet Change 386
  Summary 389
17. USING 30(b)(6) TESTIMONY AT TRIAL 391
  Introduction 393
  The 30(b)(6) Witness Testifies
    Vicariously for the Organization. 394
  Attempts to Change the Story at Trial 404
  Motion *in Limine* 408
  Summary 410
EPILOGUE 413
APPENDIX A RULE 30(b)(6) IN FIFTY STATES. 415
APPENDIX B SAMPLE 30(b)(6) NOTICE 469
APPENDIX C DOCUMENT DEPOSITION NOTICE. 473
APPENDIX D RULE 30(b)(6) DEPOSITIONS FOR EMAIL 479
APPENDIX E CONTENTION 30(b)(6) DEPOSITION 487
APPENDIX F CORPORATE STRUCTURE 30(b)(6)
  DEPOSITION NOTICE. 491
INDEX. 497
ABOUT THE AUTHOR. 515

Acknowledgments

"No man is an island."[1] Without the insights of my friends and colleagues throughout the country, this book could not have happened. Seasoned lawyers have helped shape the strategies and techniques that I attempt to share in this book: my law partner Joel Smith; my friends and fellow trial lawyers, Phillip Miller and Paul Scoptur, authors of *Advanced Depositions Strategy and Practice*; David Ball, author of *David Ball on Damages* and *Reptile*; Carl Bettinger, author of *Twelve Heroes, One Voice*; David Wenner and Greg Cusimano, the creators of the Jury Bias Model, and Pat Malone, author of *Rules of the Road* and *The Fearless Cross-Examiner*; as well as all the countless great lawyers who contributed ideas to this project. Thank you.

A final thanks to two very gifted lawyers in our law firm, Kara Rahimi and Andrew Gross, as well as my law clerks, Courtney Baga, Christie Welsh, Laurie Thomas, and Sean Lanterman, who helped with legal research, writing, citations, and editing; and a final thanks to Taylor Burrows for her meticulous proofreading and commonsense insights. I don't think I would have finished this project if I'd had to do it all myself.

Everyone who reads this book needs to join me in thanking Tina Ricks, my editor, who relentlessly pushed me to work into the wee hours of the mornings to make some very dense material understandable. Final thanks to the Trial Guides team that made this book actually find its way onto paper: Patricia Esposito, our goalie and copyeditor; Lucie Haskins, who indexed 500 pages of complex material; Melissa Gifford, who designed the pages; Michael Fofrich, who designed a cover that told the story; Justin Kahn, who edited 850 footnotes; Molly Hunt, who proofed everything; and finally our production editor, Travis Kremer, for making it all happen.

---

1. John Donne, "Meditation XVII," in *Devotions upon Emergent Occasions* (1624).

Publisher's Note

This book is intended for practicing attorneys. It does not offer legal advice or take the place of consultation with an attorney who has appropriate expertise and experience.

Attorneys are strongly cautioned to evaluate information, ideas, and opinions set forth in this book in light of their own research, experience, and judgment. Readers should also consult applicable rules, regulations, procedures, cases, and statutes (including those issued after the publication date of this book), and make independent decisions about whether and how to apply such information, ideas, and opinions for particular cases.

Quotations from cases, pleadings, discovery, and other sources are for illustrative purposes only and may not be suitable for use in litigation in any particular case.

All individual and business names that appear in illustrative examples have been fictionalized, and any resemblance between these fictional names and real persons is strictly coincidental and unintentional. Real names are used only in reported cases for which citations are given in the footnotes. The publisher disclaims any liability or responsibility for loss or damages resulting from the use of this book or the information, ideas, and opinions contained in this book.

Citations and Secondary Materials

Annotations throughout this book quote or reference judicial opinions that may cite and rely on secondary materials to support the decision or point being made. For consistency, this book attempts to mirror the citation formatting of the secondary material used by the court at the time of the decision.

One should be aware that the current citation of the secondary sources, including the name of the text, the authors, the section numbers, and names of the sections may have changed since the time the court quoted or relied on the material.

If you plan on citing the sources used in this text, make sure that the case law is still current and that the citation formatting required by your jurisdiction is used.

As with any book relating to legal concepts, please be aware that the law may have changed.

Introduction

If strength were all, tiger would not fear scorpion.

—Charlie Chan[1]

For thirty-seven years, in state and federal courts, I have litigated and tried countless cases involving trucking collisions, motorcycle and car wrecks, medical malpractice, nursing home abuse, product liability, construction injuries, child abuse, contracts, and civil rights violations. When those cases involved corporate or institutional defendants, I was inevitably thrown into a world of litigation obstruction and evasion. The effort to identify the factual basis for positions that corporate adversaries asserted more often than not became a game of cat and mouse.

These defendants' answers to discovery were largely nonresponsive, evasive, and misleading. They littered their responses to written discovery with boilerplate objections and followed these

---

1. *Charlie Chan's Secret*, directed by Gordon Wiles (1936; 20th Century Fox).

objections with partial answers, subject to those objections. They delayed document production or provided incomplete documents. Witnesses purported to know nothing. With every effort to unearth the facts, the cost of litigation became more prohibitive. Corporate litigation seemed insurmountable. I dreaded every time I had to face a corporate defendant.

Like other lawyers, I had a vague understanding that under Federal Rule of Civil Procedure 30(b)(6), and the comparable rules in state courts, a corporation was supposed to designate someone to provide the information I requested. In theory, the rule was supposed to cut through the evasion. Like everyone else, I was frustrated because those depositions never worked! I talked to other lawyers to learn if I was doing something wrong. My experience was not solitary. The recurrent complaint was that the 30(b)(6) corporate witnesses were seldom prepared and the depositions were therefore ineffective.

I scoured the 30(b)(6) case law in search of a solution to my frustration when litigating with major corporate and governmental entities. What I discovered was that the Federal Rule of Civil Procedure 30(b)(6), *Deposition by Issue Designation*, was the most misunderstood and underused discovery weapon available to lawyers who face corporate and governmental adversaries. I learned that the rule can be devastating to those adversaries when we use it properly. The key was to figure out how to use the rule effectively.

Once I came to understand the legal framework, I discovered that harnessing the power of 30(b)(6) required much more than asking for substantive information. Because evasion has become an art form, not only did I need well-crafted 30(b)(6) notices to access the information, but I also needed to know how to ask the correct foundational questions to build a record that exposed the adversary's obstruction. I discovered that Rule 30(b)(6) is like jujitsu. The power comes from deflecting our adversary's obstructive conduct back on them.

By understanding the theoretical framework of Rule 30(b)(6) and then using the tools you will find in the book, you will be able to build a record to expose the evasion, to compel disclosure of critical information, and oftentimes to secure sanctions. Focused 30(b)(6) representative deposition notices and discovery strategies force these institutions to produce information at a fraction of the litigation cost. This book is a tool that will enable you to face Goliath without fear. It is a tool that will enable you to get the evidence you need to achieve fair settlements and to win at trial. The strategies and techniques discussed in this book can take your practice to a higher level. Good luck.

—MRK

1

Deposing Organizations

We're in a battle for our lives for things that really matter to us. There's a shell game going on like I've never seen before.

—Senator John Kerry[1]

Introduction. 7
Learning about 30(b)(6) 8
Deposing Organizations in State Courts. 10
The Steps of Rule 30(b)(6) 11
    Step 1: Figure Out Your Case. 11
    Step 2: Craft the 30(b)(6) Notice. 11
    Step 3: Serve the 30(b)(6) Notice and
        Start Maneuvering 12
    Step 4: Take the Deposition. 12
    Step 5: Write a Brief. 13

---

1. John Kerry (presentation, Massachusetts College of Liberal Arts, North Adams, MA, June 3, 2005).

Step 6: Depose Again and Lock Down............13
Step 7: Block Attempts to Alter Testimony 14
Step 8: Use 30(b)(6) Testimony in
   Summary Judgments or Trial 14
SUMMARY 14

Introduction

A great case needs great evidence. But you can't get great evidence if your opponent has it locked up. A well-crafted 30(b)(6) deposition unlocks the door.

Developing an effective 30(b)(6) deposition technique first requires that you understand the case law. Without a thorough understanding of the legal framework, it is impossible to execute an effective 30(b)(6) strategy. Although courts throughout the country have been deflecting obstructive 30(b)(6) witness tactics for decades, a significant percentage of the practicing bar continues to be unaware or misinformed about the law of 30(b)(6) depositions. To be an effective advocate, it is critical to understand the rules of engagement before the battles begin.

We need to understand the duties of both the requesting and responding parties; the rules controlling logistics, such as location, length, and number of depositions; the permissible scope of inquiry and what objections are appropriate; as well as the consequences of failing to produce the information requested. Therefore, at the outset, this book strives to arm you with a comprehensive legal framework of the law of 30(b)(6), Deposition by Issue Designation.

With an understanding of the established legal parameters, with the help of friends and colleagues throughout the country, I set out to develop, test, and then refine, through countless depositions, a disciplined methodology for harnessing the power of 30(b)(6). My colleagues and I learned that the power of the rule starts with knowing what you want and then crafting airtight 30(b)(6) deposition notices to ensure that the courts will enforce the rules. Then we developed the bulletproof foundational outlines to expose the evasive response to our deposition notices.

I have written this book to share what I have learned. The book is organized using a generally linear process of evaluating information sources from organizations, such as corporations, partnerships, or the government. Then the book shows how to develop a discovery plan to efficiently get the information you want using Rule 30(b)(6).

Learning about 30(b)(6)

This book has a two-fold design: you will both learn the law and find cases throughout the book that will arm you with the necessary legal principles for virtually any problem you face with 30(b)(6). However, you will need more than legal principles and oratory eloquence to prevail. You will also need a factual record. Courts apply established legal principles to a factual record. Therefore, throughout the book I share suggestions to develop the questioning technique necessary to build a factual record that supports your legal position.

Although the majority of the case law in this book involves corporate deponents, the principles I discuss in this book are not limited to corporations. Rather, this book explores techniques that you can apply to crafting depositions for all varieties of organizations and entities.

Getting information from an institutional adversary is challenging at best. It is literally not possible to take the deposition of a corporation or an organization; when an organization is involved, you must obtain the information you seek from actual people who are authorized to speak for the organization.[2] The challenge is to identify who in the organization has the case-critical information and whose testimony can bind the organization.

Large organizations seldom have a single repository of information. Individual witnesses typically do not have access to all information known to the organization. Often people within the organization provide conflicting testimony, and the witness may not have the authority to bind the party organization to a position.

Those challenges are compounded when, more often than not, the organization's defense strategy is to engage in a calculated course of litigation obstruction to prevent access to the information that the institution controls. Written discovery seldom yields fruitful

---

2. *United States v. Taylor*, 166 F.R.D. 356, 361 (M.D.N.C. 1996) (citing 8A Wright, Miller & Marcus, § 2103, at 30).

information. Attorneys make blanket objections to relevance and undue burden; documents that they produce and responses to questions are evasive and covered with objections, even though courts repeatedly hold that they are improper.[3] To uncover the truth, you must cut through the self-serving filters of what information a responding party chooses to disclose. As a result, depositions are the battleground where the vast majority of litigation actually takes place.[4]

Finding the appropriate people to depose becomes even more important when you are faced with rules or scheduling orders that limit the number of depositions allowed, such as the federal presumptive limit of ten depositions.[5] The first line of defense in any case involving institutional defendants is to limit the plaintiff's access to information. A common litigation strategy is to identify or proffer witnesses who are unable to provide the necessary information, and then to object to any depositions beyond the presumptive limit. Identifying the correct witnesses early in the litigation can avoid unnecessary and costly litigation.

The Federal Rules of Civil Procedure provide for two separate methods you may use to depose an organization. Rule (30)(b)(1) allows you to depose an organization through a *particular* officer, director, or managing agent of the organization.[6] Rule 30(b)(1) binds parties whose depositions you take through officers or

---

3. *Athridge v. Aetna Cas. & Sur. Co.*, 184 F.R.D. 181, 190 (D.D.C. 1998); *Walker v. American Radiographics, Inc.*, 2010 WL 5437254, at *1 (S.D. Fla. 2010); *Network Tallahassee, Inc. v. Embarq Corp.*, No. 4:10CV38-RH WCS, 2010 WL 4569897, *1 (N.D. Fla. Sept. 20, 2010).
4. *Hall v. Clifton Precision Tool*, 150 F.R.D. 525, 531 (E.D. Pa. 1993).
5. Fed. R. Civ. P. 30(2)(A)(i). The Rules Committee considered reducing the presumptive limit from ten depositions to five. However, in April 2014 the proposal was dropped in favor of education and more efficient use of discovery mechanisms, like those this book discusses and advocates for.
6. *Cadent Ltd. v. 3M Unitek Corp.*, 232 F.R.D. 625, 627 (C.D. Cal. 2005).

managing agents.[7] However, when gathering testimony using a Rule 30(b)(1) deposition, if the employee or member of the organization is not an officer or managing agent, that deposition represents the personal knowledge of the deponent and does not bind the organization.[8] Alternatively, Rule 30(b)(6) requires that the *organization designate and prepare people* to speak on its behalf regarding "matters" specified in the deposition notice.

Although both deposition methods bind the organization, there is an important conceptual distinction. A deposition you take under Rule 30(b)(1) is a deposition of a person and, therefore, represents the knowledge of that particular person; whereas, a deposition you take under Rule 30(b)(6) is conceptually the testimony of the organization itself and thereby represents the cumulative knowledge of the organization. This book explores both methods at length.

Deposing Organizations in State Courts

Depositions of institutional witnesses are not limited to litigation in the federal court system. Throughout the country, states have adopted rules for taking depositions of organizations. Many of those states have mirrored Federal Rule 30(b)(6) or have established procedures that accomplish the same goals sought by the federal courts. When the state rule is based on its federal counterpart, those states often interpret their state rule using the federal authority for guidance.

A detailed discussion of each state's interpretations of Rule 30(b)(6) is available in Appendix A.

---

7. *Rubin v. Gen. Tire & Rubber Co.*, 18 F.R.D. 51, 55 (S.D.N.Y. 1955) ("the Courts have inferred from Rule 37(d) that the deposition of a corporation that is a party may be taken through its officers or managing agents.").
8. *Progress Bulk Carriers v. Am. S.S. Owners Mut. Prot. & Indem. Ass'n, Inc.*, 939 F. Supp. 2d 422, 430 (S.D.N.Y. 2013) aff'd, No. 12 CIV. 264 ALC FM, 2014 WL 896739 (S.D.N.Y. Feb. 21, 2014).

The Steps of Rule 30(b)(6)

Following are the steps you are likely to encounter as you prepare for and conduct a Rule 30(b)(6) deposition. Keep in mind that you might not do all of these, and some may repeat. The steps might not all come in this order. Much of this depends on your opponent's decisions, and on the court's rulings. You could begin at Step 1 and then skip some of the intervening steps. But in general, here are the steps of a Rule 30(b)(6) deposition.

Step 1: Figure Out Your Case

The first step, which you can't skip under any circumstances, is figuring out your case. What exactly is it that you need to prove? What are the defenses likely to be, and how will you preempt them? I cover this to a certain extent in chapter 2, "Building a Record," but many other writers have covered this to a greater extent. I am a fan of these books:

- David Ball, *David Ball on Damages*, 3rd ed. (Portland, OR: Trial Guides, 2013)
- Rick Friedman and Patrick Malone, *Rules of the Road*, 2nd ed. (Portland, OR: Trial Guides, 2010)
- Neil Feigenson, *Legal Blame*, Revised ed. (American Psychological Association, 2001)
- Carl Bettinger, *Twelve Heroes, One Voice*, (Portland OR: Trial Guides, 2011)

What these books teach is that you need to know where you're going and how you're going to get there. Who is the villain in your case? What did they do? What are you trying to prove?

Step 2: Craft the 30(b)(6) Notice

Once you know what you're trying to accomplish, you craft the 30(b)(6) notice. How you craft the notice will have a direct impact on whether or not you will be able to compel the organization to provide the information you need to prevail at trial. Equally important is the ability to craft a deposition notice that will enable you to bind that organization to the positions they have taken. The book teaches you all the rules and the strategies you need to use those rules. Chapter 7, "Crafting the 30(b)(6) Notice" teaches you how to properly craft the notice. Chapter 8, "Rule 30(b)(6), Rule 30(b)(2), and Rule 34 Document Depositions," and chapter 9, "Electronic Discovery," teach you how to craft a notice for documents or electronically stored information.

Step 3: Serve the 30(b)(6) Notice and Start Maneuvering

Portions of this step may or may not happen. After you serve the 30(b)(6) notice, lawyers representing the organization may try to prevent you from taking your deposition or may try to limit your deposition in whatever way they can. There may be negotiations and motions for protective orders. Before you even begin a deposition, you may find yourself needing to write a brief in response to their motions for a protective order. This book provides the legal arguments and supporting cases for virtually every problem that you will encounter—with ready access to the cases to help you write that inevitable brief to compel the necessary testimony from the organization. The cases you will need for brief writing are all throughout the book.

Step 4: Take the Deposition

Once you have established the right to question the 30(b)(6) witness, you will often find yourself in the middle of a 30(b)(6) deposition where your witness is unprepared. They might not know the answers to questions that they should have known in order to respond to your deposition notice, or they will simply be outright evasive. You may also encounter lawyers representing those organizations who will attempt to obstruct you from asking the necessary questions to get the information you need. If you are faced with these problems, your job is to establish a record of how the organization and their witness didn't comply with the 30(b)(6) rules. In this book, you will learn about the responsibilities of the responding organization, the cases necessary for your brief, and how to craft questions to build a record to support your motion to compel additional testimony. Chapter 10, "Duty to Attend," and chapter 11, "Duty to Prepare," deal with the organization's responsibilities. Chapter 12, "Scope of Inquiry," and chapter 13, "Deposition Obstruction," deal with various types of obstruction, and chapter 14, "Motions to Compel and Sanctions," teaches you about the types of motions you may need to write.

In this book we talk about building a record. To fully build a record, you need to understand how to craft your questions. *Advanced Depositions Strategy and Practice* by Paul Scoptur and Phillip Miller (Portland, OR: Trial Guides, 2013) is the book I look to for structuring my questions to help me build the record I need to support my 30(b)(6) motion practice.

Step 5: Write a Brief

If the organization didn't designate a witness, or the witness was unprepared, or you face obstruction, you will need to bring a motion to compel. Once again you will need to write a brief, using the record you created in either your pre-deposition correspondence or in the deposition to show that the organization didn't follow Rule 30(b)(6). If you want the judge to rule in your favor, you have to not only spell out the organization's responsibilities, but also provide the court with a clear record of how they didn't follow the rules. As with other steps, this book includes the case law and the strategies you need to show how the organization's conduct is inappropriate. Throughout the book, you will find the law for virtually any issue that may come up.

Step 6: Depose Again and Lock Down

If the court orders the organization to provide a fully prepared witness, this additional testimony is your time to lock down your opponent's position for trial. Your job is to get a record that this is what there is—there is no other information your opponent can produce. You're building a record to bind the organization. Chapter 15, "Binding Effect," will show you how to build a solid record so the organization can't change their testimony.

Step 7: Block Attempts to Alter Testimony

There may be times when the organization attempts to change their testimony. This step may or may not happen. If you understand the law and you build an appropriate record, it will become difficult if not impossible for them to change their testimony or produce new information that they should have disclosed earlier. If you build a record as discussed in chapter 15, "Binding Effect," and if you understand the law of changing testimony in chapter 16, "Changing the Testimony," you can prevent organizations from changing their testimony according to the rules.

Step 8: Use 30(b)(6) Testimony in Summary Judgments or Trial

Once you have a killer 30(b)(6) transcript, you have to get that information in front of a jury. Chapter 17, "Using 30(b)(6) Testimony at Trial," will explain the evidentiary issues you need to understand to use your testimony at trial.

Summary

- Effective 30(b)(6) depositions require that you first understand your case.

- Rule 30(b)(6) depositions represent the institutional knowledge of the organization.

- Rule 30(b)(1) depositions of officers, directors, or managing agents represent the individual's knowledge (not the organization's knowledge).

- Rule 30(b)(6) requires that the organization designates and prepares a witness to speak on their behalf regarding the issues you've designated.

- Both Rule 30(b)(6) and Rule 30(b)(1) bind the organization.

- Almost every state has a rule which mirrors federal Rule 30(b)(6) and use federal law to interpret their state rules. Rule 30(b)(6) is not just about federal court.

2

Building a Record

Give me six hours to chop down a tree and I will spend the first four sharpening the axe.

—Abraham Lincoln

Introduction	19
Set Up the Legal Framework	19
Lock Down Facts	20
Establish Standards of Conduct	22
Establish Motive	24
Neutralize Defenses	25
Summary	27

Introduction

Before you can craft an effective strategy for deposing corporations or any other organization, you must understand the legal framework for your case. You need to know precisely what you must prove and what defenses you must redress before you take a single deposition. With a clear understanding of the legal framework of the litigation, you can develop a discovery plan to not only lock down the facts necessary to prove your case, but also establish motive and neutralize the anticipated defenses.

Set Up the Legal Framework

The simplest place to start your preparation is to review the jury instructions that apply to your case. The instructions identify the elements of the *prima facie* case. The instructions, however, are merely the starting point. The case law that provides the basis for those instructions will reveal the issues that you must anticipate when attempting to prove claims or defenses at trial. With an understanding of the *prima facie* case and the associated issues, you will then be able to identify what facts you need to establish the elements you require to defeat a summary judgment motion, and you will be able to lock down those facts through depositions.

Institutions defend their cases by limiting access to information and then narrowing issues with summary judgment motions by asserting that there is no factual basis for a claim. Do not assume that facts are established or that they will be developed at trial. Courtrooms throughout the country are littered with cases where lawyers thought the case facts would come out at trial but found instead that they were dismissed by summary judgment. If case critical facts are not in a deposition transcript, expect a summary judgment motion claiming that there is no factual basis for your claim.

Lock Down Facts

Although lawsuits often involve factual disputes, not all facts are in dispute. In addition to helping you gather information and identify what facts your opponent will refute, depositions can help you identify what facts are missing from your trial story and, finally, what facts are *un*disputed. The goals of your depositions are not only to discover facts, but also to verify facts and lock down your adversary's positions on known facts. Using the legal framework and the techniques detailed in this book, you will be able to compel corporate or other institutional adversaries to specify what factual position they will advance at trial.

By taking control of depositions from the outset, you will establish a clear record of case critical facts, enabling you to eliminate defenses and allowing you to strategically bring forth your own summary judgment motions. If you know what you are looking for, you will know what to ask. *The goal must always be to establish a factual record.* For detailed guidance on structuring questions to lock down that record, see Phillip Miller and Paul Scoptur, *Advanced Depositions Strategy and Practice* (Portland, OR: Trial Guides, 2013), the premier guide on deposition technique.

Jurors tend to believe that attorneys will promote the contentions, evidence, and arguments that best advance their case. As a result, jurors discount the self-serving evidence a party offers voluntarily and place greater weight on evidence the adversary develops through cross-examination.[1] Therefore, the most persuasive evidence for your case will come from the information you develop through your adversaries' depositions. Rule 30(b)(6) depositions enable you to prove your case against a corporation, government agency, or organization through their own witnesses. Establishing facts through your adversaries highlights the factual dispute and narrows the debate to the significance of the established conduct.

---

1. Robert H. Klonoff and Paul L. Colby, *Sponsorship Strategy: Evidentiary Tactics for Winning Jury Trials* (Lexis Law Pub., 1990).

Example: Minnow Cove Resort

For example, you represent Mary who was injured when she fell down the stairs at a cabin at Minnow Cove Resort. Minnow Cove is a small fishing resort in Northern Minnesota. It is a small family-run business structured as a corporation. It has a single shareholder, Bob Sanderson. He is the only officer in the corporation.

You must establish that the resort owner did not maintain the cabins in a reasonably safe manner. The post-injury investigation revealed that the stairs did not comply with the building codes. You have learned from your legal research that if the stairs were built before 2008, the building code would not be applicable. Therefore, you must establish when the stairs were built. Without that information, you will not be able to defend against the opponent's motion to exclude the use of the code violations in your case. By asking a managing agent, in this case Bob Sanderson, the necessary questions, you can neutralize motions based on lack of a record.

Q: When were the stairs built?

A: It was part of a remodel project in 2009.

Q: What was the remodel project?

A: We put a second floor on the cabin.

Q: Who was the contractor?

A: We didn't use one.

Q: Who did the construction?

A: I did.

Q: Who designed the stairs?

A: I did it.

Q: Did anyone help you design or build it?

A: I did all of it myself.

The questions seem simple, yet they are important to establish not only that the construction followed the effective date of the building code, but also that the managing agent of the corporation designed and built the stairs. You now have the sound bites necessary to establish that the building code does apply to this premises liability case.

Establish Standards of Conduct

The legal framework and the record of established facts will get you over the first hurdle of the lawsuit—summary judgment. Establishing a *prima facie* case alone, however, does not ensure that you will prevail at trial. At trial you must both convince and motivate the jury to find in your favor. Jurors' thinking will not be limited to the elements in their instructions. They will bring their life experiences to the deliberation room and evaluate not only the credibility of the evidence, but also the motives of the parties.[2]

When evaluating liability, jurors will apply the factual scenario they find most believable to the standards of conduct (rules) that our society requires to maintain order. Rick Friedman's and Pat Malone's excellent work *Rules of the Road* teaches us how to develop understandable rules prescribing conduct that the defendant cannot credibly dispute.[3] You can best learn the art of crafting rules by mastering the lessons in *Rules of the Road*. This book does not attempt to duplicate Friedman's and Malone's instruction on how to establish such rules. Rather, this book focuses on how to depose the institutional defendant, which among other things will provide the vehicle for that defendant to either endorse the rules or risk losing credibility. Just as establishing facts through the adversary's witness narrows the debate, so too does establishing standards of conduct (rules). As the chances for debate narrow, your chances of success increase.

---

2. Phillip H. Miller and Paul J. Scoptur, *Advanced Depositions Strategy and Practice* (Portland: Trial Guides, 2013).
3. Rick Friedman and Patrick A. Malone, *Rules of the Road: A Plaintiff Lawyer's Guide to Proving Liability*, 2nd ed. (Portland: Trial Guides, 2010).

Example: Minnow Cove Resort

Using our Minnow Cove example, you can establish the standard of conduct through the managing agent, Bob Sanderson:

Q: What are building codes?

A: When people build something, they have to go by certain codes.

Q: Are those codes important?

A: Yes.

Q: Why?

A: I suppose, for safety.

Q: Were you aware that the building codes were necessary for safety at the time that you built the stairs in Cabin 8?

A: Yes.

Q: Do you believe that people who build stairs for hospitality industries should follow the building codes?

A: Yes.

Q: You knew that when you built the stairs. Right?

A: Yes.

Q: Do you think if somebody chose to build a staircase in a resort without following the building codes, would that be reckless?

A: Yes, it would.

Establish Motive

Agreeing on the standards of acceptable behavior (rules) and agreeing on what happened are important starting points for developing the case, but they are not always sufficient. Once the case goes before the jury, the decision process is not limited to the strict legal elements of the case. Jurors are motivated by their personal values and views. The story you tell them must be about more than just *what* happened; it needs to be about *why* it happened. Jurors need to be *engaged* in the story. They must feel that they are part of something important. They will want to *resolve a conflict*, to right a wrong. To that end they need to know *why this happened*.[4]

Simply violating a rule is not motivating. "Accidents happen" is a common attitude among jurors. Many jurors refuse to find liability, regardless of the law, because they perceive the event as "just an accident." It is the defendant's decision to violate the rule that will motivate the jurors to find in your favor. A conscious decision is no longer an accident. It is a decision to harm someone. Knowledge and control drive liability verdicts.[5]

Every story needs a villain. Alleging abstractly that a corporation did something wrong can be legally sufficient to impose liability,[6] but may not be sufficient to persuade a jury. It is much harder to craft a trial story if the villain does not have a face because the jury will not know who made the decision to violate the rule. By identifying a person within that organization, you give the story a villain the jury can hold accountable. Therefore, it is important to use your corporate depositions to identify the villain within the organization: Who made the decision to violate an accepted standard of behavior that resulted in harm? With a villain, the jury will be motivated to act in a way that can right the wrong.

---

4. Phillip H. Miller and Paul J. Scoptur, *Advanced Depositions Strategy and Practice* (Portland: Trial Guides, 2013).
5. *Id.*
6. *Scampone v. Highland Park Care Ctr.*, LLC, 618 Pa. 363, 57 A.3d 582 (2012).

Example: Minnow Cove Resort

If we look to our Minnow Cove example, we need to evaluate why the building codes weren't followed:

Q: Did you know that there were building codes that dealt with stairs?

A: Yes.

Q: Did you use the building codes when you built the stairs?

A: No.

Q: Why not?

A: Because our county doesn't have a building inspector—they don't have a building code enforcer.

Bob Sanderson knew the building codes were for the safety of his customers, but he cut corners because he didn't think he would get caught. As a result, all of his customers were put at risk and Mary was harmed.

NEUTRALIZE DEFENSES

Success at trial requires much more than considering how you will win your case. It also requires considering all the ways you might lose your case. You will seldom find success if you are not prepared to respond to the *legal defenses* that your adversary will raise over the course of the litigation. Predicting the defenses you are likely to encounter requires strategic analysis and legal research. Because every case is different, there is no laundry list. However, here are some common legal defenses to consider: comparative fault, no duty, immunity, open and obvious defects, superseding cause, and other ways the defense undermines proximate cause. If you anticipate the defense, you can build a record to preempt the defense long before you face a motion or trial.

Example: Minnow Cove Resort

In our Minnow Cove case, you learned through your research that your client couldn't sue the property owner if the danger was open and obvious. Therefore, you must neutralize the defense through the company's managing agent.

Q: Do you understand that it is your responsibility to repair hazardous conditions on your business property?

A: Yes.

Q: Do you agree that reasonable business owners must not create dangerous conditions for their customers?

A: Sure.

Q: Did you consider the condition of the stairwell in Cabin 8 to be an open and obvious danger to your customers?

A: No.

With that sound bite, it will be impossible for the defense to bring a motion for summary judgment claiming the danger was open and obvious.

To preempt defenses effectively, you must also be prepared to respond with facts to evidentiary issues that the defense will raise. Again, there is no laundry list. The defense may attempt to limit the use of documents or physical evidence, claiming a lack of foundation or a break in the chain of custody. The defense may claim hearsay that will require you to provide a record establishing that the information you are providing falls within an exception to the hearsay rules. Often the counsel will debate the role of regulations or policies and procedures in establishing standards of care. The court might well exclude a regulation if you do not provide a record that clearly establishes that the standard of care requires the organization's employees to follow a specific regulation. In negligence *per se* cases, the record must establish that the regulation or law was intended for the benefit of a class of people that includes your client. The list is endless. Therefore, you must carefully analyze your case at the outset to forecast what issues your adversary will raise later on. If you anticipate what is coming, you can craft a plan to eliminate the evidentiary issues.

Ultimately, the court will resolve legal issues through motion practice. Therefore, it is critical that you build a factual record, through the deposition testimony, to satisfy the elements of your claim and to neutralize your adversary's position. Knowing the case law that applies to your client's suit enables you to strategically develop the deposition testimony that the court needs, to then allow the case to proceed to a jury verdict.

Summary

- Know the legal elements of your case.
- Anticipate legal defenses.
- Do not wait until trial to establish key facts and principles.
- Do not rely on written discovery to establish key facts and principles.
- Use depositions to lock down facts.
- Use depositions to establish rules.
- Use depositions to establish motive.
- Identify the villain.

3

Details of Rule 30(b)(6)
Deposing Organizations by Issue Designation

Cut to the chase.

—Hal Roach Sr.[1]

Introduction..................................31
Rule 30(b)(6) by Issue Designation 31
    What Rule 30(b)(6) Actually Says 32
    Rule 30(b)(6) Benefits Both Sides 33
    Rule 30(b)(6) Depositions Cannot
        Name Individuals 36
Depose Nonparties with Rule 30(b)(6) 37
Subpoenas Are Issued by the Presiding Court.........41
Location of a Nonparty 30(b)(6) Deposition 42
Objections to Nonparty Subpoenas 45

---

1. *Cut to the Chase!: The Charley Chase Collection* (Milestone Films, 2012), DVD.

Subpoenas for Documents and
    Testimony Are Separate....................47
YOU CAN DEPOSE NONCORPORATE
    ORGANIZATIONS WITH 30(b)(6)..................48
DEPOSE GOVERNMENT ENTITIES WITH 30(b)(6)...........54
DEPOSE FOREIGN ORGANIZATIONS WITH 30(b)(6) 55
SUMMARY 55

Introduction

In this chapter, I will discuss what Rule 30(b)(6) is, when it is appropriate to use a 30(b)(6) deposition, and how you can use 30(b)(6) with both institutional parties and organizations that are not parties to the litigation. Unlike taking testimony of specific people, depositions under Rule 30(b)(6) require organizations to designate people to provide information in response to designated issues. Under Federal Rule 30(b)(6), you can take designee depositions of both parties and nonparties, including local and international governments.[2] Because nonparty depositions fall under Rule 45, which governs subpoenas, this chapter will discuss the interrelationship between Rule 30(b)(6) and Rule 45. I will cover deposition location requirements, when and how objections must be made, and which court maintains jurisdiction over those objections.

Rule 30(b)(6) by Issue Designation

Depositions typically ask any given witnesses what they know. The problem in litigation involving corporations and organizations is that any given witness probably does not have the entire *institutional knowledge* of the corporation or organization. As a result, the individual person's testimony is often incomplete or conflicts with others' recollections within the institution. Conflicting testimonies make it impossible for you to know, until the time of trial, which version of the facts the organization will adopt. The solution lies in a special form of deposition: 30(b)(6) *depositions by issue designation*.[3] Depositions you conduct under Rule 30(b)(6) focus on *information you are seeking from the organization as a whole, rather than the knowledge of one person you are deposing.*

---

2. Some State Rules omit the right to use a subpoena for nonparties under their comparable rules—*see* Appendix A for a complete list of state rules for 30(b)(6).
3. *See, e.g., Great Am. Ins. Co. of N.Y. v. Vegas Constr. Co.*, 251 F.R.D. 534, 539 (D. Nev. 2008).

Example: ACME Trucking Co.

For example, you represent a client injured in a collision with a commercial truck owned by ACME Trucking Co. If you try to learn whether the company had conducted a background check on the driver of that commercial truck, Sam Bachelor, by taking the deposition of the company safety director, that person could tell you he doesn't remember what the results of any investigation revealed. However, if you create a notice for the 30(b)(6) deposition of ACME Trucking Co., requesting that they describe the company hiring protocols and the results of any background check of the involved driver, they are required to gather all of the information and provide it to you at the deposition. "I don't know" is no longer an option for the company.

With that sound bite, it will be impossible for the defense to bring a motion for summary judgment claiming the danger was open and obvious.

What Rule 30(b)(6) Actually Says

Rule 30(b)(6) is titled "Notice or Subpoena Directed to an Organization" and reads as follows:

> In its notice or subpoena, a party may name as the deponent a public or private corporation, a partnership, an association, a governmental agency, or other entity and must describe with reasonable particularity the matters for examination. The named organization must then designate one or more officers, directors, or managing agents, or designate other persons who consent to testify on its behalf; and it may set out the matters on which each person designated will testify. A subpoena must advise a nonparty organization of its duty to make this designation. The persons designated must testify about information known or reasonably available

to the organization. This paragraph (6) does not preclude a deposition by any other procedure allowed by these rules.[4]

Once you properly invoke Rule 30(b)(6), the responding organization must designate and prepare one or more people to testify on its behalf about the topics that you, as the requesting party, identify. The responding party has notice and the opportunity to prepare, and so the responding party is then bound by its designated representatives' testimony.[5]

The purpose of the rule is to streamline the discovery process. Rather than forcing you as the requesting party to pursue an endless stream of witnesses to discover the information you need, Rule 30(b)(6) requires the responding organization to designate and prepare the witness for specific areas of inquiry before the deposition.

Rule 30(b)(6) Benefits Both Sides

Rule 30(b)(6) was intended to benefit both sides—the requesting party, as well as the responding party. The responding organization benefits by being able to control whom it wishes to designate and prepare to testify on its behalf.[6] This provides both practical and tactical benefits. For instance, if the person who possesses the requested knowledge in the organization is inarticulate or has a criminal history or is unavailable, the responding organization may designate and prepare a more desirable witness. Additionally, the responding organization can minimize the number of witnesses who will be deposed by sufficiently preparing its designated

---

4. Fed. R. Civ. P. 30(b)(6).
5. *Cadent Ltd v. 3M Unitek Corp.*, 232 F.R.D. 625, 628 (C.D. Cal. 2005) ("This means that under Rule 32(a), depositions of corporate officers under Rule 30(b)(1), as well as Rule 30(b)(6) depositions, may be used at trial against the corporate party.") (citing *Coletti v. Cudd Pressure Control*, 165 F.3d 767, 773 (10th Cir. 1999); *Crimm v. Missouri Pac. R.R. Co.*, 750 F.2d 703, 708–09 (8th Cir. 1984)).
6. *United States v. Taylor*, 166 F.R.D. 356, 360 (M.D.N.C. 1996).

witness. By controlling who will be deposed, the responding organization can reduce any potential disruption of its operations.

At the same time, 30(b)(6) benefits the requesting party. The rule is designed to avoid the *bandying* that occurs in organizations when the requesting party deposes officers or employees, but each witness claims not to know facts that someone in the organization clearly knows.[7] The purpose of 30(b)(6) depositions "is to curb any temptation by the corporation to shunt a discovering party from 'pillar to post' by presenting deponents who each disclaim knowledge of facts known to someone in the corporation."[8] "Without the rule, a corporation could hide behind the alleged failed memories of its employees."[9]

The advisory comments to the rule clearly set forth this cut-to-the-chase policy:

> [A] 30(b)(6) deposition more efficiently produces the most appropriate party for questioning, curbs the elusive behavior of corporate agents who, one after another, know nothing about the facts clearly available within the organization and suggest someone else has the requested knowledge, and reduces the number of depositions for which an organization's counsel must prepare agents and employees.[10]

In spite of the Rules of Civil Procedure's policies for sharing information, strategies to hide or skew the truth unfortunately

---

7. Fed. R. Civ. P. 30 advisory committee's note (1970 Amendments); *United States v. Taylor*, 166 F.R.D. 356, 361 (M.D.N.C. 1996); see also, *Great Am. Ins. Co. of New York v. Vegas Const. Co.*, 251 F.R.D. 534, 538 (D. Nev. 2008).
8. *Great Am. Ins. Co. of New York v. Vegas Const. Co.*, 251 F.R.D. 534, 539 (D. Nev. 2008) (citing *Federal Deposit Ins. Corp. v. Butcher*, 116 F.R.D. 196, 199 (E.D. Tenn. 1986)).
9. *QBE v. Jorda*, 277 F.R.D. 676, 688 (S.D. Fla. 2012) (citing *Ierardi v. Lorillard, Inc.*, No. 90–7049, 1991 WL 66799, *2 (E.D. Pa. Apr. 15, 1991)).
10. Fed. R. Civ. P. 30 advisory committee's note, Sub. (b)(6) (1970 Amendment).

continue to pervade modern litigation. Rule 30(b)(6) depositions enable you to discover information you need for trial by defeating the responding organization's shell game strategies to hide the ball.

The rule's effectiveness bears heavily upon the parties' reciprocal obligations. First, as the requesting party, you must reasonably define the subjects of your intended inquiry so that the responding organization can select and prepare the most suitable deponents. In turn, the responding organization, that now knows the specific areas of inquiry, must produce one or more deponents whom they have suitably prepared to respond to questioning within that scope of inquiry.[11] The ultimate goal is to streamline your ability to discover potentially relevant information.

Technique: Issuing a 30(b)(6) Notice

When issuing a notice of deposition under Rule 30(b)(6), rather than identifying a specific person to testify, the notice should read as follows:

```
Pursuant to Federal Rule of Civil
Procedure 30(b)(6), Big Box Stores is
required to designate and fully prepare
one or more officers, directors, managing
agents, or other persons who consent to
testify on behalf of Big Box Stores, and
whom Big Box Stores will fully prepare
to testify regarding all information that
is known or reasonably available to Big
Box Stores' organization regarding the
following designated matters:
```

---

11. *See, e.g.*, *Prokosch v. Catalina Lighting, Inc.*, 193 F.R.D. 633, 638 (D. Minn. 2000).

By requiring the responding organization to designate who will testify, the burden of producing the correct person shifts to that organization. As in jujitsu, this redirects the responsibility for any obstruction of information to the responding organization, because the court will hold the organization accountable for failing to produce the correct person.[12]

Rule 30(b)(6) Depositions Cannot Name Individuals

You can use Rule 30(b)(6) for deposing *entities* about specific issues. You cannot use Rule 30(b)(6) to require specific people to prepare to testify about specific issues. A 30(b)(6) deposition notice cannot name a person to answer the matters of examination. If you title a deposition notice as 30(b)(6), but you name a specific person as the deponent, that notice is deficient and your opponent can file a motion to quash it.[13] If your notice names specific people, even if they are officers, directors, or managing agents, then you must issue that as Rule 30(b)(1). A 30(b)(1) notice cannot include specific matters that you want to examine.[14]

The distinction between these two rules lies in the duty to prepare. Under both 30(b)(6) and 30(b)(1), the organization is bound by its officers' testimony. However, the organization is only required to prepare for the specific matters named in the 30(b)(6) notice. The individual person named in a 30(b)(1) notice is not required to prepare. Therefore, if you take testimony under 30(b)(1), the deponents are only required to testify as to their personal knowledge and are not required to prepare for any specific matters.

---

12. *See, e.g., Pioneer Drive, LLC v. Nissan Diesel America, Inc.*, 262 F.R.D. 552, 557–61 (D. Mont. 2009).
13. *Youell v. Grimes*, No. 00-2207-JWL, 2001 WL 1273260, *1 (D. Kan. Apr. 13, 2001).
14. *Id.* at *2.

Example: ACME Trucking Co.

For example, you may always take the 30(b)(1) deposition of our ACME Trucking Co. driver, Sam Bachelor, as an individually named deponent. However, if you name Sam Bachelor in your 30(b)(6) deposition notice, requesting that he be prepared to fully answer specific areas of examination, that deposition notice is defective on its face because Sam Bachelor is not an organization. Your opponent will always prevail on the motion to quash that deposition notice.

DEPOSE NONPARTIES WITH RULE 30(b)(6)

Federal Rule 30(b)(6) depositions are not restricted to parties in the lawsuit. In a given lawsuit, there may be organizations that are not parties in the lawsuit but that have knowledge you need for the lawsuit. For example, consider the following nonparties:

- A vendor that provided the training and training materials for a product that a party used.

- An accounting firm that has filed tax returns or regulatory compliance documents on behalf of a party.

- A subrogated insurance company or its collection agent who refuses to provide the basis of claims.

- An architectural firm that has blueprints of a property in a premises liability case.

- A contractor that provided a property inspection.

- A consulting firm that evaluated corporate operational systems.

- A hospital billing department that charged a patient for care under a negotiated reimbursement contract.

- An IT company responsible for a party's company computer systems.
- A real estate appraiser in a bad faith claim.
- A vehicle service company that inspected a vehicle before the collision.
- A risk management company that performed a previous industrial safety inspection.
- A security company that manages surveillance of a party's premises.

You may require a nonparty organization to provide Rule 30(b)(6) testimony by issuing a subpoena for that organization to testify.[15] The language of the rule is as follows:

> **Notice or Subpoena Directed to an Organization.**
> A subpoena shall advise a nonparty organization of its duty to make such a designation. The persons so designated shall testify as to matters known or reasonably available to the organization.[16]

When you request a nonparty's testimony, a subpoena replaces the 30(b)(6) notice. The advisory committee notes explain that "the subpoena, rather than a notice of examination, is served on a nonparty."[17]

---

15. *Price Waterhouse LLP v. First Am. Corp.*, 182 F.R.D. 56, 61 (S.D.N.Y. 1998). Some states omit this language from their rules. *See* Appendix A for a complete list of 30(b)(6) rules by state.
16. Fed. R. Civ. P. 30(b)(6).
17. Fed. R. Civ. P. 30(b)(6) advisory committee's note (1971 Amendment).

Details of Rule 30(b)(6) 39

The subpoena must meet the same requirements as the 30(b)(6) notice by stating the following:

- the named deponent organization
- the matters of examination
- the court that issued the subpoena
- the title of the action
- the civil-action number[18]

The subpoena must also advise the nonparty entity of its duty to designate a person as a witness and of the witness's duty to appear and testify at the specified time and place.[19]

While it has become common practice to attach a 30(b)(6) notice to a subpoena when you are requesting testimony of a nonparty organization, the rule requires that you list all of the 30(b)(6) notice requirements in the subpoena document itself.

Technique: Include Requirements in the Subpoena

In view the language of the rule, the best practice is to include the requirements of the 30(b)(6) in the body of the subpoena itself. For example,

```
Pursuant to Federal Rule of Civil Procedure
30(b)(6), you are hereby advised as a
nonparty organization of your duty to
designate one or more officers, directors,
or managing agents, or other persons who
consent to testify on your behalf and whom
```

---

18. Fed. R. Civ. P. 45(a)(1)(A).
19. Fed. R. Civ. P. 45(a)(1)(iii).

> Omnicare Pharmacy and Supply Services, LLC, will fully prepare to testify regarding the following designated matters and as to such information that is known or reasonably available to the organization:
>
> **MATTERS OF EXAMINATION**
>
> 1.
> 2.

If you need the nonparty 30(b)(6) witness to also produce documents at the time of testimony, Rule 30(b)(2) requires that you serve a subpoena *duces tecum* in conjunction with the subpoena to testify.

> **30(b)(2) Producing Documents.** If a subpoena *duces tecum* is to be served on the deponent, the materials designated for production, as set out in the subpoena, must be listed in the notice or in an attachment.

Example: ACME Trucking Co.

Using our example of ACME Trucking Co., you may learn that the company claimed to have relied on an independent security company, Background Checks, Inc., to conduct background checks on all of their potential drivers. ACME Trucking Co. claims to have lost the background check records of the driver in your crash. Using 30(b)(6) language in your subpoena and subpoena *duces tecum*, you can require Background Checks, Inc., to gather and provide all information and documents about the background check of the ACME Trucking Co. driver.

Subpoenas Are Issued by the Presiding Court

You can issue a subpoena for deposition testimony of a nonparty in accordance with Federal Rule 30(b)(6).[20] Although Rule 30(b)(6) provides the procedure for requiring a nonparty organization to designate people to be deposed, it does not explain the mechanics of how to compel the testimony from a nonparty.[21] To that end, Rule 45 governs how to serve the subpoena to obtain testimony from nonparty entities.

Subpoenas for nonparties to attend a deposition must be issued by the court where the action is pending and are covered under Rule 45(a)(2):[22]

> The amended Rule 45(a)(2) makes it clear that the presiding court may issue nationwide deposition subpoenas so long as the deposition is to take place within one hundred miles of the witness's residence or regular place of business.[23]

This is a departure from the earlier requirement that subpoenas for nonparty depositions had to be issued from the jurisdiction in which the deposition would be taken. The 2013 amendment resolved the conflicts between courts that manage, enforce, and punish discovery, and assisted in streamlining interjurisdictional litigation practice in federal courts.[24]

---

20. *Price Waterhouse LLP v. First Am. Corp.*, 182 F.R.D. 56, 61 (S.D.N.Y. 1998).
21. *Id.* at 63 (citing *Cates v. LTV Aerospace Corp.*, 480 F.2d 620 (5th Cir. 1973)).
22. Fed. R. Civ. P. 45(a)(2) ("Issuing Court. A subpoena must issue from the court where the action is pending.") (Amended in 2013.)
23. *VirtualAgility, Inc. v. Salesforce.com, Inc.*, 2014 WL 459719, at *4 (E.D. Tex. Jan. 31, 2014).
24. Fed. R. Civ. P. 45(a) advisory committee's note (2013 Amendment).

Location of a Nonparty 30(b)(6) Deposition

When you are seeking 30(b)(6) testimony from an entity that isn't a party, Rule 45(c) controls where the deposition will occur.[25] The rule establishes limitations on how far away the nonparty's deposition can be:

> A subpoena may command a person to attend a trial, hearing, or deposition only as follows: (A) within one hundred miles of where the person resides, is employed, or regularly transacts business in person; or (B) within the state where the person resides, is employed, or regularly transacts business in person, if the person (i) is a party or a party's officer; or (ii) is commanded to attend a trial and would not incur substantial expense.[26]

When you are using Rule 30(b)(1) to depose an employee of the nonparty entity, how you interpret the Rule is straightforward. Rule 45(c) requires that you conduct the deposition within one hundred miles of where the *person resides, is employed, or regularly transacts business*.[27]

Rule 45, however, is silent about the deposition location when you depose an organization under Rule 30(b)(6). Since the nonparty entity is the deponent, there is a potential tension between Rule 30(b)(6) and Rule 45. On the one hand, because the entity is the deponent, that entity's headquarters would logically be (and often is) the appropriate location to include in the subpoena for

---

25. Fed. R. Civ. P. 45(c).
26. *Id.*
27. Fed. R. Civ. P. 45(c)(1)(A).

a 30(b)(6) deposition.[28] On the other hand, if the entity designates a witness who is not within the territorial limitations, then Rule 30(b)(6), which is a deposition of the entity, conflicts with Rule 45's requirement that the deposition take place within one hundred miles of where the *person* resides.

Understanding how the conflict in the rules was reconciled requires that you understand the principles underlying both rules. Rule 30(b)(6) provides a procedure for the entity to determine the proper person to depose.[29] It does not deal with the issue of where the deposition takes place.[30] Rule 45(c) covers the location of a deposition for a nonparty witness.[31] It protects nonparties from burdensome discovery in an action in which they have little interest.[32] Therefore, you cannot require a person whom a nonparty organization designates to testify under Rule 30(b)(6) to travel outside of the limits imposed by Rule 45(c).[33] As a result, it is the responding organization that controls where the deposition will take place. The deposition must take place within one hundred miles of where the nonparty designated witness resides or works.

If the requesting party issues a subpoena to attend a deposition outside of the territorial limitations, Rule 45(d)(3) requires a court to quash or modify the subpoena. Rule 45(d)(3)(A)(ii) states that if a nonparty does not obey the subpoena, they are excused if the subpoena required them to attend outside the territorial limits under Rule 45(c)(1)(A).[34] The entity that the requesting

---

28. *VirtualAgility, Inc. v. Salesforce.com, Inc.*, 2014 WL 459719, at *4 (E.D. Tex. Jan. 31, 2014).
29. *Cates v. LTV Aerospace Corp.*, 480 F.2d 620, 623 (5th Cir. 1973).
30. *Id.*
31. *Id.*
32. *Price Waterhouse LLP v. First Am. Corp.*, 182 F.R.D. 56, 63 (S.D.N.Y. 1998).
33. *Cates v. LTV Aerospace Corp.*, 480 F.2d 620, 623 (5th Cir. 1973).
34. Fed. R. Civ. P. 45(d).

party subpoenaed does not need to object, because the notice is void due to distance.[35]

The 2013 advisory committee's notes explain that, in some situations, the court has the discretion to order nonparty depositions outside of the territorial limitations established in Rule 45:

> Under Rule 45(c)(1)(B)(ii), nonparty witnesses can be required to travel more than one hundred miles within the state where they reside, are employed, or regularly transact business in person only if they would not, as a result, incur "substantial expense." When travel over one hundred miles could impose substantial expense on the witness, the party that served the subpoena may pay that expense and the court can condition enforcement of the subpoena on such payment.[36]

The court may allow the deposition despite a distance over one hundred miles if the court finds that travel expenses won't be substantial, or the court may allow the deposition under condition that the requesting party pays for the deponent's travel expenses.[37]

---

35. *Sykes Int'l, Ltd. v. Pilch's Poultry Breeding Farms, Inc.*, 55 F.R.D. 138, 139 (D. Conn. 1972) ("A subpoena requiring attendance at Hartford served on Humphreys in the Netherlands would be void and without force. No order is required to protect Mr. Humphreys from undue burden or expense.") (citing *Doble v. United States District Court*, 249 F.2d 734 (9th Cir. 1957); *Farr v. Delaware, L. & W. R. R.*, 7 F.R.D. 494 (S.D.N.Y. 1944)); *see also*, *Hallamore Corp. v. Capco Steel Corp.*, 259 F.R.D. 76, 80 (D. Del. 2009) ("Although a motion to quash would have been the preferable course of action for [subpoenaed corporation], this court cannot enforce a subpoena issued incorrectly."); *Kupritz v. Savannah Coll. of Art and Design*, 155 F.R.D. 84, 88 (E.D. Pa. 1994).
36. Fed. R. Civ. P. 45(c) advisory committee's note (2013 Amendment).
37. *Id.*

Example: ACME Trucking Co.

Again let's use our ACME Trucking Co. example, involving ACME's background check vendor, Background Checks, Inc. Your lawsuit is in Minnesota, but Background Checks, Inc., has its corporate headquarters in Missouri. The presumption would be that their 30(b)(6) deposition would take place in Missouri. Background Checks, Inc., designates an employee who lives and works in New Mexico. You will need to conduct the deposition within one hundred miles of that employee's residence or place of business in New Mexico.

OBJECTIONS TO NONPARTY SUBPOENAS

Your adversary cannot object to a subpoena that you issue to a nonparty entity. Only the nonparty can object and prevent disclosure.[38] If the subpoenaed, nonparty, 30(b)(6) deponent objects to attending the deposition, the burden is on that nonparty to file a timely *motion to quash* in the court where the action is pending, under Rule 45(d)(3).[39] The nonparty may base its motion to quash on the grounds that the subpoena does the following:

- Fails to allow reasonable time to comply
- Is beyond the prescribed geographic limit
- Seeks protected or privileged information
- Imposes an undue burden or expense
- Seeks a trade secret

---

38. *McCoy v. Sw. Airlines Co., Inc.*, 211 F.R.D. 381, 384 (C.D. Cal. 2002); *Brown v. Braddick*, 595 F.2d 961, 967 (5th Cir. 1979) (citing Wright & Miller); § 2459 Subpoena for the Production of Documents and Things—Quashing or Modifying a Subpoena, 9A *Fed. Prac. & Proc. Civ.* § 2459 (3d ed.); *see also*, *Baptiste v. Centers, Inc.*, 118 Fair Empl. Prac. Cas. (BNA) 1682, 2013 WL 3196758 (M.D. Fla. 2013).
39. Fed. R. Civ. P. 45(d)(3)(B) ("[In] the court for the district where compliance is required").

A notice of objection is not sufficient to stay the deposition. To be timely, the responding nonparty entity must file its motion to quash a subpoena before the subpoena's return date (that is, before the date of the deposition's notice).[40] The nonparty's failure to serve timely objections waives all grounds for objection, including attorney–client privilege.[41]

On the other hand, a subpoena *duces tecum* may simply command the responding nonparty to produce documents or other tangible items, and does not necessarily involve testimony. In that case, the notice must allow a fourteen-day opportunity for the entity you subpoena to file written objections.[42] Although a few courts have permitted objections beyond the fourteen-day window (if the deponent shows extraordinary circumstances and good cause),[43] normally courts require parties to serve all objections within the fourteen-day window.[44] Once the nonparty serves its objection to producing the documents, it is not required to produce those documents. The requesting party must file a motion to compel.[45]

---

40. *Estate of Ungar v. Palestinian Auth.*, 451 F. Supp. 2d 607, 609–10 (S.D.N.Y. 2006) (citing *Sony Music Entertainment. Inc.*, 326 F. Supp. 2d 556, 561 (S.D.N.Y. 2004); *In re Welling*, 40 F. Supp. 2d 491, 491 (S.D.N.Y. 1999); *cf. Langford v. Chrysler Motors Corp.*, 513 F.2d 1121, 1126 (2d Cir. 1975)); *United States ex rel. Pogue v. Diabetes Treatment Centers of America, Inc.*, 238 F. Supp. 2d 270, 278 (D.D.C. 2002).
41. *McCoy v. Sw. Airlines Co., Inc.*, 211 F.R.D. 381, 384 (C.D. Cal. 2002); *Creative Gifts, Inc. v. UFO*, 183 F.R.D. 568, 570 (D.N.M. 1998); *In re DG Acquisition Corp.*, 151 F.3d 75, 81 (2d Cir. 1998) (citations omitted); *Pennwalt Corp. v. Durand–Wayland, Inc.*, 708 F.2d 492, 494, n. 5 (9th Cir. 1983).
42. Fed. R. Civ. P. 45(d)(2)(B).
43. *See, e.g.*, *Motorola Credit Corp. v. Uzan*, 293 F.R.D. 595, 601 (S.D.N.Y. 2013); *In re Sur. Ass'n of Am.*, 388 F.2d 412, 413 (2d Cir. 1967).
44. *McCoy v. Sw. Airlines Co., Inc.*, 211 F.R.D. 381, 385 (C.D. Cal. 2002); *Creative Gifts, Inc. v. UFO*, 183 F.R.D. 568, 570 (D.N.M. 1998).
45. Fed. R. Civ. P. 45(d)(2)(B)(1).

Subpoenas for Documents and Testimony Are Separate

If you serve a nonparty with a subpoena to testify in a deposition, as well as a subpoena *duces tecum* demanding production of documents at that deposition, the responding party's objections to the subpoena *duces tecum* requesting documents does not prevent the subpoena for the deposition requiring testimony. Even when you join both subpoenas into a single deposition notice, the subpoena compelling testimony and the subpoena compelling documents are distinct from each other. The responding entity must apply the objection rules for each subpoena independently. If the responding entity objects to the subpoena for documents, then you as the requesting party must bring forth the motion to compel the entity to produce those documents. By contrast, the responding entity must bring forth the motion to quash the subpoena compelling testimony. In summary, when you provide a combined subpoena for testimony and documents and the responding party objects to your document request, the respondent's witness still must attend the deposition; however, the witness is not required to bring the documents to the deposition.

Example: ACME Trucking Co.

Once again let's use our ACME Trucking Co. and Background Checks, Inc., example:

ACME Trucking Co.'s lawyers are not allowed to object to the subpoena requiring the 30(b)(6) testimony of Background Checks, Inc.

If Background Checks, Inc., wishes to object to attending the deposition for any reason other than the witness's location outside the one-hundred-mile limit, it must file a motion to quash the subpoena with the court where the case is pending, before the date of the deposition notice. If the deposition location is beyond the one-hundred-mile limit, Background Checks' obligation to bring a motion is waived.

On the other hand, if Background Checks, Inc., wishes to object to producing the documents that you have subpoenaed, they do not need to bring a motion for protective order. They merely need to file a written objection within fourteen days. Then it is your obligation to bring a motion in the court where the case is pending to compel production of the documents.

You Can Depose Noncorporate Organizations with 30(b)(6)

Rule 30(b)(6) is not restricted to corporations. You can also use rule 30(b)(6) to secure relevant information from any organization. The rule itself is called "Notice or Subpoena Directed to an Organization," and reads as follows:

> In its notice or subpoena, a party may name as the deponent a public or private corporation, a partnership, an association, a governmental agency, or other entity[.][46]

Although 30(b)(6) traditionally permitted deposing governmental agencies and business units, such as corporations and partnerships, the modern rule has much broader application. It has been well settled through case law that these same 30(b)(6) principles that apply to partnerships, which are expressly included in the rule, also apply to joint ventures[47] and trusts.[48]

The language of Rule 30(b)(6) states that the rule applies to all associations and other entities. An *association* is a broad term,

---

46. Fed. R. Civ. P. 30(b)(6).
47. *Starlight Intern, Inc. v. Herlihy*, 186 F.R.D. 626, 638 (D. Kan. 1999); *Resolution Trust Corp. v. Farmer*, No. CIV. A. 92-3310, 1994 WL 317458, *1 (E.D. Pa. June 24, 1994).
48. w*Taylor v. Shaw*, 2007 WL 710186, *2 (D. Nev. March 7, 2007).

referring to "mere collections of individuals" that have joined together for a common purpose,[49] such as people involved in office sharing agreements[50] or on church boards.[51] The term *association*, as commonly used, applies to "a body of acting together, without a charter, but upon the methods and forms used by incorporated bodies, for the prosecution of some common enterprise."[52]

Most significantly, Rule 30(b)(6) does not require the organization to have legal status. In 2007, Rule 30(b)(6) was amended to include the words "or other entity." The advisory committee comments to the amendment state that the change was made to "ensure that the deposition process could be used with *any* organization 'no matter what abstract fictive concept' describes it."[53] The advisory committee went on to say the following:

> Nothing is gained by wrangling over the place to fit into current rule language such entities as limited liability companies, limited partnerships, business trusts, more exotic common-law creations, or forms developed in other countries.[54]

As a practical matter, serving an entity with a 30(b)(6) deposition notice is more complicated. Rule 45(b) requires you to arrange

---

49. *Carolina Casualty Co. v. Elliot*, 2010 WL 5089988, *1 (E.D. Wis. Dec. 7, 2010) (citing *Navarro Sav. Ass'n v. Lee*, 446 U.S. 458, 461 (1980)); *see also*, 6 Am. Jur. 2d Associations and Clubs § 1.
50. *Carolina Casualty Co. v. Elliot*, 2010 WL 5089988, *1 (E.D. Wis. Dec. 7, 2010).
51. *Executive Bd. of Mo. Baptist Convention v. Carnahan*, 170 S.W.3d 437, 445 (Mo. App. 2005).
52. *Id.* (citing *Clark v. Grand Lodge of Bhd. of R.R. Trainmen*, 328 Mo. 1084, 43 S.W.2d 404, 408 (1931)).
53. 7–30 *Moore's Federal Practice*—Civil § 30.25 (quoting Fed. R. Civ. P. 30(b)(6) advisory committee's note (2007)); *Carolina Casualty Co. v. Elliot*, 2010 WL 5089988, *1 (E.D. Wis. Dec. 7, 2010).
54. Fed. R. Civ. P. 30(b)(6) advisory committee's note (2007). *See, e.g.*, *Taylor v. Shaw*, 2007 WL 710186, *5 (D. Nev. Mar. 7, 2007) (permitting 30(b)(6) deposition of a trust).

"delivery" of the subpoena, which courts have held requires personal service.[55] Courts have looked to Rule 4 of the Federal Rules of Civil Procedure, which governs serving complaints and answers to complaints, to evaluate whether the requesting party has served subpoenas sufficiently. The federal service rule states the following:

> **Rule 4(h) Serving a Corporation, Partnership, or Association.** Unless federal law provides otherwise or the defendant's waiver has been filed, a domestic or foreign corporation, or a partnership *or other unincorporated association* that is subject to suit under a common name, must be served:
>
> (1) In a judicial district of the United States:
>
> > (b) by delivering a copy of the summons and of the complaint to an **officer, a managing or general agent, or any other agent authorized by appointment or by law** to receive service of process and—if the agent is one authorized by statute and the statute

---

55. *Ott v. City of Milwaukee*, 682 F.3d 552, 557 (7th Cir. 2012); *In re Edelman*, 295 F.3d 171 (2d Cir. 2002); *China v. U.S. Department of Defense*, 23 Fed. Appx. 721, 725 (9th Cir. 2001); *Handy v. Diggins*, 2012 WL 2890961, *1 (D. Colo. 2012); *Special Markets Ins. Consultants, Inc. v. Lynch*, 2012 WL 1565348, *1, n.1 (N.D. Ill. 2012); *United States v. Elsass*, 109 A.F.T.R.2d 2012-1880, 2012 WL 1409624, *2 (S.D. Ohio 2012); *Fiorentino v. Cabot Oil & Gas Corp.*, 2012 WL 959392, *2 (M.D. Pa. 2012); *S.E.C. v. Art Intellect, Inc.*, 2012 WL 776244, *3 (D. Utah 2012); *Novovic v. Greyhound Lines, Inc.*, 2012 WL 252124, *7 (S.D. Ohio 2012); *Prescott v. County of Stanislaus*, 2012 WL 10617, *2 (E.D. Cal. 2012); *Doe v. Catholic Soc. of Religious and Literary Educ.*, 2009 WL 4506560, *1 (S.D. Tex. 2009).

so requires—by also mailing a copy of each to the defendant.⁵⁶

Rule 4(e) incorporates a forum state's procedural law for service of summons and complaints:

> (e) **Serving an Individual Within a Judicial District of the United States.** *Unless federal law provides otherwise,* an individual . . . may be served in a judicial district of the United States by: (1) following state law for serving a summons in an action brought in courts of general jurisdiction in the state where the district court is located or where service is made.⁵⁷

Because courts have extended this rule to include how you should properly serve subpoenas, it uses state procedures to resolve the ambiguity about who is subject to service on behalf of the entity. State statutes list agents, such as presidents, managers, and secretaries, whom you may serve on behalf of an entity. Follow these same rules to serve subpoenas on unincorporated entities.

---

56. Fed. R. Civ. P. 4(h)(1). *Ultradent Products, Inc. v. Hayman*, M8–85 RPP, 2002 WL 31119425, *3 (S.D.N.Y. Sept. 24, 2002) ("It follows that sufficient notice is given a corporate nonparty when the same method of service of process is used to obtain the court's jurisdiction over it [for a subpoena])." *See also, In re Grand Jury Subpoenas Duces Tecum Addressed to Canadian Int'l Paper Co.*, 72 F. Supp. 1013, 1021 (S.D.N.Y. 1947).
57. Fed. R. Civ. P. 4(e).

Technique: State Service of Process Rules for Nonparties

Following are examples of state procedures for serving subpoenas on organizations in order to take a nonparty Rule 30(b)(6) deposition.

Alabama

Alabama law provides for service on "Corporations and other Entities: Upon a domestic or foreign corporation or upon a partnership, limited partnership, limited liability partnership, limited liability company, or unincorporated organization or association, *by serving an officer, a partner (other than a limited partner), a managing or general agent,* or any agent authorized by appointment or by law to receive service of process."[58]

For example, federal regulations govern these Nursing Home Family Councils.[59] To serve a Nursing Home Family Council with a 30(b)(6) deposition notice in Alabama, you need to identify someone who is an officer or agent. Most Family Councils have regular elections for a chair, president, vice-chair, secretary, and treasurer.[60] To serve this entity under Alabama law, you can serve any of these leaders.

California: Serving an Association

California Civil Procedure allows you to serve an unincorporated association through "the president or other head of the association, a vice president, a secretary or assistant secretary, a treasurer or assistant treasurer, a general manager, or a person authorized by the association to receive service of process."[61]

For example, a condominium or apartment association is required to have a president, secretary, and treasurer under the Davis–Stirling Act.[62] In California, you can serve the association by serving one of those leaders.

---

58. Ala. R. Civ. Proc. 4(c)(6).
59. 42 C.F.R. § 483.15(c), Participation in Resident and Family Groups.
60. "Organizing Family Councils in Nursing Homes," *California Advocates for Nursing Home Reform*, accessed August 15, 2014, http://www.canhr.org/familycouncils/fc_organizing.htm.
61. Cal. Civ. Proc. § 416.40 (b).
62. Cal. Civ. Code § 4800 (West 2014).

California: Serving a Member of an Association

California allows the court to permit service on any individual member of a voluntary, unincorporated association if the leadership is unknown or nonexistent.

For example, the North American Soccer League is an unincorporated association of soccer exhibitors. The California rules permits the court to order that the entity serving the subpoena can deliver a copy of the process to any one or more of the association's members designated in the order. In addition, they can mail a copy of the process to the association at its last known address. Serving a subpoena in this manner constitutes personal service on an unincorporated association.[63]

Washington

An unincorporated region of the United States may be subject to a subpoena. Most states have a home rule. Most states have a home rule providing county commissions, boards, or councils the same powers as city councils over these unincorporated areas.[64]

For example, the State of Washington's constitution permits counties to adopt a home rule in their charters and to elect leadership: council members, sheriff, treasurer, clerk, and other roles. The King County Washington Charter, for example, gives the city council the power to investigate complaints and to subpoena witnesses.[65] Therefore, when investigating your suit, serve the county council for the unincorporated area in accordance with their charter.

---

63. *California Clippers, Inc. v. U.S. Soccer Football Ass'n.*, 314 F. Supp. 1057, 1062 (N.D. Cal. 1970).
64. "History of County Government: A Surge Toward Home Rule," *National Association of Counties*, accessed August 21, 2014, http://www.naco.org/Counties/learn/Pages/HistoryofCountyGovernmentPartII.aspx; "County Forms of Government," *The Municipal Research and Services Center*, last modified March 16, 2015, http://www.mrsc.org/subjects/governance/locgov12.aspx.
65. King Cnty., Wash. Code Charter (2013).

Depose Government Entities with 30(b)(6)

Rule 30(b)(6) requires government agencies to provide testimony about all information known to that agency.[66] The agency has a duty to make available people who can give complete, knowledgeable, and binding answers on the agency's behalf.[67] You can serve this notice on lower-level government committees as well as broader departments.[68] However, the deposition is only binding on the agency on which you serve the notice—you must subpoena related government entities separately.

> **Example:** The US Navy
>
> For example, you could not obtain documents and information from the nonparty Secretary of the Navy in Washington, D.C., if you issued a subpoena to a lower-level branch, the Navy plant representative at the defendant's office, LTV Aerospace Corporation in Grand Prairie, Texas.[69] You must direct the subpoena to the actual entity that controls the documents.

---

66. *See, e.g., United States ex. rel. O'Keefe v. McDonnell Douglas Corp.*, 961 F. Supp. 1288, 1290 (E.D. Mo. 1997); *Johns v. United States*, 1997 WL 732423, *2 (E.D. La. Nov. 21, 1997); *United States v. Davis*, 1993 WL 414761, *4, n.10 (D.R.I. Apr. 14, 1993); *Ghandi v. Police Dept. of Detroit*, 74 F.R.D. 115, 121 (E.D. Mich. 1977); *see also, United States v. District Council of New York*, 1992 WL 208284, *5 (S.D.N.Y. Aug. 18, 1992).
67. *Zip-O-Log Mills, Inc. v. United States*, 113 Fed. Cl. 24, 32 (2013).
68. *See, e.g., Mitsui & Co. (U.S.A.), Inc. v. Puerto Rico Water Resources Authority*, 93 F.R.D. 62, 67 (D.P.R. 1981) (government-owned corporation); *Ghandi v. Police Dep't of Detroit*, 74 F.R.D. 115, 122 (E.D. Mich. 1977) (holding that the Federal Bureau of Investigation was a "governmental agency" within meaning of 30(b)(6)).
69. *Cates v. LTV Aerospace Corp.*, 480 F.2d 620, 622 (5th Cir. 1973).

Depose Foreign Organizations with 30(b)(6)

Rule 30(b)(6) applies to both foreign and domestic corporations.[70] In addition, Rule 30(b)(6) also applies to foreign governments.[71] Rule 30(b)(6) does not contain any geographic component restricting its application to entities within the United States.[72] Because the language of Rule 30(b)(6) includes "governmental agency," without geographical restrictions, the rule applies to foreign sovereigns as well.[73]

Summary

- Rule 30(b)(6) designates issues, not people.

- Rule 30(b)(6) requires organizations to prepare the witness as to all knowledge that the organization reasonably knows regarding the matters of examination.

- Rule 30(b)(6) applies to nonparties as well as parties.

- A nonparty deposition must be within one hundred miles of where the *designated witness* resides, is employed, or regularly transacts business.

- Rule 30(b)(6) can be used with any organization or entity.

---

70. *See, e.g.*, *Monetti, S.p.A. v. Anchor Hocking Corp.*, 1992 WL 77677, *2 (N.D. Ill. Apr. 6, 1992); *Work v. Bier*, 106 F.R.D. 45, 52 (D.D.C. 1985); *Slauenwhite v. Bekum Maschinenfabriken, GMBH*, 104 F.R.D. 616, 618 (D. Mass. 1985) (citing *Adidas (Canada) Ltd v. SS Seatrain Bennington*, 1984 WL 423, Nos. 80 Civ. 1922 & 82 Civ. 0375 (PNL) (S.D.N.Y. Slip op. May 30, 1984)).
71. *Rubin v. Islamic Republic of Iran*, 2007 WL 2219105, *5 (N.D. Ill. 2007); *McKesson Corp. v. Islamic Republic of Iran*, 185 F.R.D. 70, 79–80 (D.D.C. 1999).
72. *McKesson Corp. v. Islamic Republic of Iran*, 185 F.R.D. 70, 80 (D.D.C. 1999).
73. *Rubin v. Islamic Republic of Iran*, 2007 WL 2219105, *5 (N.D. Ill. 2007) (citing *McKesson Corp. v. Islamic Republic of Iran*, 185 F.R.D. 70, 79–80 (D.D.C. 1999)).

- The entity does not need legal status to be subject to 30(b)(6).
- Rule 30(b)(6) can be used with foreign organizations and governments.
- The 30(b)(6) notice cannot name a person.

4

Rule 30(b)(6) Logistics

Location, Duration, and Number of Depositions

Forget logistics, you lose.
—Lieutenant General Frederick Frank,
Operation Desert Storm

Introduction	59
Sequence of Depositions	59
Location of a Party Deposition	61
Location of a Nonparty Deposition	64
Multiple Witnesses for a Single 30(b)(6) Notice	65
Multiple 30(b)(6) Notices	68
Designee v. Individual Depositions	72
Calculation of Time Limitations	75

Video Depositions..............................76
Summary......................................79

Introduction

Debates about when, where, who, and how many become another source of delay and consternation for lawyers attempting to schedule 30(b)(6) depositions. This chapter will answer these logistical questions involving 30(b)(6) depositions and provide the legal authority you can use for your briefs, if motions become necessary.

Sequence of Depositions

You can schedule depositions in any order you want. Rule 26(d) provides the following:

> Unless the court upon motion, for the convenience of parties and witnesses and in the interests of justice, orders otherwise, methods of discovery may be used in any sequence, and the fact that a party is conducting discovery, whether by deposition or otherwise, shall not operate to delay any other party's discovery.[1]

The advisory committee's comments to Rule 26(d) state that Rule 26(d) was enacted "to eliminate any fixed priority in the sequence of discovery."[2] The defense and the plaintiff can conduct their discovery simultaneously. One party should not wait to begin its discovery based on the other's completion, unless special considerations warrant the delay.[3]

An attorney representing a party or witness whom you have served with a valid notice of deposition may not unilaterally refuse

---

1. Fed. R. Civ. P. 26(d).
2. *Keller v. Edwards*, 206 F.R.D. 412, 415 (D. Md. 2002).
3. *Cont'l Illinois Nat. Bank & Trust Co. of Chicago v. Caton*, 130 F.R.D. 145, 148 (D. Kan. 1990).

to produce his client until certain conditions are fulfilled.[4] Unless, in the interest of justice or for the witness's convenience, the court orders otherwise, you, as the party who initiates the discovery, may schedule depositions in any sequence.[5]

If either side files a motion to compel their adversary's sequence of depositions, the burden is on the party that filed the motion to establish good cause factually that it's in the interest of justice to alter the series of depositions. Tactical advantage is not considered good cause. It is not in the interest of justice for the court to choose sides and uphold one party's request for a tactical advantage over the other.[6] Therefore, courts do not routinely grant protective orders altering the sequence of depositions.[7]

Example: Big Box Store

For example, you represent Maria Franklin, who was assaulted in the parking lot of a Big Box Store. You know Big Box Stores, Inc. has a video of the event and has interviewed employees about what happened. You want to take a 30(b)(6) deposition at the outset to learn Big Box Stores' position about what happened. Big Box's lawyers say they will not produce a designated witness in response to your 30(b)(6) notice until you have taken the deposition of all of the employees they interviewed. Armed with the authority you have learned in this chapter, you will be able to compel the testimony in the sequence you requested.

---

4. *Hill v. Forward Air Solutions, Inc.*, 2011 WL 1130868, at *2 (W.D.N.C. 2011) (citing *Keller v. Edwards*, 206 F.R.D. 412, 416 (D. Md. 2002)).
5. Fed. R. Civ. R. 26(d)(2); *United States v. Bartesch*, 110 F.R.D. 128, 129 (N.D. Ill. 1984). The 1970 Amendments to the Federal Rules of Civil Procedure established this provision. The advisory committee notes to the 1970 Amendments explain the effect of Rule 26(d): "The principal effects of the new provision are first, to eliminate any fixed priority in the sequence of discovery, and second, to make clear and explicit the court's power to establish priority by an order issued in a particular case."
6. *Stein v. Tri-City Healthcare Dist.*, No. 12-CV-2524-BTM BGS, 2014 WL 458021, *2 (S.D. Cal. Feb. 4, 2014).
7. *Id.* at *1.

LOCATION OF A PARTY DEPOSITION

The deposition notice must include the "time and place of the deposition."[8] The Federal Rules of Civil Procedure do not cover where the deposition of a party, under either Rule 30(a)(1) or 30(b)(6), should be conducted.[9] Therefore, the requesting party may choose the place for the deposition.[10] If the responding party doesn't like the location, it may petition the court for a protective order, under Rule 26(c)(2), to pick a different place.[11] The burden is on the responding party to show specific harm or prejudice to the court.[12] If the responding party can't demonstrate specific harm, the court will not grant a protective order.[13]

Usually parties will hold depositions of corporate representatives where the corporation conducts its business.[14] If there is a dispute over where the principal place of business is, the responding party must demonstrate that the corporation's principal place of business is different from where the requesting party wants to hold the deposition.[15] To determine the principal place of business, courts use the "total activity" test, which considers multiple factors, such as the location of the corporation's nerve center,

---

8. Fed. R. Civ. P. 30(b)(1).
9. *In re Outsidewall Tire Litig.*, 267 F.R.D. 466, 470 (E.D. Va. 2010).
10. *Turner v. Prudential Ins. Co. of Am.*, 119 F.R.D. 381, 383 (M.D.N.C. 1988) (citing 8 C. Wright & A. Miller, *Federal Practice and Procedure* § 2112 at 403 (1970)).
11. *Id.*
12. *Cadent Ltd. v. 3M Unitek Corp.*, 232 F.R.D. 625, 629 (C.D. Cal. 2005).
13. *Id.*
14. *Webb v. Ethicon Endo-Surgery, Inc.*, 2015 WL 317215, at *7 (D. Minn. Jan. 26, 2015); *Irrigation Tech. Leasing Associates, Inc. v. Superior Farming Co.*, No. 90 CIV. 7982 (JMC), 1992 WL 350806, *1 (S.D.N.Y. Nov. 17, 1992) (citing 4 J. Moore et al., *Moore's Federal Practice* ¶ 26.70[1–4] at 26–456 to 457 & n. 1 (2d ed. 1992)).
15. *Starlight Intern, Inc. v. Herlihy*, 186 F.R.D. 626, 644 (D. Kan. 1999).

administrative offices, production facilities, employees, and so on, and balances these factors in light of the facts of each case.[16]

The courts generally presume that a defendant's 30(b)(6) deposition should take place at its principal place of business.[17] However, courts also recognize that factors such as the following might justify a change in location:[18]

- The location of counsel for the parties in the forum district.[19]

- The number of corporate representatives a party is seeking to depose.[20]

- The likelihood of significant discovery disputes arising, which the forum court would need to resolve.[21]

- The amount the witnesses engage in travel for business purposes to the forum jurisdiction.[22]

- The equities with regard to the nature of the claim and the parties' relationship.[23]

---

16. *Id.*; *see also*, *Amoco Rocmount Co. v. Anschutz Corp.*, 7 F.3d 909, 915 (10th Cir. 1993) (as clarified on reh'g (Oct. 22, 1993) (quoting *White v. Halstead Indus.*, 750 F. Supp. 395, 398 (E.D. Ark. 1990))).
17. *E.I. DuPont de Nemours & Co. v. Kolon Indus., Inc.*, 268 F.R.D. 45, 54 (E.D. Va. 2010).
18. *Id.*; *see also*, *Cadent Ltd. v. 3M Unitek Corp.*, 232 F.R.D. 625, 629 (C.D. Cal. 2005) citing *Turner*, 119 F.R.D. at 383; *Rapoca Energy Co., L.P. v. AMCI Export Corp.*, 199 F.R.D. 191, 193 (W.D. Va. 2001).
19. *E.I. DuPont de Nemours & Co. v. Kolon Indus., Inc.*, 268 F.R.D. 45, 54 (E.D. Va. 2010); *Cadent Ltd. v. 3M Unitek Corp.*, 232 F.R.D. 625, 630 (C.D. Cal. 2005).
20. *E.I. DuPont de Nemours & Co. v. Kolon Indus., Inc.*, 268 F.R.D. 45, 54 (E.D. Va. 2010).
21. *Id.*
22. *Id.*; *see also*, *In re Outsidewall Tire Litig.*, 267 F.R.D. 466, 472 (E.D. Va. 2010); *Afram Export Corp. v. Metallurgiki Halyps, S.A.*, 772 F.2d 1358, 1365–66 (7th Cir. 1985).
23. *E.I. DuPont de Nemours & Co. v. Kolon Indus., Inc.*, 268 F.R.D. 45, 54 (E.D. Va. 2010); *Cadent Ltd. v. 3M Unitek Corp.*, 232 F.R.D. 625, 629 (C.D. Cal. 2005) (citing *Armsey v. Medshares Mgmt. Servs.*, 184 F.R.D. 569, 571 (W.D. Va. 1998); *Resolution Trust Corp. v. Worldwide Ins. Management Corp.*, 147 F.R.D. 125, 127 (N.D. Tex. 1992)).

- The danger associated with traveling to the location of the testimony.[24]
- The location of documents the parties will need.[25]
- The relative financial positions of the parties.[26]

The court may consider all relevant facts and equities within its broad discretion for determining both the appropriate place for examination and its conditions, such as who pays for travel expenses.[27] Ultimately, the court must consider each case on its own facts and on the equities of the particular situation.[28] As a result, you may often find yourself deposing corporate defendants in places other than the principal place of business for the convenience of all parties and in the general interests of judicial economy.[29]

---

24. *Cadent Ltd. v. 3M Unitek Corp.*, 232 F.R.D. 625, 630 (C.D. Cal. 2005) (citing *United States v. $160,066.98 from Bank of America*, 202 F.R.D. 624, 627–28 (S.D. Cal. 2001)).
25. *Mill-Run Tours, Inc. v. Khashoggi*, 124 F.R.D. 547, 551 (S.D.N.Y. 1989); *Turner v. Prudential Ins. Co. of Am.*, 119 F.R.D. 381, 382–83 (M.D.N.C. 1988).
26. *Cadent Ltd. v. 3M Unitek Corp.*, 232 F.R.D. 625, 629 (C.D. Cal. 2005) (citing *Baker v. Standard Indus., Inc.*, 55 F.R.D. 178, 179 (D.P.R. 1972), Wright, Miller & Marcus, *Federal Practice and Procedure: Civil 2d* § 2112 at 84–85 (1994 rev.)); *Tomingas v. Douglas Aircraft Co.*, 45 F.R.D. 94, 96–97 (S.D.N.Y. 1968).
27. *Branyan v. Koninklijke Luchtvaart Maatschappij*, 13 F.R.D. 425, 429 (S.D.N.Y. 1953).
28. *Turner v. Prudential Ins. Co. of Am.*, 119 F.R.D. 381, 383 (M.D.N.C. 1988) (citing *Farquhar v. Shelden*, 116 F.R.D. 70 (E.D. Mich. 1987), and *Leist v. Union Oil Co. of California*, 82 F.R.D. 203 (E.D. Wis. 1979)).
29. *Cadent Ltd. v. 3M Unitek Corp.*, 232 F.R.D. 625, 629 (C.D. Cal. 2005) (citing *Sugarhill Records Ltd. v. Motown Record Corp.*, 105 F.R.D. 166, 171 (S.D.N.Y. 1985)); *Custom Form Mfg., Inc. v. Omron Corp.*, 196 F.R.D. 333, 338 (N.D. Ind. 2000); *see also*, *Leist v. Union Oil Co. of California*, 82 F.R.D. 203, 204 (E.D. Wis. 1979).

Example: Home Products Store

For example, you represent Dan Wellington, who was injured when a display collapsed on him at a Home Product Store in Boston. You want to take a 30(b)(6) deposition dealing with the events that caused the injury in Boston. Home Product Stores, Inc.'s headquarters are in Minneapolis, MN. Therefore, the presumption is for the 30(b)(6) deposition to take place in Minneapolis. However, the case's venue is in Boston, all lawyers are in Boston, the documents relative to the incident are in Boston, and all witnesses are in Boston. The parties may agree or the court may rule that it is more appropriate for you to take the deposition in Boston.

LOCATION OF A NONPARTY DEPOSITION

As we discussed in chapter 3, "Details of Rule 30(b)(6)," an organization that isn't a party in the lawsuit can be subject to a subpoena to designate a witness under Rule 30(b)(6). Rule 45 establishes the territorial limitations where you can hold depositions of a nonparty. You must conduct the deposition within one hundred miles of where the witness resides, is employed, or regularly transacts business in person.[30] When you request a 30(b)(6) deposition of a nonparty organization, the court typically uses the location of that entity's headquarters to calculate the territorial limitation for where the deposition will take place.[31] However, if the entity designates a witness who is outside of that area, the location of the designated witness controls the deposition location.[32]

---

30. Fed. R. Civ. P. 45(c).
31. *See, e.g., VirtualAgility, Inc. v. Salesforce.com, Inc.*, 2014 WL 459719, at *3 (E.D. Tex. Jan. 31, 2014).
32. *Cates v. LTV Aerospace Corp.*, 480 F.2d 620, 623 (5th Cir. 1973).

Multiple Witnesses for a Single 30(b)(6) Notice

The organization you are deposing may designate multiple people to respond to the matters you are asking about. The organization has a duty to do so if they need multiple people to respond to all of the matters of examination.[33] Rule 30(b)(6) states, "The named organization must then *designate one or more* officers, directors, or managing agents, or designate other persons who consent to testify on its behalf[.]"[34] However, regardless of the number of witnesses the organization designates, the Rule 30(b)(6) deposition counts as a single deposition.[35]

> [T]he Advisory Committee Notes to the 1993 amendments to the Federal Rules, which expressly state that for purposes of calculating the number of a depositions in a case, a 30(b)(6) deposition is separately counted as a single deposition, regardless of the number of witnesses designated.[36]

It is critical that you understand this distinction because responding parties may try to claim that you have exceeded the presumptive ten-deposition limit established in Rule 30(a)(2)(A)(i) when they designate multiple witnesses to respond to one 30(b)(6) notice.[37]

---

33. *QBE v. Jorda*, 277 F.R.D. 676, 688 (S.D. Fla. 2012); *Ecclesiastes 9:10–11–12, Inc. v. LMC Holding Co.*, 497 F.3d 1135, 1147 (10th Cir. 2007); *Marker v. Union Fidelity Life Ins. Co.*, 125 F.R.D. 121, 127 (M.D.N.C. 1989); *Alexander v. F.B.I.*, 186 F.R.D. 137, 142 (D.D.C. 1998).
34. Fed. R. Civ. P. 30(b)(6).
35. *Quality Aero Technology, Inc. v. Telemetrie Elektronic GMBH*, 212 F.R.D. 313 (E.D.N.C. 2002).
36. *Id.* at 319 (citing Fed. R. Civ. P. 30(b)(6) advisory committee's note (1993 Amendment).
37. Fed. R. Civ. P. 30(a)(2)(A)(i).

Further, a responding organization's argument that each matter in issue constitutes a separate deposition is "baseless, and has no support in the rules, or the case law interpreting them."[38]

> The calculation for deposition time limits found in Rule 30(d)(1) is different when taking 30(b)(6) depositions. Rule 30(d)(1) provides a presumptive time limit of seven hours for each deposition. However, for purposes of 30(b)(6) depositions, each designee is subject to the seven-hour time limit separately, regardless of how many designees the corporation appoints.[39]

The advisory committee's notes state the following:

> For purposes of this durational limit, the deposition of each person designated under Rule 30(b)(6) should be considered a separate deposition. The presumptive duration may be extended, or otherwise altered, by agreement. Absent agreement, a court order is needed. The party seeking a court order to extend the examination, or otherwise alter the limitations, is expected to show good cause to justify such an order.[40]

For example, if you have listed four topics and the responding organization designates three witnesses to testify about those four topics, the four topics count as one deposition. However, each witness can testify up to seven hours for a total of twenty-one hours.

If your opponent designates a single person to testify in response to your 30(b)(6) deposition notice, Rule 30(d)(1) states,

---

38. *Meltzer/Austin Restaurant Corp. v. Benihana Nat. Corp.*, 2013 WL 2607589, *11 (W.D. Tx. June 10, 2013).
39. Fed. R. Civ. P. 30(d).
40. Fed. R. Civ. P. 30(d) advisory committee's note (2000 Amendment).

"a deposition is limited to one day of seven hours." Both the advisory committee and the courts have determined that when calculating that seven-hour time limit, only actual testimony time is included, "lunch and other breaks are not counted."[41] The express language of the 2000 committee comments, states:

> This limitation contemplates that there will be reasonable breaks during the day for lunch and other reasons, and that the only time to be counted is the time occupied by the actual deposition.[42]

If the testimony of that single person requires more than seven hours to respond to the matters of examination, you may make a motion to allow for additional time.[43]

Technique: Multiple Witnesses and Areas of Examination

Consider this example: You represent John Williams who died as a result of a fentanyl overdose at Rosetown Senior Living. You sued Rosetown Senior Living. In that lawsuit you served a 30(b)(6) deposition notice identifying three separate areas of examination:

1. The medication administration policies and procedures in effect at Rosetown Senior Living between May 9, 2012, and January 26, 2013.

---

41. *Wilson v. Kautex, A Textron Co.*, 2008 WL 189568, at *3 (N.D. Ind. Jan. 17, 2008); see also Fed. R. Civ. P. 30(d) advisory committee's note (2000 Amendment).
42. Fed. R. Civ. P. 30(d) advisory committee's note (2000 Amendment).
43. *Canal Barge Co. v. Commonwealth Edison Co.*, 2001 WL 817853, *4 (N.D. Ill. 2001) (allowing deposition of one designee to last for three, seven-hour days to question about fifty-six different barges).

2. The controlled substance documentation system that Rosetown Senior Living used between May 9, 2012, and January 26, 2013.

3. The controlled substance administration to John Williams between May 9, 2012, and January 26, 2013.

Rosetown Senior Living designates three separate people to testify at the 30(b)(6) deposition. Even though they have produced three people, their combined testimony to your 30(b)(6) notice of deposition constitutes a single deposition. However, even though a single deposition has a presumptive seven-hour limit, because the defendant designated three people, you may depose each witness for up to seven hours.

Multiple 30(b)(6) Notices

Rule 30(2)(A)(i) sets a limit of ten depositions, unless the court grants leave for more.[44] Rule 30(b)(6) is silent as to the number of 30(b)(6) depositions you may take within that presumptive limit. The advisory committee's notes to the 1993 amendments to the Federal Rules state as follows: "[A] deposition under Rule 30(b)(6) should, for purposes of this limit, be treated as a single deposition even though more than one person may be designated to testify."[45] Following the reasoning of the advisory committee, the court in *Quality Aero Technology v. Telemetrie Elektronic* stated that "there is no aspect of the rules, which either restricts a party to a single 30(b)(6) deposition or restricts the allotted time for taking a 30(b)(6) deposition."[46]

---

44. Fed. R. Civ. P. 30(2)(A)(i).
45. Fed. R. Civ. P. 30 advisory committee's note (1993 Amendment).
46. *Quality Aero Technology v. Telemetrie Elektronic, GMBH*, 212 F.R.D. 313, 319 (E.D.N.C. 2002).

In *Quality Aero* the court rejected the argument that Rule 30(a)(2)(A)(ii) requires the court's leave for additional depositions if "the *person* to be examined already has been deposed in the case."[47] The court recognized that Rule 30(b)(6) depositions of organizations are different from 30(b)(1) depositions of people because Rule 30(b)(6) focuses on the "matters for examination" rather than the knowledge of a single person.[48] Because Rule 30(a)(2)(A)(ii) does not discuss "organizations," courts have found that additional 30(b)(6) notices that contain new "matters of examination" are permissible.[49]

There has been some inconsistency in the ways courts have approached the relationship of the single deposition Rule 30(a)(2)(A)(ii) and Rule 30(b)(6). In *Ameristar Jet Charter, Inc. v. Signal Composites, Inc.*, the court interpreted the term "person," contained in Rule 30(a)(2)(A)(ii), to include organizations.[50] The *Ameristar Jet* court's interpretation has been subject to debate.[51] In *Loops LLC v. Phoenix Trading, Inc.*, the court

---

47. *Id.* (discussing Fed. R. Civ. P. 30(a)(2)(A)(ii)).
48. Fed. R. Civ. P. 30(b)(6).
49. *Quality Aero Technology v. Telemetrie Elektronic, GMBH*, 212 F.R.D. 313, 319 (E.D.N.C. 2002); *Cornell Research Foundation, Inc. v. Hewlett-Packard Co.*, 2006 WL 5097357 (N.D.N.Y. Nov. 13, 2006); *Loops LLC v. Phoenix Trading, Inc.*, 2010 WL 786030, *2 (W.D. Wash. March 2, 2010); *I/P Engine, Inc. v. AOL, Inc.*, 283 F.R.D. 322, 324 (E.D. Va. 2012).
50. *Ameristar Jet Charter, Inc. v. Signal Composites, Inc.*, 244 F.3d 189, 192–93 (1st Cir. 2001).
51. In *Ameristar Jet Charter, Inc. v. Signal Composites, Inc.*, 244 F.3d 189 (1st Cir. 2001) the magistrate issued a protective order quashing a second a nonparty 30(b)(6) subpoena, involving identical matters in issues, after the magistrate recommended that summary judgment be granted. On appeal, the first circuit did not rule that leave of court is necessary every time a second 30(b)(6) deposition is sought. Rather, as the court in *Quality Aero Technology v. Telemetrie Elektronic, GMBH*, 212 F.R.D. 313, 319 (E.D.N.C. 2002) explained: "The First Circuit's holding that the district court had properly granted a protective order, rather than an interpretation of the rule was a predictable result of the standard of review: 'we will intervene in such matters [discovery] only upon a clear showing of manifest injustice, that is, where the lower court's discovery order was plainly wrong and resulted in substantial prejudice to the aggrieved party'" (internal citations omitted) 244 F.3d at 191. *AG-Innovations, Inc. v. United States*, 82 Fed. Cl. 69, 98

rejected *Ameristar Jet*, stating there is no reason to count the depositions as two simply because the plaintiffs divided the topics into two subgroups rather than lumping them into one.[52] Similarly, in *I/P Engine, Inc. v. AOL, Inc.*, the court ruled that the "Rule 30(b)(6) depositions of the five corporate defendants count, at most, as one deposition each for this purpose, no matter how many separate depositions of the 30(b)(6) designees are actually conducted."[53]

In jurisdictions where the court has required leave to issue additional 30(b)(6) notices, courts routinely will grant the leave when a party presents new matters of examination. The advisory committee to the Federal Rules cautioned that courts "must be careful not to deprive a party of discovery that is reasonably necessary to afford a fair opportunity to develop and prepare the case."[54] With an eye to full disclosure, the courts should grant leave when the deposition notices do not duplicate each other.

Regardless of the jurisdiction, litigation should not be a game of cat and mouse. The purpose of discovery is to allow you a broad search for facts, which will then aid you in preparing and presenting the case.[55] The responding party should not be permitted to read the rules narrowly to prevent access to relevant information. At the same time, the requesting party must be vigilant not to issue a 30(b)(6) notice that duplicates earlier 30(b)(6) requests. If you are able to stage discovery with well-crafted 30(b)(6) notices, it can proceed in an orderly fashion, typically on an issue-by-issue basis, without unjustifiable expense to either party. Requiring every issue to be included in a single 30(b)(6) notice would result in an unwieldy deposition event.

(2008). The court explained that Ameristar Jet Charter was inapplicable when the 30(b)(6) testimony involved new matters in issue and/or it involved a party.
52. *Loops LLC v. Phoenix Trading, Inc.*, 2010 WL 786030, *2 (W.D. Wash. March 2, 2010).
53. *I/P Engine, Inc. v. AOL, Inc.*, 283 F.R.D. 322, 324 (E.D. Va. 2012).
54. Fed. R. Civ. P. 26 advisory committee's note to 1983 amendments.
55. *Int'l Paper Co. v. United States*, 36 Fed.Cl. 313, 317 (1996).

Example: Valley Nursing Home

You represent Tom who developed pressure sores in a Valley Nursing Home. Pressure sores that are as serious as Tom's can occur only if he did not receive proper care over an extended period of time. You suspect that Valley Nursing Home was understaffed as a result of cost-savings decisions. You also believe that because Valley Nursing Home was understaffed, management didn't have time to look at the reports that would identify care delivery problems in the organization. You want to learn the following:

1. What type of reports can Valley Nursing Home's electronic time clock generate to evaluate staffing patterns?

2. How did Valley Nursing Home make its staffing decisions?

3. What types of reports does Valley Nursing Home keep for tracking pressure sores?

4. What types of reports does Valley Nursing Home use in its day-to-day operations?

5. What is the corporate management structure?

6. What is Valley Nursing Home's position on how Tom's pressure sores developed?

If you wanted to look for answers to the questions in each of these areas with a traditional approach of deposing individual witnesses, it could result in dozens of depositions grouped together by subject matter. Rule 30(b)(6) is a better approach, because by requiring Valley Nursing Home to pull together the answers for each area of inquiry, you can reduce the total number of depositions. Yet, at the same time, each of these areas deals with very different parts of the lawsuit. It doesn't make sense to deal with management structure in the same deposition you are using to unravel how reports are generated from the payroll clock. Nor does it make sense to discuss staffing decisions in the same deposition you are using to discover Valley Nursing Home's position about the factual treatment record and the patho-physiology of how the sores developed.

In order to have time to evaluate the evidence before going to the next phase of the depositions, you want to sequence when you take the testimony. It makes sense to first learn what types of data systems exist in the company so that you can tailor your document/data request to avoid receiving millions of unmanageable data points in response. You may then want to learn how the company is organized and how it shares information throughout the organization. Then you can understand what information was available to Valley Nursing Home before you take the testimony, as well as cross-examine, the designated witnesses about what they claim happened. The sequenced discovery is much more manageable for everyone and, therefore, the preferable approach. In order to achieve this sequence, you must phase the discovery with multiple 30(b)(6) depositions.

Designee v. Individual Depositions

You may experience a situation in which you have taken a 30(b)(6) deposition on a specific issue, such as a documents deposition, and then you wish to take the deposition of that person as a fact witness regarding other matters. You have an adversary who refuses to provide that witness, saying, "You don't get another bite of the apple." You need to know the legal principles when conferring with your adversary, and if unsuccessful, you need to be able to provide the court with the cases to support your motion.

A deposition under Rule 30(b)(6) is substantially different from a witness's deposition as an individual.[56] Unlike the 30(b)(1) testimony of an individual, a 30(b)(6) witness testifies as a representative of the entity. The 30(b)(6) witness's answers bind the entity, and the entity is responsible for producing a witness who is prepared to provide all the relevant information that the entity knows or reasonably should know.[57] Because 30(b)(1) and 30(b)(6) depositions impose different obligations and involve different

---

56. *Sabre v. First Dominion Capital, LLC*, 2001 WL 1590544, *1 (S.D.N.Y. Dec. 12, 2001); *Lacaillade v. Loignon Champ-Carr, Inc.*, No. 10-CV-68-JD, 2011 WL 6020703, *4 (D.N.H. Dec. 2, 2011).
57. *Sabre v. First Dominion Capital, LLC*, 2001 WL 1590544, *1 (S.D.N.Y. Dec. 12, 2001) (citing 8A Charles A. Wright, Arthur R. Miller, Richard L. Marcus, *Federal Practice & Procedure* § 2103 (2d ed. 1994)).

ramifications, a party may depose a single witness on the same topics, once in the 30(b)(6) deposition and again as an individual in a separate 30(b)(1) deposition.[58]

The 30(b)(6) representative and 30(b)(1) individual depositions differ in both the witness's knowledge base and in how you can use the testimony in court. When the deponent testifies in an individual capacity, the testimony provides only that witness's *personal* knowledge, perceptions, and opinions.[59] There is no obligation to prepare. Therefore, that witness could choose (or be directed) not to prepare. Then the witness can display a real or feigned lack of knowledge when you question him. By contrast, the information you seek in a 30(b)(6) deposition requires that the witness prepare in order to provide all information that the organization knows or that is reasonably available to the organization, and to provide the organization's positions. Because deponents in a Rule 30(b)(6) deposition must prepare, you can discover information that would otherwise not be forthcoming.

Further, the binding effect of a testimony you take from the individual witness differs from the testimony you take of that same witness in a 30(b)(6) designee capacity.[60] As I discuss in chapter 15, "Binding Effect," when the witness testifies in an individual capacity, the witness is subject to impeachment. However, if the witness is a designee, the organization is bound by the testimony. Unless the organization can prove that the witness could not have

---

58. *Commodity Futures Trading Comm. v. Midland Rare Coin Exch. Inc.*, 1999 WL 35148749, *4 (S.D. Fla. July 28, 1999); *Landmark Screens, LLC v. Morgan, Lewis & Brokius LLP*, 2010 WL 3221859, *2 (N.D. Cal. Aug. 13, 2010); *Ice Corp. v. Hamilton Sundstrand Corp.*, 2008 WL 4724471, *3–4 (D. Kan. Oct. 24, 2008); *Sabre v. First Dominion Capital, LLC*, 2001 WL 1590544, *2 (S.D.N.Y. Dec. 12, 2001).
59. *In re C.R. Bard, Inc. Pelvic Repair Systems Product Liability Litigation*, 2013 WL 1722998, *1 (S.D.W.Va. 2013) (citing *United States v. Taylor*, 166 F.R.D. 356, 361 (M.D.N.C. 1996)); *see also, In re Motor Fuel Temperature Sales Practices Litig.*, 2009 WL 5064441, *2 (D. Kan. Dec. 16, 2009).
60. *Lacaillade v. Loignon Champ-Carr, Inc.*, 2011 WL 6020703, *2 (D.N.H. Dec. 2, 2011).

known the information or that it was inaccessible, that organization cannot submit new or different allegations that could have been made at the time of the 30(b)(6) deposition.[61]

Often you may need the same witness to testify on separate occasions, once as an individual and again as a 30(b)6) witness. Organizations cannot refuse to designate a 30(b)(6) witness in response to the matters of examination by claiming that you already explored the facts in a previous individual 30(b)(1) deposition.

"To the extent [the organization] argues that plaintiffs have already taken the deposition testimony of several individuals concerning these subjects, its objection is immaterial."[62] As the discovering party, you have a right to know whether your adversary has adopted any of the testimonies individuals have given, or whether they will be advancing a different interpretation of the events.[63]

Refusing to designate a 30(b)(6) witness because the topics in the deposition notice have already been covered in earlier 30(b)(1) deposition, is sanctionable conduct.[64] Insisting that the prior testimony was sufficient to satisfy the requesting party's inquiries is an improper attempt to shift the burden of production to the requesting party.[65]

In addition, the responding party cannot refuse to produce a witness because that witness was or will be deposed in their individual capacity under Rule 30(b)(1).

---

61. *Rainey v. Am. Forest & Paper Ass'n, Inc.*, 26 F. Supp. 2d 82, 94 (1998) citing *Ierardi*, 1991 WL 158911, *3; *Taylor*, 166 F.R.D. at 362.
62. *Smith v. Gen. Mills, Inc.*, 2006 WL 7276959, at *5 (S.D. Ohio Apr. 13, 2006) (quoting *Sabre v. First Dominion Capital, LLC*, Case No. 01 Civ 2145, 2002 U.S.App. LEXIS 22193, at *7–8 (S.D.N.Y. Nov. 7, 2002)).
63. *Smith v. Gen. Mills, Inc.*, 2006 WL 7276959, at *5 (S.D. Ohio Apr. 13, 2006).
64. *Foster-Miller, Inc. v. Babcock & Wilcox Canada*, 210 F.3d 1, 17 (1st Cir. 2000).
65. *Id.* (citing *Mitsui & Co. (U.S.A.), Inc. v. Puerto Rico Water Resources Authority*, 93 F.R.D. 62, 66–67 (D.P.R. 1981)).

> Just because [the responding entity] may choose to designate certain individuals as its corporate designees whose fact depositions have already occurred does not insulate [the responding entity] from the requirements of Rule 30(b)(6). Such a finding would eviscerate Rule 30(b)(6).[66]

There is a conceptual difference between testifying as an individual and as a 30(b)(6) designee. When testifying as a designee, it's with the corporation's knowledge, not the individual's knowledge. Because there are different preparation standards when a witness testifies as an individual as opposed to a 30(b)(6) designee, the witness's testimony as an individual doesn't prohibit you from taking their deposition later as a 30(b)(6) designee.[67]

Calculation of Time Limitations

The depositions of a person who receives notice as an individual witness under Rule 30(b)(1) and who serves as a corporate representative under Rule 30(b)(6) are considered separate depositions and, therefore, are subject to independent seven-hour time limits.[68]

---

66. *ICE Corp. v. Hamilton Sundstrand Corp.*, No. 05-4135-JAR, 2007 WL 1732369, *3 (D. Kan. June 11, 2007).
67. *See In re C.R. Bard, Inc. Pelvic Repair Systems Product Liability Litigation*, 2013 WL 1722998, *1 (S.D.W.Va. 2013) (citing *Foster–Miller, Inc. v. Babcock & Wilcox Canada*, 210 F.3d 1, 17 (1st Cir. 2000), citing *Lending Tree, Inc. v. LowerMyBills, Inc.*, 2006 WL 2443685, *2 (W.D.N.C. Aug. 22, 2006)); *AG-Innovations Inc. v. US*, 82 Fed Cl. 69, 81 (2008) (citing *Alloc, Inc. v. Unilin Decor N.V.*, Nos. 02–C–1266, 03–C–342, 04–C–121, 2006 WL 2527656, *2 (E.D. Wis. Aug. 29, 2006)).
68. *Wesley v. Gates*, No. C 08-2719 SI, 2009 WL 1955997, *1 (N.D. Cal. July 2, 2009) (citing *Sabre v. First Dominion Capital, LLC*, No. 01-CIV-5145-BSJHBP, 2001 WL 1590544, *1–2 (S.D.N.Y. Dec. 12, 2001)).

Example: Valley Nursing Home

In the Valley Nursing Home case with Tom's pressure sores, the nursing home may designate the director of nursing to respond to your 30(b)(6) question regarding staffing decisions. As the case progresses, you may decide you want to take the deposition of that same director of nursing as an individual under Rule 30(b)(1). That is permissible. Just because the person was designated as a 30(b)(6) witness, it doesn't preclude deposing her as an individual. Each time you take a deposition, it is a separate seven-hour time calculation.

Video Depositions

Having the ability to show the court and jury a witness's demeanor, tone, appearance, and conduct is critical to helping them determine that witness's credibility. Therefore, videotaping the deposition testimony can be a very important tool for persuasion. A video showing a witness's changed testimony has far greater impact than an attorney reading it. The Rules of Civil Procedure unquestionably permit videotaping.

Rule 30(b)(3)(A) covers your right to record depositions: "Unless the court orders otherwise, testimony may be recorded by audio, audiovisual, or stenographic means."[69]

In *Rice's Toyota World, Inc. v. Southeast Toyota Distributors, Inc.*, the court explained the importance of video depositions in the fact-finding process:

> A video deposition better serves these objectives by permitting the fact-finder to utilize a greater portion of his perceptive processes than when merely reading or listening to a stenographic deposition. While we

---

69. Fed. R. Civ. P. 30(b)(3)(A).

often make decisions by written word alone, when it comes to determining facts by comparing the testimonies of one or more persons, we do a better job by being able to employ as many of our senses as possible. Personally observing the witness is preferable. Next in rank would be viewing a video deposition where one directly uses the combined senses of hearing and seeing without the filtering process that occurs when one listens to a deposition being read or reads it himself from the cold record which excludes pitch and intonation of voice, rapidity of speech, and all the other aural and visual clues. Thus, it is not surprising to find . . . [a] "legion of cases" which have extolled the advantages of video depositions and preference for their use in a trial, noting that a witness's demeanor reflected in his motions, expressions, voice inflections, etc., give the fact-finder a unique advantage in evaluating evidence, resulting in appellate courts granting greater deference to such findings. Video depositions can markedly increase accuracy and trustworthiness. In addition, to the extent that a video deposition reduces tedium, the fact-finder's concentration and attention will be enhanced, again to the benefit of the decision process.[70]

The majority of federal decisions, in recognizing the importance of videotaped testimonies at trial, have allowed counsel to include audiovisual recordings with stenographic recordings in depositions.[71]

---

70. *Rice's Toyota World, Inc. v. Southeast Toyota Distributors, Inc.*, 114 F.R.D. 647, 649 (M.D.N.C. 1987).
71. *Id.* at 647; *see also, Pioneer Drive, LLC v. Nissan Diesel America, Inc.*, 262 F.R.D. 552, 555–56 (D. Mont. 2009); *Marlboro Products Corp. v. North Am. Philips Corp.*, 55 F.R.D. 487, 489–90 (S.D.N.Y. 1972); *Carpenter v. Forest Meadows Owners Association*, No. 1:09-CV-01918, 2011 WL 3207778, at *8 (E.D. Cal, July 27, 2011)

In *Pioneer Drive, LLC v. Nissan Diesel America, Inc.*, the court held that an independent professional was not required to video record a deposition that was also being recorded by a stenographer.[72] The court determined that "[t]he Federal Rules of Civil Procedure allow, at the very least, counsel to videotape a deposition in concert with a stenographer recording it."[73] The court reasoned the following:

> [The] defendant's concerns over accuracy and objectivity were misplaced from the start. *There was an authorized officer to stenographically record the examination present at the deposition.* This provided both an assurance of an accurate record of the deposition, as well as a benchmark upon which the video record could be challenged if that was necessary.[74]

(denying motion to prohibit use of a video recorded deposition where the plaintiff's attorney who was operating the video equipment failed to repeat the instructions required by Fed. R. Civ. P. 30(b)(5)(B) because "the written deposition transcript [recorded by an independent stenographer] ensures there has been no falsification of the recordings."); *Anderson v. Dobson*, 627 F. Supp. 2d 619, 624–25 (W.D.N.C. 2007) (holding that recording a deposition by a party's attorney is not a per se violation of the Rules and denying a motion to strike the video deposition absent "any indication of irregularities in the video recording process"); *Duncan v. Husted*, No. 2:13-CV-1157, 2011 WL 1540550, at *1–2 (S.D. Ohio April 7, 2015) (permitting the plaintiff to operate recording equipment to record a deposition provided that an independent notary performs the other duties required by Rules 28 and 30); *American General Life Ins. Co. v. Billard*, No. C10-1012, 2010 WL 4367052, at *5–6 (N.D. Iowa, Oct. 28, 2010) (party's attorney "is under no obligation to hire a professional videographer" so long as the attorney adheres to the requirements of Fed. R. Civ. P. 30(b)(5)); *Maranville v. Utah Valley University*, No. 2:11CV958, 2012 WL 1493888, at *2 (D. Utah April 27, 2012); *Carpenter v. Forest Meadows Fed Owners Ass'n*, No. 1:09-CV-01918, 2011 WL 32077778, at *7–8 (E.D. Cal. July 27, 2011); *Roberts v. Homelite Div. of Textron, Inc.*, 109 F.R.D. 664, 667 (N.D. Ind. 1986); *Ott v. Stipe Law Firm*, 169 F.R.D. 380, 381 (E.D. Okla. 1996).
72. *Pioneer Drive, LLC v. Nissan Diesel America, Inc.*, 262 F.R.D. 552, 555–56 (D. Mont. 2009).
73. *Id.*
74. *Id.* (Emphasis added.)

Interpreting Federal Rules of Civil Procedure 28(a) and (c), the court "[agreed] with those courts that have concluded that neither Rule 28(a) nor Rule 28(c) specifically prohibit a party's attorney from operating the video camera during the course of a video deposition otherwise conducted in compliance with Rule 30."[75]

Summary

- A party initiating discovery can select the sequence of the depositions they are requesting.

- A party may unilaterally choose the location for deposing an opposing party.

- A deponent may move for a protective order to establish an alternative deposition location.

- There is a rebuttable presumption that a defendant's 30(b)(6) deposition should take place at its principal place of business.

- A nonparty 30(b)(6) deposition must be taken within one hundred miles of the designated witness's home or principal place of business.

- A responding organization may designate multiple people to respond to the matters of examination.

- A party must limit depositions to seven hours unless a stipulation or order extends the time.

- For purposes of the durational limit, the deposition of each person designated under Rule 30(b)(6) should be considered a separate deposition.

- Non-duplicative, multiple 30(b)(6) depositions.

---

75. *Id.*

- The 30(b)(6) deposition of a witness is a separate deposition from the deposition of that same person as an individual witness.

- A 30(b)(6) witness serves as a binding representative of an entity and has an obligation to comprehensively prepare for the deposition.

- Federal courts permit counsel to video record depositions in addition to taking a stenographic record.

5

Deposing Officers, Directors, and Managing Agents
30(b)(1) Depositions

What did the president know and when did he know it?

—Howard Baker[1]

Introduction. 83
A Managing Agent's Word Binds an Organization. 84
Where Do Depositions Take Place?. 87
Is Your Witness a Managing Agent? 88
Former Officers, Directors,
　and Managing Agents 93
Deposing Executives. 101
　　Is This Executive's Deposition Necessary?. 102

---

1. Hearing before the Select Comm. on Presidential Campaign Activities of the U.S.S., 93d Cong. (1973) (statement of Sen. Howard Baker, ranking member).

Who Establishes That This
    Deposition Is Necessary?.....................104
        Some Jurisdictions Have No Executive Protection ..105
        Some Jurisdictions Have Varying Levels
            of Executive Protection: The Apex Doctrine......106
Rule 30(b)(6): An Alternative to
    Deposing the Executive 110
Summary 111

Introduction

You may, at times, find it strategically necessary to establish that a particular managing member of an organization had (or did not have) specific information. In those instances, you must depose those managing agents in their individual capacity, using Rule 30(b)(1).

If the person you name is an officer, director, or managing agent, her testimony will bind the corporation. If you don't know the name of the person, Rule 30(b)(1) allows you to describe a particular class or group that the person belongs to. Rule 30(b)(1) states the following:

> **Notice in General:** A party who wants to depose a person by oral questions must give reasonable written notice to every other party. The notice must state the time and place of the deposition and, if known, the deponent's name and address. *If the name is unknown, the notice must provide a general description sufficient to identify the person or the particular class or group to which the person belongs.*[2]

However, if you choose to name a category of witnesses, using Rule 30(b)(1), there is a risk that, if the category is too specific (for example, *records custodian* or *product designer*), you may not get the information you are looking for. The deponent may fit your designated title, but not have the information you want. Further, if you limit the notice to "the person with the most knowledge," your deposition will be limited to what that one specific person knows, rather than what the organization knows. The person with the most knowledge may still only know a small fraction of what the organization knows.

---

2. Fed. R. Civ. P. 30(b)(1). (Emphasis added.)

When taking the 30(b)(1) deposition of a person, here are some questions to consider:

- Will the person's testimony bind the organization?
- Where will the deposition take place?
- Will you be able to take the deposition of the person you specified?

This chapter will explain the legal principles you need to evaluate these issues and will provide techniques for building the record you will need to bring forth your motions.

A Managing Agent's Word Binds an Organization

It is well recognized that an officer's, director's, or managing agent's deposition binds an organization to their testimony. When an employee named in a deposition notice "is a director, officer, or managing agent of [a corporate party], such employee will be regarded as a representative of the corporation."[3] Therefore, her testimony will bind the organization. Because directors, officers, and managing agents are representatives of their entities, you do not need a subpoena to compel their testimony.[4] On the other hand, although responding parties commonly make low-level employees of the company available for depositions, strict application of the rules means you do need a subpoena to compel their testimony because they are not officers, directors, or managing agents of the company.

---

3. *Cadent Ltd. v. 3M Unitek Corp.*, 232 F.R.D. 625, 628 (C.D. Cal. 2005); *Moore v. Pyrotech Corp.*, 137 F.R.D. 356, 357 (D. Kan. 1991); *United States v. One Parcel of Real Estate at 5860 North Bay Rd.*, 121 F.R.D. 439, 440–41 (S.D. Fla. 1988).
4. *Cont'l Fed. Sav. & Loan Ass'n v. Delta Corp. of Am.*, 71 F.R.D. 697, 699 (W.D. Okla. 1976) (citing Wright & Miller, *Federal Practice and Procedure: Civil* § 2107).

Example: Johnson Tie-Rods

You are involved in a manufacturing defect product liability case against Johnson Tie-Rods, a manufacturer of snowmobile tie-rods. If you want to take the deposition of the VP of Operations, you don't need a subpoena to compel that testimony because he is an officer of the company. On the other hand, if you want to take the deposition of a specific worker on the assembly line, you must use a subpoena to compel that deposition because the witness is not an officer, director, or managing agent.

When you are analyzing the rules about corporate employee depositions, existing officers and directors are easy to identify, as are low-level employees. However, determining whether the employee is a managing agent could lead you into much debate and litigation. In this chapter, I will discuss the legal principles for determining a witness's status as a managing agent. The burden is on you as the requesting party to establish that the witness is a director, officer, or managing agent. If you cannot establish this status, then you need a subpoena to compel the person's attendance, which invokes the territorial limitations of Rule 45. If the company is not a party to the lawsuit, you must serve subpoenas on their employees to compel their individual 30(b)(1) testimony.

Rule 30(b)(1) depositions of directors, officers, or managing agents are an alternative and *additional* method to 30(b)(6) for binding an organization. Using Rule 30(b)(6) does not prevent you from using other rules to depose entities.[5] Rule 30(b)(6)

---

5. *Crest Infiniti, II, LP v. Swinton*, 174 P.3d 996, 999-1000 (Okl. 2007); *Operative Plasterers' & Cement Masons Intern. Ass'n v. Benjamin*, 144 F.R.D. 87, 89 (N.D. Ind. 1992); *Founding Church of Scientology of Washington, D.C. v. Webster*, 802 F.2d 1448, 1451 (D.C. Cir. 1986) (citing 4A J. Moore, *Moore's Federal Practice* ¶ 30, 51, at 30–41 (2d ed. 1984)); *Coletti v. Cudd Pressure Control*, 165 F.3d 767, 773 (10th Cir. 1999).

explicitly provides for this: "This paragraph [6] does not preclude a deposition by any other procedure allowed by these rules."[6]

Further,

> ... [t]he Advisory Committee's note accompanying the rule made clear that the new 30(b)(6) procedure does not supplant, but "supplements the existing practice whereby the examining party designates the corporate official to be deposed." The [30(b)(1)] procedure, long known to the bar, thus remains available for litigants to employ if they see fit.[7]

Depositions you take of officers, directors, and managing agents under Rule 30(b)(1), like 30(b)(6) depositions, are not hearsay. This is because courts consider them as an admission by a party–opponent under Federal Rule of Evidence 801(d)(2).[8] This means that using either Rule 30(b)(1) or Rule 30(b)(6) depositions of managing agents will bind the organization, and you may evoke them against the organization at trial.[9] Rule 32(a)(3) states the following:

> **Deposition of Party, Agent, or Designee.** An adverse party may use for *any purpose* the deposition of a party or anyone who, when deposed, was the party's officer, director, managing agent, or designee under Rule 30(b)(6) or 31(a)(4).[10]

---

6. Fed. R. Civ. P. 30(b)(6). (Emphasis added.)
7. Fed. R. Civ. P. 30(b)(6) advisory committee's note (1970 Amendment); *Founding Church of Scientology of Washington, D.C. v. Webster*, 802 F.2d 1448, 1451 (D.C. Cir. 1986); *see also, Moore v. Pyrotech Corp.*, 137 F.R.D. 356, 357 (D. Kan. 1991); *Sugarhill Records Ltd. v. Motown Record Corp.*, 105 F.R.D. 166, 168-169 (S.D.N.Y. 1985); 8 C. Wright and Miller, *Fed. Prac. & Proc.*, § 2103, at 373–74 (1970).
8. *Stearns v. Paccar, Inc.*, 1993 WL 17084, *4 (10th Cir. 1993).
9. *Cadent Ltd. v. 3M Unitek Corp.*, 232 F.R.D. 625, 628 (C.D. Cal. 2005); *Coletti v. Cudd Pressure Control*, 165 F.3d 767, 773 (10th Cir. 1999); *Crimm v. Mo. Pac. R.R. Co.*, 750 F.2d 703, 708–09 (8th Cir. 1984).
10. Fed. R. Civ. P. 32(a)(3). (Emphasis added.)

Using Rule 32(a)(3), a party can introduce

> as a part of his substantive proof, the deposition of his adversary, and it is immaterial that the adversary is available to testify at the trial or has testified there.[11]

Further, you can use the testimony to impeach the corporation or organization.[12]

Example: Johnson Tie-Rods

> Let's use our Johnson Tie-Rods example, where you have taken the deposition of the VP of Operations regarding the company's quality control procedures for manufacturing tie-rods. In addition, you took the depositions of three factory workers, establishing that the manufacturing process did not comply with the quality control protocols. You may introduce the deposition of the VP of Operations at trial regardless of whether or not he is available because he is an officer of the company. On the other hand, the line workers are not officers, directors, or managing agents. Therefore, their depositions are hearsay (out of court statements) and cannot be introduced at trial unless you prove that the witnesses are unavailable for trial.

WHERE DO DEPOSITIONS TAKE PLACE?

If the deponent is a party, then you, as the requesting party, may set the place for deposition. However, that location is subject to the court's power to grant a protective order under Rule 26(c)(2), designating a different place. The general rule is that you should

---

11. *King & King Enters. v. Champlin Petroleum Co.*, 657 F.2d 1147, 1163–64 (10th Cir. 1981).
12. *United States v. Taylor*, 166 F.R.D. 356, 361 (M.D.N.C. 1996); *see* Fed. R. Evid. 613.

take the deposition of a corporate officer or managing agent within the jurisdiction of the corporation's principal place of business.[13] If the witness is not an officer, director, or managing agent, then you will need to use the territorial limitations found in Rule 45's requirements for subpoenas.

IS YOUR WITNESS A MANAGING AGENT?

When the witness that you designate in a 30(b)(1) deposition notice is an existing director or officer, her status as a *managing agent* is clear, therefore establishing the binding effect of their testimony on the corporation. However, if the witness is not an officer or director, determining whether the witness is a managing agent is not as straightforward. There is no definitive definition of the term *managing agent*.

As the examining party, the burden is on you to establish factually, through the deposition testimony, whether or not the witness is a managing agent.[14] You need to prove that the witness is a managing agent in order to bind the organization with that testimony.

The deponent's title, for example, *manager*, does not determine whether or not a witness is a managing agent. Nor does the fact that the witness does not have the title of *manager* establish that she is not a managing agent. The court bases managing agent status on a person's authority and knowledge of work related to litigation; this person does not need to hold a managerial title within the corporation. The term *managing agent* does not have a literal interpretation,

---

13. *Trans Pac. Ins. Co. v. Trans-Pac. Ins. Co.*, 136 F.R.D. 385, 392–93 (E.D. Pa. 1991) (citing *Salter v. Upjohn Co.*, 593 F.2d 649, 651 (5th Cir. 1979); *Oxford Industries, Inc. v. Luminco, Inc.*, 1990 WL 269728, 1990 U.S. Dist. LEXIS 17392 (E.D. Pa. Dec. 21, 1990); *Farquhar v. Shelden*, 116 F.R.D. 70, 72 (E.D. Mich. 1987); *Zuckert v. Berkliff Corp.*, 96 F.R.D. 161, 162 (N.D. Ill. 1982); *Mitchell v. American Tobacco Company*, 33 F.R.D. 262 (1963); *Mill Run Tours v. Khashoggi*, 124 F.R.D. 547, 550 (S.D.N.Y. 1989); and *Work v. Bier*, 107 F.R.D. 789, 792 n. 4 (D.D.C. 1985)).
14. *JSC Foreign Econ. Ass'n Technostroyexport v. Int'l Dev. & Trade Servs., Inc.*, 220 F.R.D. 235, 237 (S.D.N.Y. 2004).

but rather depends largely on whether the interests of the person align with the principal, and on the nature of the person's "functions, responsibilities, and authority respecting the subject matter of the litigation."[15] The focus is on what the employee *actually does* for the organization, rather than her title.[16]

Knowing whether or not the witness will identify with the organization, or the adversary, is paramount in determining managing agent status.[17] Courts have used various factors to determine if there is a factual basis for designating a witness as a managing agent. Because the factual circumstances differ greatly among cases, the test for managing agent status is a functional one and the court determines the status on a case-by-case basis.[18]

Courts generally agree on the broad principles for deciding whether a person is a managing agent of a corporation. To establish managing agent status, a party must prove the following:

1. The corporation has invested the employee with discretion to exercise her judgment.

2. The company depends on the employee to carry out the employer's directions.

3. The employee identifies with the interests of the corporation as opposed to the interests of the adverse party.[19]

---

15. *Tomingas v. Douglas Aircraft Co.*, 45 F.R.D. 94, 96 (S.D.N.Y. 1969) (citing *Kolb v. A. H. Bull S.S. Co.*, 31 F.R.D. 252, 254 (E.D.N.Y. 1962)).
16. *Young & Assoc. Pub. Relations v. Delta Air Lines, Inc.*, 216 F.R.D. 521, 523 (D. Utah 2003).
17. *In re Honda Am. Motor Co., Inc. Dealership Relations Litig.*, 168 F.R.D. 535, 541 (D. Md. 1996).
18. *Id.* at 540 (citing *Founding Church of Scientology of Washington, D.C. v. Webster*, 802 F.2d 1448, 1452 (D.C. Cir. 1986)).
19. *In re Honda Am. Motor Co. Dealership Relations Litig.*, 168 F.R.D. 535, 540 (D. Md. 1996) (citing *Reed Paper Co. v. Proctor & Gamble Distrib. Co.*, 144 F.R.D. 2, 4 (D. Me. 1992)); *Colonial Capital Co. v. General Motors Corp.*, 29 F.R.D. 514, 516–17 (D. Conn. 1961); *Sugarhill Records Ltd. v. Motown Record Corp.*, 105 F.R.D. 166, 170 (S.D.N.Y. 1985); Afram Lines, 159 F.R.D. at 413; *Indep. Prods. Corp. v. Loew's, Inc.*, 24 F.R.D. 19, 25 (S.D.N.Y. 1959).

Within these broad categories, courts have considered numerous factors. Some of the factors in this list may seem repetitious, but each of the following points references what a specific court stated. The important things is to ask the questions to try to identify what are the employee's actual duties, relationship to the business, and relationship to the issues in the case.

- The degree of supervisory authority the employee has in the relevant area.[20]

- The employee's general responsibilities regarding the matters at issue in the litigation.[21]

- The employee's reliability in giving testimony, at her principal's direction, in response to the demand of a party engaged in litigation with the principal.[22]

- The employee, or employees, who are in higher authority than the deponent and are in charge of or possess the information about the matters at issue.[23]

- The employee's interests in relation to, or identifying with, those of the principal.[24]

---

20. *Sugarhill Records Ltd. v. Motown Record Corp.*, 105 F.R.D. 166, 170 (S.D.N.Y. 1985).
21. *In re Honda Am. Motor Co. Dealership Relations Litig.*, 168 F.R.D. 535, 540, 541 (D. Md. 1996); *Sugarhill Records Ltd. v. Motown Record Corp.*, 105 F.R.D. 166, 170 (S.D.N.Y. 1985).
22. *Terry v. Modern Woodmen of America*, 57 F.R.D. 141, 143 (W.D. Mo. 1972); *Tomingas v. Douglas Aircraft Co.*, 45 F.R.D. 94, 96 (S.D.N.Y. 1969) (citing *United States v. The Dorothy McAllister*, 24 F.R.D. 316, 318 (S.D.N.Y. 1959)); *Rubin v. General Tire & Rubber Co.*, 18 F.R.D. 51, 56 (S.D.N.Y. 1955).
23. *Terry v. Modern Woodmen of Am.*, 57 F.R.D. 141, 143 (W.D. Mo. 1972); *Tomingas v. Douglas Aircraft Co.*, 45 F.R.D. 94, 96 (S.D.N.Y. 1969) (citing *United States v. The Dorothy McAllister*, 24 F.R.D. 316, 318 (S.D.N.Y. 1959)); *Rubin v. General Tire & Rubber Co.*, 18 F.R.D. 51, 56 (S.D.N.Y. 1955).
24. *Young & Assoc. Pub. Relations v. Delta Air Lines, Inc.*, 216 F.R.D. 521, 523 (D. Utah 2003) (citing *Stearns v. Pacer, Inc.*, 986 F.2d 1429, 1429 (10th Cir. 1993) (citing *Crimm v. Mo. Pacific R. Co.*, 750 F.2d 703, 708–09 (8th Cir. 1984)).

- The nature of the employee's functions, responsibilities, and duties.[25]

- The extent of the employee's power to exercise judgment and discretion.[26]

- Whether any employee or employees higher in authority than deponent were in charge of the matter or possessed all of the necessary information sought in the deposition.[27]

- Whether the employee has general powers from the corporation to exercise her judgment and discretion in dealing with corporate matters.[28]

- Whether the employee could be depended upon to carry out her employer's direction to give testimony at the demand of a party engaged in litigation with the employer.[29]

- The employee's ability to help with fact-finding on the matter at issue, in comparison to other people associated with the corporation.[30]

- Whether the employee can be expected to identify himself with the interests of the corporation rather than with those of the opposing party.[31]

---

25. *Id.*; *see also*, *Terry v. Modern Woodmen of Am.*, 57 F.R.D. 141, 143 (W.D. Mo. 1972) (citing *Tomingas v. Douglas Aircraft Co.*, 45 F.R.D. 94, 96 (S.D.N.Y. 1968)).
26. *Young & Assoc. Pub. Relations v. Delta Air Lines, Inc.*, 216 F.R.D. 521, 523 (D. Utah 2003). (citing *Stearns v. Pacer, Inc.*, 986 F.2d 1429 (10th Cir. 1993) (citing *Crimm v. Missouri Pacific R. Co.*, 750 F2d 703, 708–09 (8th Cir. 1984)).
27. *Id.*
28. *Young & Assoc. Pub. Relations v. Delta Air Lines, Inc.*, 216 F.R.D. 521, 523 (D. Utah 2003) (citing *Reed Paper Co. v. Proctor & Gamble Distrib. Co.*, 144 F.R.D. 2, 4 (8th Cir. 1984)).
29. *Id.*
30. *Rundquist v. Vapiano Se*, 277 F.R.D. 205, 208 (D.D.C. 2011).
31. *Young & Assoc. Pub. Relations v. Delta Air Lines, Inc.*, 216 F.R.D. 521, 523 (D. Utah 2003) (citing *Reed Paper Co. v. Proctor & Gamble Distrib. Co.*, 144 F.R.D. 2, 4 (8th Cir. 1984)).

- Whether the employee's authority included exercising personal discretion in making decisions without obtaining additional authorization from superiors in dealing with corporate matters.[32]
- The employee's appearance, for example, whether the person "appears to be clothed with at least the apparent authority, if not actual authority, of a managing officer or agent."[33]
- The adversary counsel's possible representation of the employee.[34]

No single factor will determine the outcome. Witnesses may not even be managing agents in the course of their everyday duties for the defendant corporation, but nonetheless, they may be managing agents for the purpose of giving testimony regarding the subject matter of the litigation.[35] The issue is not whether the deponent has the power to bind the organization in the contractual sense, but whether the organization has invested the person with general powers to exercise her judgment and discretion on the organization's behalf.[36]

---

32. *Young & Assoc. Pub. Relations v. Delta Air Lines, Inc.*, 216 F.R.D. 521, 523 (D. Utah 2003).
33. *Terry v. Modern Woodmen of Am.*, 57 F.R.D. 141, 143 (W.D. Mo. 1972).
34. *Stearns v. Paccar, Inc.*, 1993 WL17084, *4 (10th Cir. 1993) (Presence of the counsel could arguably elevate the witness to a managing agent, thereby binding the company: "At the time of her deposition, [the deponent] was accompanied by [the corporation's] counsel, who made deposition objections with only [the corporation]'s interests in mind.").
35. *See Tomingas v. Douglas Aircraft Co.*, 45 F.R.D. 94, 96 (S.D.N.Y. 1969).
36. *See In re Honda Am. Motor Co. Dealership Relations Litig.*, 168 F.R.D. 535–540, 541 (D. Md. 1996) (citing *Colonial Capital Co. v. General Motors Corp.*, 29 F.R.D. 514, 516–17 (D. Conn. 1961)).

Largely because of the vast variety of factual circumstances, determining whether a witness has managing agent status remains a functional one to be determined largely on a case-by-case basis.[37]

Example: *Tomingas v. Douglas Aircraft Co.*

In the case of *Tomingas v. Douglas Aircraft Co.*, Douglas Aircraft Co. was the defendant in an aviation crash case. Douglas was the manufacturer of an aircraft that crashed in Canada. Douglas's engineers assisted the Canadian government in investigating the crash and were in charge of identifying pieces of wreckage. Although those engineers weren't involved in managing any part of the company, the court determined that they possessed enough identity of interests with their employer to make them managing agents able to give testimony regarding the accident investigation. The court required Douglas to produce engineers for depositions who, as managing agents, would bind the organization.[38]

FORMER OFFICERS, DIRECTORS, AND MANAGING AGENTS

In order to bind an organization, the witness must be a managing agent *at the time* of the deposition, as opposed to the time when the activities disputed in the litigation occurred.[39] Therefore, as a general rule, former employees cannot be managing agents of a

---

37 *E.I. Dupont de Nemours and Co. v. Kolon Industries, Ins.*, 268 F.R.D. 45, 48 (2010) (citing *Founding Church of Scientology, Inc. v. Webster*, 802 F.2d 1448, 1452 (D.C. Cir. 1986)).
38. *Tomingas v. Douglas Aircraft Co.*, 45 F.R.D. 94 (S.D.N.Y. 1969).
39. *Martin Cty. Coal Corp. v. Universal Underwriters Ins. Servs., Inc.*, 2010 WL 4629761, *2 (E.D. Ky.) (citing *In re Honda Am. Motor Co. Dealership Relations Litig.*, 168 F.R.D. 535, 540–541 (D. Md. 1996)).

corporation,[40] and you cannot compel a corporation to produce its former officers or directors using 30(b)(1).[41] Instead, you must subpoena such witnesses as with any other nonparty witness.[42] Consequently, although persuasive, the testimony of the former employee generally does not bind the organization.

There are exceptions to the general rule for determining whether a *former* managing agent will bind the corporation. The "timing and circumstances of reassignment or termination" of the corporation's employees "render the true status of the proposed deponents highly suspect, and allow for a strong inference that [the corporation] is moving its employees around like chessmen, conveniently shielding them from access."[43] For example, if a corporation terminates an employee in order to avoid disclosure in an existing or potential litigation, the former employee may still bind the corporation.[44] The same is true if there is evidence that the employee has been or might be reappointed to another position in the corporation.[45] Further, if a person continues to act as a managing agent despite no longer being an employee,

---

40. *Rundquist v. Vapiano Se*, 277 F.R.D. 205, 208 (D.D.C. 2011) (citing *Simms v. Center for Correctional Health and Policy Studies*, 272 F.R.D. 36, 41 (D.D.C. 2011)).
41. *Rundquist v. Vapiano Se*, 277 F.R.D. 205, 208 (D.D.C. 2011); *In re Honda Am. Motor Co., Dealership Relations Litig.*, 168 F.R.D. 535, 540–541 (D. Md. 1996).
42. *Rundquist v. Vapiano Se*, 277 F.R.D. 205, 208 (D.D.C. 2011); *In re Honda Am. Motor Co., Dealership Relations Litig.*, 168 F.R.D. 535, 541 (D. Md. 1996).
43. *Rundquist v. Vapiano Se*, 277 F.R.D. 205, 208 (D.D.C. 2011) (citing *E.I. DuPont de Nemours and Co. v. Kolon Indus., Inc.*, 268 F.R.D. 45, 50–51 (E.D. Va. 2010)).
44. *In re Honda Am. Motor Co., Dealership Relations Litig.*, 168 F.R.D. 535, 541 (D. Md. 1996) (citing *Indep. Prods. Corp. v. Loew's, Inc.*, 24 F.R.D. 19, 23–24 (S.D.N.Y. 1959)).
45. *Id.* (citing *Curry v. States Marine Corp. of Del.*, 16 F.R.D. 376, 377 (S.D.N.Y. 1954)).

that person can also be considered a managing agent.[46] In circumstances where a person did not hold any office or formal position within the corporation, but still controlled the affairs of the organization, such as a founder of a religious organization[47] or a 100 percent stockholder, that person can be considered a *de facto* managing agent.[48]

The party that claims a witness is a managing agent carries the burden of establishing the factual basis for the status.[49] However, during the discovery process, if parties dispute a person's acceptability as a managing agent for deposition, the court should resolve any doubts in favor of the examining party since the trial court will ultimately determine whether the witness's testimony will bind the defendant.[50]

---

46. *Rundquist v. Vapiano Se*, 277 F.R.D. 205, 208 (D.D.C. 2011) (citing *In re Honda Am. Motor Co., Dealership Relations Litig.*, 168 F.R.D. 535, 541 (D. Md. 1996) and *E.I. DuPont de Nemours and Co. v. Kolon Indus., Inc.*, 268 F.R.D. 45, 48–49 (E.D. Va. 2010)); *Founding Church of Scientology of Washington, D.C., Inc. v. Webster*, 802 F.2d 1448,1455–57 (D.C. Cir. 1986) ("The test is a practical one, focusing on how active and substantial the individual's control is.").

47. *Founding Church of Scientology of Washington, D.C. v. Webster*, 802 F.2d 1448, 1452 (D.C. Cir. 1986) ("For the purpose of determining whether an individual is a 'managing agent' within the meaning of the discovery rules, the alter ego theory provides a useful analogy.").

48. *See* Petition of Manor Investment Co., 43 F.R.D. 299, 300–301 (S.D.N.Y. 1967) ("If he has general powers to exercise his judgment and discretion in dealing with corporate matters, he may be deemed a 'managing agent.' In each instance a realistic appraisal of his activities determines the true nature of his relationship to the corporation.").

49. *Young & Assoc. Pub. Relations v. Delta Air Lines, Inc.*, 216 F.R.D. 521, 524 (D. Utah 2003).

50. *Tomingas v. Douglas Aircraft Co.*, 45 F.R.D. 94, 97 (S.D.N.Y. 1969) (citing *United States v. The Dorothy McAllister*, 24 F.R.D. 316, 318 (S.D.N.Y. 1959)); *Rubin v. General Tire & Rubber Co.*, 18 F.R.D. 51, 56 (S.D.N.Y. 1955).

Example: Portland Parts, Inc.

For example, you represent a manufacturer called Temco Parts, Inc. involved in a contract dispute with one of its component part suppliers, Portland Parts, alleging that Portland Parts did not meet specifications for a component part. The CFOs of each company signed the contract. Conversations that occurred during the signing of the contract are important to the case. However, the Portland Parts's CFO has resigned and taken a job with another company. Because he is a former employee, you must subpoena him to testify, and his deposition testimony is not binding on the company.

Technique: Establish the Witness's Status

The key to successfully binding the corporation using Rule 30(b)(1) is to establish a deposition record that factually presents the witness as an officer, director, or managing agent at the operative times. Your first line of inquiry is to establish whether the witness is a current officer or director:

Q: Are you currently an officer or director of Portland Parts?

Q: Which office do you hold?

If the witness is a current officer or director, then that witness will bind the corporation. However, if the witness is a former officer or director, then your inquiry must focus on whether that witness still identifies with the corporation.

Q: Have you ever been an officer or director in Portland Parts?

Q: When?

Q: When did your role as an officer or director in Portland Parts end?

Q: Why?

Q: What is your current relationship with Portland Parts?

Q: Do you own any stock in Portland Parts?

Q: How much?

Q: Do you have the ability to vote at shareholder meetings?

Q: Do you receive any salary, income, or dividends from Portland Parts?

Q: How much?

Q: Do you still feel connected to Portland Parts?

Q: Tell us about that please.

Q: Are you represented in this deposition by Portland Parts's lawyers?

Q: Did you meet with Portland Parts's lawyers to prepare for your deposition?

Q: What did you discuss?

Will this last question elicit an attorney–client privilege objection and instruction not to answer?

If the attorney representing the organization asserts attorney–client privilege, that attorney has bolstered the argument that the testimony will bind the company. On the other hand, if you challenge whether there is a privilege, you are lessening your argument of the binding effect of that testimony.

If the witness is not an officer or director of the corporation, then your inquiry must focus on whether the witness is a managing agent for the matter that is the subject of the litigation.

Q: What is your job today?

Q: Who is your employer?

Q: What is your job title?

Q: Describe your job for us, please.

Q: Are you currently a managing agent of Portland Parts?

Q: Please describe the functions, the responsibilities, and the duties of your job.

Q: Do you have the power to exercise judgment and discretion in your job?

Q: Tell us about that, please.

Q: What is your role regarding [the particular matter of inquiry you're seeking in the deposition]?

Q: Do you have supervisory authority with respect to [the particular matter of inquiry you're seeking in the deposition]?

Q: Is there any person or are there any people higher in authority than you in charge of [the particular matter of inquiry you're seeking in the deposition]?

Q: Who?

Q: Are Portland Parts' lawyers at this deposition representing you?

Q: What is your relationship with Portland Parts?

Q: Do you still feel connected to Portland Parts?

Q: Tell us about that, please.

Q: Do you identify with Portland Parts in any way?

Q: Tell us about that, please.

If the witness was a managing agent during the time critical to the litigation, but is no longer acting in that capacity, then you need to develop a record that establishes why the witness changed positions.

Q: What was your job during [the critical time frame]?

Q: Who was your employer?

Q: What was your job title at that time?

Q: Describe that job for us, please.

Q: Please describe the functions, the responsibilities, and the duties of that job.

Q: Did you have the power to exercise judgment and discretion in that job?

Q: Tell us about that, please.

Q: Did you have supervisory authority with respect to [the particular matter of inquiry you're seeking in the deposition]?

Q: Was there any person or were there any people higher in authority than you in charge of [the particular matter of inquiry you're seeking in the deposition]?

Q: Who?

Q: When did you leave that job?

Q: Why did you leave that position?

Q: Whose decision was it for you to leave that position?

Q: Do you continue to have any supervisory authority involving [the particular matter of inquiry you're seeking in the deposition]?

Q: Do you currently have a role in Portland Parts?

Q: What role?

Q: Is there any plan for you to return to your former position at Portland Parts?

Q: What is your current relationship with Portland Parts?

Q: Are Portland Parts' lawyers at this deposition representing you?

Q: Did you meet with Portland Parts' lawyers to prepare for your deposition?

Q: What did you discuss?

Will this last question elicit an attorney–client privilege objection and instruction not to answer? Consider the following points I explained earlier:

    If the attorney representing the organization asserts attorney–client privilege, that attorney has bolstered the argument that the testimony will bind the company. On the other hand, if you challenge whether there is a privilege, you are lessening your argument of the binding effect of that testimony.

    If the witness is not an officer or director of the corporation, then your inquiry must focus on whether the witness is a managing agent for the matter that is the subject of the litigation.

Q: Do you still feel connected to Portland Parts?

Q: Tell us about that, please.

Q: Do you identify with Portland Parts in any way?

Q: Tell us about that, please.

Unlike a 30(b)(6) designated witness, a 30(b)(1) witness has no duty to prepare for the deposition. Rather, the 30(b)(1) deponent's obligation is to testify completely as to the information she knew at the time of the deposition. The problem that ultimately arises in litigation is that the witness refreshes her recollections before the trial and offers a more complete or altered testimony that the counsel must permit. On the other hand, a 30(b)(6) witness must be *fully prepared* to provide all information that the organization knows regarding the matters of examination. As I discuss in chapter 16, "Changing the Testimony," if the organization's designated witness attempts to change her testimony, the burden shifts to that organization to prove that the information was unavailable at the time of the deposition. If the organization cannot do so, the court should not allow the altered testimony.

When you depose officers, directors, or managing agents in the course of any litigation, their testimony will bind the organization. Using 30(b)(1) is a tactical choice. If you want to prove that a specific person within the organization did or did not know something, then use 30(b)(1). However, if you want to discover particular information or establish a company's position, then use 30(b)(6).

To make use of the tactical distinction between 30(b)(1) and 30(b)(6), you need to determine what you hope to learn: specific information known within the organization and how the organization will interpret facts and documents, or what a *single* employee did or did not know. If you want the totality of what the organization knows, you will find Rule 30(b)(6) generally more effective in forcing the organization to provide all that information. On the other hand, if you need to establish that a specific person within the organization knew or did not know specific information, then you should use 30(b)(1).

Example: Montgomery Medical Systems

For example, you represent the family of a nursing home resident who died by strangulation in a bed rail manufactured by Montgomery Medical Systems. Your research reveals that, four years before the manufacture of the Montgomery Medical Systems bed that killed your client, the FDA had sent out notices to Montgomery Medical Systems, alerting them to the dangers of entrapment. If you want to establish that Montgomery Medical Systems received the notice, you should take a 30(b)(6) deposition of Montgomery Medical Systems, focusing on all notices the company received from the FDA regarding bed-rail entrapment dangers. On the other hand, if you want to learn whether anyone in Montgomery Medical Systems gave those notices to the design engineers, you should take the individual 30(b)(1) deposition of the design engineer to see if she knew about the FDA warnings. If the engineer didn't know about the warnings, you can establish that the company withheld the notices. This fact expands your theory of liability beyond a simple negligent design defect. The cause of action would now focus on intentional corporate management decisions resulting in an unreasonably dangerous design.

Deposing Executives

You may encounter situations in which you want to depose high-level officers in the organization, such as a CEO. The tactical decision to issue a 30(b)(1) deposition notice of that high-ranking corporate officer may result in motions to quash the notice. Institutions often argue that taking the deposition of their high-ranking people would create a significant burden on their organization.

All depositions create a burden; therefore, as in all motions for protection under Rule 26(c), only unreasonable burdens will sustain an order for protection. When courts face motions to quash the deposition of a high-ranking employee, they must weigh the respective needs and burdens of both parties. Therefore, the threshold question for the courts to analyze is whether that specific person's deposition is necessary.

Is This Executive's Deposition Necessary?

If the high-ranking official has the information you need, it is unusual "for a court to prohibit the taking of a deposition altogether absent extraordinary circumstances."[51] For example, when the high-ranking person *has* the crucial information necessary to the case, or it is critical to establish that the high-ranking person *did not* possess information,[52] the court will allow the deposition to proceed.

> ### Example: Automobile Manufacturing Case
>
> You have been asked to represent twelve families in wrongful death lawsuits against an automobile manufacturer for not recalling their cars that had defective brakes. The question you want to resolve is whether the manufacturer failed to recall eight hundred thousand cars due to management decisions. The upper-level executives hold the crucial information on the recall; therefore, deposing the upper-level executives is important.

On the other hand, if the person you want to depose doesn't have personal knowledge relating to the litigation, the deposition may have no purpose. In that case, deposing this executive creates a "potential for abuse," which the court will balance with the

---

51. *Apple Inc. v. Samsung Electronics Co., Ltd.*, 282 F.R.D. 259, 263 (N.D. Cal. 2012) citing *WebSideStory, Inc. v. NetRatings, Inc.*, 06CV408 WQH (AJB), 2007 WL 1120567, at *2 (S.D. Cal. Apr. 6, 2007)); *see also, In re Google Litig.*, C 08-03172 RMW (PSG), 2011 U.S. Dist. LEXIS 120905, *10 (N.D. Cal. Oct. 19, 2011); *Celerity, Inc. v. Ultra Clean Holding, Inc.*, 2007 U.S. Dist. LEXIS 8295, 2007 WL 205067, *3 (N.D. Cal. 2007); *Blankenship v. Hearst Corp.*, 519 F.2d 418, 429 (9th Cir. 1975).
52. *Travelers Rental Co. v. Ford Motor Co.*, 116 F.R.D. 140, 144 (D. Mass. 1987) ("[T]he lack of knowledge claimed by these high executives may, in and of itself, be relevant evidence.").

principle that "a party seeking to prevent a deposition carries a heavy burden to show why discovery should be denied."[53]

Example: Automobile Repair Case

> For example, if your lawsuit is against an automobile distributor for not properly repainting the car after repairing a fender bender, the upper-level executives for the auto manufacturer would have no knowledge of what occurred, and their depositions would not be appropriate.

Once the court establishes the executive's testimony as relevant, courts have recognized that mere representation by the company's lawyers that the executive doesn't have information is insufficient to quash the deposition notices:

> [E]ven where . . . a high-ranking corporate officer denies personal knowledge of the issues at hand, this "claim . . . is subject to testing by the examining party."[54]

Similarly, the U.S. District Court in Massachusetts has recognized the following:

---

53. *Apple Inc. v. Samsung Electronics Co., Ltd.*, 282 F.R.D. 259, 263 (N.D. Cal. 2012) (citing *Celerity, Inc. v. Ultra Clean Holding, Inc.*, 2007 U.S. Dist. LEXIS 8295, 2007 WL 205067, at *3 (N.D. Cal. 2007) and *Blankenship v. Hearst Corp.*, 519 F.2d 418, 429 (9th Cir. 1975)); *see also, In re Google Litig.*, C 08-03172 RMW (PSG), 2011 U.S. Dist. LEXIS 120905, *10 (N.D. Cal. Oct. 19, 2011); *WebSideStory, Inc. v. NetRatings, Inc.*, 06CV408 WQH (AJB), 2007 U.S. Dist. LEXIS 20481, 2007 WL 1120567, *2 (S.D. Cal. Apr. 6, 2007).
54. *Six West Retail Acquisition v. Sony Theatre Management Corp.*, 203 F.R.D. 98, 102 (S.D.N.Y. 2001) (quoting *Consolidated Rail Corp. v. Primary Industries Corp.*, No. 92 Civ. 4927, 1993 WL 364471, at *1 (S.D.N.Y. Sept. 10, 1993)); *Johnson v. Jung*, 242 F.R.D. 481, 484 (N.D. Ill. 2007).

> Ford responds to plaintiff's recital of facts indicating the involvement of these four persons in the resale program with "know nothing" affidavits of each. Perhaps they could better be described as "remember nothing" affidavits. In the face of the showing made by the plaintiff, they are plainly insufficient to support a motion to quash. The plaintiff is entitled to "test" the claim of lack of knowledge or lack of recollection by deposing the witness. . . . In fact, the ability to "test" is even more important in the case of a claimed lack of recollection than lack of knowledge, since recollection can frequently be refreshed during an examination.[55]

If the executive has the knowledge, we want to take their deposition. The question is, who has the responsibility of establishing that the executive should be protected or not from having their deposition taken?

Who Establishes that This Deposition is Necessary?

Courts vary on the standards they impose when determining whether you can depose a high-level executive. Some courts say it is the executive's responsibility to prove the deposition is inappropriate. Others presume that the executive shouldn't be deposed and that the requesting party must prove why the deposition is necessary.

In some places, executives have special protections, and in some jurisdictions, they don't. Some jurisdictions have no protections, and some jurisdictions have varying levels of what has

---

55. *Travelers Rental Co. v. Ford Motor Co.*, 116 F.R.D. 140, 143 (D. Mass. 1987) (citing *Amherst Leasing Corp. v. Emhart Corp.*, 65 F.R.D. 121, 121–23 (D. Conn. 1974) and *Parkhurst v. King*, 266 F. Supp. 780 (E.D. Pa. 1967)).

become known as the *Apex Doctrine*. Research your jurisdiction carefully on this issue.

Some Jurisdictions Have No Executive Protection

Some jurisdictions reject the special protections for high-ranking executives.[56] They have determined that special protections for executives are inconsistent with the existing policy for broad discovery rules and, therefore, require the party opposing the deposition to prove the protective order is necessary, as covered in Rule 26.[57] Those courts have found that setting a discovery bar higher than what the Federal Rules of Civil Procedure describe is inconsistent with the federal rules.[58]

---

56. *Serrano v. Cintas Corp.*, 699 F.3d 884, 902 (6th Cir. 2012) ("[W]e conclude that the magistrate judge erred as a matter of law in relying on 'apex doctrine' to grant the protective order. In doing so, the magistrate judge . . . failed to analyze, as required by Rule 26(c)(1), what harm [the executive] would suffer by submitting to the deposition. This error of law constitutes an abuse of discretion that warrants vacating the magistrate judge's order."); *Crest Infiniti II, LP v. Swinton*, 174 P.3d 996, 1004 (Okla. 2007) ("We decline to adopt a form of the apex doctrine that shifts a burden to the party seeking discovery. In Oklahoma the burden of showing 'good cause' is statutorily placed on the party objecting to discovery and is part of that party's motion for a protective order."); *State ex rel. Ford Motor Co. v. Messina*, 71 S.W.3d 602, 606–07 (Mo. 2002).
57. *Serrano v. Cintas Corp.*, 699 F.3d 884, 901–02 (6th Cir. 2012); *State ex rel. Ford Motor Co. v. Messina*, 71 S.W.3d 602, 606–07 (Mo. 2002). Oklahoma and Missouri have expressly rejected the Apex Doctrine as contrary to their discovery rules. *Crest Infiniti, II, LP v. Swinton*, 174 P.3d 996, 998 (Okl. 2007) ("The burden to show that a deposition of a corporate official is for the purpose of annoyance, harassment, embarrassment, oppression or undue delay, burden or expense, is upon the party or individual objecting to discovery; further, the Court declines to adopt the apex doctrine."); *Citigroup Inc. v. Holtsberg*, 915 So. 2d 1265, 1269 (Fla. Dist. Ct. App. 4th Dist. 2005) ("[N]o reported Florida appellate court opinion has expressly adopted the doctrine; a district court of appeal cannot adopt a doctrine which arguably conflicts with the discovery rules."); *Citigroup, Inc. v. Holtsberg*, 915 So.2d 1265 (S. Fla. Dist. Ct. App. 4th Dist. 2005); "Discovery— Oral Depositions," 4 *Am. Jur. Trials* 119 (originally published in 1966).
58. *Citigroup, Inc. v. Holtsberg*, 915 So. 2d 1265 (S. Fla. Dist. Ct. App. 4th Dist. 2005); "Discovery—Oral Depositions," 4 *Am. Jur. Trials* 119 (originally published in 1966).

For example, the U.S. District Court in Northern Illinois stated the following:

> In short, highly placed executives are not immune from discovery, and the fact that an executive has a busy schedule cannot shield that witness from being deposed.[59]

The court reasoned thus:

> If the President of the United States is not immune from responding to reasonably scheduled discovery, . . . neither is the General Secretary and CEO of the General Board of Pension and Health Benefits of the United Methodist Church.[60]

Some Jurisdictions Have Varying Levels of Executive Protection: The Apex Doctrine

Other courts have developed rules, known as the *Apex Doctrine*, which give high-ranking executives levels of protection from depositions. These rules focus on which party has the burden of establishing whether deposing a high-ranking executive is appropriate or whether the notice of deposition should be quashed.[61] Jurisdictions vary as to which party bears that burden.

---

59. *Johnson v. Jung*, 242 F.R.D. 481, 486 (N.D. Ill. 2007) (citing *General Star Indemnity Co. v. Platinum Indemnity Ltd.*, 210 F.R.D. 80, 83 (S.D.N.Y. 2002) and *Six West Retail Acquisition v. Sony Theatre Management Corp.*, 203 F.R.D. 98, 102 (S.D.N.Y. 2001)).
60. *Johnson v. Jung*, 242 F.R.D. 481, 486 (N.D. Ill. 2007) (citing *Clinton v. Jones*, 520 U.S. 681, 117 S.Ct. 1636, 137 L.Ed.2d 945 (1997), 8 C. Wright, A. Miller & R. Marcus, *Federal Practice and Procedure* § 2037 at 500–502 (1970), and *CBS, Inc. v. Ahern*, 102 F.R.D. 820, 822 (S.D.N.Y. 1984)).
61. *United States v. Morgan*, 313 U.S. 409, 421–22 (1941); *Salter v. Upjohn Co.*, 593 F.2d 649, 651–52 (5th Cir. 1979); *In re Continental Airlines*, 305 S.W.3d 849, 852–53 (Tex. Ct. App. 2010); *Alberto v. Toyota Motor Sales USA Inc.*, 796 N.W.2d 490, 493–94 (Mich. Ct. App. 2010).

Executives Must Prove the Deposition is Unnecessary

Some jurisdictions place the burden on the party opposing the discovery. In these jurisdictions, the executive's deposition is presumed to be appropriate, unless the executive proves that it is not. For example, the U.S. District Court of the Southern District of New York stated the following:

> In resisting the deposition, [the opposing party] argues first that plaintiff has not demonstrated that [the corporation's CEO] has relevant personal knowledge of any of the facts of the case. But it is not plaintiff's burden to do so. An order barring a litigant from taking a deposition is most extraordinary relief. . . . It is the party seeking such an order that bears the burden of proving that the proposed deponent has nothing to contribute.[62]

In other jurisdictions, once the corporation receives a notice of executive deposition, the corporate party can respond with a detailed affidavit describing the job title and duties, both at the current time and at the time of the events at issue, to challenge that deposition.[63] If the statement demonstrates the executive's lack of familiarity and lack of unique or superior knowledge about the facts of the case, the burden then shifts to the party

---

62. *Speadmark Inc. v. Federated Department Stores Inc.*, 176 F.R.D. 116, 118 (S.D.N.Y. 1997) (citing *Investment Properties Int'l, Ltd. v. IOS, Ltd.*, 459 F.2d 705, 708 (2d Cir. 1972) and *Naftchi v. New York University Medical Center*, 172 F.R.D. 130, 132 (S.D.N.Y. 1997)).
63. *Lederman v. N.Y.C. Dep't of Parks & Rec.*, 731 F.3d 199, 203 (2d Cir. 2013); *Maxtena, Inc. v. Marks*, 289 F.R.D. 427, 440 (D. Md. 2012); *Alex & Ani, Inc. v. MOA Int'l Corp.*, 2011 U.S. Dist. LEXIS 146581, 9 (S.D.N.Y. Dec. 20, 2011); *Byrd v. District of Columbia*, 259 F.R.D. 1, 8 (D.D.C. 2009); *Reif v. CNA*, 248 F.R.D. 448, 454 (E.D. Pa. 2008); *Bogan v. City of Boston*, 489 F.3d 417, 423 (1st Cir. 2007); *Thomas v. International Bus. Machs.*, 48 F.3d 478, 483 (10th Cir. 1995); *Baine v. General Motors Corp.*, 141 F.R.D. 332, 335 (M.D. Ala. 1991); *Salter v. Upjohn Co.*, 593 F.2d 649, 651 (5th Cir. 1979).

seeking discovery to justify that the executive's testimony is necessary.[64] If the party seeking discovery fails to show that the deposition is necessary, the court will grant a protective order for the corporation.

The Requesting Party Must Prove the Executive's Deposition is Necessary

Other jurisdictions apply a rebuttable presumption that all executives are protected from having their depositions taken.[65] This means that if you are seeking the deposition of a high-ranking executive, you must establish that the discovery meets Rule 26 requirements before you issue a motion to compel, regardless of your opponent's actions.[66] When seeking to depose a high-level executive in rebuttable presumption states, you must demonstrate that you need the executive testimony by meeting a two-prong test:

---

64. *Citigroup, Inc. v. Holtsberg*, 915 So. 2d 1265 (S. Fla. Dist. Ct. App. 4th Dist. 2005) (denying protective order where responding party did not submit such an affidavit); *Thomas v. Int'l Bus. Machs.*, 48 F.3d 478, 482 (10th Cir. 1995) (denying deposition of CEO who had no personal knowledge); *Lewelling v. Farmer's Ins. Of Columbus, Inc.*, 879 F.2d 212, 218 (6th Cir. 1989).
65. *Apple Inc. v. Samsung Electronics Co., Ltd*, 282 F.R.D. 259, 263 (N.D. Cal. 2012) (citing *In re Google Litig.*, C 08–03172 RMW (PSG), 2011 WL 4985279, at *2, 2011 U.S. Dist. LEXIS 120905, at *10 (N.D. Cal. Oct. 19, 2011); *Celerity, Inc. v. Ultra Clean Holding, Inc.*, 2007 U.S. Dist. LEXIS 8295, 2007 WL 205067, at *3 (N.D. Cal. 2007); *Blankenship v. Hearst Corp.*, 519 F.2d 418, 429 (9th Cir. 1975); *WebSideStory, Inc. v. NetRatings, Inc.*, 06CV408 WQH (AJB), 2007 U.S. Dist. LEXIS 20481, 2007 WL 1120567, at *2 (S.D. Cal. Apr. 6, 2007).
66. *Apple Inc. v. Samsung Electronics Co., Ltd.*, 282 F.R.D. 259, 263 (N.D. Cal. 2012); *Bank of the Ozarks v. Capital Mortgage Corp.*, 2012 WL 2930479, *2 (E.D. Ark. July 18, 2012); *Cardenas v. Prudential Ins. Co. of Am.*, 2003 WL 21293757, *1–3 (D. Minn. May 16, 2003); *In re United States*, 197 F.3d 310, 312–13 (8th Cir. 1999); *Liberty Mut. Ins. Co. v. Superior Court*, 10 Cal. App. 4th 1282, 1289, 13 Cal. Rptr. 2d 363, 367 (1992); *State ex rel. Ford Motor Co. v. Messina*, 71 S.W.3d 602, 606–07 (Mo. 2002); *Crown Cent. Petrol. Corp. v. Garcia*, 904 S.W.2d 125, 128 (Tex. 1995); *Mule v. Chrysler Corp.*, 106 F.R.D. 364, 366 (D.R.I. 1988).

1. You must show that the executive has unique or superior knowledge relevant to the litigation.

2. You must show that you have exhausted alternative discovery methods for that information.[67]

Arguing that the high-ranking executive's testimony is necessary simply because the highest-ranking corporate officer of any corporation has the ultimate responsibility for all corporate decisions is not sufficient to meet the requirements of the first prong (unique and superior knowledge).[68]

Some courts have also held that mere receipt of memos and other correspondences does not demonstrate unique or superior knowledge.[69] Therefore, you must establish a record from the low-level employees that the executive was involved in the events that gave rise to the litigation in an individual capacity, or that the executive's lack of knowledge is critical to the elements of the case.

The second prong requires you to exhaust alternative discovery methods.[70] Courts frequently demand that you seek discovery first by deposing lower-level employees.

To satisfy the second requirement, you must establish a record by deposing lower-level employees. These depositions must demonstrate the executive's direct involvement in the events leading to the litigation, the lower-level employees' lack of knowledge about the events, or holes in the information about that event that the executive must fill. In practice, lower-level employees often lack knowledge, follow instructions to say "not sure," or deny knowledge to escape accountability. Those employees will often testify that their superiors in the organization have the

---

67. *Apple Inc. v. Samsung Electronics Co.*, Ltd, 282 F.R.D. 259, 263 (N.D. Cal. 2012) (citing *In re Google Litig.*, C 08–03172 RMW (PSG), 2011 WL 4985279, at *2, 2011 U.S. Dist. LEXIS 120905, at *10 (N.D. Cal. Oct. 19, 2011)).
68. *In re Daisy Mfg. Co., Inc.*, 17 S.W.3d 654, 659 (Tex. 2000).
69. *Liberty Mut. Ins. Co. v. Superior Court*, 10 Cal. App. 4th 1282, 1289, 13 Cal. Rptr. 2d 363, 367 (1992).
70. *Baine v. Gen. Motor Corp.*, 141 F.R.D. 332, 335 (M.D. Ala. 1991).

knowledge necessary to respond. If your deposition request meets both requirements, then the court will permit the deposition.[71]

Rule 30(b)(6): An Alternative to Deposing the Executive

If your opponent wants to litigate over whether or not you can depose the high-ranking person under the various interpretations of the Apex Doctrine, you can use the alternative approach of crafting a Rule 30(b)(6) deposition notice to get the same information. In *Banks v. Office of the Senate Sergeant-At-Arms,* the court determined that a party is "entitled to know what [the executive] knew, and when he knew it."[72] If you need an executive's personal knowledge, craft a focused "matters of examination" for the 30(b)(6) deposition notice to get that same information. When an organization receives a 30(b)(6) notice, they must interview the executive and use their own records to determine what information relative to the issues in the litigation the executive knew and when the executive knew it. Therefore, a 30(b)(6) deposition notice can accomplish what you need where the Apex Doctrine may limit discovery.

> **Example:** *Banks v. Office of the Senate Sergeant-At-Arms*
>
> In *Banks v. Office of the Senate Sergeant-At-Arms*, the court recognized that Rule 30(b)(6) allowed the plaintiff to inquire about what the high-ranking executive's role was in the decision to terminate an employee. Based on the specific matter of inquiry in the deposition notice, the court permitted the plaintiff in this employment discrimination case to question "(a) who made the decision to terminate [the plaintiff] and

---

71. *Apple Inc. v. Samsung Electronics Co., Ltd.*, 282 F.R.D. 259, 263–64 (N.D. Cal. 2012) (citing *In re Google Litig.*, C 08–03172 RMW (PSG), 2011 WL 4985279, at *2, 2011 U.S. Dist. LEXIS 120905, at *10 (N.D. Cal. Oct. 19, 2011)).
72. *Banks v. Office of the Senate Sergeant-At-Arms*, 241 F.R.D. 370, 374 (D.D.C. 2007).

(b) what information that decision-maker indicated he was taking into account to decide to fire [the plaintiff]."[73] In addition, the plaintiff's specific matter of inquiry allowed questioning on the following:

1. The identity of the decision-makers who were considering the plaintiff and the competing candidate for the employment position.
2. The process they used.
3. Their roles in selecting the candidate for the position.[74]

Summary

- Rule 30(b)(1) depositions of officers, directors, and managing agents bind corporations.

- Rule 30(b)(1) depositions are effective when you need to know about a specific person's knowledge or lack of knowledge.

- Rule 30(b)(6) depositions are effective when you need to know about the organization's knowledge or position.

- *Managing agent* status depends on the witness's relationship to the litigation and the witness's authority and knowledge of the relevant issues.

- The paramount test of a managing agent status is whether the person identifies with the organization's interests.

- Thorough factual records will help you establish that the witness has the requisite managing agent status.

- Jurisdictions vary in their rulings about deposing high-level executives under the Apex Doctrine.

- Rule 30(b)(6) helps you avoid the Apex Doctrine challenges.

---
73. *Id.* at 373–74.
74. *Id.* at 370, 374.

6

DEPOSING LOW-LEVEL EMPLOYEES

The greatest secrets are always hidden in the most unlikely places.

—Roald Dahl, *Charlie and the Chocolate Factory*

INTRODUCTION	115
INFORMAL COMMUNICATION EMPLOYEES	116
Before the Suit: Rule 4.2	118
During the Lawsuit: Contact with Current Employees	119
FORMER EMPLOYEES	123
RESPONSIBILITIES DURING THE INVESTIGATION	126
INVOLUNTARY REPRESENTATION	130
SUMMARY	134

Introduction

Rank-and-file employees are often a key source of information regarding the true workings of a business. As the people who witness actual day-to-day operations, they can provide firsthand knowledge of not only the events associated with an injury, but also the internal business operations that gave rise to the harm.

You do not always need to use formal depositions to seek information from lower-level employees. Because of the potential volatility of these witnesses, your opponent will frequently attempt to limit or delay your access to these witnesses. The extent to which attorneys are permitted to have *ex parte* communications (conversations without your adversary present) with current and former employees of an adverse party is governed by the state rules of professional conduct. When regulating the conduct of the members of its bar, federal courts look to the state rules of professional conduct for their jurisdiction, but also consider the ABA Model Rules of Professional Conduct.[1]

Whether you can interview employees of an adversary, or potential adversary, depends on multiple factors, including who the person is, the person's current employment status, and what the person's access was to privileged information. In the following pages, I will discuss what is and is not appropriate when you want to contact employees and former employees of the organization without your adversary being there.

---

1. *Olson v. Snap Products, Inc.*, 183 FRD 539, 541 (D. Minn. 1998), citing *United States v. Agosto*, 675 F.2d 965, 969 (8th Cir. 1982), *cert. denied*, 459 U.S. 834, 103 S.Ct. 77, 74 L.Ed.2d 74 (1982).

Informal Communication Employees

ABA Model Rules of Professional Conduct Rule 4.2, which governs contact with an adverse party's former and existing employees, was substantially amended in 2002. Various states have adopted and applied this rule in different ways. Further, many of the cases discussing the extent of permissible *ex parte* communication predate the adoption of Rule 4.2. Therefore, as you analyze the law for any given jurisdiction, focus not only on the rule, but also the relationship of that judicial authority to the current Rule of Professional Conduct.

Rule 4.2 of Professional Conduct requires the following:

> **Communication with a Person Represented By Counsel:** In representing a client, a lawyer shall not communicate about the subject of the representation with a person the lawyer knows to be represented by another lawyer in the matter, unless the lawyer has the consent of the other lawyer or is authorized to do so by law or a court order.[2]

Since Rule 4.2 of the Rules of Professional Conduct prohibits "communication with a person represented by counsel" in litigation with a corporation, the question becomes whether the courts consider individual employees as represented by the corporation's counsel. Applying the rule is contingent upon the type of employee and the time in the litigation.

Comment [7] to Rule 4.2 states the following:

> In the case of a represented organization, this rule prohibits communications with a constituent of the organization who supervises, directs, or regularly consults with the organization's lawyer concerning the matter or has authority to obligate the

---

2. Model Rules of Prof'l Conduct R. 4.3 cmt. 1 (2007).

organization with respect to the matter or whose act or omission in connection with the matter may be imputed to the organization for the purposes of civil or criminal liability. Consent of the organization's lawyer is not required for communication with a former constituent. If a constituent of the organization is represented in the matter by his or her own counsel, the consent by that counsel to a communication will be sufficient for the purposes of this Rule.[3] In communication with current or former constituents of an organization, a lawyer must not use methods of obtaining evidence that violate the legal rights of the organization. See rule 4.4.[4]

Rule 4.2 balances your need for information and the organization's need to protect legitimate interests.[5] Rule 4.2 protects an organization's attorney–client relationship because it prohibits *ex parte* communication with employees "who are so closely tied with the organization or the events at issue that it would be unfair to interview them without the presence of the organization's counsel."[6] Preventing employees from disclosing unfavorable facts merely because they occurred in the workplace, however, is not a legitimate reason for an organization to claim that Rule 4.2 prevents communication with those employees.[7] The no-contact rule does not exist "to protect a corporate party from the revelation of prejudicial facts."[8]

---

3. Compare Model Rules of Prof'l Conduct Rule 3.4(f).
4. Model Rules of Prof'l Conduct R. 4.2 cmt. 7 (2007), *see* Model Rules of Prof'l Conduct Rule 4.4.
5. *Clark v. Beverly Health & Rehab. Servs., Inc.*, 440 Mass. 270, 797 N.E.2d 905, 913 (2003).
6. *Id.*
7. *Id.* (citing *Messing, Rudavsky & Weliky, P.C. v. President & Fellows of Harvard College*, 436 Mass. 347, 764 N.E.2d 825 (2002)).
8. *Dent v. Kaufman*, 185 W. Va. 171, 406 S.E.2d 68 (1991).

Before the Suit: Rule 4.2

Courts have ruled that Rule 4.2 applies only *after* litigation has begun.[9] Rule 4.2 does not apply before the lawsuit begins, because the rule applies only to people represented by a lawyer "in the matter."[10] Before the lawsuit begins, when you are conducting interviews as part of a pre-suit investigation, there is not a "matter" within the meaning of Rule 4.2.[11] If the courts interpreted Rule 4.2 to prevent pre-suit investigations, that would conflict with Rule 11 of the Federal Rules of Civil Procedure, which requires a reasonable investigation before a suit begins.[12]

Further, courts have rejected arguments contending that the Rules of Professional Conduct prohibit pre-suit *ex parte* communications because, in pre-suit investigations, the attorney "should have known" that the other person *would* be represented if a lawsuit began.[13] The language of the rule, however, only prohibits *ex parte* contact when counsel knows the other person is currently represented by counsel.[14]

---

9. *See, e.g., Weider Sports Equipment Co., Ltd v. Fitness First, Inc.*, 912 F. Supp. 502, 506 (D. Utah 1996); *Johnson v. Cadillac Plastic Grp., Inc.*, 930 F. Supp. 1437 (Dist. Colo. 1996); and *Terra International, Inc., v. Mississippi Chemical Corp.*, 913 F. Supp. 1306 (W.D. Iowa 1996).
10. *Jorgensen v. Taco Bell Corp.*, 50 Cal. App. 4th 1398, 1401, 58 Cal. Rptr. 2d 178, 180 (1996).
11. *Id.*
12. *Johnson v. Cadillac Plastic Group, Inc.*, 930 F. Supp. 1437 (D. Colo. 1996).
13. *Jorgensen v. Taco Bell Corp.*, 50 Cal. App. 4th 1398, 1401, 58 Cal. Rptr. 2d 178, 180 (1996), citing Triple A, supra, 213 Cal. App. 3d at p. 140, 261 Cal. Rptr. 493; *Continental, supra*, 32 Cal. App. 4th 119–121, 37 Cal. Rptr. 2d 843.
14. *Snider v. Superior Court*, 113 Cal. App. 4th 1187 (2003); *Jorgensen v. Taco Bell Corp.*, 50 Cal. App. 4th 1398, 1401, 58 Cal. Rptr. 2d 178, 180 (1996).

Example: Holy Cross Nursing Home

Imagine a situation where you have been asked to investigate potential claims against Holy Cross Nursing Home for the wrongful death of Dean Jacoby. The family has heard from employees of the Holy Cross Nursing Home that Dean was dropped during a transfer from the bed to the wheelchair because there was only one aide available at the time. From your review of his medical records, you know there were orders requiring that two people be involved in any transfer. You want to find out what happened, and why, before your decide whether to file a lawsuit against Holy Cross Nursing Home. In this example, you are allowed to contact the employees who told the family that Dean was dropped during a single-aide transfer before starting a lawsuit.

During the Lawsuit: Contact with Current Employees

Once a lawsuit has begun against an organization, the question becomes whether the organization's employees are considered "represented by the counsel." Rule 4.2 permits you to directly contact some categories of witnesses without their counsel present. Whether the employees want to talk to you is up to them. However, before you attempt to contact them, you should study the ethics rules in your particular jurisdiction, because the rules vary from jurisdictions to jurisdiction. It is important to identify the most recent version of the state rules of professional responsibility because there have been significant changes throughout the country following the adoption of ABA Rule of Professional Responsibility 4.2 in 2002. Many of the cases discussing the standards for *ex parte* communication predate the rule's changes. Therefore, your research must identify the version of the rule as well as what rule the common law is interpreting. The ABA Rules of Professional Responsibility explain which categories of employees you may speak to.

Control-Group Employees

If the employee you want to speak to within an organization is a member of the *control group* (the employee supervises, directs, or regularly consults with the organization's lawyer), the court considers that employee to be represented by the organization's attorney. Comment 7 to Rule 4.2 provides the following:

> In the case of a represented organization, this Rule prohibits communications with a constituent of the organization who supervises, directs, or regularly consults with the organization's lawyer concerning the matter or has authority to obligate the organization with respect to the matter or whose act or omission in connection with the matter may be imputed to the organization for purposes of civil or criminal liability.[15]

Low-Level Employees

General counsel or retained counsel represent the company. They do not represent all employees of the company.[16] Low-level employees do not have the authority to bind the organization. As a result, the court does not consider the low-level employees the *party*. Although those low-level employees may have information that could be harmful to their employer, their statements are unlikely to *bind* the employer.[17] The majority of jurisdictions permit *ex parte* communication with existing low-level employees. However, determining what constitutes a low-level employee varies by jurisdiction.

---

15. Model Rules Rules of Prof'l Conduct R. 4.2 cmt. 7 (2007).
16. *Terra Int'l, Inc. v. Miss. Chem. Corp.*, 913 F. Supp. 1306, 1317 (N.D. Iowa 1996).
17. *Niesig v. Team I*, 558 N.E.2d 1030 (N.Y. 1990); *Messing, Rudavsky & Weliky, P.C. v. President & Fellows of Harvard Coll.*, 436 Mass. 347, 764 N.E.2d 825 (2002); *Andrews v. Goodyear Tire & Rubber Co.*, 191 F.R.D. 59 (D.N.J. 2000).

Some jurisdictions have held that the plaintiff's counsel can contact all current employees *ex parte*, except for those employees in the corporation's control group, that is, senior corporate management officials.[18] In *Johnson v. Cadillac Plastic Group Inc.*, the court stated that having the status of management-level employee alone does not make the person a *party* for the purposes of Rule 4.2.[19]

> If [an] employee [who is not authorized to commit the organization on the matter of representation] has information adverse to corporate policy or practice which is at issue in any litigation, the employee must be free to speak and the courts should have access to the evidence. Any concept of ethics which is to the contrary must be premised on a very special justification. The admissions restriction portion of the comments to Rule 4.2 of the ABA Model Rules of Professional Conduct is not supported by such justification.[20]

Another view involves a stricter reading of Rule 4.2 and the Official Comments founded prior to the 2002 Amendments. This view holds that the plaintiff's counsel can contact current employees, unless those employees have the power to bind the corporation,

---

18. *See, e.g., Palmer v. Pioneer Inn Assoc. Ltd.*, 257 F.3d 999, 1001 (9th Cir. 2001) ("Under the managing-speaking test, *ex parte* interviews are barred for employees holding managerial positions giving them authority to speak for and bind the corporation."; *Johnson v. Cadillac Plastic Group Inc.*, 930 F. Supp. 1437, 1442 (D. Colo. 1996); *Bey v. Village of Arlington Heights*, 50 Fair Empl. Prac. Cas. (BNA) 1375 (N.D. Ill. Aug. 9, 1989); *Fair Automotive Repair, Inc. v. Car-X Service Systems, Inc.*, 471 N.E.2d 554, 560–61 (Ill. Ct. App. 1984); *Porter v. Arco Metals Co., Div. of Atl. Richfield Corp.*, 642 F. Supp. 1116 (D. Mont. 1986); *Andrews v. Goodyear Tire & Rubber Co.*, 191 F.R.D. 59, 76–78 (D.N.J. 2000); *Bouge v. Smith's Mgmt. Corp.*, 132 F.R.D. 560, 567, 569–71 (D. Utah 1990).
19. *Johnson v. Cadillac Plastic Group Inc.*, 930 F. Supp. 1437, 1442 (D. Colo. 1996).
20. *Id.* (quoting *Bouge v. Smith's Mgt. Corp.*, 132 F.R.D. 560, 566 (D. Utah 1990)).

make admissions for the corporation, or conduct acts that they can attribute to the corporation.[21]

Still another view, commonly known as the *alter ego test*, was adopted by the *Restatement (Third) of Law Governing Lawyers*. This view holds that the court will allow you contact with some employees, but not with employees whose interests are indistinguishable from the corporation and/or whose own interests are directly at stake in the litigation.[22] Other jurisdictions use a case-by-case balancing test.[23] Finally, a handful of jurisdictions have case law that prohibits you from *ex parte* contact with current employees without notifying the attorney representing the organization.[24] However, many of those cases predate the amendment to Rule 4.2. Therefore, you must evaluate both the ethics rule and the cases for any given jurisdiction when determining whether it is appropriate to speak to the low-level employees.

Example: Holy Cross Nursing Home

Using our Dean Jacoby and Holy Cross Nursing Home example, you have started a lawsuit and want to know if any nursing home employees were complaining to management about being understaffed. Through the payroll records you received in discovery, you have a list of employees. Your next step is to determine whether or not you can contact them. Through your legal research, you learn that your state has adopted ABA Rule 4.2.

---

21. *See, e.g.*, *Weibricht v. So. Ill. Transfer, Inc.*, 241 F.3d 875, 881–82 (7th Cir. 2001), amended, No. 00-1563, 2001 U.S. App. Lexis 5642 (7th Cir. Mar. 27, 2001); *Hill v. Shell Oil Co.*, 209 F. Supp. 2d 876, 878–79 (N.D. Ill. 2002); *Orlowski v. Dominick's Finer Foods, Inc.*, 937 F. Supp. 723 (E.D. Ill. 1996).
22. *See, e.g.*, *Niesig v. Team I*, 558 N.E.2d 1030, 1035–38 (1990); *Strawser v. Exxon Co., U.S.A.*, 843 P.2d 613, 621–23 (Wyo. 1992); *Dent v. Kaufman*, 185 W. Va. 171, 406 S.E.2d 68, 71–72 (1991).
23. *See, e.g.*, *NAACP v. State of Florida*, 122 F. Supp. 2d 1335, 1341 (M.D. Fla. 2000).
24. *See, e.g.*, *Lewis v. CSX Transp., Inc.*, 202 F.R.D. 464, 466–67 (W.D. Va. 2001); *Cagguila v. Wyeth Labs., Inc.*, 127 F.R.D. 653, 654–55 (E.D. Pa. 1989).

Therefore, you know that the court allows you to contact certain types of employees. The aides you want to question about issues of understaffing are not part of the control group, and so you are free to contact them. Although the court does not require the employees to talk to you, a number are willing to talk, and you learn that they struggle with patient care because the nursing home will not hire enough people to do the job properly.

FORMER EMPLOYEES

The ABA Committee on Ethics and Professional Responsibility issued the formal opinion permitting *ex parte* communication with unrepresented former employees of corporations. The ABA Committee stated the following:

> [I]t is the opinion of the Committee that a lawyer representing a client in a matter adverse to a corporate party that is represented by another lawyer may, without violating Model Rule 4.2, communicate about the subject of the representation with an unrepresented former employee of the corporate party without the consent of the corporation's lawyer.[25]

Then the Committee amended the Comments to Rule 4.2 to clearly establish that *ex parte* communication with former employees is permissible. Comment 7 verifies the ruling:

> Consent of the organization's lawyer is not required for communication with a former constituent.[26]

---

25. ABA Formal Op. 91–359 (1991); *see also, FleetBoston Robertson Stephens, Inc. v. Innovex, Inc.*, 172 F. Supp. 2d 1190, 1194 (D. Minn. 2001).
26. Model Rules Rules of Prof'l Conduct R. 4.2 cmt. 7 (2007).

Consistent with the ABA position, courts have long recognized that informal interviews are exceptionally efficient for gathering meaningful facts. Informal interviews are generally more conducive to full disclosure and are far less costly than the more structured processes of formal discovery, or even informal investigation with the opposing counsel present.[27] Further, costly formal depositions that may deter witnesses with limited resources, or even somewhat less formal and costly interviews attended by the adversary's counsel, are no substitute for such off-the-record private efforts to learn and assemble, rather than perpetuate, information.[28]

The majority of jurisdictions have held that you can conduct interviews of a corporate defendant's former employees.[29] Courts

---

27. *Clark v. Beverly Health & Rehab. Servs., Inc.*, 440 Mass. 270, 277, 797 N.E.2d 905, 910 (2003) (citing *Niesig v. Team I*, 76 N.Y.2d 363, 372, 559 N.Y.S.2d 493, 558 N.E.2d 1030 (1990), *Cram v. Lamson & Sessions Co., Carlon Div.*, 148 F.R.D. 259, 261 (S.D. Iowa 1993), and *Siguel v. Trustees of Tufts College*, Civ. A. No. 88-0626-Y (D. Mass. Mar. 12, 1990)).
28. *Clark v. Beverly Health & Rehab. Servs., Inc.*, 440 Mass. 270, 797 N.E.2d 905 (2003); *see also*, *Cram v. Lamson & Sessions Co., Carlon Div.*, 148 F.R.D. 259, 261 (S.D. Iowa 1993); *Siguel v. Trustees of Tufts College*, Civ. A. No. 88-0626-Y (D. Mass. Mar.12, 1990).
29. *See, e.g.*, *FleetBoston Robertson Stephens, Inc. v. Innovex, Inc.*, 172 F. Supp. 2d 1190, 1194 (D. Minn. 2001); Ellen Messing & James Weliky, Contacting Employees of an Adverse Corporate Party: A Plaintiff's Attorney's View, 19 Lab. Law. 353, 362 (2004) ("[c]onsent of the organization's lawyer is not required for communication with a former constituent"); ABA Formal Op. 91-359 (Apr. 2, 1991); Supreme Court of Ohio, Board of Commissioners of Grievances and Discipline, Op. No. 96-1 (Feb. 2, 1996); *Continental Ins. Co. v. Super. Ct.*, 37 Cal. Rptr. 2d 843 (Cal. App. 1995) (interpreting analogous CAL. RULES OF PROF'L CONDUCT R. 2–100, questioning holding of *Bobele v. Super. Ct.*, 245 Cal. Rptr. 144 (Cal. Ct. App. 1988)); *Nalian Truck Lines, Inc. v. Nakano Warehouse & Transp. Co.*, 6 Cal. App. 4th 1256, 1261–64 (Cal. Ct. App. 1992); *Sequa Corp. v. Lititech*, 807 F. Supp. 653, 659–61 (D. Colo. 1992); *DuBois v. Gradco Sys., Inc.*, 136 F.R.D. 341, 344–45 (D. Conn. 1991) (citing, at note 4, Bar Association opinions reaching the same result from Illinois, Pennsylvania, Minnesota, Nassau County (NY), Virginia, Colorado, the City of New York, and Florida); *Diossi v. Edison*, 583 A.2d 1343, 1345 (Del. Super. Ct. 1990); *H.B.A. Management v. Estate of Schwartz*, 693 So. 2d 541, 542 (Fla. 1997); *In re Domestic Air Transp. Anti-Trust Litig.*, 141 F.R.D. 556, 561–62 (N.D. Ga. 1992); *P.T.*

have opined that immunizing former employees from all *ex parte* interviews would permit the organization to monitor the flow of non-privileged information to a potential adversary at the expense of uncovering material facts. Fairness in our established system of adversary representation would be the casualty.[30] When evaluating the propriety of *ex parte* communications with former employees, there is no control group analysis. Former employees, unlike current ones, cannot be construed as parties or agents of a corporate party and, thus, are not within the scope of the rule.[31]

Barnum's Nightclub v. Duhamell, 766 N.E.2d 729, 732–37 (Ind. App. 2002); *Brown v. St. Joseph County*, 148 F.R.D. 246, 251–53 (N.D. Ind. 1993); *Cram v. Lamson & Sessions Co.*, 148 F.R.D. 259, 261–63 (S.D. Iowa 1993); *Centennial Management Services, Inc. v. Axa Re Vie*, 193 F.R.D. 671, 683–84 (D. Kan. 2000); *Ramada Franchise Systems, Inc. v. Tresprop, Ltd.*, 75 F. Supp. 2d 1205 (D. Kan. 1999); *Humco, Inc. v. Noble*, 31 S.W.3d 916, 919–20 (Ky. 2000); *Intergen N.V. v. Grina*, No. 01-11774-REK, 2002 U.S. Dist. LEXIS 5512, at *3 (D. Mass. Mar. 29, 2002) (ruling that "no former employee has current 'speaking authority' for any corporation of which he was an employee formerly," thus finding that under *Messing, Rudavsky & Weliky*, 764 N.E.2d 825, contact with former employees was permitted); *Smith v. Kansas City So. Ry. Co.*, 87 S.W.3d 266, 271–72 (Mo. App. 2002) (*ex parte* contact permissible with former employees not expressly represented by own counsel or company counsel); *In re Tyco Int'l Ltd. Securities Litig.*, No. 00-MD-1335-B, 2001 U.S. Dist. LEXIS 819, at *9 (D.N.H. Jan. 30, 2001); *Polycast Tech. Corp. v. Uniroyal, Inc.*, 129 F.R.D. 621, 628 (S.D.N.Y. 1990); *Reynolds v. Ingram*, No. 5:98-CV-895-BO(2), 2000 U.S. Dist. LEXIS 7261, at *5 (E.D.N.C. March 31, 2000); Fulton, 829 P.2d at 960; *United States v. Beiersdorf-Jobst, Inc.*, 1997 WL 640799, at *2–4 (N.D. Ohio 1997); *Action Air Freight, Inc. v. Pilot Air Freight Corp.*, 769 F. Supp. 899, 902–04 (E.D. Pa. 1991), appeal dismissed, 961 F.2d 207 (3d Cir. 1992); *Sherrod v. Furniture Center*, 769 F. Supp. 1021 (W.D. Tenn. 1991); *Shearson Lehman Bros., Inc. v. Wasatch Bank*, 139 F.R.D. 412, 418 (D. Utah 1991); *Patriarca v. Center for Living & Working, Inc.*, 778 N.E.2d 877 (Mass. 2002) (noting that "the majority of courts that have decided this issue have concluded that former employees, for the most part, do not fall within the constraints of rule 4.2," but finding no need to decide the issue on facts presented); *see also*, Mass. Bar Ass'n Ethics Op. 02-03 (rule does not include former employees within its ambit).

30 *Clark v. Beverly Health & Rehab Servs.*, Inc., 440 Mass. 270, 278, 797 N.E.2d 905, 911 (2003) (citing *Niesig v. Team I*, 76 N.Y.2d 363 371 559 N.Y.S.2d 493 558 N.E.2d 1030 (1990)).

31 *Breedlove v. Tele-Trip Co., Inc.*, 1992 WL 202147, at *1 (N.D. Ill. 1992).

In *Fleetboston Robertson Stephens, Inc. v. Innovex, Inc.*, the court held that even the highest level of former employee, the former CEO, could be interviewed *ex parte* as long as the counsel made no inquiry into privileged matters.[32]

Example: Holy Cross Nursing Home

For example, going back to the Dean Jacoby and Holy Cross Nursing Home lawsuit, you have learned that the CFO from Holy Cross Nursing Home has left the company. He is retired and living in south Florida. You decide to play the long shot and contact him to see if he would be willing to discuss whether the Board of Directors were limiting how much the nursing home could spend on hiring staff. He is willing to talk to you. Because he is a former employee, you are entitled to speak with him about anything except privileged communications with the company lawyers. In the conversation, you learn that he left the company because he was disgusted with how the board was diverting money from patient care into profits. You have now corroborated the anecdotal stories you have learned about from the low-level employees.

Responsibilities During the Investigation

Communications with unrepresented witnesses, including former and current employees of an adverse organization, require fairness as described under Rule 4 of the Rules of Professional Conduct. Rule 4.1 states as follows:

> *Rule 4.1* In the course of representing a client a lawyer shall not knowingly:

---

32. *Fleetboston Robertson Stephens, Inc. v. Innovex, Inc.*, 172 F. Supp. 2d 1190, 1194 (D. Minn. 2001).

(a) make a false statement of material fact or law to a third person; or

(b) fail to disclose a material fact when disclosure is necessary to avoid assisting a criminal or fraudulent act by a client, unless disclosure is prohibited by Rule 1.6.[33]

Rule 4.3 requires that you disclose your interests to an unrepresented person:

Rule 4.3 In dealing on behalf of a client with a person who is not represented by counsel, a lawyer shall not state or imply that the lawyer is disinterested. When the lawyer knows or reasonably should know that the unrepresented person misunderstands the lawyer's role in the matter, the lawyer shall make reasonable efforts to correct the misunderstanding. The lawyer shall *not give legal advice* to an unrepresented person, other than the advice to secure counsel, if the lawyer knows or reasonably should know that the interests of such a person are or have a reasonable possibility of being in conflict with the interests of the client.

The purpose of these rules is to prohibit an attorney from unfairly taking advantage of unrepresented parties when acting on behalf of a client, while still allowing leeway for the proper search for truth.[34] Under Rule 4.3 you are responsible for identifying your

---

33. Model Rules Rules of Prof'l Conduct R. 4.1.
34. *FleetBoston Robertson Stephens, Inc. v. Innovex, Inc.*, 172 F. Supp. 2d 1190, 1194–95 (D. Minn. 2001) (citing 52 M. S. A., Rules of Prof. Conduct, Rule 4.2, MN ST RPC Rule 4.2, 4.3, 4.4); *Olson v. Snap Products, Inc.*, 183 F.R.D. 539, 544–45 (D. Minn. 1998)).

client and explaining that your client has interests opposed to those of the unrepresented person.[35] Some courts have gone on to impose further requirements, including informing the employee of his right to refuse the interview.[36]

Technique: Establish that Communication Is Voluntary

Under Rule 4.1 and 4.3, you need to inform witnesses of their rights. When possible, it is good advice to establish a record of the voluntary nature of the *ex parte* communication with your adversary's low-level or former employee. Despite the legal and ethical right to interview these witnesses, some aggressive litigators will challenge that right. In some instances, the witness may even be under improper pressure to falsely state that the conversation was not voluntary. If you make a record at the beginning of the recorded interview, this will reduce any future attempts to challenge the interview's propriety.

Here are some sample questions:

Q: What is your name please?

Q: Are you currently working for ACME Trucking or any company related to ACME Trucking?

Q: My name is Mark Kosieradzki. My law firm is investigating a matter on behalf of Violet Jones concerning events that occurred at ACME Trucking. Would it be OK if I ask you some questions?

Q: You and I have not talked before today. Is that correct?

Q: I came here just a few minutes ago. Did we discuss Violet Jones or ACME Trucking before we started recording?

Q: Are you meeting with me voluntarily?

---

35. Model Rules Rules of Prof'l Responsibility R. 4.3 cmt. 1 (2007) (emphasis added).
36. Ohio Sup. Ct. Ethics Op. 2005-3 (2005); *Cole v. Appalachian Power Co.*, 903 F. Supp. 975, 980 (S.D.W.Va. 1995); *McCallum v. CSX Trans., Inc.*, 149 F.R.D. 104, 112 (M.D.N.C. 1993); *Monsanto Co. v. Aetna Cas. & Sur. Co.*, 593 A.2d 1013, 1018 (Del. Super. 1990).

Q: Have I offered you any promises or inducements for taking the time to talk with me?

Q: Do you feel threatened or pressured in any way to provide information?

Q: Do you understand that you don't have to talk to me if you don't want to?

Q: I understand that you used to work at ACME Trucking. Is that correct?

Q: What was your position there?

Q: Did you have any management or administrative functions?

Q: Are you currently working? For whom?

Q: While you were working for ACME Trucking, were you ever told that particular types of communication or information were privileged?

Q: If the answers to any of the questions I ask you involve any privileged information, please let me know, so we won't discuss the privileged matters. Will you do that please?

Q: Are you represented by a lawyer?

If the answer is yes, stop questioning. If the answer is no, continue.

Q: Have you met with any lawyers on behalf of ACME Trucking or its owners?

Q: Has anyone asked you not to talk to us?

Q: Who?

Q: When?

Q: Is it OK if I ask you some questions?

Involuntary Representation

If witnesses do not want to provide informal statements, then you will need to formally depose them. When you send subpoena notices requesting depositions to non-managing agents and servants of an institutional party, you should submit the notices to them as individuals, using Rule 30(b)(1) and a Rule 45, to compel their testimony.[37]

In many cases, the corporation's attorney will appear at the deposition, asserting that he represents the witness. The ABA Committee on Ethics and Professional Responsibility formal ethics opinion prohibits that practice, stating that Model Rule 4.2 "does not contemplate that a lawyer representing the entity can invoke the rule's prohibition to cover all employees of the entity, by asserting a blanket representation of all of them."[38] Consistent with the ABA opinion, courts throughout the country have held that an attorney for a corporate defendant cannot merely assert automatic representation on the former employee:[39]

> An organization may not assert a preemptive and exclusive representation by the organization's lawyer of all current (or former) employees as a means to invoke Rule 4.2 and insulate them all from *ex parte* communication with the lawyers of potential adversary parties.[40]

---

37. Fed. R. Civ. P. 45.
38. ABA Formal Op. 95–396, § VI (1995).
39. *Terra Int'l v. Mississippi Chem. Corp.*, 913 F. Supp. 1306, 1317 (N.D. Iowa 1996); *Carter-Herman v. City of Philadelphia*, 897 F. Supp. 899, 903 (E.D. Pa. 1995); *Brown v. Saint Joseph County*, 148 F.R.D. 246, 251 (N.D. Ind. 1993); *Michaels v. Woodland*, 988 F. Supp. 468, 472 (D.N.J. 1997); *Breedlove v. Tele-Trip Co., Inc.*, 1992 WL 202147, at *1 (N.D. Ill. 1992).
40. *Patriarca v. Ctr. for Living & Working, Inc.*, 438 Mass. 132, 135–36, 778 N.E.2d 877, 880 (2002).

Any other interpretation of Rule 4.2 would empower an organization to "thwart the purpose of Rule 4.2 simply by unilaterally pronouncing its representation of all of its employees."[41] Courts have recognized that allowing an employer or its lawyers to assert automatic representation is potentially coercive. For example, employers might try to stifle criticism or the revelation of negative evidence by controlling *ex parte* contacts with the opposing counsel, or they might impose a blanket representation "agreement" on all employees.[42]

> [T]he broad interpretation of the Comment [Comment 7 to Rule 4.2] would allow the employer to unilaterally impose a novel, limited form of attorney–client relationship on its employees, against those individuals' will and against their perceived or even actual interests, while serving the interests of the employer and the employer's attorneys (including their interest in suppressing evidence of discrimination). Such a position is both illogical and unethical.[43]

Further, a former employee may have interests adverse to those of their former employer. A blanket rule that would require the former employee to accept the organization's representation would deny that person the right to an attorney of his choice.[44] As such, "regardless of how much [an employer] may wish to provide its

---

41. *Carter-Herman v. City of Philadelphia*, 897 F. Supp. 899, 903 (E.D. Pa. 1995).
42. *Terra Int'l v. Mississippi Chem. Corp.*, 913 F. Supp. 1306, 1317 (N.D. Iowa 1996).
43. Ellen J. Messing and James S. Weliky, "Contacting Employees of an Adverse Corporate Party: A Plaintiff's Attorney's View," *The Labor Lawyer* 19, no. 3 (2004): 369–70.
44. *Clark v. Beverly Health & Rehab. Servs., Inc.*, 440 Mass. 270, 797 N.E.2d 905 (2003) citing *Patriarca v. Center for Living & Working, Inc.*, 438 Mass. 132, 136, 778 N.E.2d 877 (2002).

former and current employees with individual legal representation, an attorney–client relationship cannot be created unilaterally or imposed upon the employees without their consent."[45]

Offering representation to potential witnesses raises ethical issues under Rule 7 of the Professional Rules of Conduct.[46] Rule 7.3 prohibits lawyers from soliciting prospective clients in person, outside of the specified advertising alternatives. Rule 7.3(a) states the following:

> A lawyer shall not by in-person, live-telephone, or real-time electronic contact solicit professional employment when a significant motive for the lawyer's doing so is the lawyer's pecuniary gain, unless the person contacted: (1) is a lawyer; or (2) has a family, close personal, or prior professional relationship with the lawyer.[47]

Lawyers representing organizations have argued that, when the organization is paying for all the efforts their attorney has used in communicating with a potential witness, the representation is not for the attorney's pecuniary gain because the putative client is not paying. In *Terra Inter., Inc. v. Mississippi Chemical Corp.*, the court cautioned, "To the extent an employer tried to do either of these things, the court may have the inherent power to consider whether formation of the 'representation' is a sham designed merely to defeat *ex parte* contacts."[48]

---

45. *Brown v. Saint Joseph County*, 148 F.R.D. 246, 251 (N.D. Ind. 1993).
46. Model Rules Rules of Prof'l Responsibility 7.3
47. *Id.*
48. *Terra Int'l v. Mississippi Chem. Corp.*, 913 F. Supp. 1306, 1317 (N.D. Iowa 1996).

Technique: Establishing Involuntary Representation

Communications between a corporation's counsel and a corporation's former employee generally should be treated no differently than communications with any other third-party fact witness.[49] Courts have repeatedly rejected corporations' gratuitous claims of privilege in their attempts to solicit former employees for representation.[50] For representation to exist, the employee must specifically *request* the personal representation.[51] Communications that occur before establishing an attorney–client relationship are not privileged, even if the parties establish an attorney–client relationship later.[52] At the beginning of the deposition, you can make a record to evaluate if this was an unsolicited representation:

Q: How did you first learn you were going to testify?

Q: Was it when you were served by the paper work from my office?

Q: Were you represented by a lawyer at that time?

Q: What did you do?

Q: What did you understand the deposition paper work to mean?

Q: Why didn't you call a lawyer?

Q: When did ACME Trucking's lawyer first contact you?

Q: Did you receive any letters from them before the call?

---

49. *Infosystems, Inc. v. Ceridian Corp.*, 197 F.R.D. 303, 305–06 (E.D. Mich. 2000).
50. *Morisky v. Pub. Serv. Elec. & Gas Co.*, 191 F.R.D 419, 424 (D.N.J. 2000); *E.E.O.C. v. CRST Van Expedited, Inc.*, No. C07-0095, 2009 WL 136025, at *3 (N.D. Iowa Jan. 20, 2009) (counsel's communications with former employees of client's corporation should be treated no differently from communications with any other third-party fact witnesses).
51. *Tuttle v. Combined Ins. Co.*, 222 F.R.D. 424, 429 (E.D. Cal. 2004); *United States v. Keplinger*, 776 F.2d 678, 701, *cert. denied*, 476 U.S. 1183, 106 S.Ct. 2919, 91 L.Ed.2d 548 (1986).
52. *E.E.O.C. v. CRST Van Expedited, Inc.*, No. C07-0095, 2009 WL 136025, at *3 (N.D. Iowa Jan. 20, 2009) (citing *EEOC v. Johnson & Higgins, Inc.*, 1998 WL 778369, at *1 (S.D.N.Y.)).

Q: What did the letter say?

Q: What did you do when you got the letter?

Q: Did they offer to represent you?

Q: Did you hire them?

Q: Did you sign any written agreement to pay them?

Q: When did that occur?

Once you have established a record that the witness did not retain the attorney, you can ask questions about communications between the lawyer and the witness. Attorney-client privilege applies only when there is an attorney-client relationship. If your opponent instructs the witness not to answer your questions, you now have the power to bring forth a motion to compel answers and to impose sanctions. You may also discover whether the attorney has sent letters to the witnesses (and perhaps others) directing him or her not to communicate with you if contacted. If that is the case, the lawyer can be sanctioned and removed from the case. He may even face potential ethics sanctions.

Summary

- You may communicate with all company employees before the lawsuit begins.

- Tell witnesses why you are talking to them and inform them it is their choice to speak with you.

- You may generally speak with low-level employees during litigation.

- You may always speak with all former employees.

- Keep in mind that attorneys for companies cannot impose automatic representation on former and low-level employees.

7

CRAFTING THE 30(b)(6) NOTICE
The Requesting Party's Duties

The quality of your answers is in direct proportion to the quality of your questions.

—Albert Einstein

INTRODUCTION 137
REASONABLE PARTICULARITY AND
    PAINSTAKING SPECIFICITY 137
QUALIFIERS 142
WHAT CAN YOU ASK IN THE
    MATTERS OF EXAMINATION? 145
    Facts 146
    Sources of Information 147
    Positions, Subjective Beliefs, and Opinions 150
    Interpretation of Documents 151

> Interpretation of Events........................152
> Contentions and Affirmative Defenses............154
>
> You Decide the Method of Discovery..............156
>
> Summary...160

Introduction

The key to a successful 30(b)(6) deposition begins with a properly crafted deposition notice. The purpose of the 30(b)(6) deposition notice is to let the responding organization know what you will be asking them so they can properly prepare. There are different lines of cases that define the level of particularity that is required in a 30(b)(6) notice. In this chapter, I will discuss how to craft your requests to conform to either line of cases, and what topics you can request information about.

When crafting a deposition notice that seeks discovery through a Rule 30(b)(6) deposition, the rule states the following:

> **Describe with *reasonable particularity* the matters for examination.** The named organization must then designate one or more officers, directors, or managing agents, or designate other persons who consent to testify on its behalf; and it may set out the matters on which each person designated will testify.[1]

Courts have differed on what *reasonable particularity* means, describing it with varying theoretical tests. Ultimately, however, the court bases its decisions on practical concerns: Will the topics in the notice let the designated witness know how to prepare?

Reasonable Particularity and Painstaking Specificity

Courts have two lines of interpretation for the term *reasonable particularity*. The more stringent approach calls for you as the requesting party to designate, "with painstaking specificity, the particular subject areas that are intended to be questioned, and

---

1. Fed. R. Civ. P. 30(b)(6). (Emphasis added.)

that are relevant to the issues in dispute."[2] In those cases, you are responsible for preparing "a roster of information which is reasonably specific and intelligible to the defendants so that they know about which specific representations their designee needs to acquire knowledge."[3]

The other approach rejects the *painstaking specificity* standard, reasoning that applying the *reasonable particularity* phrase contained in the rule provides sufficient notice for preparing for a deposition. However, the topics in your notice must clearly outline what the designated witness must prepare.[4] If the court can discern what you are seeking from the "plain language" of your notice, then the court will deem that the notice has "reasonable particularity."[5]

Regardless of which line of cases your jurisdiction follows, your discovery request should be sufficiently definite and limited, so that it will "apprise a person of ordinary intelligence" of what information you are requesting. For example, a matter that directly asks for "facts, information, or documents that relate to a particular allegation" is *reasonably particular,* because a party ought to know,

---

2. *Hartford Fire Ins. Co. v. P & H Cattle Co.*, No. CIV.A. 05-2001-DJW, 2009 WL 2951120, at *10 (D. Kan. Sept. 10, 2009); *McBride v. Medicalodges, Inc.*, 250 F.R.D. 581, 584 (D. Kan. 2008); *Lipari v. U.S. Bancorp*, N.A, No. CIVA 07-2146-CM-DJW, 2008 WL 4642618, at *1 (D. Kan. Oct. 16, 2008); *EEOC v. Thorman & Wright Corp.*, 243 F.R.D. 421, 426 (D. Kan. 2007); *see also, Sprint Communications Co., L.P. v. Theglobe.com, Inc.*, 236 F.R.D. 524, 528 (D. Kan. 2006); *Prokosch v. Catalina Lighting, Inc.*, 193 F.R.D. 633, 638 (D. Minn. 2000).
3. *Brunet v. Quizno's Franchise Co.*, No. 07-CV-01717, 2008 WL 5378140, at *4 (D.C. Dec. 23, 2008).
4. *See, e.g.*, *Espy v. Information Technologies, Inc.*, No. 08-2211, 2010 WL 1488555, at *2 (D. Kan. Apr. 13, 2010); *Starlight Int'l Inc. v. Herlihy*, 186 F.R.D. 626, 638 (D. Kan. 1999); *Heartland Surgical Specialty Hosp., LLC v. Midwest Div., Inc.*, No. 05-2164-MLB-DWB, 2007 WL 1054279, at *3–4 (D. Kan. Apr. 9, 2007).
5. *Hartford Fire Ins. Co. v. P & H Cattle Co.*, No. CIV.A. 05-2001-DJW, 2009 WL 2951120, at *10 (D. Kan. Sept. 10, 2009) (citing *Regan–Touhy v. Walgreen Co.*, 526 F.3d 641, 649–50 (10th Cir.2008) (quoting 8A Wright & Miller, Federal Practice and Procedure § 2211)); *Steil v. Humana Kan. City, Inc.*, 197 F.R.D. 442, 444 (D. Kan. 2000).

and can easily discern, the evidence that they base their allegation on.[6] Allegation inquiries "do not appear overly broad as they specifically limit the scope to specific allegations with regard to factual circumstances surrounding [a particular event] in the case."[7]

The practical test of a 30(b)(6) notice's effectiveness is whether the *matters of examination* that you list provide the responding organization with what it needs to sufficiently prepare. If you give the defendant sufficient notice to determine the matters for which they have to prepare, then the court expects their designated witness to be fully prepared to testify regarding those topics. Even if a precise question isn't listed in the notice, the analysis focuses on whether the matter of examination was clear enough that a reasonable person should have understood it and should have been prepared to discuss that topic. If the requesting lawyers clarified what they intended by the notice with a letter, courts have found that the notice and reasonable particularity requirements were met through the letter.[8] Ultimately, the question is whether the court is able to determine whether the witness has produced the information you requested during a motion to compel.[9]

Regardless of whether your jurisdiction follows a *reasonable particularity* or *painstaking specificity* interpretation of cases, from a tactical standpoint, the clearer the notice, the greater likelihood that the court will require the responding party to give you the information you request. That being said, you should also write the notice sufficiently broad, so that the defending adversary can't claim surprise by your questions at the deposition.

---

6. *Hartford Fire Ins. Co. v. P & H Cattle Co.*, No. CIV.A. 05-2001-DJW, 2009 WL 2951120, at *1 (D. Kan. Sept. 10, 2009).
7. *Id.*
8. *Alexander v. F.B.I.*, 186 F.R.D. 137, 139 (D.D.C. 1998); cf. *United States v. Taylor*, 166 F.R.D. 356, 361 (M.D.N.C. 1996).
9. *Hartford Fire Ins. Co. v. P & H Cattle Co.*, No. CIV.A. 05-2001-DJW, 2009 WL 2951120, at *10 (D. Kan. Sept. 10, 2009), (citing *Regan-Touhy v. Walgreen Co.*, 526 F.3d 641, 649–50 (10th Cir. 2008) (quoting 8A Wright & Miller, *Federal Practice and Procedure* §2211)).

Technique: Requesting Information about Surveillance Videos

When a surveillance system captures the events that are the subject of a litigation, discovering that surveillance image is critical. Often, organizations that have surveillance images that could be helpful to your case do not preserve the images. Therefore, your discovery must focus not only on determining whether a video exists, but also whether it has been transferred to a third party and who has viewed it. You will need to create a foundational record to establish the basis for a spoliation claim. Using Rule 30(b)(6), you can learn about the surveillance system and why the image is no longer available. If your jurisdiction requires the notice to be crafted with only reasonable particularity, a broad inquiry regarding the video system should place the responding party on sufficient notice to understand that the inquiry will delve into all aspects of the surveillance system. For example, your 30(b)(6) notice could be a broad request like this:

```
1. Electronic surveillance system used at
   the Big Box store in Moses Lake, WA,
   on May 4, 2012.
```

However, if the responding party claims not to know the answers to your questions because the company didn't foresee that line of inquiry from your notice, you will need to make a motion to the court to compel further answers. If the court agrees that the responding party could not foresee your questions from your notice, you may be out of luck. Therefore, the more specific you are in the notice, the more likely the court will require the responding party to provide the information.

If you choose to draft the notice using a *painstaking specificity* standard, it is best to start with the broader matter of inquiry and then drill down with greater specificity. When you couple the broader *reasonable particularity* notice language with a roster of more detailed inquiries, you will defuse the responding party's ability to allege that they don't know how to prepare. Using the same example regarding surveillance systems, an alternative approach to crafting the notice could include the following matters of examination:

1. Electronic surveillance system used at the Big Box store in Moses Lake, WA, on May 4, 2012.

2. The **position/location**[10] of all video cameras at the Big Box store in Moses Lake, WA, on May 4, 2012.

3. The **method of operation** of the video surveillance system at the Big Box store in Moses Lake, WA, on May 4, 2012.

4. The **location and storage** of video or digital images captured by the video surveillance system at the Big Box store in Moses Lake, WA, on May 4, 2012.

5. The identity of all **people** involved in the maintenance and operation of the video/security system at the Big Box store in Moses Lake, WA, on May 4, 2012.

6. The job descriptions and responsibilities of all **people** involved in the maintenance and operation of the video/security system at the Big Box store in Moses Lake, WA, on May 4, 2012.

7. The identity of all people who have **viewed** the video/digital images captured at the Big Box store in Moses Lake, WA, on May 4, 2012.

---

10. Author's note: I like to use bold key words and phrases in my deposition notices so that I can easily see the general point I'm focusing on while questioning the witness.

8. All **policies** regarding the retention of surveillance videos following notice of an incident at the Big Box store in Moses Lake, WA, on May 4, 2012.

9. The role of Claims Management, Inc., in monitoring, reviewing, and **preserving** the images captured on the electronic **surveillance system** used at the Big Box store in Moses Lake, WA, on May 4, 2012.

Qualifiers

Attorneys often like to use an expansive term, such as *including but not limited to,* which qualifies their requests. These types of phrases sometimes leave the requesting lawyers thinking they have covered their bases to get all the information they need. The problem is an expansive phrase like *including but not limited to* leaves the responding lawyer unclear as to what the witness must be prepared to answer. If the responding party "cannot identify the outer limits of the areas of inquiry noticed, compliant designation is not feasible."[11] Courts have found that a notice that states "including *but not limited to*" the areas you want to ask about is too broad. The notice is overbroad because the responding organization cannot identify the outer limits of the areas they need to prepare for.[12] However, if you give sufficient additional

---

11. *Steil v. Humana Kan. City, Inc.*, 197 F.R.D. 442, 444 (D. Kan. 2000) (citing *Reed v. Bennett*, 193 F.R.D. 689, 692 (D. Kan. 2000)).
12. *Hartford Fire Ins. Co. v. P & H Cattle Co.*, No. CIV.A. 05-2001-DJW, 2009 WL 2951120, at *1 (D. Kan. Sept. 10, 2009); *Reed v. Bennett*, 193 F.R.D. 689, 692 (D. Kan. 2000); *Steil v. Humana Kansas City, Inc.*, 197 F.R.D. 442, 444 (D. Kan. 2000).

explanations in the deposition notice to guide the responding party to prepare, the courts may allow the depositions.[13]

Technique: Designing a 30(b)(6) Notice that Is Not Overbroad

In the case of *Hartford Fire Ins. Co. v. P & H Cattle Co.*, the court was asked to determine if the following 30(b)(6) notice was overbroad:

> "Topic 8: The document retention policies applicable to any [Heartland] Financial Records, [Heartland] Patient Records, [Heartland] Financial Reports, or [Heartland] Plans and Forecasts."
>
> "Topic 9: The destruction, alteration, or loss of any [Heartland] Financial Records, [Heartland] Patient Records, [Heartland] Financial Reports, or [Heartland] Plans and Forecasts."
>
> "[Heartland] Financial Records" is defined by the notice as "records of Heartland Surgical Specialty Hospital, LLC's income, expenses, assets, liabilities, accounts receivable, accounts payable, profits, losses, or other financial information."
>
> The term "[Heartland] Patient Records" is defined as "records of Heartland Surgical Specialty Hospital, LLC's patient encounters and patient billing, including but not limited to patient names and

---

13. *Hartford Fire Ins. Co. v. P & H Cattle Co.*, No. CIV.A. 05-2001-DJW, 2009 WL 2951120, at *1 (D. Kan. Sept. 10, 2009).

addresses, admissions, diagnoses, referring physicians, treating physicians, treatments, fees and charges, discounts, invoices, claims submitted to insurers and other third-party payers, amounts collected from patients, and amounts collected from third-party payers."

The term "[Heartland] Financial Reports" is defined as "reports that state, summarize, or analyze information contained in [Heartland] Financial Records or [Heartland] Patient Records, including but not limited to general ledger, income statements, balance sheets, financial statements, reports on uses and sources of capital, reports on changes in financial position, and reports on owners' equity or payments to owners."

The term "Heartland Plans and Forecasts" is defined as "any budget, plan, projection, forecast, or pro forma statement of Heartland Surgical Specialty Hospital, LLC's patient volume, income, expenses, assets, liabilities, accounts receivable, accounts payable, profits, losses, or other financial information."[14]

---

14. *Heartland Surgical Specialty Hosp., LLC v. Midwest Div., Inc.*, No. 05-2164-MLB-DWB, 2007 WL 1054279, at *4 (D. Kan. Apr. 9, 2007).

When the court faced this matter of inquiry, it ruled that the definitions in the request provided sufficient particularity, so it was not overbroad.

> [T]he definitions of patient records and financial reports do use the phrase "including but not limited to," but are then followed by an extensive example list of the records and reports for which information is sought by Defendants. However, it is clear both from the language used in topics 8 and 9 and from the definitions provided what specific information is being sought.[15]

What Can You Ask in the Matters of Examination?

The courts accept that you can question an organization using a 30(b)(6) deposition to require them to tell you about their claims or defenses if they intend to use any of that information in the litigation.[16] "[N]umerous courts have ruled that a Rule 30(b)(6) notice of deposition that seeks the factual bases for another party's claims or defenses is proper."[17] Nevertheless, in practice,

---

15. *Id.* at *8, n.5–7.
16. *United States v. Taylor*, 166 F.R.D. 356, 361 (M.D.N.C. 1996) (citing *United States v. Mass. Indus. Fin. Agency*, 162 F.R.D. 410, 412 (D. Mass. 1995)); *Toys "R" Us, Inc. v. N.B.D. Trust Company*, No. 88C10349, 1993 WL 543027, at *2 (N.D. Ill. Sept. 29, 1993); *Lapenna v. Upjohn Co.*, 110 F.R.D. 15, 21 (E.D. Pa. 1986).
17. *Smith v. General Mills, Inc.*, 2006 WL 7276959 (2006) citing *Security Ins. Co. of Hartford v. Trustmark Ins. Co.*, 218 F.R.D. 29, 33–35 (D. Conn. 2003) (third-party defendant required to name Rule 30(b)(6) witness to testify as to its denials to the third-party complaint); *U.S. v. McDonnell Douglas Corp.*, 961 F. Supp. 1288, 1290 (E.D. Mo. 1997) (overruling work product objections to Rule 30(b)(6) deposition question and ruling that defendant was entitled to inquire into the factual bases of the government's allegations); *Resolution Trust Corp. v. Sands*, 151 F.R.D. 616, 620 (N.D. Tex. 1993) (requiring party to "designate someone to state the facts upon which the [other party] bases its claims" of negligence, gross negligence and

responding organizations try to limit the areas of inquiry. It is therefore important for you to know the laws if you are to respond to those objections.

Rule 30(b)(6) itself does not limit the matters of examination that a requesting party may seek in any way. However, the case law has established that the matters of examination can request not only facts within the organization's knowledge, but also its subjective beliefs, opinions,[18] and interpretation of documents and events.[19]

Facts

Facts are the most obvious subject matter that you can ask about in a 30(b)(6) deposition.

Technique: Foreign Object after Surgery Case

The deposition notice can detail, in its matters of examination, facts that the organization knows and that are reasonably available regarding specified topics. For example, Megan Wilson sued two physicians and Shady Grove Adventist Hospital for medical malpractice as a result of injuries she suffered when a foreign object was left in her stomach while undergoing a hysterectomy at the time of the birth of her child. Megan was unconscious during the procedure. Depositions were necessary to learn what happened in the operating room. The lawyers representing Megan decided to issue a 30(b)(6) deposition on the hospital to find out what the hospital claimed had happened. The defense objected, claiming the plaintiff had to serve interrogatories or take the depositions of everyone in

---

breach of fiduciary duty); *Protective Nat'l Ins. Co. v. Commonwealth Ins. Co.*, 137 F.R.D. 267, 272–77 (D. Neb. 1989) (party entitled to discover through Rule 30(b)(6) deposition the factual bases for contentions in counterclaim); *Bd. of Regents v. Nippon Telephone and Telegraph Corp.*, 2004 U.S. Dist LEXIS 28819, ——15–17 (W.D. Tex. June 1, 2004) (improper to refuse to provide Rule 30(b)(6) testimony regarding the factual bases of its affirmative defenses).

18. *See, e.g., Lapenna v. Upjohn Co.*, 110 F.R.D. 15, 20 (E.D. Pa. 1986); *Kendall v. United Air Lines, Inc.*, 9 F.R.D. 702, 703 (S.D.N.Y. 1949); 4 J. Moore, J. Lucas & G. Grotheer, *Moore's Federal Practice* ¶ 26.56[3], at 142–43 (2d ed. 1984).

19. *QBE Insurance Corporation v. Jorda Enterprises, Inc.*, 277 F.R.D. 676, 687 (S.D. Fla. 2012); *United States v. Taylor*, 166 F.R.D. 356, 361 (M.D.N.C. 1996); *Ierardi v. Lorillard, Inc.*, No. 90–7049, 1991 WL 158911 (E.D. Pa. Aug. 13, 1991).

the operating room to develop that story. The court disagreed, ruling that the plaintiff could take the 30(b)(6) deposition. The court expressly stated these matters of examination:

```
1. Any and all facts leading up to, con-
   cerning, or surrounding any sponge,
   soaking towel, or foreign object left
   in Megan Wilson's body after her giv-
   ing birth and undergoing an operation
   and/or procedures to remove a placenta
   at Shady Grove Adventist Hospital on
   or about March, 2001.[20]
```

Sources of Information

You can ask about *sources of information* in your 30(b)(6) deposition. *Sources of information* about the defendants' claims and defenses are relevant and, therefore, you are allowed to discover them.[21] Rule 26(b)(1) provides for the following:

> Parties may obtain discovery regarding any non-privileged matter that is relevant to any party's claim or defense—including the existence, description, nature, custody, condition, and location of any documents or other tangible things and the identity and location of persons who know of any discoverable matter.[22]

By understanding the sources of information, you can then vet those sources to ensure that the opposing party fully discloses all information.

---

20. *Wilson v. Lakner*, 228 F.R.D. 524, 525 (D. Md. 2005).
21. *E.E.O.C. v. Caesars Entertainment, Inc.*, 237 F.R.D. 428, 434 (D. Nev. 2006).
22 Fed. R. Civ. P. 26(b)(1).

Technique: Exploring Punch-In/Punch-Out Time Clock Systems

Consider this example. You are involved in a nursing home negligence case. The defense is relying on the nursing home chart to prove the staff provided proper care. You want to make sure that the information in the chart is accurate. You want to learn whether the caregivers were *actually* present at the time they made entries in the medical charts, and if a sufficient number of employees were working to be able to adequately accomplish their required tasks.

Payroll punch-in/punch-out time clock system records are one of the best sources for this information. If you craft a 30(b)(6) notice with painstaking specificity, it is possible not only to get the data, but also identify the systems that can generate reports from the software. This eliminates the expense of independently organizing the data. An example of the matters of inquiry to identify that information could be the following:

> Pursuant to Federal Rule of Civil Procedure 30(b)(6), Cedar Gardens Homes is required to designate and fully prepare one or more officers, directors, managing agents, or other people who consent to testify on behalf of Cedar Gardens Homes, and whom Cedar Gardens Homes will fully prepare to testify regarding all information that is known or reasonably available to Cedar Gardens Homes' organization regarding the following designated matters:
>
> 1. The name of Cedar Gardens Homes' "punch-in/punch-out" time clock system.
>
> 2. The name of the software Cedar Gardens Homes uses for the "punch-in/punch-out" time clock system.

3. The location of all electronically stored data from the "punch-in/punch-out" time clock system.

4. All methods of accessing the database for the "punch-in/punch-out" time clock system.

5. Identification numbers and passwords necessary to access the database.

6. How the "punch-in/punch-out" time clock system works.

7. The contact information of all people and entities responsible for maintaining the "punch-in/punch-out" time clock system.

8. The contact information of all people and entities that used the "punch-in/punch-out" time clock system.

9. All reports that can be generated by the "punch-in/punch-out" time clock system.

10. The functionality of all management and/or analytics components of the "punch-in/punch-out" time clock system.

11. All ways Cedar Gardens Homes used the "punch-in/punch-out" time clock system.

12. The method of querying the "punch-in/punch-out" clock system.

Positions, Subjective Beliefs, and Opinions

You can ask about an organization's positions, subjective beliefs, and opinions in your 30(b)(6) depositions. Ever since the landmark case of *United States v. Taylor,* courts have universally established that the Rule 30(b)(6) witness must present the organization's *position* on the matters of examination contained in the notice.[23] This extends not only to facts, but also to subjective beliefs and opinions,[24] as well as interpretation of documents and events.[25]

Example: Adams Aviation

You are involved in a lawsuit against Adams Aviation (an aviation manufacturing company), based on their failure to retrofit a plane in response to a Federal Aviation Administration report of malfunction or defect. Adams Aviation has been sold to Blue Sky Systems. Adams Aviation doesn't admit or deny getting the report. Rather, Adams Aviation claims they no longer have access to the documents that were handed over to Blue Sky Systems.

You believe you can establish your claim through the Federal Aviation Administration documents. You want to lock down Adams Aviation's position so they cannot offer any evidence, direct or rebuttal, or argument at trial as to that topic. By using a Rule 30(b)(6) deposition, you can force Adams Aviation to take a position. If that position is "we don't know," they will not be able to rebut the evidence you introduce from the government proving they did. You've eliminated the "I said, he said" debate.

---

23. *United States v. Taylor,* 166 F.R.D. 356, 362 (M.D. N.C. 1996); *United States v. Massachusetts Indus. Finance Agency,* 162 F.R.D. 410, 412 (D. Mass. 1995); *Lapenna v. Upjohn Co.,* 110 F.R.D. 15, 21 (E.D. Pa. 1986); *Toys "R" Us, Inc. v. N.B.D. Trust Company,* No. 88C10349, 1993 WL 543027, at *2 (N.D. Ill. Sept. 29, 1993).
24. *Lapenna v. Upjohn Co.,* 110 F.R.D. 15, 20 (E.D. Pa. 1986) (citing *Kendall v. United Air Lines, Inc.,* 9 F.R.D. 702 (S.D.N.Y. 1949)). *See also,* 4 J. Moore, J. Lucas & G. Grotheer, *Moore's Federal Practice* ¶ 26.56[3], at 142–43 (2d ed. 1984).
25. *Ierardi v. Lorillard, Inc.,* No. 90-7049, 1991 WL 158911, at *2 (E.D. Pa. Aug. 13, 1991); 4 J. Moore, J. Lucas & G. Grotheer, *Moore's Federal Practice* ¶ 26.56[3], at 142–43 (2d ed. 1984).

Interpretation of Documents

You can ask how an organization *interprets* documents in your 30(b)(6) deposition. Since "documents can always be interpreted in various ways . . . plaintiffs are entitled to discover the interpretation that [the organization] intends to assert at trial."[26] Inquiries about information in the documents are "useful to testify as to interpretation of papers, and any underlying factual qualifiers of those documents."[27]

Technique: Health Insurance Denial

Requesting an organization to interpret any document germane to the litigation is appropriate for a 30(b)(6) inquiry. For example, John Dinkins made a claim against his group health insurer, Starlight Health Plans, seeking benefits for a blood brain barrier disruption (BBBD) treatment. Starlight Health Plans denied the treatment, claiming it didn't fall under his coverage. John Dinkins has hired you to sue Starlight Health Plans to provide the lifesaving medical care. You want to determine every coverage reason for the denial. Using a 30(b)(6) deposition, you can flesh out the defense's reasoning.

> Pursuant to Federal Rule of Civil Procedure 30(b)(6), Starlight Health Plans is required to designate and fully prepare one or more officers, directors, managing agents, or other people who consent to testify on behalf of Starlight Health Plans, and whom Starlight Health Plan will fully prepare to testify regarding

---

26. *Id.*
27. *Dongguk Univ. v. Yale Univ.*, 270 F.R.D. 70, 74 (D. Conn. 2010) (citing *Beckner v. Bayer CropScience, L.P.*, 2006 U.S. Dist. LEXIS 44197, *27, 29–30 (D.W.Va. June 28, 2006)).

all information that is known or reasonably available to Starlight Health Plans' organization regarding the following designated matters:

1. Any and all facts leading up to, concerning, or surrounding the claim by John Dinkins for blood brain barrier disruption (BBBD) treatment.

2. The applicability of the Group Health Insurance Plan issued to the plaintiff through his employment with Terminex Co., believed to be numbered E9384.

Interpretation of Events

You can ask how an organization interprets events in your 30(b)(6) deposition. As the requesting party, you should not be obligated to depose a string of employees, none of whom is able to speak for the organization, to determine how an incident in question occurred.[28] Rule 30(b)(6) requires organizations to be more than mere document gatherers; they must produce live witnesses who know or who can reasonably find out what happened in given circumstances.[29] The organization must explain how it expects to construe the varying facts of the position it advocates.[30]

---

28. *Wilson v. Lakner*, 228 F.R.D. 524, 529 (D. Md. 2005).
29. *Id.*
30. *United States v. Taylor*, 166 F.R.D. 356, 363 (M.D.N.C. 1996); *In re Neurontin Antitrust Litig.*, MDL 1479, 2011 WL 253434, at *7 (D.N.J. Jan. 25, 2011) aff'd MDL 1479, 2011 WL 2357793 (D. N.J. June 9, 2011).

Technique: Garage Door Injury

You represent Robert Samuelson, a deliveryman who was bringing a load of freight to a Big Box store. As he entered the building, the garage door came down on his head, causing a traumatic brain injury. You want to find out what Big Box Stores, Inc. claims happened and whether they have any defenses regarding design or misuse of the garage door. You can use 30(b)(6) to compel Big Box Stores, Inc. to reveal their position on how the event occurred and whether they can deflect responsibility to another entity.

> Pursuant to Federal Rule of Civil Procedure 30(b)(6), Big Box Stores, Inc., is required to designate and fully prepare one or more officers, directors, managing agents, or other people who consent to testify on behalf of Big Box Stores, Inc., and whom Big Box Stores, Inc., will fully prepare to testify regarding all information that is known or reasonably available to Big Box Stores, Inc.'s, organization regarding the following designated matters:
>
> - Big Box Stores, Inc.'s, position and/or opinion as to how the incident occurred in which Robert Samuelson was struck on or about the head by the steel roller door at the Big Box store.
>
> - Any error, malfunction, failure, misuse, and/or abuse that caused or contributed to the incident in which Robert Samuelson was struck on or about the head by the steel roller door at the Big Box store.

Contentions and Affirmative Defenses

You can ask about *contentions, denials,* and *affirmative defenses* in your 30(b)(6) deposition. In response to your complaint, the defense may present denials, affirmative defenses, and contentions. *Contentions* are allegations or responses in the pleadings that the parties base their claims and defenses on. *Affirmative defenses* are legal positions in which your opponent says there is no basis to the claim. *Denials* are a denial of a fact that you have asserted in a complaint.

Asking questions about an organization's basis for their legal positions is appropriate in a Rule 30(b)(6) deposition.[31] Facts and documents about an organization's claims and defenses are relevant, and you are allowed to discover them under Rule 26.[32] Courts have required parties to name Rule 30(b)(6) witnesses to testify about denials in their pleadings,[33] as well as to testify about the factual bases of their affirmative defenses.[34] Courts often reject the defense's objections to a Rule 30(b)(6) deposition that inquires into the factual bases of their allegations call for work product.[35] Conversely, a corporate plaintiff must state the facts on which it bases its claims, as asserted in its complaint.[36] Therefore, you may ask about the factual basis for an organization's denials, affirmative defenses, and contentions in a 30(b)(6) deposition.[37]

---

31. *Canal Barge Co. v. Commonwealth Edison Co.*, No. 98 C 0509, 2001 WL 817853, at *2 (N.D. Ill. July 19, 2001); *United States v. Taylor*, 166 F.R.D. 356, 362 (M.D.N.C. 1996).
32. *Smith v. General Mills, Inc.*, 2006 WL 7276959 (2006); *E.E.O.C. v. Caesars Entm't Inc.*, 237 F.R.D. 428, 434 (M.D. Nev. 2006).
33. *Security Ins. Co. of Hartford v. Trustmark Ins. Co.*, 218 F.R.D. 29, 33–35 (D. Conn. 2003).
34. *Telephone and Telegraph Corp.*, 2004 U.S. Dist LEXIS 28819, ——15–17 (W.D. Tex. June 1, 2004).
35. *U.S. v. McDonnell Douglas Corp.*, 961 F. Supp. 1288, 1290 (E.D. Mo. 1997).
36. *Resolution Trust Corp. v. Sands,* 151 F.R.D. 616, 620 (N.D. Tex. 1993).
37. *Security Ins. Co. of Hartford*, 218 F.R.D. 29 (D. Conn. 2003); *E.E.O.C. v. Caesars Entm't Inc.*, 237 F.R.D. 428, 434 (D. Nev. 2006); *Ieradi v. Lorillard,*

Technique: Designing a 30(b)(6) Contention Notice

Understanding the factual basis for an affirmative defense or contention is critical when you are preparing for trial. You can design 30(b)(6) deposition notices to focus on facts, witnesses, and documents, rather than legal opinions. In their answers, defendants will base their affirmative defense on specific sources of information. In your 30(b)(6) deposition notice, focus the matters of examination on these sources. The template for the matters of examination is as follows. You can replace [Defendant] with your defendant's name:

> Pursuant to Federal Rule of Civil Procedure 30(b)(6), [Defendant] is required to designate and fully prepare one or more officers, directors, managing agents, or other persons who consent to testify on behalf of [Defendant], and whom [Defendant] will fully prepare to testify regarding all information that is known or reasonably available to [Defendant]'s organization regarding the following designated matters:
>
> 1. All facts, witnesses, and documents on which [Defendant] bases your contention set forth in Paragraph No. __ of the Answer to Plaintiff's Complaint, stating that: [insert contention language].

Inc., No. 90–7049, 1991 WL 158911 (E.D. Pa. Aug. 13, 1991); *Protective Nat'l Ins. Co. v. Commonwealth Ins. Co.*, 137 F.R.D. 267, 272–77 (D. Neb. 1989).

Technique: Contention—Someone Else Is at Fault

In the typical answer to a complaint, you will often find your opponent allege that someone else caused the harm. Use the following template for affirmative defense 30(b)(6) notices and simply extract the precise language from your opponent's answer and insert it into your 30(b)(6) deposition notice.

> All facts, witnesses, and documents on which you base your contention set forth in Paragraph No. 15 of the Answer to the Plaintiff's Complaint stating that "the plaintiff's damages were caused by the conduct and/or lack of due care of people other than the defendant, whether individual, corporate, associate, or otherwise, and whether named or unnamed in the Plaintiff's Complaint, for whose conduct the defendant is not responsible."

By limiting your request to facts, witnesses, and documents, linked to the precise language from the defendant's answer, your request will comply with the legal requirements for contention discovery.

You Decide the Method of Discovery

Rule 30(b)(6) does not contain any requirement that you must first try to discover the facts underlying a claim by other means than a deposition.[38] If you serve a party with a Rule 30(b)(6) deposition notice or subpoena request, they are not allowed "to

---

38. *S.E.C. v. Kramer*, 778 F. Supp. 2d 1320 (M.D. Fla. 2011) (citing 8A Wright, Miller & Marcus § 2103).

elect to supply the answers in a written response to an interrogatory."[39] Because depositions provide a means to obtain more complete information, they are the process that the courts favor for gathering information.[40]

"The organization must designate a person to speak on its behalf, and it is this position that the attorney must advocate."[41] The organization that intends to assert claims and defenses in litigation is responsible to adequately prepare a person to testify as to those claims and defenses.[42] Contentions are based on the facts of a case; "the attorney for the corporation is not at liberty to manufacture the corporation's contentions."[43] A corporation cannot "have [its] attorney assert that the facts show a particular

---

39. *Marker v. Union Fidelity Life Ins.*, 125 F.R.D. 121, 126 (M.D.N.C. 1989).
40. *Great American Ins. Co. v. Vegas Const. Co., Inc.*, 251 F.R.D. 534, 539 (D. Nev. 2008) (citing *Marker v. Union Fidelity Life Insurance*, 125 F.R.D. 121, 126 (M.D.N.C. 1989)); see also, *Ieradi v. Lorillard, Inc.*, No. 90-7049, 1991 WL 158911, at *1 (E.D. Pa. Aug. 13, 1991) (citing *Marker v. Union Fidelity Life Ins. Co.*, 125 F.R.D. 121, 126 (M.D.N.C. 1989).
41. *United States v. Taylor*, 166 F.R.D. 356, 363 (M.D.N.C. 1996); *Corus Eng. Steels Ltd. v. M/V Atlantic Forrest*, Civ. A., No. 01-2-76, at *2, 2002 WL 31308335 (E.D. La. Oct. 11, 2002); *Twentieth Century Fox Film Corp. v. Marvel Enter., Inc.*, No. 01 Civ. 3016 (AGS), 2002 WL 1835439, at *3 (S.D. N.Y. Aug. 8, 2002); *A.I.A. Holdings, S.A. v. Lehman Bros., Inc.*, No. 97CIV-4978, 2002 WL 1041356, at *3 (S.D.N.Y. May 23, 2002); *Paul Revere Life Ins. Co. v. Jafari*, 206 F.R.D. 126, 127 (D. Md. 2002); *United Tech. Motor Sys., Inc. v. Borg-Warner Auto., Inc.*, No. Civ. A. 97-71706, 1998 WL 1796257, at *2 (E.D. Mich. Sept. 04, 1998); *Exxon Research & Eng'g Co. v. United States*, 44 Fed. Cl. 597, 599–600 (Fed. Cl. 1999).
42. *In re ClassicStar Mare Lease Litig.*, 2009 WL 1313311, at *2 (E.D. Ky. May 12, 2009).
43. *United States v. Taylor*, 166 F.R.D. 356, 363 (M.D.N.C. 1996); *Corus Eng. Steels Ltd. v. M/V Atlantic Forrest*, Civ. A., No. 01-2-76, at *2, 2002 WL 31308335, at *2 (E.D. La. Oct. 11, 2002); *Twentieth Century Fox Film Corp. v. Marvel Enter., Inc.*, No. 01 Civ. 3016 (AGS), 2002 WL 1835439, at *3 (S.D. N.Y. Aug. 8, 2002); *A.I.A. Holdings, S.A. v. Lehman Bros., Inc.*, No. 97CIV-4978, 2002 WL 1041356, at *3 (S.D.N.Y. May 23, 2002); *Paul Revere Life Ins. Co. v. Jafari*, 206 F.R.D. 126, 127 (D. Md. 2002); *United Tech. Motor Sys., Inc. v. Borg-Warner Auto., Inc.*, No. Civ. A. 97-71706, 1998 WL 1796257, at *2 (E.D. Mich. Sept. 04, 1998); *Exxon Research & Eng'g Co. v. United States*, 44 Fed. Cl. 597, 599–600 (Fed. Cl. 1999).

position on a topic when, at the Rule 30(b)(6) deposition, the corporation asserts no knowledge and no position."[44]

The witness must be prepared to provide all facts that the organization knows. It does not matter that the witness learned the facts from documents protected as work product, because the facts in those documents are not subject to protection.[45] In *Wilson v. Lakner*, the court cautioned the attorneys preparing their witness to testify:

> Defense counsel may wish to exercise caution in preparing the witness or witnesses with privileged documents—otherwise the privilege may be waived as to those documents—but it is simply no answer to a 30(b)(6) deposition notice to claim that relevant documents or investigations are privileged and that therefore no knowledgeable witness can be produced.[46]

Similarly the mere fact that the lawyer for the responding party prepared the witness for a 30(b)(6) deposition does not create an attorney–client privilege as to the facts of the case that the lawyer and the witness discussed.[47] In order to avoid the risk of waiving their attorney-client privilege, many law firms now prepare a person who then prepares the designee for the 30(b)(6) deposition.

Courts consistently allow lawyers to ask to ask about contention facts in 30(b)(6) depositions.[48] Any limitations on conten-

---

44. *Canal Barge Co. v. Commonwealth Edison Co.*, No. 98 C 0509, 2001 WL 817853, at *2 (N.D. Ill. July 19, 2001) (citing *United States v. Taylor*, 166 F.R.D. 356, 363, n. 8 (M.D.N.C. 1996)).
45. *Security Ins. Co. of Hartford*, 218 F.R.D. 29, 34 (D. Conn. 2003).
46. *Wilson v. Lakner*, 228 F.R.D. 524, 529 (D. Md. 2005).
47. *Id.* at 524, fn. 10.
48. *Security Ins. Co. of Hartford*, 218 F.R.D. 29 (D. Conn. 2003). *See, e.g., Radian Asset Assur., Inc. v. Coll. of the Christian Bros. of New Mexico*, 273 F.R.D. 689, 692 (D.N.M. 2011); *E.E.O.C. v. Caesars Entm't, Inc.*, 257 F.R.D. 428,

tion questions arise out of either the work product doctrine, or overbroad and overburdensome claims.[49]

The majority of courts have held that nothing prevents a deposition either in lieu of or in conjunction with interrogatories.[50] In *Sec. Ins. Co. of Hartford v. Trustmark Ins. Co.*, the court explained its position on deposition questions:

> As courts have held contention interrogatories seeking the factual bases for allegations would not encroach on protected information, it is not apparent how the same information would be otherwise unavailable through questions posed to a deponent in the course of a deposition.[51]

In a limited number of complex cases, such as patent, anti-trust, or surety bond evaluations, which necessarily involve mixed questions of law and fact, some courts have prevented 30(b)(6) inquiries where the inquiries would elicit the views and conclusions of the counsel.[52] However, even in complex cases, if contentions

---

432–34 (D. Nev. 2006); *AMP, Inc. v. Fujitsu Microelectronics, Inc.*, 853 F. Supp. 808, 831 (M.D. Pa. 1994).
49. *See, e.g., E.E.O.C. v. Caesars Entm't, Inc.*, 257 F.R.D. 428, 432–34 (D. Nev. 2006) (denying "defendant's request for a protective order to limit the scope of Rule 30(b)(6) deposition questioning to preclude inquiry into the factual bases for defendant's asserted position statements and affirmative defenses").
50. *Sec. Ins. Co. of Hartford v. Trustmark Ins. Co.*, 218 F.R.D. 29, 33 (D. Conn. 2003); *Protective Nat'l Ins. Co. v. Commonwealth Ins. Co.*, 137 F.R.D. 267, 272–77 (D. Neb. 1989).
51. *Sec. Ins. Co. of Hartford v. Trustmark Ins. Co.*, 218 F.R.D. 29, 34 (D. Conn. 2003); *see also, United States v. Boyce*, 148 F. Supp. 2d 1069, 1086 (S.D. Cal. 2001).
52. *JP Morgan Chase Bank v. Liberty Mut. Ins. Co.*, 209 F.R.D. 361, 362 (S.D.N.Y. 2002); *SEC v. Morelli*, 143 F.R.D. 42, 47 (S.D.N.Y. 1992); *TV Interactive Data Corp. v. Sony Corp.*, C 10-475 PJH MEJ, 2012 WL 1413368, at *2 (N.D. Cal. Apr. 23, 2012); *Exxon Research & Eng'g Co. v. United States*, 44 Fed. Cl. 597, 599–600 (Fed. Cl. 1999) (disallowing contention deposition on condition that interrogatory responses are forthcoming, but allowing for potential subjective testimony of patent claim in deposition of in-house attorney who

and affirmative defenses are factually based, the organization is required to designate a witness to provide that factual basis in response to a 30(b)(6) deposition notice.[53] The distinction turns on whether the matters of examination are seeking valid factual bases for contentions or whether they appear to seek the counsel's legal theory or strategy.[54]

Summary

- A 30(b)(6) notice must identify matters of examination with reasonable particularity.

- The requesting party must give the responding party sufficient notice to be able to prepare.

- The responding party must be able to identify the outer limits of the areas of inquiry.

- The term *including but not limited to* makes it impossible to identify the outer limits of the inquiry and is therefore overbroad.

- Matters of examination may request facts, sources of information, subjective beliefs, opinions, and interpretations of documents and events.

- A 30(b)(6) notice may inquire about the factual basis for affirmative defenses and contentions.

---

does not work for the firm handling the litigation if the contention interrogatories are not sufficient to get the requested information).
53. *Canal Barge Co. v. Commonwealth Edison Co.*, No. 98 C 0509, 2001 WL 817853, at *2 (N.D. Ill. July 19, 2001); *AMP, Inc. v. Fujitsu Microelectronics, Inc.*, 853 F. Supp. 808, 831 (M.D. Pa. 1994) (compelling a corporate patent defendant to produce a 30(b)(6) witness to answer questions regarding contentions and affirmative defenses in the defendants' answer and counterclaim).
54. *See Radian Asset Assur., Inc. v. Coll. of the Christian Bros. of New Mexico*, 273 F.R.D. 689, 691–92 (D.N.M. 2011) (examining the distinction between cases that permit and those that disallow contention inquiries).

8

Rule 30(b)(6), Rule 30(b)(2), and Rule 34 Document Depositions

Documents don't lie.
Documents don't forget.
Documents don't change their story.
Documents don't try to cover up after the fact.

—John Frost

Introduction. 163
Problems with Rule 34 Document Requests 163
Combining Rules 30(b)(2), 30(b)(6), and 34 to Get
    Complete Responses to Document Requests 165
Objections to Document Requests. 166
    Must Respond within Thirty Days. 166
    Objection Rules. 167
    "Subject to and Without Waiving". 170

What Is Possession, Custody, and Control? 172
    Defining Possession, Custody, or Control 172
Produced Documents Must Be Organized 174
The Solution: Rule 30(b)(6), Rule 30(b)(2),
    and Rule 34 Document Deposition 175
    Organizations Cannot Insist on
        Alternative Discovery 176
    Discovery about Discovery Is Permissible. 177
Rule 30(b)(2): Producing Documents on Time. 180
Rule 30(b)(6) 181
Foundation Concerning the Document Search. 184
    Matter of Inquiry 1: Do the Documents Exist? 185
    Matter of Inquiry 2: What Are the Systems,
        Processes, and Purposes for Creation,
        Duplication, and Storage of Documents? 187
    Matter of Inquiry 3: What Are the
        Document Destruction and Retention Policies? . . .191
    Matter of Inquiry 4: Where Are the
        Documents Located? 193
    Matter of Inquiry 5: How Are
        the Documents Organized, Indexed, and Filed? . . .194
    Matter of Inquiry 6: How Did the
        Organization Search for the Documents? 196
    Matter of Inquiry 7: Is the Document
        Set Complete?. 200
Preempt Improper Objections 202
Duty to Supplement 203
Summary 204

Introduction

Truth is found in the documents. In the landmark case of *Zubulake v. UBS Warburg,* Judge Shira Ann Scheindlin recognized the essence of what we are trying to accomplish in this chapter: "Documents create a paper reality we call proof."[1] However, our challenge is not only to identify the documents that uncover the truth, but also to compel our opponents to *thoroughly* produce those documents.

Typically, to obtain documents, you serve your opponent with a Rule 34 Request for Production of Documents. Rule 34 requires that, among other things, parties to a lawsuit will provide for the "production, inspection, and copying of documents."[2] The rule specifies the procedure and time requirements you should use when requesting the documents from a party.[3] Parties responding to your Rule 34 request have a duty to complete a reasonable investigation to satisfy your discovery request.[4]

Problems with Rule 34 Document Requests

Unfortunately, traditional requests for documents from your opponent often result in evasive and incomplete responses, littered with boilerplate objections. There are several recurrent problems when your opponent responds to a Rule 34 request for production of documents:

- **Problem 1.** The opposing counsel does not adequately verify that the document set is complete. This is because your opponent, the producing counsel, does not have the client's institutional knowledge. Instead, the producing counsel

---

1. *Zubulake v. UBS Warburg, LLC*, 220 F.R.D. 212, 214 (S.D.N.Y. 2003).
2. Fed. R. Civ. P. 34(a).
3. Fed. R. Civ. P. 34(b).
4. *Prokosch v. Catalina Lighting, Inc.*, 193 F.R.D. 633, 636–37 (D. Minn. 2000).

can only repeat what information and documents the client identified, which may or may not be accurate or complete.

- **Problem 2.** Your opponent may respond to your Rule 34 request in a way that is untimely, evasive, filtered, or that contains litanies of patterned objections, such as "overbroad," "vague," "irrelevant," and "not calculated to lead to the discovery of admissible evidence."

- **Problem 3.** Your opponent produces documents with the statement that the documents are "subject to and without waiving" that objection. With this tactic, lawyers put the boilerplate comment at the beginning of their response and then do an incomplete job of hunting for documents. Later, when they produce additional documents that you haven't seen, they assume this language allows this conduct. Although such objections have become commonplace, courts have determined them to be a prohibited abusive practice. In *Network Tallahassee, Inc. v. Embarq Corp.*, the court stated, "This is an abusive practice that has become commonplace and should end."[5]

- **Problem 4.** Your opponent produces documents in a random and disorganized fashion.

By using Rules 30(b)(2), 30(b)(6), and 34 together, you can take a document deposition that identifies missing records and creates a factual record upon which the court can base its rulings on objections your opponent raises.

This chapter will explain the following:

- What rules you need to know for document production.

- How you can use Rule 30(b)(6), Rule 30(b)(2), and Rule 34 together to get documents when you need them.

---

5. *Network Tallahassee, Inc. v. Embarq Corp.*, 2010 WL 4569897 (N.D. Fla. Sept. 20, 2010).

- How you can use Rule 30(b)(6) to ensure that a witness can identify the following:
  » The existence of the documents
  » Why they were created
  » Where they are stored
  » How they were organized
  » How the search was conducted
  » The completeness of the documents
  » How to neutralize spurious objections

Combining Rules 30(b)(2), 30(b)(6), and 34 to Get Complete Responses to Document Requests

When used together, Rule 30(b)(2), Rule 30(b)(6), and Rule 34 become the vehicle to establish whether your opponent's production response was complete. Using these rules together, you can call a document deposition, where you depose a *document production* witness. *The primary purpose of the document production witness is to establish if the records are complete.* The document deposition not only identifies missing records, but it also enables both parties to create a factual record upon which the court can base its rulings on objections that the responding party might make. *Once the court establishes that the produced documents are complete, you may examine additional witnesses as to the content of those records.*

The procedure is patently simple:

- Rule 34 identifies the categories of documents that your opponent must produce.

- Rule 30(b)(2) requires the deponent to produce the documents *at the deposition*.

- Rule 30(b)(6) requires the deponent to identify available documents, describe how the organization searched for those documents, and attest to the completeness of the documents produced.

In the document deposition, an organization is directed to do the following:

1. Provide a witness.

2. Require the witness to bring the requested documents to the deposition.

3. Ensure that the witness will testify to establish and verify the documents' existence, the purpose of the documents' creation, the documents' location and organization, the search for those documents, and the completeness of the documents produced.

By using a Rule 30(b)(6), Rule 30(b)(2), and Rule 34 document deposition, it is possible to establish whether the documents that the organization produced are complete.

Objections to Document Requests

Your opponents may object to your document requests. Following are the rules for document production. These are the rules of engagement that your opponents have to follow. You can use these rules and case law to show a judge why your opponents' objections are improper or are waived because your opponents didn't make the objections at the appropriate time.

Must Respond within Thirty Days

Rule 34(b)(2)(A) requires the party to whom you directed the document request to respond in writing within thirty days after you served the request.[6] Therefore, you must give the responding party at least thirty days to assemble and produce the documents you requested.[7]

Objection Rules

This section outlines the rules a responding party must follow if it objects to a production of documents request.

State Objections with Particularity

If the responding party objects to producing any of the documents you requested, the responding party must state those objections *with particularity*.[8] *With particularity* means that both the requesting party and the court must be able to understand the legal and factual basis for the objection from the contents of their response.[9]

Waiving Untimely Objections

If your opponents do not object to your request for documents in a timely manner, they waive the right to object.

- Rule 33(b)(4), which deals with interrogatories, has a provision that automatically waives untimely objections.

- Rule 34 does not have this provision for untimely objections. However, courts have reasoned that a Rule 33(b)(4) type of waiver should be implied into all procedural rules involving the use of various discovery mechanisms.[10]

---

6. Fed. R. Civ. P. 34(b)(2)(A).
7. *Brown v. Greyhound Lines, Inc.*, 1995 WL 811965 (S.D. Tex. Aug. 25, 1995).
8. Fed. R. Civ. P. 34(b)(2)(B).
9. *See Athridge v. Aetna Cas. & Sur. Co.*, 184 F.R.D. 181, 190 (D. D.C. 1998).
10. *Horrace Mann Ins. Co. v. Nationwide Mutual Ins. Co.*, 283 F.R.D. 536, 538 (D. Conn. 2006) (citing *Byrd v. Reno*, No. 96-2375, 1998 WL 429676, at *6 (D. D.C. Feb. 12, 1998)) (holding that an argument that an untimely objection is waived should be analyzed the same under Rule 34 as it is under Rule 33); *Deal v. Lutheran Hosp. & Homes*, 127 F.R.D. 166, 168 (D. Ala. 1989) (holding that the waiver analysis should be "similar if not identical" under Rules 33, 34, 36, and 45(d)(1)).

To overcome the waiver, the objecting party must establish good cause for its failure to timely state its objection.[11] The court does not consider counsel's inadvertence, excusable neglect, and lack of prejudice as reasons for not complying with the deadline to state objections.[12]

Waiving All Objections

Some courts have applied the waiver of untimely objections rule to *all objections*, not just the substantive objections. A party's failure to object within the thirty-day window can lead to serious problems: "A party who fails to file timely objections waives all objections, including those based on privilege or work product."[13]

Boilerplate Objection Language

Boilerplate objections have become commonplace responses to document requests. For example, at the beginning of the response to every request, your opponent might include language like this:

- Vague

- Overburdensome

---

11. *See, e.g., Starlight Int'l, Inc. v. Herlihy*, 181 F.R.D. 494, 496 (D. Kan. 1998).
12. *Id.* at 496–97 (citing *Broitman v. Kirkland*, 86 F.3d 172, 175 (10th Cir. 1996); *Deghand v. Wal-Mart Stores, Inc.*, 904 F. Supp. 1218, 1221 (D. Kan. 1995)).
13. *Horrace Mann Ins. Co. v. Nationwide Mutual Ins. Co.*, 283 F.R.D. 536, 538 (D. Conn. 2006) citing *Ramirez v. County of Los Angeles*, 231 F.R.D. 407, 409 (C.D. Cal. 2005); *Microsoft Corp. v. Multi-Tech Sys., Inc.*, No. CIV. 00-1412ADMRLE, 2002 WL 273146, at *1 (D. Minn. Feb. 26, 2002); *see also, Pham v. Hartford Fire Ins. Co.*, 193 F.R.D. 659, 662 (D. Colo. 2000) (finding claim of privilege waived where the defendant failed to file objections to interrogatories until 71 days after the interrogatories were served); *Smith v. Conway Org., Inc.*, 154 F.R.D. 73, 76 (S.D. N.Y. 1994) (deeming waived a work-product objection asserted nearly four months after the document request was served). *See also, Meridian Trust Co. v. Provident Life and Cas. Ins. Co.*, No. 91-4504, 1992 WL 73094, at *1 (E.D. Pa. April 1, 1992) (citing *Weber v. Chateaugay Corporation*, 1990 WL 87310, *4 (E.D. Pa. 1990); *Klitsch v. General Motors Corp.*, 1990 WL 192037, *1 (E.D. Pa. 1990); *Krewson v. City of Quincy*, 120 F.R.D. 6, 7 (D. Mass. 1988); *Perry v. Golub*, 74 F.R.D. 360, 363–64 (N.D. Ala. 1976); *Davis v. Romney*, 53 F.R.D. 247, 248 (E.D. Pa. 1971)).

- Irrelevant
- Not calculated to lead to admissible evidence
- Not proportional to the needs of the case

If your opponents insert these objections into a response to a Rule 34 request for documents, those boilerplates are not enough to relieve them of their duty to respond.[14] As in all written discovery, it is the objecting parties' burden to provide a *factual basis* for their objections in their written responses. The court can then use this factual basis to make a reasoned ruling from the face of the response. If your opponents do not produce the factual basis for an objection within thirty days, the court is supposed to rule that the objection is waived. In other words, it's not enough just to object. Your opponents have to say *why* they object.[15]

For example, your opponents stating, "It's overburdensome," in the response isn't good enough. They have to say, "It's overburdensome because the defendant has ten thousand filing cabinets in a warehouse, there is no index, and it will take us four months to find the information."

Example: Bagel Depot, Inc.

You have a lawsuit against a Bagel Depot shop, where a customer was injured when a light fixture fell on her. You want the personnel file of a former employee who was in charge of building maintenance at this shop from three years ago. Bagel Depot, Inc. responds to the document request with a response that says, "Objection, overburdensome." That objection is within the thirty-day limit, but it is insufficient because there is no factual basis for it. Bagel Depot, Inc. hasn't said *why* the request is overburdensome.

---

14. *Burlington Northern v. U.S. Dist. Ct. of Montana*, 408 F.3d 1142, 1149 (9th Cir. 2005).
15. *Id.*

"Subject to and Without Waiving"

It has become commonplace for lawyers responding to written discovery to begin their written responses to your discovery requests with an objection, and then the statement claiming to produce "subject to and without waiving our objection." This means your opponents are planning to give you some of the documents, but because they have an objection, they may not be giving you everything. They won't verify that the document set is complete. Your opponents may believe that because of this clause, "subject to and without waiving our objection," they can produce additional documents at trial that were requested here. Your opponents may think that this statement protects them. Unless you challenge their response, it might.

In *Athridge v. Aetna,* the court clearly identified the misleading nature of the "produce subject to and without waiving" response. The court recognized the following:

> . . . that this type of answer "hides the ball." It leaves the plaintiff wondering what documents are produced and what documents are being withheld. Furthermore, it permits the defendant to be the sole arbiter of that decision. Such an objection is really no objection at all, as it does not address why potentially responsive documents are being withheld.[16]

Such discovery responses lead the requesting party to believe that the responding party's document production and interrogatory answers are comprehensive, when, in fact, the responder has discreetly withheld documents and information.

In *Network Tallahassee, Inc., v. Embarq Corp.,* the court identified the underlying policy problem of such a response, using this explanation:

---

16. *Athridge v. Aetna Cas. & Sur. Co.*, 184 F.R.D. 181, 190 (D. D.C. 1998).

> [A]n unscrupulous attorney could withhold properly discoverable information—a smoking-gun document, for example—and assert later that he did nothing dishonest because he had, after all, objected to the discovery request and simply withheld the information based on the (unwaived) objection.[17]

Network Tallahassee went on with this order:

> A party met with a response of this kind may insist that the objections be explicitly waived or withdrawn in writing and, if they are not, may move to compel. The motion will always be granted, and fees will always be assessed, at least absent a reasonable explanation that is difficult to imagine. But *this order provides fair warning: a party cannot properly engage in this practice. The party may object to discovery or not, but the party cannot have it both ways.*[18]

However, once the objection-without-waiving statement is made, the burden is now on you, the requesting party, to challenge this language in a timely fashion. If you don't challenge the objection-without-waiving language promptly, you will lose your right to raise that problem later on or to ask for a more complete document set.[19]

Although the law clearly prohibits "subject to and without waiving" objections, your arguments to the court are more likely to prevail if you can show that the objection did obscure the fact that your opponent *did not* produce relevant information. Without a record, the court has little or nothing upon which to base its ruling, other than a self-serving affidavit that your opponent submitted.

---

17. *Network Tallahassee, Inc., v. Embarq Corp.*, 2010 WL 4569897, *1 (N.D. Fla. Sept. 20, 2010).
18. *Id.* (Emphasis added.)
19. *See Lapenna v. Upjohn Co.*, 110 F.R.D. 15, 24 (E.D. Pa. 1986).

Example: Bagel Depot, Inc.

Using the Bagel Depot, Inc. example, your opponents claim it is overburdensome to find the personnel file because the corporation's personnel records are paper files stored in a warehouse in Texas. There are 10,000 filing cabinets with information about 400 stores and 180,000 employees. On its face, their position sounds rational. However, using a Rule 30(b)(6), Rule 30(b)(2), and Rule 34 document deposition, the designated Bagel Depot, Inc. witness testifies that there is an indexing system to locate the file and that the company could produce it within the hour. With what you learn at the document deposition, there is a clear record that the overburdensome argument is without merit. It is not overburdensome to locate the former building maintenance employee's personnel file. A motion is no longer necessary because you have neutralized the objection.

What Is Possession, Custody, and Control?

Rule 34(a)(1) requires the responding party to produce documents in its *possession, custody,* or *control*. You may find that your opponent responds to Rule 34 requests with this statement: "The defendant does not have the requested documents in its possession." Again, this type of insidious response often masks the defendant's failure to have fully responded to your request.

The courts have defined *possession* and *control* differently than your opponent has asserted. You can include quotes from the following cases in your brief to explain why the documents you want are actually in your opponent's control, and why you have a right to see them.

Defining Possession, Custody, or Control

Rule 34 requires the responding party to produce all documents that are in its "possession, custody, or control."[20] In *Calzaturio*

---

20. Fed. R. Civ. P. 34(a)(1); *Calzaturio S.C.A.R.P.A. S.P.A. v. Fabiano Shoe Co., Inc.*, 201 F.R.D. 33, 38 (D. Mass. 2001).

S.C.A.R.P.A. S.P.A. v. Fabiano Shoe Co., Inc., the court explained, "Control is defined not only as actual possession, but also as the legal right, authority, or practical ability to obtain the requested documents from a nonparty."[21] Courts have interpreted Rule 34 to "require production if the party has practical ability to obtain the documents from another, irrespective of his legal entitlement to the documents."[22] Therefore,

> under Rule 34, "control" does not require that the party have legal ownership or actual physical possession of the documents at issue; rather, documents are considered to be under a party's control when that party has the right, authority, or practical ability to obtain the documents from a nonparty to the action.[23]

---

21. *Calzaturio S.C.A.R.P.A. S.P.A. v. Fabiano Shoe Co., Inc.*, 201 F.R.D. 33, 38 (D. Mass. 2001); *see also, Prokosch v. Catalina Lighting, Inc.*, 193 F.R.D. 633, 636 (D. Minn. 2000) (citing *Florentia Cont. Corp. v. RTC*, No. 92 Civ. 1188, 1993 WL 127187, at *3 (S.D.N.Y. Apr. 22, 1993)); *Alexander v. F.B.I.*, 194 F.R.D. 299, 301 (D. D.C. 2000); *In re Bankers Trust Co.*, 61 F.3d 465, 469 (6th Cir. 1995) (citing *Resolution Trust Corp. v. Deloitte & Touche*, 145 F.R.D. 108, 110 (D. Colo. 1992)); *Weck v. Cross*, 88 F.R.D. 325, 327 (N.D. Ill. 1980); *Searock v. Stripling*, 736 F.2d. 650, 653 (11th Cir. 1984).
22. *Prokosch v. Catalina Lighting, Inc.*, 193 F.R.D. 633, 636 (D. Minn. 2000) (citing *U.S. v. Skeddle*, 176 F.R.D. 258, 261, n.5 (N.D. Ohio 1997) (citations omitted)); *Scott v. Arex*, 124 F.R.D. 39, 41 (D. Conn. 1989); Gary J. Mennitt, Document Discovery: Possession, Custody or Control, N.Y.L.J. 214 (Nov. 21, 1995).
23. *Prokosch v. Catalina Lighting, Inc.*, 193 F.R.D. 633, 636 (D. Minn. 2000) (citing *Bank of New York v. Meridien BIAO Bank Tanzania, Ltd.*, 171 F.R.D. 135, 146 (S.D.N.Y. 1997)); *see also, In re NASDAQ Market-Makers Antitrust Litigation*, 169 F.R.D. 493, 530 (S.D.N.Y. 1996); *Golden Trade S.r.L. v. Lee Apparel Co.*, 143 F.R.D. 514, 525 (S.D.N.Y. 1992); *Scott v. Arex*, 124 F.R.D. 39, 41 (D. Conn. 1989); *M.L.C., Inc. v. North American Philips Corp.*, 109 F.R.D. 134, 136 (S.D.N.Y. 1986).

Example: Paula's Pizza

For instance, *control* of documents would include records in the possession of a subsidiary corporation or records turned over to other entities, such as an independent accounting firm or consultant. In a lawsuit against Paula's Pizza, a small, tightly held corporation, you have requested the company's tax returns. Your opponent responds that Paula's Pizza doesn't have them anymore. In the document deposition, you can ask, "Who does have the tax returns?" At that point you may find that Paula's Pizza's accountants (a separate accounting company) have the tax returns. You may then ask, "Did anyone request those tax returns from the accountants?" With the answer being "no," you have established that Paula's Pizza had misled you and the court with its evasive answer.

Produced Documents Must Be Organized

Dump-truck production is yet another recurrent problem when organizations respond to Rule 34 requests. Organizations often produce massive volumes of documents in a random, disorganized manner. As a result, the ability to evaluate those documents in the context of other documents becomes challenging and burdensome. The rules prohibit dump-truck production. Rule 34(b)(2)(E)(i) establishes how the responding party must organize documents for production under Rule 34:

1. Produce the documents as kept in the usual course of business.

2. Organize the documents to correspond with the categories in the request.

3. Label the documents to correspond with the categories in the request.[24]

---

24. Fed. R. Civ. P. 34(b)(2)(E)(i).

The rules for production are well established. However, experience tells us that our success with motions to compel is often a function of not only the law, but also the factual record that the court uses to consider the motion. Therefore, the question is this: How do you make a record about a defendant organization's responses to document requests? The answer is simple: a document deposition.

The Solution: Rule 30(b)(6), Rule 30(b)(2), and Rule 34 Document Deposition

The Federal Judicial Center in its *Manual for Complex Litigation* has recognized the challenges that accompany Rule 34:

> In litigation with voluminous documents, requests for production and responses can become mired in confusion unless carefully administered. Requests can be overlooked, responses can be lost in the shuffle, failures to respond can be obscured, and uncertainty can arise over what was requested and what was produced.[25]

The document deposition ensures that all parties have the same documents, with the same Bates numbers, and the same exhibit numbers. Using this deposition simplifies litigation management and trial. More importantly, depositions are the best vehicle for establishing if documents exist and if the document production is complete. "Because of its nature, the deposition process provides a means to obtain more complete information and is, therefore, favored."[26] In *Cache La Poudre Feeds, LLC v. Land O'Lakes, Inc.*,

---

25. Manual for Complex Litigation 76 (3d ed. Thompson West).
26. *Great American Ins. Co. v. Vegas Const. Co., Inc.*, 251 F.R.D. 534, 539 (D. Nev. 2008) (citing *Marker v. Union Fidelity Life Insurance*, 125 F.R.D. 121, 126 (M.D.N.C. 1989)); *see also In re China Merchants Steam Nav. Co.*, 259 F. Supp. 75 (S.D.N.Y. 1966).

the court affirmed the use of a Rule 30(b)(6) deposition to explore the procedures that the defendant employed to identify, preserve, and produce responsive documents.[27]

The goal of the document deposition is not to explore the documents' substantive content. Rather, the goals are to do the following:

- Identify all documents within the designated categories.
- Neutralize spurious objections.
- Establish if the search is complete, which documents have been produced, and which ones are missing.
- Build a record to compel production.

You can use the document deposition to accomplish all these goals.

Organizations Cannot Insist on Alternative Discovery

A party you have served with a deposition notice or subpoena request does not have the right "to elect to supply the answers in a written response to an interrogatory" instead of the deposition.[28] As the requesting party, you have the right and responsibility to determine which method of examination, whether by oral examination or written interrogatories, will best provide the information you need to properly prepare the litigation. In *Goldberg v. Raleigh Manufacturers,* the court succinctly stated the following:

> [I]t has long been recognized that there are far greater advantages in obtaining the facts and circumstances involved in a confronting examination than in a written one.[29]

---

27. *Cache La Poudre Feeds, LLC v. Land O'Lakes, Inc.*, 244 F.R.D. 614, 619 (D. Colo. 2007).
28. *Great American Ins. Co. v. Vegas Const. Co.*, 251 F.R.D. 534, 539 (D. Nev. 2008).
29. *Goldberg v. Raleigh Manufacturers*, 28 F. Supp. 975, 977 (D. Mass. 1939).

The cases clearly state that our adversaries can't pick the way in which we ask for the information. We get to choose how we want to get the information.

Discovery about Discovery Is Permissible

Your opponent may object that the Rule 30(b)(2), Rule 30(b)(6), and Rule 34 document deposition is impermissible because "discovery on discovery" is not relevant. Historically, Federal Rule 26(b)(1) said a party was entitled to discovery of the following:

> [T]he existence, description, nature, custody, condition, and location of any books, documents, or other tangible things and the identity and location of persons who know of any discoverable matter.[30]

The advisory committee note explained the following:

> Discovery of such matters is so deeply entrenched in practice that it is no longer necessary to clutter the long text of Rule 26 with these examples. The discovery identified in these examples should still be permitted under the revised rule when relevant and proportional to the needs of the case.[31]

It is clear from the advisory committee's comment to the amendment to Rule 26 that discovery on discover was and is appropriate.[31]

In *Ruiz-Bueno v. Scott,* the court described the legal principles supporting discovery about discovery. The court explained that the description or location of documents is relevant because the information can assist a party in structuring its discovery or

---

30. Fed. R. Civ. P. 26(b)(1).
31. Fed. R. Civ. P. 26(b)(1) advisory committee's note (2015 Amendment); *See also, Moore's Answer Guide*: Federal Discovery Practice, 2016 ed., §2.06 [2].

in pursuing discovery effectively and efficiently.[32] *Ruiz-Bueno* ruled, "Discovery into how the discovery was conducted is permissible."[33]

However, courts have also allowed discovery about discovery when the responses are *not* in question.[34] Courts have approved inquiry as to who provided the information and who participated in a document search.[35] In *S2 Automation LLC v. Micron Technology, Inc.,* the court approved inquiry into the "search strategy" for identifying pertinent documents, including the procedures the defendant used and how the defendant interacted with its counsel to facilitate the production process.[36]

Example: Cedar Gardens Homes

You have a lawsuit involving a medication aide in an assisted living facility called Cedar Gardens Homes. A male medication aide gave a sleeping pill to an eighty-eight-year-old woman and raped her. The Cedar Gardens Homes ultimately found out about the rape and fired the aide. You want to have the aide's personnel file to answer questions about the aide's history and position:

- Where did he come from?
- Who hired him?
- Did he have any problems at his previous job?
- Did the nursing home company know about any background issues?
- When did they know about these issues?
- Did they fire him because of the rape?

---

32. *Ruiz-Bueno v. Scott*, 2013 WL 6055402, *1 (S.D. Ohio Nov. 15, 2013).
33. *Id.*
34. *Id.*
35. *Id.* at *3; *see also, Strauss v. Credit Lyonnais, S.A.*, 242 F.R.D. 199, 232 (E.D.N.Y.2007); *McNearney v. Washington Dept. of Corrections*, 2012 WL 3155099, *6 (W.D. Wash. Aug. 2, 2012).
36. *See S2 Automation LLC v. Micron Technology, Inc.*, 2012 WL 3656454, *32 (D.N.M. Aug.9, 2012).

- What facts did they know about the rape?

You get a copy of the aide's personnel file, but there's nothing about the rape or firing in the file. Clearly something is amiss. In a document deposition, you can ask the following:

Q: What documents are contained in the personnel file?

Q: Why aren't there documents about rape and termination in the file?

When you ask these questions, the deponent answers:

A: Oh, the misbehavior and firing is in the termination file. You didn't ask for the termination file.

You don't need to suspect that there is something amiss, however, to ask more questions about the overall document set. The rules allow you to discover how the opposing party has conducted document searches and how it has named and stored the documents. Here are some questions you might ask:

Q: What documents fall within this category?

Q: What are the policies for their naming and storage?

Q: What are the procedures for their naming and storage?

Q: What is the purpose of creating the documents?

Q: How are they created?

Q: Why are they created?

Q: Where are they located?

For example, your opponents might store data on a cell phone and a laptop. How is that data organized? You want to preempt your opponents' objections. You want to know how they search for information in the cell phone or laptop.[37]

---

37. *See* chapter 9, "Electronic Discovery."

Rule 30(b)(2): Producing Documents on Time

A recurrent problem with Rule 34 requests for documents is that the responding organization does not produce the documents *when* you need them. The defendant might make repeated promises, such as "we are working on it" or "we will get them to you soon." All the while, the litigation languishes. By using Federal Rule of Civil Procedure 30(b)(2), you can establish a deadline for your opponent to produce documents.

Rule 34 states that your opponent must produce documents within thirty days. Your opponent may give excuses, essentially saying, "the check's in the mail." Rule 30(b)(2), however, states that the witness must bring the documents to the deposition. By using a Rule 30(b)(2) deposition, *you* set a date for the deposition and, as a result, the date on which your opponent must produce the documents.

When using Rule 30(b)(2) with a party, you must serve a Rule 34 request for documents together with the 30(b)(6) deposition notice.[38] The deponent must then bring the documents you requested to the deposition so you can examine, copy, and inquire about them. However, when you are using the Rule 30(b)(2) deposition protocol, you must follow Rule 34's requirements, including thirty days' notice. So unlike a typical 30(b)(6) deposition which you can set at any reasonable time, when you are using Rule 34, you must give at least thirty days' notice. When you use a combination of Rule 34 and Rule 30(b)(2), the deponents have to bring the documents you requested, and they have to appear on your schedule. These two rules together enable you to take control of the timing for your opponent to produce documents. You can use Rule 30(b)(2) with nonparties as well as parties to the litigation.

---

38. Fed. R. Civ. P. 30(b)(2).

- **Nonparty request for documents.** When requesting documents or tangible items from a nonparty, rather than using a Rule 34 document request, you must serve a subpoena *duces tecum,* using Rule 45(a)(1)(A)(iii) to compel the nonparty to produce the documents.

- **Party request for documents.** When requesting documents or tangible items from a party, use Rule 34.[39]

Rule 30(b)(6)

The next question is, whom do you depose? The answer is in Rule 30(b)(6). "Records custodian" depositions are seldom of any value. Because Rule 30(b)(1) covers the custodian deposition, the custodian has no duty to prepare. As a result, that witness will not have the answers you need in order to establish what records exist or whether the production is complete. The witness's response is always the same: "to the best of my knowledge." That answer leaves you wondering, what else is out there?

The goal of the 30(b)(6) document deposition is to determine if the produced document set is complete and to build a record to compel the defendant to produce missing documents. Rather than naming a specific person or listing a job title, such as custodian of records, by using Rule 30(b)(6), you can tailor the matters of examination to focus on the completeness of the production set, rather than on the content of the records.

The goal of the document deposition is not to explore the substantive content of the documents produced. Rather, the goals are to do the following:

- Identify all documents within the designated categories.

- Neutralize spurious objections.

---

39. *See* chapter 10, "Duty to Attend," which explains in detail how the rules require responding organizations to attend the deposition.

- Establish completeness of the search, which documents have been produced, and which ones are missing.
- Build a record to compel production.

Technique: Draft the Matters of Examination

Because the goal of the 30(b)(6) document deposition is to determine if the produced document set is complete and to build a record to compel production of missing documents, the matters of examination must, therefore, focus on those goals. The 30(b)(6) matters of examination for the document production witness are as follows:

1. The existence of the documents and/or electronically stored data requested in the schedule of documents below, pursuant to Fed. R. Civ. P. 34.

2. The systems, process, and purpose for the creation, duplication, and storage of the documents and/or electronically stored data requested in the schedule of documents below, pursuant to Fed. R. Civ. P. 34.

3. Any and all document and/or electronically stored data retention and destruction policies that would relate to any of the documents requested in the schedule of documents below, pursuant to Fed. R. Civ. P. 34.

4. The location of the documents and/or electronically stored data requested in the schedule of documents below, pursuant to Fed. R. Civ. P. 34.

> 5. The organization, indexing, and filing of the documents and/or electronically stored data requested in the schedule of documents below, pursuant to Fed. R. Civ. P. 34.
>
> 6. The method of search for the documents and/or electronically stored data requested in the schedule of documents below, pursuant to Fed. R. Civ. P. 34.
>
> 7. The completeness of the documents and/or electronically stored data produced pursuant to Fed. R. Civ. P. 34.
>
> **TAKE NOTICE** that, pursuant to Fed. R. Civ. P. 30(b)(2), [Requesting Party] requests that the [Responding Party]'s designee, responsive to this deposition notice, produce, at the time of the deposition, the documents identified in the Schedule of Documents contained in this deposition notice.
>
> **SCHEDULE OF DOCUMENTS**
>
> 1. [ADD]
> 2. [ADD]
> 3. [ADD]

If there are omissions within the produced documents, you can question the 30(b)(6) witness to figure out what he omitted and why. If your opponent objects, you can vet whether those objections are legitimate. The document deposition provides an efficient and distinct advantage over the more common approach of requesting your opponent to produce documents under Rule 34 alone.

Foundation Concerning the Document Search

The effectiveness of the Rule 30(b)(6) document deposition is a product of asking the right questions to make a foundational record as to whether the organization has conducted a valid search. The goal of the records deposition is to verify whether your opponent has produced complete records. Therefore, you must establish that the organization has fully prepared its designated witness to provide all information that the organization reasonably knows regarding the matters of examination in the 30(b)(6) notice. Vetting objections and verifying complete disclosure requires a record of the locations, organization, search methods, and completeness of the records you requested. In practice, the designated witness is seldom fully prepared and is often an institutional professional witness, unable to adequately respond to the matters you listed in the 30(b)(6) notice. Almost universally, we discover records that the organization did not produce.

In order to establish that the defendant is providing *all* documents, you first need to establish that the document deposition witness is able to provide all information that the company knows about each of the matters of examination. By asking simple foundational questions, it is possible to first determine if the organization produced an appropriate witness.

> **Technique:** Is the Witness Prepared?
>
> The purpose of the deposition is to establish a record as to whether the organization has *fully prepared* the witness to provide all information that the responding organization knows or reasonably has available on the matters of

examination. Look for these key pieces of information about the documents in your list:

- Do the documents exist?
- What are the systems, processes, and purposes for creation, duplication, and storage of documents?
- What are the document destruction and retention policies?
- Where are the documents located?
- How are the documents organized, indexed, and filed?
- How did the organization search for the documents?
- Is the document set complete?

Matter of Inquiry 1: Do the Documents Exist?

Is This the Right Witness?

Before you can ask about the documents, you must first establish that the witness knows about the subject matter and has verified that she has been provided all information that the organization knows. With the following line of questions, we are building a record as to what knowledge this witness has about the records we are looking for. In addition, we want to learn who else has information about the records and what the organization did to ensure that the witness has all the information the organization knows.

Q: What has Cedar Gardens Homes done to gather all the knowledge, known or reasonably available to Cedar Gardens Homes, with respect to the existence of the documents in Request #_____?

Q: How was the knowledge, known or reasonably available to Cedar Gardens Homes, made known to you?

Q: What is your experience working with the documents identified in Request #_____?

Q: Are there any other people who have knowledge about the documents identified in Request #_____?

Q: List their names, please.

Q: Is there anyone else?

Q: Who else knows what documents exist for Request #_____?

Q: List their names, please.

Q: Is there anyone else?

Q: Have you talked to any of these people to ensure you have one hundred percent of the information known to Cedar Gardens Homes about the existence of the documents listed in Request #_____?

Q: Why not?

Q: What did they tell you?

Q: What has Cedar Gardens Homes done to make sure you have all of the knowledge, known or reasonably available to Cedar Gardens Homes, with respect to identifying the documents which would be responsive to Request #_____?

What Documents Exist?

Once you have established that the witness has all information known to the organization about the existence of the documents you requested, you must then learn what documents exist in the defined category.

Using our personnel file example, you discovered that by redefining portions of the personnel file as a "termination file," the human resources department (or the organization's lawyers) tried to evade honestly providing the records we were obviously looking for. Therefore, the next portion of the document deposition is to ensure that all parties are using the same terms to describe the documents you requested and the opposing party produced.

Q: What do you understand the documents named Request # _____ to be?

Q: Describe the documents in Request #_____.

Q: What kinds of documents are they?

Q: How does Cedar Gardens Homes categorize them?

Q: Have you listed for the jury every document that would fall under Request #_____?

Q: Any others?

Q: What about _____?

Q: Why didn't you list that document?

Q: Any others?

Q: Are there any documents that you thought might be responsive to this request that you decided not to include?

Q: What are they?

Matter of Inquiry 2: What Are the Systems, Processes, and Purposes for Creation, Duplication, and Storage of Documents?

By understanding how and why the documents are prepared, you are on the first leg of establishing their relevance in your case, as well as where to find them, and whether you received a complete set.

Example: George's Grocery Emporium, Inc.

For example, in an employment sexual harassment case against George's Grocery Emporium, Inc., understanding the purpose of having sexual harassment policies shows that the company had knowledge of the foreseeable risk of sexual harassment, understood why sexual harassment is bad, and had adopted company standards to follow to prevent sexual harassment.

By knowing how policies are created, typically on a word processing program, you can learn through the metadata[40] when the organization created the policy, who created it, and whether it was changed following the event that is the basis of your lawsuit.

Who Knows How the Documents Are Created?

Q: What has Big Box Stores done to gather all the knowledge, known or reasonably available to them, with respect to the systems, process, and purpose for the creation, duplication, and storage of the documents or electronically stored data requested in categories _____ through _____?

Q: How was the knowledge, known or reasonably available to Big Box Stores, made known to you?

Q: What was your role in gathering all the knowledge, known or reasonably available to Big Box Stores, with respect to the systems, process, and purpose for the creation, duplication, and storage of the documents or electronically stored data requested in categories _____ through _____?

Q: What is your experience working with the creation, duplication, and storage of the documents identified in Request #_____?

Q: What is your experience working with the electronic creation, duplication, and storage of the documents identified in Request #_____?

Q: Who are all the people with knowledge of the electronic creation, duplication, and storage of the documents in Request #_____?

---

40. *See* chapter 9, "Electronic Discovery" for a discussion of metadata.

Q: Who were all the people involved in gathering the information regarding electronic creation, duplication, and storage of the documents identified in Request #_____?

Q: What has Big Box Stores done to make sure you have all the knowledge, known or reasonably available to Big Box Stores, with respect to the electronic creation, duplication, and storage of the documents in Request #_____?

As you are learning which other people were involved in the search for information and in the witness preparation, you are identifying potential witnesses to fill in the holes of the testimony. If these other people haven't been interviewed in preparing for the deposition, then you have a record to establish that the designated witness may not have all the information that the organization knew.

Where Are the Documents Created?

This next line of questions is designed to identify which computers the organization can search to find the documents, if necessary. In addition, if you discover inconsistencies in the story you are receiving from the 30(b)(6) witness, you need to know who was involved in creating the documents. Then, if it becomes necessary, you know whom to depose as an individual 30(b)(1) witness. Also, if the 30(b)(6) witness is inadequately prepared, you have a record of what sources of information your opponent did not contact.

Q: How were the documents created?

Q: Were they created manually or electronically?

Q: Were they created in the ordinary course of business?

Q: Why are these documents created or generated?

Q: Who created the documents?

Q: Are there any electronic versions of any of the documents in Request #_____?

Q: Which computers were they created on?

Q: Who could tell us?

Q: Did you talk to them?

Q: Why not?

Q: What did they say?

Are the Documents Duplicated?

In the contemporary business world, companies create and store documents in multiple locations. There are times when someone attempts to alter or destroy paper or electronic records. By knowing the multiple places where an organization might keep its records, it is possible to find versions that weren't altered.

For example, nursing homes create admissions assessments of incoming patients' skin conditions. If the patient has a pressure sore, the staff documents it in the patient's chart, so the nurses can compare the progress of the wound against a baseline. Alternatively, if the patient doesn't have a pressure sore on admission, the staff documents that as well, so the nursing staff knows if there is a change in condition when a wound develops. That record is sometimes sent to the director of nursing or placed in a wound rounds book. With these records, the nursing staff has a way of tracking the patient's condition from the time of the admission until discharge.

If a patient develops a pressure sore while at the nursing home, the question is whether the sore developed due to lack of care. When it is because of lack of care, sometimes caregivers try to cover up their negligence by altering the admissions assessment to say the patient had the wound upon admission. However, if they don't change every record, their cover-up will be exposed. Therefore, it is necessary to find all copies of records to make sure they are the same.

Q: Are the documents in Request #_____ duplicated?

Q: Under what circumstances are they duplicated?

Q: How and where are they stored?

Q: Are they stored manually or electronically?

What Is the Purpose of the Documents?

By establishing the business purposes for the records, you establish their relevance. If you establish that they are created in the normal course of business, you establish the record for their admissibility.

Q: What is the purpose for the creation and use of the documents or electronically stored data requested in categories _____ through _____?

Q: Tell us about that, please.

Matter of Inquiry 3: What Are the Document Destruction and Retention Policies?

Organizations typically keep records as long as those records have business utility or a legal requirement to be preserved. Periodically, however, organizations purge records because of the cost of storage. These companies have schedules for retention and destruction. If the records you have requested are missing or destroyed, even though they still fall within the company's retention schedule, you are able to build a record to establish spoliation of relevant evidence.

For example, many companies have video surveillance cameras. They typically have a retention policy that requires them to preserve the video if a customer complains of an adverse event, such as a fall or an assault. If a company ignores the preservation policy for that video or writes over the video, you have the ability to make a record of the requirement to preserve, the purpose of that requirement, the company's exclusive control, and the fact that the company chose to violate its own policy to preserve evidence.

Q: What has Cedar Gardens Homes done to gather all the knowledge, known or reasonably available to Cedar Gardens Homes, with respect to the destruction and retention policies for documents in Request #_____?

Q: How was the knowledge, known or reasonably available to Cedar Gardens Homes, made known to you?

Q: What is your experience working with destruction and retention policies for documents identified in Request #_____?

Q: Who are all the people with knowledge of destruction and retention policies for documents in Request #_____?

Q: Who were all the people involved in gathering the information regarding destruction and retention policies for documents identified in Request #_____?

Q: What has Cedar Gardens Homes done to make sure you have all the knowledge, known or reasonably available to Cedar Gardens Homes, with respect to destruction and retention policies for documents in Request #_____?

Q: Does Cedar Gardens Homes have a document retention and destruction policy?

Q: Written policy?

Q: Where is the written policy kept?

Q: How is the policy supposed to work?

Q: What is the custom and practice for destruction of documents that are not identified in the written retention and destruction policy?

Q: Have any documents in the Request category #_____ been destroyed before your search began?

Q: Does Cedar Gardens Homes have a litigation hold policy?

Q: Did anyone send a litigation hold notice in this case?

Q: When?

Q: Who?

Matter of Inquiry 4: Where Are the Documents Located?

Using our medical record example, by identifying the various locations where the documents were supposed to be located, you can then ask if the assisted living facility searched every one of those locations. If not, you have not received a complete set of records.

Q: What has Cedar Gardens Homes done to gather all the knowledge, known or reasonably available to Cedar Gardens Homes, with respect to the location of documents in Request #_____?

Q: How was the knowledge, known or reasonably available to Cedar Gardens Homes, made known to you?

Q: What is your experience working with locating documents identified in Request #_____?

Q: Who knows about where the documents in Request #_____ are kept?

Q: Who else?

Q: Who is in charge of storing the documents?

Q: Did you talk to the person in charge?

Q: Why not?

Q: Who were all the people involved in gathering the information regarding the location of documents in Request #_____?

Q: What has Cedar Gardens Homes done to make sure you have all the knowledge, known or reasonably available to Cedar Gardens Homes, with respect to the location of documents in Request #_____?

Q: Where are the documents in Request #_____ located?

Q: Is there more than one location?

Q: Where?

Matter of Inquiry 5: How Are the Documents Organized, Indexed, and Filed?

Using our example of Big Box Stores having 10,000 filing cabinets with information about 400 stores and 180,000 employees, the *overburdensome* objection can be compelling. However, by asking the witness whether Big Box Stores has an indexing system to locate documents, you may discover that the objection is spurious. You can neutralize that objection by showing that the indexing system can make document retrieval simple and fast.

Q: What has Big Box Stores done to gather all the knowledge, known or reasonably available to Big Box Stores, with respect to the organization, indexing, and filing of documents in Request #_____?

Q: How was the knowledge, known or reasonably available to Big Box Stores, made known to you?

Q: What is your experience regarding the organization, indexing, and filing of documents identified in Request #_____?

Q: Who else has experience regarding the organization, indexing, and filing of documents identified in Request #_____?

Q: Who were all the people involved in gathering the information regarding organization, indexing, and filing of documents identified in Request #_____?

Q: What has Big Box Stores done to make sure you have all the knowledge, known or reasonably available to Big Box Stores, with respect to the organization, indexing, and filing of documents in Request #_____?

Q: How are the documents in Request #_____ kept in the ordinary course of business?

Q: Copies in other locations?

Q: Where?

Q: Who could tell us?

Q: Did you talk to him?

Q: Why not?

Q: Who sees the documents in Request #_____?

Q: How are the documents distributed?

Q: Are the documents distributed to other employees?

Q: Other departments?

Q: Organizations or people outside of the company?

Q: Are their internal controls to limit who sees the documents identified in Request #_____?

Q: What kinds of controls?

For each location in which the documents in Request #_____ are kept:

Q: How are they filed?

Q: How are they indexed?

Q: Who is responsible for them?

Q: How can you retrieve the documents?

Q: Is there a document management system or database or other electronic indexing system?

Q: Is it burdensome to search that database?

Matter of Inquiry 6: How Did the Organization Search for the Documents?

Ultimately, you want to learn whether the organization has searched all the locations for all the documents that it knows about.

The classic example of an inadequate search involves responses to requests for email. You are representing a victim of a physical assault in the parking lot of a Big Box Store. In your inadequate security lawsuit, you ask for the following:

> All emails, to be provided in their native PST format, that contain information regarding security systems for the Big Box Store, as well as violent crimes, alleged violent crimes, and purse snatchings at the store.

The response states that a search of the store manager's computer did not identify any responsive email. Through the document deposition, you learn that, during relevant times, the store had replaced the manager's computer. Further, you learn that all emails, including deleted emails, were stored on an archive server. The company did not search that server. Following the deposition, a search of the archive reveals emails that predate the assault incident and reveals the manager's requests to upper management for funding for more security because of her concerns for the safety of customers in the parking lot where the assault occurred. The funding request was denied.

How Did the Organization Search for the Documents?

Q: Who conducted the search for the documents in Request #_____?

Q: Anyone else?

Q: How did Big Box Stores conduct the search for the requested documents?

Q: Was it electronic or manual?

Q: Did the organization generate or prepare any reports showing the search result?

Q: Where did they look?

Q: Other locations?

Q: Computer servers?

Q: Individual computers?

Q: Laptops?

Q: Hard drives?

Q: Other storage media?

Q: Smartphones/PDA?

Q: Company-issued phones?

Q: Who has possession?

Q: Carrier?

Q: Phone number?

Q: When was the search conducted?

Q: When was the document or electronically stored information found?

Were There Previous Searches for These Documents?

If the organization conducted previous searches, you may be able to establish that the organization was concerned with the conduct of their company long before you became involved. If you determine documents are missing from the search, copies may be found in the files of the prior search.

Q: Before producing the documents for this deposition, had Big Box Stores previously been asked to search for any of these documents?

Q: Who asked?

Q: Governmental agency?

Q: Related to this incident?

Q: Other lawsuits?

Q: When?

Q: What did Big Box Stores do with them?

Q: Did the organization keep a file of what was sent?

Q: Keep a record of what was sent?

Q: Were any documents sent out without retaining copies?

Q: Were any documents destroyed after copies were sent?

How Did You Prepare?

The organization has the duty to fully prepare the witness to provide all information that the organization knows. By exploring the organization's preparation process, you can find out whether the organization fully explored all avenues of information when it prepared its witness. In addition, if the witness does not know how the organization conducted its search, then the witness cannot certify that the search was complete.

Example Q and A: How Did You Search?

Imagine a case where you are trying to prove a nursing home had not hired enough staff to care for the needs of a patient. The patient developed pressure sores because the nursing staff ignored him. To evaluate how many staff members were necessary to care for the patients, you must also know how many patients were in the nursing home. This is known as a *resident census*. Therefore, you ask for the production of the census records.

Q: Tell us everything that was done to prepare you for this deposition.

A: I am just here to tell you what I know.

Q: Who else at the nursing home is involved in the archive of resident census records, which were requested in the notice of this deposition?

A: John Albrecht, our documents manager; Sally McCarthy, his administrative assistant; as well as their filing clerks.

Q: In preparing for this deposition, did you talk to John Albrecht, Sally McCarthy, or any of the filing clerks?

A: No.

Q: Are there any written procedures that describe the protocol for archiving documents at Cedar Gardens Home?

A: I don't know.

Q: Who would know?

A: I am sure Mr. Albrecht and Ms. McCarthy could both tell you what policies they use to archive those documents.

Q: Would Mr. Albrecht and Ms. McCarthy have more knowledge than you about the organization, indexing, and filing of the documents requested to be provided with this deposition?

A: Yes.

Q: Did you look for the resident census records?

A: No.

Q: Why not?

A: That's not part of my job.

Q: Who did?

A: I asked John Albrecht to gather the documents for me.

Q: How did he conduct the search?

A: I suppose he asked one of his clerks to gather the documents.

Q: Who did the actual search?

A: I don't know.

Q: Where did they look?

A: I suppose they looked in the filing cabinets.

Q: Do you know?

A: Not really.

Q: Is there more than one location where the documents could be located?

A: I don't know.

If you establish that the witness does not have the information necessary to respond to the method of search, then the witness cannot verify that the search was complete. The testimony establishes a record that the witness is either not prepared, or that the search was not truly complete. Both provide the requisite foundation for a motion to compel and a motion for sanctions. With a solid record, the opposing attorney will generally recognize the danger of putting the failure to comply with the rules before the court. As a result, you will seldom need motions to compel.

Matter of Inquiry 7: Is the Document Set Complete?

Once you have asked all of these foundational questions in matters 1 through 6, you want the witness to verify, under oath, that the records the organization has produced are one hundred percent complete.

Are the Documents Complete? (Repeat for Each Request #)

This series of questions is to determine whether documents produced in response to Request #_____ are complete.

Q: What is Exhibit #_____?

Q: Does Exhibit #_____ contain 100 percent of the documents responsive to Request#_____?

Q: Is Exhibit #_____ 100 percent of what was found in the search?

Q: Have you brought everything found in the search?

Q: Has anyone decided not to include any document in response to Request #_____?

Q: Who decided not to include a document?

Q: When was a document excluded?

Q: What was excluded?

Q: Why was it excluded?

Q: Is it listed on a privilege log?

Q: Was anything removed or withdrawn from the documents found at any time after the search?

Q: Who removed anything?

Q: What was removed?

Q: Why was it removed?

Q: Is it listed on privilege log?

Q: Where was Exhibit #____ found?

Q: Were copies found in different locations?

Q: Are all copies included?

Q: Is Exhibit #____ organized in the identical way the documents are kept in the *ordinary course* of Cedar Gardens Homes' business?

Q: How is it different?

Q: Who organized the documents in the manner provided to us?

Q: How are the documents organized in the *ordinary course* of Cedar Gardens Homes' business?

Preempt Improper Objections

Despite universal prohibitions, it has become an all-to-common practice to routinely attempt to obstruct legitimate production requests with boilerplate objections. For example, a responding party may object to a request for "all resident census records from January 1, 2007, to June 1, 2007," on the grounds that the request is "vague, overly burdensome, and not calculated to lead to admissible evidence." You can use the document deposition to establish that such objections are spurious.

Example: Looking Up Resident Census in a Nursing Home

In a nursing home case, the nursing home company responds to your request for documents by claiming that it couldn't get the resident census information for the period of time in question. A resident census shows how many patients are in the facility. This is information that you know every nursing home looks at every day to determine its staffing levels. You design the following line of questions to show that the resident census is readily available information that the home had frequent access to every day.

Q: When I use the term *resident census*, what do you think that means?

A: The number of patients in the facility.

Q: Is this a term you use in the daily operation of a nursing home?

A: Of course.

Q: Is there anything ambiguous about the term *resident census* to you?

A: No.

Q: Resident census data is kept on the computer?

A: Yes.

Q: Do you look at that data every day?

A: Yes.

Q: Is there anything hard about looking up that data?

A: No.

Q: Just call it up on the computer?

A: Yes.

Q: How long does it take?

A: A couple of seconds.

Q: Is it burdensome for you to call up that information on the computer?

A: No.

Q: Can you print it?

A: Yes.

Q: How hard is it to print?

A: You just hit the print button with the mouse.

This type of record establishes that the nursing home's written response to the discovery request was less than candid. By creating a tight deposition record, the responding party cannot argue that the term is vague or that the production would be overly burdensome. Once you establish the relevance and simple availability of the document, motions are seldom necessary.

Duty to Supplement

If you request and receive documents from your opponent in a Rule 30(b)(6), Rule 30(b)(2), and Rule 34 document deposition, and then later your opponent discovers more documents that should have been part of the original set, then your opponent has a duty to notify you and supplement the document set.

Your opponents do not have to supplement their answers to your deposition questions. However, they must supplement the document requests. "The producing party has no duty to supplement the 30(b)(6) testimony with new information."[41] Therefore, your job in the document deposition is to *find* all the documents—all the emails, all the computers, all the record storage systems, all the archives. Your job is to build a record to make sure your opponents looked completely.

Federal Rule of Civil Procedure 37(c)(1) authorizes a variety of sanctions for failing to disclose information and supplement disclosures as required by Rules 26(a) and 26(e)(1).[42] The presumptive remedy for failing to disclose information is that the court will exclude any new information discovered.[43]

When you ask defendants for documents, they have to follow the rules. They can't answer, "We don't have them." If they are unable to get the information you request, they have to show the court why they can't get it. If they didn't try to get the information properly, the court will sanction them.

Summary

- The responding party must make objections to document requests within thirty days.

- The court will waive untimely objections, including work product objections.

---

41. *See* Fed. R. Civ. P. 26(e); Fed. R. Civ. P. 26 advisory committee's note (1993 amendment).
42. *See* chapter 13, "Motion to Compel and Sanctions."
43. Fed. R. Civ. P. 37(c)(1); *see In re Ind. Serv. Orgs. Antitrust Litig.*, 168 F.R.D. 651, 653 (D. Kan. 1996); *QBE Ins. Corp. v. Jorda Enterprises, Inc.*, 277 F.R.D. 676, 688 (S.D. Fla. 2012) ("The rule provides for a variety of sanctions for a party's failure to comply with its Rule 30(b)(6) obligations, ranging from the imposition of costs to preclusion of testimony and even entry of default."); *Reilly v. Natwest Mkts. Grp. Inc.*, 181 F.3d 253, 269 (2nd Cir. 1999) (affirming order precluding five witnesses from testifying at trial); *see also, United States v. Taylor*, 166 F.R.D. 356, 363 (M.D.N.C. 1996), aff'd, 166 F.R.D. 367 (M.D.N.C. 1996) ("panoply of sanctions"); *Great Am. Ins. Co. v. Vegas Constr. Co.*, 251 F.R.D. 534, 543 (D. Nev. 2008) ("variety of sanctions").

- The responding party should organize documents in the same way as they are organized in the ordinary course of business, or to correspond with the document request.
- The responding party must produce all documents within their physical control.
- The courts define *control* not only as actual possession, but also the practical ability to obtain documents from a nonparty.
- It is an abusive discovery practice to produce documents "subject to and without waiving" objection.
- A party may object to discovery or not, but the party cannot have it both ways.
- Rule 30(b)(6), Rule 30(b)(2), and Rule 34 document depositions ensure complete production.
- Rule 30(b)(6), Rule 30(b)(2), and Rule 34 document depositions create a record upon which a court can rule on objections.
- Rule 30(b)(6), Rule 30(b)(2), and Rule 34 document deposition witnesses must be prepared to describe the following about the documents:
  » Do the documents exist?
  » What are the systems, processes, and purposes for creation, duplication, and storage of documents?
  » What are the document destruction and retention policies?
  » Where are the documents located?
  » How are the documents organized, indexed, and filed?
  » How did the organization search for the documents?
  » Is the document set complete?

9

Electronic Discovery

Just because you don't see something, doesn't mean it doesn't exist.

—Charlie Calvin[1]

Introduction............................209
Technological Framework....................210
    Where Is the Data Created and Stored?...........210
    Hidden Information......................211
Understanding the Interplay of
    Discovery Rules for Tailoring Requests........212
    Rule 34(b)(2)(E): Producing the Documents
        or Electronically Stored Information............212
    Rule 26: Professionally Working It Out...........214
    Narrowing ESI Requests with Rule 30(b)(6).......217

---

1. *The Santa Clause*, directed by John Pasquin (1994; Burbank, CA: Walt Disney Pictures.).

OVERCOMING OBJECTIONS WITH
    RULE 30(b)(6) DEPOSITIONS 221
        Making a Record 222

EMAIL 30(b)(6) TESTIMONY. 227
        Email System. 228
        Archive System 228
        Format. 229
        Retention Policy 229
        Creation and Storage. 229
        Deletion and Preservation .230
        Search Software 231
        Search Parameters 232
        Not Burdensome. 234

OVERBURDENSOME BY DESIGN 235

IDENTIFYING INCOMPLETE
    E-DISCOVERY USING 30(b)(6) 236

REQUIRING WITNESSES TO INTERPRET
    DATA DUMPS THROUGH 30(b)(6). 238

INTERNAL DATABASE REPORT CAPABILITIES. 240

USING 30(b)(6) TO PROVE SPOLIATION OF ESI 241

SUMMARY 243

Introduction

The technology revolution has drastically changed how people communicate, share, and store critical information. Modern enterprise environments now incorporate custom and third-party applications, databases, smartphones, tablets, laptops, complex server systems, external USB storage, and the ever-abstract "cloud" for their day-to-day business practice. In addition to the constant changes in devices and software, the types of data collected and stored are also changing. Not all data is created equal, which in turn affects its accessibility and is often the root of objections. Given that electronically stored information (ESI) has become an extension of a business, discovery possibilities are proportionally expanding. As the court recognized in *Johnson v. Big Lots Stores, Inc.,* "E-discovery matters are no longer the novel issues that they once were with the advent of the Internet and wide expansion of computerized data collection."[2] E-discovery must now be a part of every litigator's toolbox.

When facing the complexities of ESI, Rule 30(b)(6) depositions are a tool you can use to navigate the complicated issues associated with the discovery of ESI. This chapter is not intended to be a substitute for learning the complexities of ESI. Rather, it generally covers the ESI technological framework, the legal issues associated with the discovery of ESI, and how to use 30(b)(6) to economically narrow discovery requests and evaluate whether your adversary's objections are valid.

---

2. *Johnson v. Big Lots Stores, Inc.*, 253 F.R.D. 381, 395 (E.D. La. 2008).

Technological Framework

Before you can craft any discovery for ESI, you must understand the following:

- What information you are looking for
- How the information is created
- Where the information is stored
- How the information can be accessed

There are many different types of devices and data that you may need to discover in preparing your case. No two cases involving electronic evidence are ever the same. There is no one-size-fits-all approach to incorporating digital evidence, as the demands of each case are entirely unique.

Where Is the Data Created and Stored?

The list of devices that generate and store ESI is constantly growing. The principal sources includes the following:

- Computers (workstations and laptops)
- Tablets
- Mobile phones
- Cloud storage
- Hosted email systems (Gmail, Microsoft Exchange, Yahoo!)
- File storage (Amazon Web Services, Dropbox, Microsoft OneDrive, Google Drive)
- Server systems (file and email servers, backups, archive servers)
- Social media (Twitter, Facebook, and so on)
- External storage (external USB flash drives)
- DVR systems

- Internet of things (electronic door locks, elevators, traffic lights, cars, medical devices, thermostats).

- Source code (underlying programming language that dictates a program's functions)

Because new devices are constantly being invented, new types of information are also being invented. In the case of mobile phones, users' location information, communications, and even thoughts are all recorded with or without their knowledge. Forensic examiners may gather evidence from electronic devices based on file access, Internet browsing activity, and USB device usage to assemble a narrative or timeline of activity. This critical evidence can provide the story that is based on objective fact. Getting access to this information can make or break your case.

Hidden Information

In addition to file content, several forms of hidden data offer themselves to discovery. For nearly every type of file, contextual data is generated and stored in the ordinary course of business, but not routinely retrieved or used in day-to-day operations. The *Manual for Complex Litigation* describes five categories of hidden data that can be subject to discovery.

- *Metadata:* Virtually all (ESI) has embedded metadata. Metadata summarizes information about the data, such as who created the data and when, the history of changes to that data, to whom the data was sent, and what was done with the transmission.

- *System data:* The computer records the history of activity on the device, such as password requests, creation or deletion of files and directories, maintenance functions, and access to other electronic devices.

- *Backup data:* Created for short-term disaster recovery, backup data makes available data that would be otherwise lost.

- *Deleted files:* Deleted data is seldom actually deleted from the computer. Rather, the computer renames the data and moves it to another location within the computer's hard drive for eventual overwriting when space becomes necessary.

- *Residual data:* When data is being overwritten, portions of the information remain available for reconstruction by a forensic examiner.[3]

Understanding the Interplay of Discovery Rules for Tailoring Requests

Rules 26 and 34 dictate the manner in which you may obtain electronically stored information.[4]

Rule 34(b)(2)(E) recognizes the discovery of ESI. Rule 26 requires attorneys to work to together to design the appropriate approaches for the production of the various forms of ESI.

Rule 34(b)(2)(E): Producing the Documents or Electronically Stored Information

Unless the parties stipulate or are otherwise ordered by the court, these procedures apply to producing documents or electronically stored information. Rule 34(b)(2)(E) states the following:

(i) A party must produce documents as they are kept in the usual course of business or must organize and label them to correspond to the categories in the request;

(ii) If a request does not specify a form for producing electronically stored information, a party must produce it in a form or forms in which it is ordinarily maintained or in a reasonably usable form or forms; and

---

3. *See, generally, Manual for Complex Litigation* (4th) §11:446.
4. Fed. R. Civ. P. 34 and 26.

(iii) A party need not produce the same electronically stored information in more than one form.[5]

Given the realities of modern litigation, the rules committee recognized the very real risk that the responding party would produce raw data in an unreadable or unsearchable format, or would produce the ESI in paper-like electronic productions, such as .tiff or .pdf images, where the electronic searchability and metadata has been stripped from the ESI. In response to those concerns, Rule 34 authorizes the requesting party to designate the form in which the responding party should produce the discovery. Rule 34(b)(1)(C) states,

> The request may specify the form or forms in which electronically stored information is to be produced.[6]

Because different types of ESI may call for different forms of meaningful retrieval, the rule allows the requesting party to ask that the ESI be produced in different forms to facilitate meaningful access to the information.[7] For example, Microsoft Word documents may be supplied in their native .doc or .docx formats, Microsoft Excel spreadsheets in .xls and .xlsx formats, Microsoft PowerPoint presentations in native .ppt and .pptx formats, and email in .pst format.

Although the rule provides clear authority for discovering electronically stored information, there are often practical problems when attempting to request ESI. As the requesting party, you are often uninformed about the specifics of the ESI systems and the capabilities for cost-effective retrieval. With rapidly changing technology, there are an almost unlimited number of software applications and countless locations of data storage and retrieval

---

5. Fed. R. Civ. P. 34(b)(2)(E).
6. Fed. R. Civ. P. 34(b)(1)(C).
7. Fed. R. Civ. P. 34 Advisory Committee's note (2006 amendment).

systems, all of which you don't know at the beginning of the litigation (but your opponent does). In order to make meaningful, cost-effective ESI discovery requests, you need to understand the systems that the organization used in the past and is currently using for creating, storing, and retrieving the data.

Rule 26: Professionally Working It Out

In response to the exponentially expanding and diverse volume of electronic information, the Federal Rules of Civil Procedure were revised in 2015 to recognize the need for the parties to work together to control the cost of ESI retrieval. Rule 26(b)(1) was amended to call for relevant discovery, which is proportional to the needs of the case. Rule 26(b)(1) states the following:

> Unless otherwise limited by court order, the scope of discovery is as follows: Parties may obtain discovery regarding any nonprivileged matter that is relevant to any party's claim or defense and proportional to the needs of the case, considering the importance of the issues at stake in the action, the amount in controversy, the parties' relative access to relevant information, the parties' resources, the importance of the discovery in resolving the issues, and whether the burden or expense of the proposed discovery outweighs its likely benefit. Information within this scope of discovery need not be admissible in evidence to be discoverable.[8]

In order to achieve the goals of discovering relevant ESI in a cost-effective manner, Rule 26 requires the parties to meet at the beginning of the litigation to identify and resolve issues

---

8. Fed. R. Civ. P. 26(b)(1).

concerning the discovery of electronically stored information.[9] Rule 26(f) provides as follows:

(f) **Conference of the Parties; Planning for Discovery.**

(1) **Conference Timing.** Except in a proceeding exempted from initial disclosure under Rule 26(a)(1)(B) or when the court orders otherwise, the parties must confer as soon as practicable—and in any event at least 21 days before a scheduling conference is to be held or a scheduling order is due under Rule 16(b).

(2) **Conference Content; Parties' Responsibilities.** In conferring, the parties must consider the nature and basis of their claims and defenses and the possibilities for promptly settling or resolving the case; make or arrange for the disclosures required by Rule 26(a)(1); discuss any issues about preserving discoverable information; and develop a proposed discovery plan.

Once the parties have met and discussed their ESI requests and concerns, under Rule 26(f)(3)(C), they are required to file a discovery plan with the court:

(3) **Discovery Plan.** A discovery plan must state the parties' views and proposals on:

(C) any issues about disclosure or discovery of electronically stored information, including the form or forms in which it should be produced[.][10]

In order to have a meaningful discovery-planning meeting, the lawyers for both sides need to understand the systems used to create, store, and retrieve ESI. With this knowledge, they can work

---

9. Fed. R. Civ. P. 26(f) Advisory Committee's notes (2006 amendment).
10. Fed. R. Civ. P. 26(f).

together to properly plan the discovery of the requested information. The Advisory Committee expressly instructed that it is

> important for counsel to become familiar with those systems before the conference. With an understanding of the systems, the parties can develop a discovery plan that takes into account the capabilities of their computer systems.[11]

When the structure and capabilities of a party's information technology system are outside of the involved attorneys' knowledge and skill set, the Advisory Committee suggests involving people with special knowledge of a party's computer systems at the discovery-planning meeting.[12] By having people who know about the producing party's ESI system work together with the requesting party's forensic ESI specialist, both parties can evaluate the most effective method to retrieve the relevant ESI.

The Advisory Committee suggests that the parties, in their initial conference, should identify the following:

- The various sources of information, within a party's control, that the party will search.
- Whether the party can reasonably access this information.
- The burden or cost the party will face in retrieving and reviewing the information.
- The form or forms in which the party should produce electronically stored information.[13]

In an ideal world the responding party would provide all of this information in the Rule 26(f) discovery conference. Unfortunately, despite the obligations set forth in the advisory committee notes,

---

11. Fed. R. Civ. P. 26(f) Advisory Committee's notes (2006 amendment).
12. *Id.*
13. *Id.*

when dealing with corporations and other organizations, the discovery-planning conferences required by Rule 26(f) are not always as productive as the rules contemplated. The party that owns the information is seldom eager to disclose how to locate and retrieve it. Often, the attorneys for the responding party are unable to answer technical questions about the ESI system and are unwilling to allow informal discussions with their information technology specialists to sort out the ESI issues necessary to narrow your requests. If the lawyer for the responding organization is unable or unwilling to provide to you the information necessary for crafting a narrowed ESI request, it is best to professionally document the failure to provide that necessary information with a letter or email. The letter or email should propose solutions such as a request to meet informally with their Information Technology Specialists or a 30(b)(6) ESI deposition. By suggesting the informal meeting you have created a record that you are trying to work professionally with your adversary. If both solutions are rejected you have a record to support your motion to compel a 30(b)(6) ESI deposition.

Narrowing ESI Requests with Rule 30(b)(6)

A Rule 30(b)(6) ESI deposition is an effective tool that enables you to learn about the structure of the ESI to craft focused requests. The *Manual for Complex Litigation* (4th) states that "[n]arrowing the overall scope of electronic discovery is the most effective method of reducing costs."[14] Identifying how the organization stores and retrieves the ESI is the threshold for focusing those discovery requests.

Courts have recognized that a party can obtain information regarding its adversary's databases, information technology infrastructure, network infrastructure, software programs, messaging systems, and policies.[15] Citing the treatise *eDiscovery & Digital*

---

14. *Manual for Complex Litigation* (4th) § 11:446.
15. *Aponte-Navedo v. Nalco Chem. Co.,* 268 F.R.D. 31, 38 (D.P.R. 2010).

Evidence, the court in *Aponte-Navedo v. Nalco Chem. Co.*, stated the following:

> A party should be allowed to discover the organization of the responding party's information technology department, the hardware and software it uses, as well as its policies and practices for information processing.[16]

Numerous courts have hailed such strategies. For example, in *Ruiz-Bueno v. Scott*, the court said the following:

> [S]trictly speaking, the location or description of documents pertinent to the case is not relevant to the parties' claims or defenses, but it is the type of information which can assist a party in structuring his or her discovery or in pursuing discovery effectively and efficiently.[17]

Courts have recognized Rule 30(b)(6) depositions as a vehicle to discover what information is available to craft discovery requests and as helpful, time-reducing procedures that courts should readily allow.[18] Deposing a 30(b)(6) witness to clarify ESI structural questions is the most effective tool you have to formulate well-reasoned electronic document and forensic analysis requests for a focused ESI discovery.[19] In *Westley v. Oclaro, Inc.*, the

---

16. *Id.* (citing 1 Jay E. Grenig and William C. Gleisner, III *et al.*, *eDiscovery & Digital Evidence* § 7:10 (2009)).
17. *Ruiz-Bueno v. Scott*, No. 2:12-CV-0809, 2013 WL 6055402, at *1 (S.D. Ohio Nov. 15, 2013).
18. *Sprint Commc'ns Co., L.P. v. Theglobe.com, Inc.*, 236 F.R.D. 524, 528 (D. Kan. 2006).
19. *Aponte-Navedo v. Nalco Chem. Co.*, 268 F.R.D. 31, 38 (D.P.R. 2010) (citing 1 Jay E. Grenig and William C. Gleisner, III *et al.*, *eDiscovery & Digital Evidence* § 7:10 (2009)); *see also, Wells v. Xpedx*, No. 8:05-CV-2193TEAJ,

court described 30(b)(6) ESI depositions as a way to streamline e-discovery.[20] By taking preliminary 30(b)(6) depositions, you can effectively identify the scope of potentially relevant ESI, learn how the defendant stores and maintains data, and determine what you will need to both access and make sense of the information.[21]

You can use these depositions to identify the following:
- The data you are seeking.
- The way the organization creates the data.
- The way the organization stores the data.
- The organizational policies that govern the ESI.
- The organization's retention policy.
- The way the organization manages its electronically stored information.
- The most efficient method of retrieving the data.

Specifically, the courts have found the following areas of examination to be appropriate for your discovery. The data you are seeking:
- Data's native format and original metadata.[22]
- Databases and data structures.[23]

2007 WL 1200955, at *2 (M.D. Fla. Apr. 23, 2007); *Heartland Surgical Specialty Hosp., LLC v. Midwest Div., Inc.*, No. 05-2164-MLB-DWB, 2007 WL 1054279, at *4 (D. Kan. Apr. 9, 2007); *Cache La Poudre Feeds, LLC v. Land O'Lakes, Inc.*, 244 F.R.D. 614, 634 (D. Colo. 2007); *In re Carbon Dioxide Indus. Antitrust Litig.*, 155 F.R.D. 209, 214 (M.D. Fla. 1993).
20. *Westley v. Oclaro, Inc.*, No. 11-CV-02448 EMC NC, 2013 WL 1365910, at *3 (N.D. Cal. Apr. 3, 2013).
21. *In re Carbon Dioxide Indus. Antitrust Litig.*, 155 F.R.D. 209, 214 (M.D. Fla. 1993).
22. *Aponte-Navedo v. Nalco Chem. Co.*, 268 F.R.D. 31, 38-39 (D.P.R. 2010); *see also, Dahl v. Bain Capital Partners, LLC.*, 655 F. Supp.2d 146, 150 (D. Mass. 2009).
23. *Aponte-Navedo v. Nalco Chem. Co.*, 268 F.R.D. 31, 38 (D.P.R. 2010).

The way the organization creates the data:
- Software that creates the data.[24]
- Hardware that creates the data.[25]

The way the organization stores the data:
- How and where the organization maintains data.[26]
- Network infrastructure.[27]

The organizational policies and procedures that govern the ESI:
- Data storage policies and procedures.[28]
- Data retention policies.[29]
- Deleted data.[30]

The way the organization manages its electronically stored information:
- Organization of the information technology department.[31]
- Hardware and software necessary to access the data.[32]

---

24. *Id.*; *see also, Dahl v. Bain Capital Partners, LLC.*, 655 F. Supp.2d 146, 150 (D. Mass. 2009).
25. *Aponte-Navedo v. Nalco Chem. Co.*, 268 F.R.D. 31, 38-39 (D.P.R. 2010).
26. *In re Carbon Dioxide Indus. Antitrust Litig.*, 155 F.R.D. 209, 214 (M.D. Fla. 1993).
27. *Aponte-Navedo v. Nalco Chem. Co.*, 268 F.R.D. 31, 38 (D.P.R. 2010).
28. *Id.*
29. *Newman v. Borders, Inc.*, 257 F.R.D. 1, 3 (D.D.C. 2009), citing *Huthnance v. District of Columbia*, 255 F.R.D. 285, 287 (D.D.C. 2008) (quoting *Doe v. District of Columbia*, 230 F.R.D. 47, 56 (D.D.C. 2005)).
30. *Peskoff v. Faber*, 240 F.R.D. 26, 30 (D.D.C. 2007); *Wells v. Xpedx*, No. 8:05-CV-2193TEAJ, 2007 WL 1200955, at *1 (M.D. Fla. Apr. 23, 2007).
31. *Aponte-Navedo v. Nalco Chem. Co.*, 268 F.R.D. 31, 38 (D.P.R. 2010);
32. *In re Carbon Dioxide Indus. Antitrust Litig.*, 155 F.R.D. 209, 214 (M.D. Fla. 1993).

- Software capabilities.[33]
- Reporting capabilities.[34]

The most efficient method of retrieving the data:

- Hardware and software necessary to access the data.[35]
- Software capabilities.[36]
- Reporting capabilities.[37]

By using an ESI 30(b)(6) deposition, you will learn about the ESI structural system, that in turn will enable you to craft specific ESI requests that are designed to produce the relevant evidence necessary for your case.

Overcoming Objections with Rule 30(b)(6) Depositions

Even when you serve your carefully tailored ESI requests based on the information you learned in the Rule 26(f) discovery conference, an unfortunate reality of modern litigation is the responding party's knee-jerk response is to object to everything.

Courts universally prohibit boilerplate objections because they do not assist the requesting party or the court in determining why the responding party cannot respond to the inquiry.[38]

---

33. *Heartland Surgical Specialty Hosp., LLC v. Midwest Div., Inc.*, No. 05-2164-MLB-DWB, 2007 WL 1054279, at *4 (D. Kan. Apr. 9, 2007).
34. *Id.*
35. *In re Carbon Dioxide Indus. Antitrust Litig.*, 155 F.R.D. 209, 214 (M.D. Fla. 1993).
36. *Heartland Surgical Specialty Hosp., LLC v. Midwest Div., Inc.*, No. 05-2164-MLB-DWB, 2007 WL 1054279, at *4 (D. Kan. Apr. 9, 2007).
37. *Id.*
38. *Athridge v. Aetna Cas. & Sur. Co.*, 184 F.R.D. 181, 190 (D.D.C. 1998) citing *Pulsecard, Inc. v. Discover Card Services, Inc.*, 168 F.R.D. 295, 303 (D. Kan. 1996); *see also, Greystone Const., Inc. v. Nat'l Fire & Marine Ins. Co.*, No. CIVA07CV-00066MSKCBS, 2008 WL 795815 (D. Colo. Mar. 21, 2008).

Further, the advisory committee's note to the 2015 Amendment to Rule 26 codified the long history of case law prohibiting boilerplate objections.[39] However, such objections continue to be omnipresent in litigation. E-discovery requests are often met with objections such as these:

- Overburdensome
- Not reasonably accessible
- Disproportionate
- The produced ESI that you receive may be unilaterally limited or incomplete. For example, "Defendant has produced all *active emails*," which by definition excludes deleted emails.

Making a Record

It is your obligation to challenge those objections.[40] After you challenge the objection, the party opposing your discovery has the burden of factually demonstrating to the court that the discovery you are requesting is disproportionate to the needs of the case.[41] However, in response to your motion to compel, your opponent may file affidavits asserting the organization's extraordinary costs for data retrieval. Those affidavits are often one-sided and self-serving. Without a record showing exposing the problems with the affidavit the court will have nothing to base its ruling on except the self-serving affidavit. Therefore, you need to make a record before challenging the objection. The ESI 30(b)(6) deposition is the mechanism for making that record.

---

39. Fed. R. Civ. P. 26 advisory committee's note (2015 Amendment). *See* "Boilerplate Objection Language" in Chapter 8, "Rule 30(b)(6), Rule 30(b)(2), and Rule 34 Document Depositions."
40. *Lapenna v Upjohn Co.*, 110 F.R.D. 15, 18 (E.D. Pa. 1986).
41. *Direct Sales Tire Co. v. Dist. Court In & For Jefferson Cty.*, 686 P.2d 1316, 1321 (Colo. 1984).

Using 30(b)(6) makes sense because it would be unfair for the court to rule on the burden of retrieving the information you requested without a fully developed record. Rule 30(b)(6) depositions are a mechanism for evaluating the veracity of claims that the data is not "reasonably accessible." Courts have ordered 30(b)(6) depositions of the objecting party to determine whether the data was reasonably accessible without undue burden or cost.[42]

For example, if your opponent asserts that retrieving relevant information stored electronically would be unduly burdensome, then you can proceed with a Rule 30(b)(6) deposition to evaluate the validity of your opponent's objection.[43] That deposition may yield alternative methods for retrieving the ESI. When denying the motion for protective order, the court in *Spieker v. Quest Cherokee, LLC,* found that

> there are multiple approaches to electronic discovery and alternatives for reducing costs and it appears that defendant asserts the highest estimates possible merely to support its argument that electronic discovery is unduly burdensome.[44]

---

42. *Id.*
43. *Starbucks Corp. v. ADT Sec. Servs., Inc.*, No. 08-CV-900-JCC, 2009 WL 4730798, at 3 (W.D. Wash. Apr. 30, 2009).
44. *Spieker v. Quest Cherokee, LLC*, 2009 WL 2168892 (D. Kan. July 21, 2009).

Example: Illumination Lighting Corporation

You are representing a plaintiff who has been injured by Illumination Lighting Corporation's faulty, fallen light fixture. You want to obtain all emails relating to the testing of this fixture, an undertaking that occurred four years ago. You make a formal request and provide two reasonable and relevant search terms. The other side responds,

```
Overburdensome—the data is not readily
accessible because it is stored on mul-
tiple backup servers. The extraction of
the data will require searching hundreds
of periodic backups, which will need to
be restored and searched at a cost of
$800,000.
```

On its face, the objecting party appears reasonable. However, you want to know if there are alternative cost-effective ways to get those emails. By using a 30(b)(6) deposition to learn about their email system, you learn that the objection was a half-truth.

While it is true that there are daily periodic backups on multiple servers (comprised of terabytes of data), there is also a single email archive server that houses all emails in a single location. The archive server works by taking all incoming and outgoing emails, indexing them, and storing them in one central database simultaneous to the time the messages reach their primary email server destination. Unlike searching the multiple backup sets, search of the archive server limits the company's needs to restore and search to only one data set. The singular search of the archive server, rather than the multiple backups, costs only $11,000. By using 30(b)(6) to determine an organization's digital infrastructure, you are able to develop a record that establishes that the ESI request was in fact proportional and not overburdensome.

Technique: Email Retrieval

In many cases, electronic communications, including emails, are central to the fact-finding objective of e-discovery. When requesting email, you need to identify these specifics

- How the email was created
- Where it is stored
- What the archive system is
- What the destruction policies are
- How the search is conducted

It is not uncommon to discover that your opponent limited its search parameters, despite what you requested. Using a 30(b)(6), 30(b)(2), and Rule 34 deposition (as discussed in chapter 8), it is possible to verify that the search was complete, using the following matters of examination:

1. All email systems used in the operation of Illumination Lighting Corp., in effect for the time period spanning from 2010 to the present, including all email software and versions presently and previously used and the date of use.

2. All hardware that has been used or is currently in use as a server for the email system used at Illumination Lighting Corp., for the time period spanning from 2010 to present.

3. The backup and/or archive systems used for any email involving Illumination Lighting Corp., in effect for the time period spanning from 2010 to present.

4. The organization, indexing, and filing of all email used by Illumination Lighting Corp. for the time period spanning from 2010 to the present.

5. Any and all retention and destruction policies that would relate to any email generated or received by Illumination Lighting Corp., for the time period spanning from 2010 to present.

6. The capabilities of Illumination Lighting Corp. and/or its agents to filter, process, search, and analyze electronically stored information.

7. Illumination Lighting Corp.'s method of search of the email requested below, pursuant to Fed. R. Civ. P. 34.

8. The completeness of the email Illumination Lighting Corp. produces, pursuant to Fed. R. Civ. P. 34.

Using the 30(b)(6) deposition, you can establish whether your opponent conducted the search properly and whether that search yielded all of the information you requested. Without the deposition, you would have to accept your opponent's production as a completed disclosure, and important email communications could remain buried.

Email 30(b)(6) Testimony

When attempting to gather relevant email, you need to understand what type of email system your opponent is using, where the company stores its data and metadata, what electronic format the company uses, what the company's retention policy is, and how the company will conduct its search. With that information, you can craft search parameters that are proportional to the needs of the case. Following are a series of questions and answers related to email systems.

Q: Please read the request in Exhibit 1, Request No. 2.

A: Emails to be provided in PST format, that contains information regarding Dick Bendelson: the incident that occurred on February 16, 2014, at Superior Health Center; decisions about staffing Superior Health Center; the employee bargaining agreement; patient elopement; and responding to emergency alarms.

Q: Are you the person who has been designated to provide all information, known or reasonably available to Superior Health Center, regarding Request No. 2 contained in the 30(b)(6) deposition notice, that is Exhibit 1?

A: Correct.

Q: We have asked that Superior Health Center provide someone to tell us about the existence and search of the documents and electronically stored information with respect to that email. Are you the person Superior Health Center has designated to do that?

A: Correct.

Practice pointer: By reading the language of the request into the record, it is easy to perform a word search of the deposition transcript when you need to find the testimony in the future

Email System

Q: Let's start with this. What kind of email system does Superior Health Center use?

A: We run a Microsoft Exchange system, and it's housed here at the building where I work, which is the Human Services Building.

Q: Does Superior Health Center have a dedicated Exchange server?

A: Yep.

Q: That's solely for email?

A: Solely for email.

Archive System

Many organizations use an archive system for emails to reduce the cost of the storage and daily backups of their file servers. The archive separates individual computers and the company file servers. The email archive system will store the emails and their entire history, including attempted deletions. Searching for and retrieving emails from the archive server is substantially cheaper than searching individual computers or backup drives from a file server.

Q: Does Superior Health Center use an email management software other than Microsoft Exchange?

A: We use Mirapoint for the archiver. That's the actual system that we use to retrieve the emails when we're asked to do a search.

Q: What is the purpose of that software?

A: Mirapoint stores and maintains all emails and their metadata.

Format

The information technology specialists will need to know the electronic format of the data sets they will be searching. Therefore, you must identify that information for them.

Q: In what format does Mirapoint archive the email?

A: It's in EML format.

Retention Policy

Because organizations make business decisions as to how long they will retain their data, it is important to understand the company's retention and destruction policies. If an electronic record is destroyed before the retention period expires, you can develop evidence to support a spoliation of evidence claim.

Q: What is the retention policy for emails at Superior Health Center?

A: Right now, we're working under a seven-year policy; we like to hold emails for a seven-year retention period.

Q: Who established that seven-year retention rule?

A: Just from our Chapter 5 ordinances, we know that pretty much everything falls within seven years, and then it kind of comes down to affordability, common sense, and stuff like that.

Q: Superior Health Center is a government entity. It's required to retain its emails for seven years, correct?

A: Correct.

Creation and Storage

Whether a person creates an email on a mobile device or on an office computer, it nonetheless will be housed on a server of some sort. It may be hosted within the company, or it may be hosted in the cloud. By understanding where the email is created and ultimately stored, you can focus your search on only the devices that store the information.

Q: So let's talk about the archiving. Someone is at a laptop at Superior Health Center. They write an email, and they want to send it to another person in the facility. Are you with me?

A: Yeah.

Q: Is the email . . . is it actually created on the laptop, or does it go to the Exchange server, and is it created there?

A: It's actually created on the Exchange server.

Q: Now, once the email is sent, does it stay on the Exchange server, or does it go over to Mirapoint?

A: It does both.

Q: So what you have is the email on the Exchange server, and then simultaneously, it's preserved in the archive on Mirapoint?

A: Correct.

Deletion and Preservation

Understanding what happens to the ESI when someone tries to delete it is critical to your case. Just because the email was deleted doesn't mean it is no longer in the system. By understanding what happens after deletion, your forensic specialist can help craft the search parameters to locate deleted emails.

Q: So let's say someone wants to delete an email. They hit the delete button. What happens?

A: The deleted email ends up in their deleted box. It sits in the deleted box until they actually delete it a second time from the deleted box.

Q: I want to make sure I'm not confused. The email is created on the laptop. Correct?

A: Yes.

Q: The email is synced with the Exchange server. Correct?

A: Yes.

Q: The email is stored on the Exchange server. Correct?

A: Yes.

Q: The email is stored on the archiver. Correct?

A: Yep.

Q: Now they say, "Well, I really want to make sure I've gotten rid of this," so then they can go into the delete box, which is in the Exchange server, correct?

A: Yes.

Q: And they can delete it from the delete box.

A: Correct.

Q: What happens on the archiver?

A: The email stays there.

Q: And, of course, there will be metadata saying who attempted the deletions and when, correct?

A: Correct.

Search Software

Most archive systems have search software that will search the archive server within the parameters you agree to. Understanding what the software is enables you to learn the search capabilities of that program.

Q: So when you're doing a search for the emails, it's the archive server that you look to?

A: Yes.

Q: What kind of search engines do you have for searching the emails?

A: It's the search engine that comes with the archive server itself.

Q: How does it work?

A: It's similar to a Google search, but it's a lot simpler. It has a few drop-downs. You put in criteria; it's not complex. It's like a few drop-downs and you say, "I want to search for all emails with this date range, with this keyword in the subject or content."

Search Parameters

Courts will seldom permit unfettered access to an entire organizational computer system. You will need to focus your search on information that is relevant to the lawsuit and sensitive to the protection of confidential information that does not relate to the lawsuit. If the search has already been conducted, you can use the 30(b)(6) deposition to ensure that the search parameters were in fact what both parties agreed on.

Q: So what search parameters did the company use for producing the emails that were requested in Request No. 2?

A: The search parameters were given to me in a document. I've got a copy of it with me because I wouldn't remember it.

Q: Let's take a look at that list.

A: OK.

Q: We're going to mark this document that you have as Exhibit 10. Is Exhibit 10 the document that lists all of the search parameters you used?

A: Yes.

Q: Who developed the search parameters?

A: I don't know.

Q: So what you've done is . . . you searched for certain people identified in your list, correct?

A: Yes.

Q: What would have happened if you had searched for the keywords without limiting the search to the specific users?

A: I think we would have gotten more hits.

Q: So if Mary Wilson goes, "Ooo, I'm going to forward this on to my supervisor Stephanie Mendel," will the Stephanie Mendel email pop up?

A: No. If the train was broken, we would not see that. If Stephanie replied back to Mary, and then we have Mary as the search criterion, then we would catch that under the "Mary" search, if it met the keywords.

Q: How about if an email had said, "There was an event that occurred on February 16, 2014, at Superior Health Center"? Would that have been picked up?

A: I would have to say no, I believe not, unless one of these other words was in that same email.

Q: Were there time limitations you placed into your search query?

A: I believe it was September 1, 2013, to April 1, 2014.

Q: So if I was trying to evaluate decisions that were made on how to staff the facility over a three-year period, that would not have appeared in this email, correct?

A: Yes. That is correct.

Q: Are there any time limitations contained in Exhibit 1, which states, "Emails to be provided in PST format that contains information regarding Dick Bendelson; the incident that occurred on February 16, 2014, at Superior Health Center; decisions about staffing Superior Health Center; the employee bargaining agreement; patient elopement; and responding to emergency alarms"?

A: It doesn't appear so.

Q: Then why did you limit the search to September 1, 2013, to April 1, 2014?

A: That's what the lawyers told me to do.

Yes, this really happens. It's unbelievable, but it does. The company's lawyers in this case told the employee to limit the search.

Not Burdensome

In order to preempt a potential objection that a search is overburdensome, you can use the 30(b)(6) deposition to develop a record of how difficult the search will be.

Q: Now, if we wanted to expand the search parameters to the seven-year period, that would be something that would be easily run again, correct?

A: Correct.

Q: If we wanted to run the search parameters to the present, that would be easily run, correct?

A: Correct.

With this testimony, you have established that the search did not follow the search parameters you had requested and that the responding organization's lawyers had limited it. Also, you have definitively established that a proper search would not be overburdensome.

Overburdensome by Design

There may be times when, through your 30(b)(6) deposition, you will learn that data recovery will be expensive by design. In *Starbucks Corp. v. ADT Sec. Servs., Inc.*, the court ruled that:

> Defendant cannot be relieved of its duty to produce those documents merely because Defendant has chosen a means to preserve the evidence which makes ultimate production of relevant documents expensive.[45]

Example: *Starbucks Corp. v. ADT Sec. Servs., Inc.*

In *Starbucks Corp. v. ADT Sec. Servs., Inc.*, Starbucks requested an ESI production that ADT objected to for a variety of reasons. During the 30(b)(6) deposition of an IT person from ADT, Starbucks discovered that ADT's emails were strewn across five hundred DVD discs, requiring a robotic arm to queue the copying process, similar to a jukebox. ADT claimed that it would cost nearly $100,000 to retrieve the emails, but later upped that estimate to nearly $1 million.

Having learned about the purportedly archaic system in the 30(b)(6) deposition, the court ruled in Starbucks' favor, ordering that ADT produce the electronic information. The court said ADT could not choose a system where it reaped the business benefits of their selected technology and simultaneously used that same technology as a shield in litigation.[46]

---

45. *Starbucks Corp. v. ADT Sec. Servs., Inc.*, No. 08-CV-900-JCC, 2009 WL 4730798, at *6 (W.D. Wash. Apr. 30, 2009).
46. *Id.*

Identifying Incomplete E-Discovery Using 30(b)(6)

Even if the responding party does not make objections, its document productions may be utterly meaningless, small, or otherwise deficient. Just as you might use Rule 30(b)(6) to prevent and respond to your opposing counsels' objections, you can also use 30(b)(6) depositions to identify deficiencies in a production. As discussed in Chapter 8, "discovery about discovery" has long been approved by the courts and addressed in the Advisory Committee note which states,

> Discovery of such matters is so deeply entrenched in practice that it is no longer necessary to clutter the long text of Rule 26 with these examples.[47]

Courts have held that discovery about discovery is appropriate under Rule 26(b)(1) because it can assist a party in structuring discovery or in pursuing additional discovery effectively and efficiently.[48] In *Campbell v. Facebook*, the judge stated the following:

> Plaintiffs have a right to verify and explore the information Facebook provided through a 30(b)(6) deposition, which "permits the examining party to discover the corporation's position via a witness designated by the corporation to testify on its behalf."[49]

Courts have recognized that the litigation process requires a party to verify and explore the information provided, by using a 30(b)(6)

---

47. Fed. R. Civ. P. 26(b)(1) advisory committee's note (2015 Amendment); *See also, Moore's Answer Guide: Federal Discovery Practice, 2016 ed.*, §2.06 [2].
48. *Ruiz-Bueno v. Scott*, 2013 WL 6055402 *1 (S.D. Ohio Nov. 15, 2013).
49. *Campbell v. Facebook Inc.*, 310 F.R.D. 439 (N.D. Cal. 2015) citing *Estate of Thompson v. Kawasaki Heavy Indus., Ltd.*, 291 F.R.D. 297, 303 (N.D. Iowa 2013).

deposition.[50] With respect to the production of ESI, in *Ideal Aerosmith, Inc. v. Acutronic USA, Inc.,* the court stated,

> It is commonplace . . . to inquire of a corporate defendant the steps it took to find and produce documents relating to the litigation, as well as the corporation's electronic document storage and retrieval systems, in order to ensure that discovery was diligently completed.[51]

In *McNearney v. Washington Dept. of Corrections,* the court compelled the responding party to disclose the identity of the people who performed the ESI searches, the ESI storage locations that they searched, and the search terms that they used.[52] In *Ruiz-Bueno v. Scott,* the court compelled the responding party to explain the following:

1. What efforts it made to comply with the plaintiffs' previous discovery requests.

2. What procedures or methods it used to search for responsive electronically stored information, or ESI.[53]

Through that discovery, the requesting party was able to test if the discovery responses were complete.

---

50. *Id.* (quoting *LDA v. Virgin Enters. Ltd.*, 511 F.3d 437, 440 n. 2 (4th Cir. 2007)).
51. *Ideal Aerosmith, Inc. v. Acutronic USA, Inc.*, No. CIV.A. 07-1029, 2008 WL 4693374, at 3 (W.D. Pa. Oct. 23, 2008).
52. *McNearney v. Washington Dept. of Corrections,* 2012 WL 3155099, *6 (W.D. Wash. Aug. 2, 2012),
53. *Ruiz-Bueno v. Scott*, 2013 WL 6055402 (S.D. Ohio Nov. 15, 2013).

Example: *Ideal Aerosmith, Inc. v. Acutronic USA, Inc.*

In *Ideal Aerosmith, Inc. v. Acutronic USA, Inc.*, the plaintiff received very little valuable information in response to its ESI requests. It served a 30(b)(6) notice to learn how the defendant conducted the search. The witness that the defendant produced was unprepared and unfit to answer any questions regarding the ESI production. The defendant claimed that its witness was unable to answer the questions because the organization's independent IT consultant refused to be the 30(b)(6) witness. Rule 30(b)(6) requires the responding organization to produce a fully prepared witness regardless of the circumstances. The court ordered another 30(b)(6) deposition of an appropriate, well-prepared witness who could verify whether the defendant had diligently completed their disclosures of information. The court found Rule 30(b)(6) to be the preferred tool for determining the extent of the other side's due diligence regarding ESI productions.[54]

Requiring Witnesses to Interpret Data Dumps through 30(b)(6)

There are times when an organization will attempt to evade discovery responsibilities by providing a "data dump." That is, it provides so much data in raw form that it would be economically unfeasible to sort through it. In *Campbell v. Facebook, Inc.*, the court required Facebook to produce a 30(b)(6) witness to interpret the data for the requesting party.[55]

---

54. *Ideal Aerosmith, Inc. v. Acutronic USA, Inc.*, No. CIV.A. 07-1029, 2008 WL 4693374, at 3 (W.D. Pa. Oct. 23, 2008).
55. *Campbell v. Facebook, Inc.*, 310 F.R.D. 439 (N.D. Cal. 2015).

Example: *Campbell v. Facebook, Inc.*

Campbell v. Facebook, Inc. was a privacy class action lawsuit against Facebook, alleging that Facebook systematically intercepted private messages without user consent in violation of the Electronic Communications Privacy Act. In response to the plaintiffs' ESI request, Facebook produced the entirety of their messaging system source code, a gigantic data dump that no doubt would have taken thousands of work hours to review, not to mention the costs involved with such an undertaking. In response, the plaintiffs served a Rule 30(b)(6) deposition notice, which asked Facebook to designate a Rule 30(b)(6) witness to explain what they produced, specifically, "The identification of Facebook source code utilized to carry out each process characterized in Facebook's Responses and Objections to Plaintiffs' Interrogatories" for given topics.

Facebook was compelled, over its objections, to comply, by designating a senior software engineer in response to the 30(b)(6) notice to explain how the relevant code of the messaging service worked.[56]

The data dump, which would have brought the litigation to a crawl, was circumvented by a well-placed 30(b)(6) notice to more efficiently identify the relevant ESI—the needle in the digital haystack. In its ruling, the court reasoned that Facebook could not shift the burden to the plaintiff to analyze the source code, and that it, as manufacturer of the code, was in a much better position to evaluate it. This holding is actually a reverse proportionality ruling, preventing the plaintiff from solely bearing the expense of a costly review. This holding still achieves the ultimate objective of discovery for both parties—to have all the of information so the trial will be conducted correctly.

---

56. *Id.*

Internal Database Report Capabilities

Broad ESI requests may result in an enormous volume of information from your opponent. To control the cost of processing that information, you can craft your Rule 30(b)(6) ESI notice to identify an economical method for retrieving and organizing the data, using the database program's internal reporting functions. A number of different electronic systems, including servers and embedded systems, commonly include internal reporting and logging capabilities. If you understand how a program can produce data compilations in the ordinary business use, you can possibly authenticate data compilations in a way that satisfies the evidentiary requirements for admission at trial.

Technique: Exploring Punch-In/Punch-Out Time Clock Systems

Let's go back to our example in chapter 7, "Crafting the 30(b)(6) Notice," the section called "Technique: Exploring Punch-In/Punch-Out Time Clock Systems" where you were trying to determine whether the caregivers in a nursing home were actually present at the time they made entries in medical charts, and if a sufficient number of employees were working to be able to adequately accomplish their required tasks. You asked about the capability of the nursing home's punch-in/punch-out time clock system to generate reports. Let's say the responding party claims that it doesn't know how to access the information. You might then use an ESI 30(b)(6) notice that requests the identity of the sales representatives, trainers, and service representative(s) responsible for the particular ESI system, as well as product operating materials, training materials for its use, and information about the system. Because you can take the 30(b)(6) deposition of a nonparty, with the information you discovered in the party 30(b)(6) deposition, you will be able to establish the validity of the objections or alternatively identify the company that could access that information for you.

Using 30(b)(6) to Prove Spoliation of ESI

You may also use 30(b)(6) as a tool to discover how ESI was managed during the course of a claim.[57] Closely related to this is an issue that is especially problematic with ESI—*spoliation*—the altering or destroying of evidence relevant to a legal proceeding. Because litigants are the keepers of more ESI than ever before, there is a greater chance for spoliation. The Federal Rules Committee has placed a greater emphasis on spoliation and sanctions within the e-discovery realm with the 2015 revisions to Rule 37(e). This rule states as follows:

> (e) **Failure to Preserve Electronically Stored Information.** If electronically stored information that should have been preserved in the anticipation or conduct of litigation is lost because a party failed to take reasonable steps to preserve it, and it cannot be restored or replaced through additional discovery, the court:
>
> (1) upon finding prejudice to another party from loss of the information, may order measures no greater than necessary to cure the prejudice; or
>
> (2) only upon finding that the party acted with the intent to deprive another party of the information's use in the litigation may:
>
> (A) presume that the lost information was unfavorable to the party;
>
> (B) instruct the jury that it may or must presume the information was unfavorable to the party; or
>
> (C) dismiss the action or enter a default judgment.[58]

---

57. *Illiana Surgery & Med. Ctr., LLC v. Hartford Fire Ins. Co.*, No. 2:07-CV-003-JVB-APR, 2013 WL 2156466, at *2 (N.D. Ind. May 16, 2013).
58. Fed. R. Civ. P. 37(e).

The destruction of electronic evidence often has a drastic effect on the outcome of a case, but it can be difficult to show if an adversary has not provided any original electronic evidence for review. Rule 30(b)(6) has been used to uncover spoliation of electronic evidence.

Example: F.D.I.C. v. Horn

In *F.D.I.C. v. Horn*, a 30(b)(6) deposition of a company's lawyer showed serious deficiencies in the management of ESI at a time when a lawsuit was foreseeable.[59] Using 30(b)(6), the plaintiff's lawyer established the following:

1. There was a failure to institute any litigation hold.
2. Only three emails concerning the underlying claim existed.
3. The computers, server, Blackberry devices, and backup tapes that contained emails relating to the underlying claim had been discarded and destroyed.
4. There was currently no alternative method to locate or produce the lost communications.[60]

The court sanctioned the defendant. Without a 30(b)(6) deposition, the destruction of evidence may not have been uncovered.

---

59. *F.D.I.C. v. Horn*, No. CV 12-5958 DRH AKT, 2015 WL 1529824, at *2 (E.D.N.Y. Mar. 31, 2015).
60. *Id.*

Summary

- Rule 30(b)(6) depositions can and often should be used to streamline ESI discovery as soon as it begins.

- Courts have considered 30(b)(6) a preferred method for obtaining necessary context to narrow requests to keep them reasonable, proportional, and relevant.

- Rule 30(b)(6) depositions can be used to identify information about the following topics:

  » The data you are seeking.

  » The way the organization creates the data.

  » The way the organization stores the data.

  » The organizational policies that govern the ESI.

  » The organization's retention policy.

  » The way the organization manages its electronically stored information.

  » The most efficient method of retrieving the data.

- Rule 30(b)(6) is a useful tool for overcoming an adversary's objections to e-discovery requests, including the key tenant objections to e-discovery: "overburdensome," "not reasonably accessible," and "disproportionate."

- Rule 30(b)(6) allows the requesting party to inquire about the mechanics of collection, searching, and production for any discoverable electronic materials it obtains. Pinning down an employed methodology using 30(b)(6) may show serious deficiencies in a production.

10

Duty to Attend

Showing up is eighty percent of life.

—Woody Allen

Introduction	247
Duty to Appear	247
Duty to Move for Protective Order	248
Objection to 30(b)(6) Method of Discovery Is Without Basis	252
Objections to 30(b)(6) Notices	255
Specific People Cannot Be Named as 30(b)(6) Deponents	256
Lacking in Sufficient Particularity	256
Overbroad or Unduly Burdensome	257
Irrelevant	260
Summary	261

Introduction

Even if you have an expertly crafted 30(b)(6) deposition notice, attorneys defending the 30(b)(6) deposition will often claim the 30(b)(6) matters of examination, or even the 30(b)(6) deposition itself, is inappropriate. Regardless of the merits of their arguments, defending attorneys don't get to decide whether the deposition will proceed as scheduled. The rules establish specific duties on the responding party to appear or, as an alternative, move for a protective order before the scheduled deposition. When you are faced with those objections, or with motions, you need to understand what is objectionable, what isn't, and what the legal obligations are that your opponent will place before the court. With the legal authority and techniques in this chapter, you will be able to establish the record you need to prevail.

Duty to Appear

Many lawyers who defend 30(b)(6) depositions believe they can simply object to a deposition notice and they are relieved of their obligation to participate in that discovery unless they have an order to compel attendance. They send boilerplate letters that state, "We are in receipt of your deposition notice, which is unnecessary, premature, oppressive, and not calculated to lead to admissible evidence. Therefore, we object to that deposition and will not be presenting a witness in response to your notice." However, the rules surrounding 30(b)(6) depositions prohibit such conduct.

The responding party does not have the right to refuse to attend the deposition because it considers the deposition objectionable.[1] It is well established that "[i]t is not the prerogative of

---

1. *Mitsui & Co. (U.S.A.) v. Puerto Rico Water Res. Auth.*, 93 F.R.D. 62, 67 (D.P.R. 1981) (citing 8A C. Wright, A. Miller & R. Marcus, *Fed. Prac. & Proc. Civ.* § 2035, at 262); Fed. R. Civ. P. 37(d)(2).

counsel, but of the court, to rule on objections."[2] A party cannot cancel a deposition unilaterally.[3]

The 1970 amendment to the advisory committee notes to Rule 37 specify:

> [A] party may not properly remain completely silent even when he regards a notice to take his deposition or a set of interrogatories or requests to inspect as improper and objectionable. If he desires not to appear or not to respond, he must apply for a protective order.[4]

Under the express language of Rule 37, it is grounds for sanctions if a party refuses to attend a 30(b)(6) deposition.[5] Rule 37(d)(1)(A)(i) states,

> **Motion; Grounds for Sanctions.** The court where the action is pending may, on motion, order sanctions if: (i) a party or a party's officer, director, or managing agent—or a person designated under Rule 30(b)(6) or 31(a)(4)—fails, after being served with proper notice, to appear for that person's deposition[.]

Duty to Move for Protective Order

If your opponents think the deposition is improper or objectionable, they cannot refuse to attend. A party that for one reason or another does not want to comply with a notice of deposition must seek a protective order.[6] Rule 37(d)(2) states,

---

2. *Plaisted v. Geisinger*, 210 F.R.D. 527, 533 (M.D. Penn. 2002).
3. *Pac. Elec. Wire & Cable Co. v. Set Top Int'l Inc.*, 03 CIV. 9623 (JFK), 2005 WL 2036033, at *3 (S.D.N.Y.); *Smith v. BCE Inc.*, No. CIV.A.SA04CA0303 XR, 2005 WL 1523354, at *1 (W.D. Tex. June 22, 2005).
4. Fed. R. Civ. P. 37 advisory committee's note, Sub. (d) (1970 Amendment).
5. Fed. R. Civ. P. 37(d)(1)(A)(i).
6. *Beach Mart, Inc. v. L & L Wings, Inc.*, 302 F.R.D. 396, 406 (E.D.N.C. 2014) (citing *New England Carpenters Health Benefits Fund v. First DataBank,*

Unacceptable Excuse for Failing to Act. A failure described in Rule 37(d)(1)(A) is not excused on the ground that the discovery sought was objectionable, unless the party failing to act has a *pending* motion for a protective order under Rule 26(c).[7]

The proper procedure when objecting to a Rule 30(b)(6) deposition notice is not to serve objections on the opposing party, but rather to move for a protective order.[8]

> What is not proper . . . is to refuse to comply with the notice, put the burden on the party noticing the deposition to file a motion to compel . . . Put simply and clearly, absent agreement, a party who . . . does not wish to comply with a notice of deposition must seek a protective order.[9]

For example, once a plaintiff serves a deposition notice on a corporation, "the corporation bears the burden of demonstrating *to the court* that the notice is objectionable or insufficient."[10] The corporation cannot make its objections and then provide a witness that will testify only within the scope of its objections.[11]

Inc., 242 F.R.D. 164, 166 (D. Mass. 2007)); *Mitsui & Co. (U.S.A.) v. Puerto Rico Water Res. Auth.*, 93 F.R.D. 62, 67 (D.P.R. 1981) (citing 8A C. Wright, A. Miller & R. Marcus, *Fed. Prac. & Proc. Civ.* § 2035, at 262); Fed. R. Civ. P. 37(d)(2).
7. Fed. R. Civ. P. 37(d)(2).
8. *Beach Mart, Inc. v. L&L Wings, Inc.*, 302 F.R.D. 396, 406 (E.D. N.C. 2014) (citing *Robinson v. Quicken Loans, Inc.*, No. 3:12-CV-00981, 2013 WL 1776100 at *3 (S.D.W.Va. Apr. 25, 2013)).
9. *International Brotherhood of Teamsters, Airline Division v. Frontier Airlines, Inc.*, 2013 WL 627149 (D. Colo. Feb. 19, 2013).
10. *Beach Mart, Inc. v. L & L Wings, Inc.*, 302 F.R.D. 396, 406 (E.D.N.C. 2014) (citing *Robinson v. Quicken Loans, Inc.*, No. 3:12-CV-00981, 2013 WL 1776100 at *3).
11. *Id.*

Under Rule 37(d)(2), the objecting party must move for a protective order before the deposition.[12] However, merely filing motions for a protective order does not necessarily mean the responding party does not need to appear at the deposition.[13] In many jurisdictions, courts have ruled that it is the court's order, rather than filing a motion, that causes the deposition to be stayed. Although there are some minority jurisdictions with local rules to the contrary, Rule 30(b) places the burden on the responding party to get an order for protection before the deposition, not just to make a motion.[14] Further, if the court has not yet acted on a motion, the witness must still appear for his deposition.[15] In jurisdictions that require an order, the deposition must continue as scheduled unless there is a protective order in place.

Further, the responding party must bring a motion in a timely fashion. Even though the new Rule 26(c) does not contain a provision of timeliness, that requirement remains an implicit condition for obtaining a protective order.[16] Whether a motion is timely is

---

12. Fed. R. Civ. P. 37(d)(2).
13. *Rice v. Cannon*, 238 Ga. App. 438, 641 S.E.2d 562, 566 (2007).
14. *Hepperle v. Johnston*, 590 F.2d 609, 613 (5th Cir. 1979) (citing *Pioche Mines Consolidated, Inc. v. Dolman*, 333 F.2d 257, 269 (9th Cir. 1964)). Compare *Versage v. Marriott Int'l, Inc.*, No. 6:05-CV-974ORL19JGG, 2006 WL 3614921, at *7 (M.D. Fla. Dec. 11, 2006) (declining to stay the deposition) with *Petersen v. DaimlerChrysler Corp.*, No. 1:06-CV-00108-TC-PMW, 2007 WL 2391151, at *5 (D. Utah Aug. 17, 2007) *aff'd sub nom. Peterson v. DaimlerChrysler Corp.*, No. 1:06CV00108 TC, 2007 WL 3286694 (D. Utah Oct. 29, 2007) (discovery automatically stayed under D. Utah Local Civil Rule 26-2).
15. *Hepperle v. Johnston*, 590 F.2d 609, 613 (5th Cir. 1979) (citing *Faretta v. California*, 422 U.S. 806, 835 n. 46, 95 S. Ct. 2525, 45 L.Ed.2d 562 (1974)); *Martinez-McBean v. Government of Virgin Islands*, 562 F.2d 908, 913 (3rd Cir. 1977).
16. *Brittain v. Stroh Brewery, Co.*, 136 F.R.D. 408, 413 (M.D.N.C. 2011).

within the discretion of the court.[17] However, a motion filed the night before the deposition is not considered timely.[18]

If the responding party does not get a protective order before the discovery date, then objecting after the fact is untimely and the court will not grant the protective order.[19] Courts have found when the responding party does not object to the Rule 30(b)(6) deposition notice, this lack of objection has the same effect as if the court had issued an order allowing the discovery.[20] Rule 37(d) provides for sanctions against the responding party that disregards its obligations imposed by the discovery rules, even when there is no existing order specific to discovery.[21] Further, if an organization produces an unprepared witness, the court considers that "tantamount to a failure to appear," which is equally sanctionable.[22]

---

17. *Jolly v. Superior Court of Pinal County*, 112 Ariz. 186, 188, 540 P.2d 658, 660 (Ariz. 1975); *see also, e.g., Landsport Corp. v. Canaramp Corp.*, 2006 WL 4692567, *3 (M.D. Fla. Apr. 11, 2006).
18. *Landsport Corp. v. Canaramp Corp.*, No. 3:05CV237-J12MCR, 2006 WL 4692567, at *2 (M.D. Fla. Apr. 11, 2006); *see also, Ecclesiastes 9:10-11-12, Inc. v. LMC Holding Co.*, 497 F.3d 1135, 1147–1148 (10th Cir. 2007).
19. *QBE Ins. Corp. v. Jorda Enters.*, 277 F.R.D. 676, 682 (S.D. Fla. 2012); *Mitsui & Co. (U.S.A.) v. Puerto Rico Water Res. Auth.*, 93 F.R.D. 62, 66 (D.P.R. 1981) (citing 8B C. Wright, A. Miller & R. Marcus, *Fed. Prac. & Proc. Civ.* § 2291 at 808 (3d ed.) and *Id.* § 2035 at 262); *United States v. Portland Cement Co. of Utah*, 338 F.2d 798, 803 (10th Cir. 1964); *Truxes v. Rolan Elec. Corp.*, 314 F. Supp. 752, 759 (D.P.R. 1970).
20. *Chagas v. United States*, 369 F.2d 643, 644 (5th Cir. 1966); 8 Wright and Miller, *Fed. Prac. & Proc.*, § 2035 at 262.
21. *Mitsui & Co. (U.S.A.) v. Puerto Rico Water Res. Auth.*, 93 F.R.D. 62, 67 (D.P.R. 1981).
22. *Resolution Trust Corp. v. S. Union Co.*, 985 F.2d 196, 197 (5th Cir. 1993).

Technique: Establish an Alternative Date

If your opponent requests extensions to present its 30(b)(6) witnesses, establish an alternative date before you release the deposition date that you originally set in the deposition notice. If you don't get an alternative date first, your deposition can be unnecessarily delayed. As always, it is best to confirm your willingness to cooperate and the final agreement in a letter or e-mail.

> John,
>
> This follows our conversation of August 11 regarding your request to continue the 30(b)(6) deposition that has been scheduled for September 21. We are agreeable to working with you to find an alternative date, within a reasonable period of time. We are available September 19, 20, 23, 25, 27, and 28, as well as all dates the first week of October and October 13, 14, 15, 20, and 21. In view of the scheduling order and the discovery that remains, I am uncomfortable extending the deposition any further. Please let me know which dates work best for you. Once we have an alternative date, I will release September 21. However, until such time as we have a mutually agreeable alternative deposition date, I will insist the deposition remain as scheduled in the duly served notice of deposition.
>
> I look forward to hearing from you soon.
>
> Very truly yours,
>
> Mark Kosieradzki

Objection to 30(b)(6) Method of Discovery Is Without Basis

Rule 30(b)(6) is a powerful tool. It enables you to cut through the evasiveness and obstruction that you often find in responses to written discovery. As a result, lawyers representing organizations want to avoid 30(b)(6) depositions at all costs. If they can convince you to ask for information through interrogatories, rather than testimony, they can control the flow of information, thereby limiting access to the information you need to find.

The party *responding* to your 30(b)(6) notice does not have the right to insist on an alternative form of discovery.[23] The Federal Rules do not allow a responding party "to elect to supply the answers in a written response to an interrogatory" in response to a Rule 30(b)(6) deposition notice or subpoena request.[24] Nor can a responding party simply submit its documents as the company's position in place of producing a witness to provide the testimony requested by the deposition notice.[25] Such conduct has been described as "gamesmanship."[26]

> A party should not be prevented from questioning a live corporate witness in a deposition setting just because the topics proposed are similar to those contained in documents provided or interrogatory questions answered.[27]

The requesting party has the right to determine which method of examination, whether by oral examination or written interrogatories, will best provide the information it needs to properly prepare the litigation.[28] Courts have repeatedly recognized the importance of oral examination of witnesses:

---

23. *Starlight Int'l Inc. v. Herlihy*, 186 F.R.D. 626, 641 (D. Kan. 1999) (citing *Richlin v. Sigma Design W., Ltd.*, 88 F.R.D. 634, 637 (E.D. Cal. 1980) ("[T]he various methods of discovery as provided for in the Rules are clearly intended to be cumulative, as opposed to alternative or mutually exclusive.")).
24. *Great Am. Ins. Co. v. Vegas Constr. Co.*, 251 F.R.D. 534, 540 (D. Nev. 2008) (citing *Marker v. Union Fid. Life Ins. Co.*, 125 F.R.D. 121, 126 (M.D.N.C. 1989)).
25. *Great Am. Ins. Co. v. Vegas Constr. Co.*, 251 F.R.D. 534, 540 (D. Nev. 2008) (citing *In re Vitamins Antitrust Litig.*, 216 F.R.D. 168, 172, 174 (D.D.C. 2003)).
26. *Pioneer Drive LLC v Nissan Diesel America Inc.*, 262 F.R.D. 552, 559 (D. Mt. 2009).
27. *Dongguk v. Yale University*, 270 F.R.D. 70, 74 (D. Conn. 2010) (citing *State of New Jersey v. Sprint Corp.*, 2010 WL 610671, at *2, 2010 U.S. Dist. LEXIS 14890, at *9 (D. Kan. Feb. 19, 2010)).
28. *Goldberg v. Raleigh Manufacturers*, 28 F. Supp. 975, 977 (D. Mass. 1939).

> Oral examination of witnesses is usually favored over written interrogatories because it allows the cross-examination of evasive, recalcitrant, or hostile witnesses.[29]
>
> Because of its nature, the deposition process provides a means to obtain more complete information and is, therefore, favored.[30]
>
> When information has already been provided in other forms, a witness may still be useful to testify as to the interpretation of papers, and "any underlying factual qualifiers of those documents" (i.e., information which the defendant knows but is not apparent on the face of the documents).[31]

In the definitive treatise *Federal Practice and Procedure*, Wright, Miller, and Marcus opine that it is "difficult to show grounds for ordering that discovery not be had when it is a deposition that is sought."[32]

Further, the responding party cannot require that you take fact witness depositions—that is, 30(b)(1) depositions—in place of a 30(b)(6) deposition, which requires the organization to provide all facts known to that organization.[33] This would result in an inefficient and costly string of conflicting fact witness depositions, none of which would bind the organization.[34] Without the duty to prepare coupled with the binding effect of the 30(b)(6)

---

29. *In re China Merchants Steam Nav. Co.*, 259 F. Supp. 75, 78 (S.D.N.Y. 1966) (citing *Worth v. Trans World Films*, 11 F.R.D. 197, 198 (S.D.N.Y. 1951)).
30. *Great Am. Ins. Co. v. Vegas Constr. Co.*, 251 F.R.D. 534, 540 (citing *Marker v. Union Fidelity Life Insurance*, 125 F.R.D. 121, 126 (M.D.N.C. 1989)).
31. *Dongguk v. Yale University*, 270 F.R.D. 70, 74 (D. Conn. 2010).
32. *AG-Innovations v. U.S.*, 82 Fed. Cl. 69, 79 (2008) (citing 8 Charles Alan Wright, Arthur R. Miller & Richard L. Marcus, *Federal Practice & Procedure* § 2037 (2d ed. 1994)).
33. *Richardson v. Rock City Mech. Co.*, LLC, No. CV 3-09-0092, 2010 WL 711830, at *6 (M.D. Tenn. Feb. 24, 2010); *see also, Emon v. State Farm Mut. Auto. Ins. Co.*, No. 05-72638, 2007 WL 216138, at *1 (E.D. Mich. Jan. 26, 2007).
34. *See Wilson v Lakier*, 228 F.R.D. 524, 529 (D. Md. 2005).

testimony, a responding organization could wait until trial to cherry-pick the most convenient testimony. Rule 30(b)(6) was designed to prevent this type of "sandbagging."[35]

Objections to 30(b)(6) Notices

Procedurally, if the notice is deficient, the responding party must raise its objection with the requesting party. Rule 37(a)(1) requires the parties to confer in good faith regarding discovery disputes before seeking court action.[36] Good faith requires the responding party to promptly raise any concerns about the notice.[37] A party is not allowed to delay scheduling a deposition and then object when the deposition approaches. For example, in *Ecclesiastes 9:10–11–12, Inc. v. LMC Holding Co.*, the court deemed a four-month delay before objecting not to be in good faith.[38]

If the responding party wants to object, it is that party's responsibility to promptly notify the requesting party of its objections. If the parties cannot resolve their discovery dispute, then the objecting party must promptly move for a protective order before the scheduled deposition.[39] Following are the most common objections to the notice:

- The notice names an individual.
- The notice lacks particularity.
- The notice is overbroad and overburdensome.
- The requested information is irrelevant.

---

35. *See ICE Corp. v. Hamilton Sundstrand Corp.*, No. 05-4135-JAR, 2007 WL 1732369, at *4 (D. Kan. June 11, 2007).
36. Fed. R. Civ. P. 37(a)(1); *Ecclesiastes 9:10-11-12, Inc. v. LMC Holding Co.*, 497 F.3d 1135, 1148 (10th Cir. 2007).
37. *Id.*
38. *Ecclesiastes 9:10–11–12, Inc. v. LMC Holding Co.*, 497 F.3d 1135, 1148 (10th Cir. 2007).
39. *Chagas v. United States*, 369 F.2d 643 (5th Cir. 1966); 8 Charles Alan Wright, Arthur R. Miller & Richard L. Marcus, *Federal Practice & Procedure* § 2035, at 262 (2d ed. 1994).

Specific People Cannot Be Named as 30(b)(6) Deponents

As I discussed in chapter 3, "Details of Rule 30(b)(6)," naming a specific person in the 30(b)(6) notice makes it deficient. Rule 30(b)(6) is a specialized form of deposition designed to get information from organizations rather than individuals. If the deposition notice is a 30(b)(6) notice, but the notice also names a specific person as the witness, even if that specific person is an officer, director, or managing agent, that 30(b)(6) notice is deficient and is subject to a motion to quash.[40]

Lacking in Sufficient Particularity

If the matters of examination in the 30(b)(6) notice are not clear enough, as discussed in chapter 7, "Crafting the 30(b)(6) Notice," to enable the responding party to know the outer limits of the areas of inquiry, then it is impossible to comply with the designation requirements.[41]

For example, if the notice contains a modifier, such as "include, but are not limited to," the responding party cannot identify the outer limits of the areas for which it needs to prepare, and the notice is therefore defective.[42] If the request asks for "any and all information related to the lawsuit," the responding party has insufficient direction as to what you might ask and, therefore, they cannot realistically prepare. If your notice does not define the outer limits that the responding party must prepare to answer, then the responding party may object to the notice and move for a protective order.

---

40. *Youell v. Grimes*, No. 00-2207-JWL, 2001 WL 1273260, at *2 (D. Kan. Apr. 13, 2001).
41. *Steil v. Humana Kansas City, Inc.*, 197 F.R.D. 442, 444 (D. Kan. 2000) (citing *Reed v. Bennett*, 193 F.R.D. 689, 692 (D. Kan. 2000)).
42. *Hartford Fire Ins. Co. v. P & H Cattle Co.*, CIV.A. 05-2001-DJW, 2009 WL 2951120 (D. Kan. Sep. 10, 2009); *Reed v. Bennett*, 193 F.R.D. 689, 692 (D. Kan. 2000); *Steil v. Humana Kansas City, Inc.*, 197 F.R.D. 442, 444 (D. Kan. 2000).

Overbroad or Unduly Burdensome

A notice is overbroad only if the discovery is unduly burdensome.[43] A mere blanket assertion that the 30(b)(6) notice is overbroad or unduly burdensome does not make the deposition notice defective. If an organization objects to the 30(b)(6) notice as overburdensome, then that organization has the burden of affirmatively establishing why the discovery is objectionable.[44] That proof must include reliable evidence that demonstrates facts, particularly and specifically, to show that responding would be unduly burdensome.[45]

Even if the responding party can prove that there is a burden, that alone is not sufficient. All discovery requests, including a 30(b)(6) deposition, are burdensome. The issue is whether responding would be *unduly* burdensome. Marshaling facts is inherently burdensome. Courts have recognized that when corporations, governmental entities, or organizations are involved, the task becomes even more difficult because numerous people, in multiple places, hold relevant information.

> All discovery requests are a burden on the party who must respond thereto. Unless the task of producing or answering is unusual, undue, or extraordinary, the general rule requires the entity answering or producing the documents to bear that burden.[46]

---

43. *Beazer E., Inc. v. The Mead Corp.*, No. CIV.A. 91–408, 2010 WL 5071762 (W.D. Pa. Dec. 6, 2010).
44. *In re Rembrandt Technologies*, 2009 WL 1258761, at *3 (D. Colo. 2009); *Chamberlain v. Farmington Sav. Bank*, 247 F.R.D. 288, 290 (D. Conn. 2007).
45. *Dongguk Univ. v. Yale Univ.*, 270 F.R.D. 70, 74 (D. Conn. 2010); *Starlight Int'l Inc. v. Herlihy*, 186 F.R.D. 626, 641 (D. Kan. 1999); *Burton Mech. Contractors, Inc. v. Foreman*, 148 F.R.D. 230, 233 (N.D. Ind. 1992); *see also, In re Urethane Antitrust Litig.*, 2010 WL 4226214 (D. Kan. 2010); *Gulf Oil Co. v. Bernard*, 452 U.S. 89, 102, 101 S. Ct. 2193, 68 L. Ed. 2d 693 (1981).
46. *Nye v. Hartford Acc. & Indem. Co.*, 2013 WL 3107492, at *5 (D.S.D. June 18, 2013) (citing *Cont'l Illinois Nat. Bank & Trust Co. of Chicago v. Caton*, 136 F.R.D. 682, 684–85 (D. Kan. 1991)).

The advisory committee to Rule 30(b)(6) also recognized that the rule greatly reduces the overall cost and effort to the litigants:

> [A] 30(b)(6) deposition more efficiently produces the most appropriate party for questioning, curbs the elusive behavior of corporate agents who, one after another, know nothing about the facts clearly available within the organization and suggest someone else has the requested knowledge, and reduces the number of depositions for which an organization's counsel must prepare agents and employees.[47]

Although preparing for a 30(b)(6) deposition may be difficult, courts recognize that, in the end, Rule 30(b)(6) assists both the requesting and the responding parties with an efficient process for conducting such discovery. In the landmark decision of *United States v. Taylor*, the court stated that the duty to prepare "is merely the result of the concomitant obligation from the privilege of being able to use the corporate (or other organizational) form in order to conduct business."[48] Accordingly, courts have repeatedly recognized that the burden of compiling institutional information for litigation is a cost of operating as a corporation:

---

47. Fed. R. Civ. P. 30 advisory committee's note, Sub. (b)(6) (1970 Amendment) (emphasis added); *D.R. Horton, Inc.-Denver v. D & S Landscaping, LLC*, 215 P.3d 1163, 1168 (Colo. App. 2008); *United States v. Taylor*, 166 F.R.D. 356, 362 (M.D.N.C. 1996); *Great Am. Ins. Co. of New York v. Vegas Const. Co.*, 251 F.R.D. 534, 539 (D. Nev. 2008); *Resolution Trust Corp. v. S. Union Co.*, 985 F.2d 196 (5th Cir. 1993); *Calzaturficio S.C.A.R.P.A. s.p.a. v. Fabiano Shoe Co.*, 201 F.R.D. 33, 38 (D. Mass. 2001) (requiring "burdensome" document review).

48. *United States v. Taylor*, 166 F.R.D. 356, 362 (M.D.N.C. 1966); *AG-Innovations Inc. v. U.S.*, 82 Fed. Cl. 69, 81 (2008); *Heartland Surgical Specialty Hosp, LLC v Midwest Div, Inc.* 2007 WL 1054279, at *3 (D. Kan. April 9, 2007).

[T]he burden upon the responding party, to prepare a knowledgeable Rule 30(b)(6) witness, may be an onerous one, but we are not aware of any less onerous means of assuring that the position of a corporation that is involved in litigation can be fully and fairly explored.[49]

As a result, some burden will fall to the organization preparing to respond to a 30(b)(6) deposition in order to accomplish the goal of effective, streamlined discovery.[50] The organization can lessen that burden by designating a single witness.[51] In the long run, because Rule 30(b)(6) reduces the number of necessary depositions, the 30(b)(6) deposition actually reduces the burden and disruption to the responding party.

Example: *Wilson v. Lakner*

Going back to our example in chapter 7, "Crafting the 30(b)(6) Notice," Megan Wilson sued Shady Grove Adventist Hospital for medical malpractice during her surgical procedure. The use of a 30(b)(6) deposition eliminated the need to depose a dozen people who were in the operating room. Rather, Shady Grove Adventist Hospital produced a single witness to disclose all facts leading up to the foreign object being left in Megan Wilson's body during her operation.[52]

---

49. *Calzaturficio S.C.A.R.P.A. s.p.a. v. Fabiano Shoe Co.*, 201 F.R.D. 33, 37 (D. Mass. 2001) (citing *Poole ex rel. Elliott v. Textron, Inc.*, 192 F.R.D. 494, 504 (D. Md. 2000)); *see also*, *Prokosch v. Catalina Lighting, Inc.*, 193 F.R.D. 633, 637 (D. Minn. 2000); *Pham v. Hartford Fire Ins. Co.*, 193 F.R.D. 659, 663 (D. Colo. 2000).
50. *United States v. Taylor*, 166 F.R.D. 356, 363 (M.D.N.C. 1996).
51. *Khoa Hoang v. Trident Seafoods Corp.*, No. C06–1158 RSL, 2007 WL 2138780, at *1 (W.D. Wash. July 23, 2007).
52. *Wilson v. Lakner*, 228 F.R.D. 524, 525 (D. Md. 2005).

Irrelevant

Rule 26(b)(1), as amended in 2015 states, "Parties may obtain discovery regarding any nonprivileged matter that is relevant to any party's claim or defense and proportional to the needs of the case . . . ."[53] You are allowed to discover any information that is relevant to the subject matter involved in the pending action.[54] Relevancy encompasses "any matter that could bear on, or that reasonably could lead to other matter that could bear on, any issue that is or may be in the case."[55]

When you are conducting discovery, you are allowed to ask for information that might not be admissible in court. Your opponent is not allowed to refuse to give the information you requested without getting a court order. Rule 26(b) clearly states that inadmissibility is not a proper basis for objection to discovery.[56]

If your opponent objects based on relevance, then the burden shifts to you to show how your question is relevant before the responding party has to produce the information.[57] Then,

> once the party seeking discovery establishes the threshold relevance of the requested information, the burden shifts to the party resisting discovery to demonstrate some valid reason not to provide the discovery.[58]

---

53. Fed. R. Civ. P. 26(b)(1).
54. *Shelton v. Am. Motors Corp.*, 805 F.2d 1323, 1328 (8th Cir. 1986).
55. *Nye v. Hartford Acc. & Indem. Co.*, 2013 WL 3107492, at *4 (D. S.D. June 18, 2013) citing *E.E.O.C. v. Woodmen of the World Life Ins. Society*, No. 8-03-CV-165, 2007 WL 1217919 at *1 (D. Neb. March 15, 2007) (quoting *Oppenheimer Fund, Inc. v. Sanders*, 437 U.S. 340, 98 S. Ct. 2380, 57 L. Ed. 2d 253 (1978)).
56. *Hofer v. Mack Trucks, Inc.*, 981 F.2d 377, 380 (8th Cir. 1992) (citing *Oppenheimer Fund, Inc. v. Sanders*, 437 U.S. 340, 98 S. Ct. 2380, 57 L. Ed. 2d 253 (1978)); *Culligan v. Yamaha Motor Corp., USA*, 110 F.R.D. 122 (S.D.N.Y. 1986).
57. *Hofer v. Mack Trucks, Inc.*, 981 F.2d 377, 380 (8th Cir. 1992).
58. *Nye v. Hartford Acc. & Indem. Co.*, 2013 WL 3107492, at *5 (D.S.D. June 18, 2013).

Example: Coca-Cola Truck Accident

If you represent a passenger in a car hit by a Coca-Cola truck—to use the name of a real company in a fictional example—and you want to use the lawsuit process to get the formula for Coca-Cola, that is irrelevant. On the other hand, any information concerning the driver, the company's hiring practices, and the operation and condition of the vehicle is relevant. That information has to do with how and why the collision occurred.

Your investigation has revealed that the driver had a DUI while working. If you face an objection to your request for the company to produce the truck driver's personnel file, it is necessary to show how it is relevant. If your claim is for negligent hiring in addition to the driver's negligent driving, your argument can be that the personnel file is relevant to see if Coca-Cola investigated the qualifications of the driver before hiring him and whether this driver has had a pattern of driving abuses since he was hired. The burden will now shift back to Coca-Cola to establish valid reasons why you should not have access to that information.

SUMMARY

- The responding party cannot refuse to attend a deposition.
- The requesting party may choose the method of discovery.
- Rule 37 makes the responding party's refusal to attend a 30(b)(6) deposition sanctionable behavior.
- The responding party must get a protective order before the deposition if it does not want to respond.
- The requesting party cannot name individual people in a 30(b)(6) notice.
- The responding party must be able to ascertain the outer limits for which to prepare.
- Only *unduly* burdensome discovery is impermissible.
- The responding party, when making an objection, must establish that the matters of examination are irrelevant.

11

Duty to Prepare

If they can get you asking the wrong questions, they don't have to worry about answers.

—Thomas Pynchon[1]

Introduction..................................265
Duty to Designate..............................266
    Authority to Bind..........................269
    Multiple Designated Witnesses................271
Duty to Prepare................................272
    All Information Known or
        Reasonably Available....................275
    Witnesses..................................276
    Documents and Electronically
        Stored Information (ESI)..................279
    Preparation................................281
Privilege Waiver..............................284

---

1. Thomas Pynchon, *Gravity's Rainbow* (1973).

DUTY TO SUBSTITUTE A NEW WITNESS................287
SUMMARY......................................290

Introduction

If the responding party sends a witness to your 30(b)(6) deposition, and the witness's response to every question is, "I don't know," the responding party is violating the Federal Rules. This behavior is just as bad as refusing to attend the deposition.

When you have created a 30(b)(6) notice and identified the matters of examination with *reasonable particularity*, the responding party must produce one or more designated witnesses. Those witnesses must be fully prepared to testify regarding your matters of examination.[2] Because the universe of institutional knowledge does not typically exist in *any* one person, **Rule 30(b)(6) requires the responding party to compile the information you requested in one or more people who will testify**.[3] The responding party's responsibilities ensure that you do not have to depose an endless list of employees to locate information that is relevant.[4]

Rule 30(b)(6)'s language explicitly requires an organization to disclose all the information it knows, and courts consistently enforce this rule; however, even so, responding organizations frequently fail to meet the rule's obligations. Often, responding parties produce a designated witness who is unprepared to provide the information you requested in the notice.

If your opponent is not complying with Rule 30(b)(6), you as the requesting party must provide the court with a record to demonstrate that your opponent has failed to comply with its obligations. To do so, you must first understand those legal obligations. With that understanding, you can ask the responding party's witnesses the appropriate questions to establish that they did not meet their obligations.

---

2. Fed. R. Civ. P. 30 Advisory Committee's Note, Sub. (b)(6) (1970 Amendment); *United States v. Taylor*, 166 F.R.D. 356, 361, aff'd 166 F.R.D. 356, 367 (M.D.N.C. 1996); *Prokosch v. Catalina Lighting, Inc.*, 193 F.R.D. 633, 638 (D. Minn. 2000).
3. Fed. R. Civ. P. 30 advisory committee's note, Sub. (b)(6) (1970 Amendment).
4. *Id.*; *see also, United States v. Taylor*, 166 F.R.D. 356, 361, aff'd 166 F.R.D. 367 (M.D.N.C. 1996).

Three basic categories encompass the duties of the organization responding to a Rule 30(b)(6) notice:

1. Duty to designate
2. Duty to prepare
3. Duty to substitute

Duty to Designate

As we've learned in previous chapters, Rule 30(b)(6) provides the following:

> The named organization must then *designate* one or more officers, directors, or managing agents, or designate other persons who consent to testify on its behalf; and it may set out the matters on which each person designated will testify.[5]

The responding party must prepare and produce a witness who is able to provide binding answers on behalf of the organization.[6] The responding party has "absolutely no right . . . to refuse to designate a witness."[7] When a responding party violates this duty, the failure is a flagrant and sanctionable violation of the Federal Rules.[8] Further, courts will treat an inadequate Rule 30(b)(6) designation in the same way as a refusal or failure to answer a deposition question.[9] Failure to produce a witness who is both prepared and has authority to speak on behalf of the organization

---

5. Fed. R. Civ. P. 30(b)(6) (emphasis added).
6. *Ecclesiastes 9:10–11–12, Inc. v. LMC Holding Co.*, 497 F.3d 1135, 1148 (10th Cir. 2007).
7. *Id.*
8. *E.E.O.C. v. Thurston Motor Lines, Inc.*, 124 F.R.D. 110, 114 (M.D.N.C. 1989).
9. *Calzaturficio S.C.A.R.P.A. s.p.a. v. Fabiano Shoe Co.*, 201 F.R.D. 33, 41 (D. Mass. 2001).

is tantamount to failure to appear at the deposition.[10] Sending a witness who only repeats, "I don't know," is the same as failing to appear.

Rule 30(b)(6) does not allow the requesting party to demand the responding party produce the *person with most knowledge*—such a request is fundamentally inconsistent with the purpose and dynamics of the rule.[11] In *QBE Ins. Corp. v. Jorda Enterprises, Inc.*, the court explained that contrary to what many lawyers have long misunderstood, Rule 30(b)(6) does not require the responding party to produce the *person with most knowledge* for the deposition.[12] The responding party may even designate a person who does not have *any* personal knowledge, provided that the responding party prepares its witness thoroughly about the responding party's *institutional* knowledge. Therefore, the "most knowledgeable" misnomer is illogical for a Rule 30(b)(6) deposition.[13]

The *person with most knowledge* description is a historical artifact. Before the 1970 amendment that added Rule 30(b)(6) to the Rules of Civil Procedure, lawyers used Rule 30(b)(1) to identify witnesses by description:

> If the name is unknown, the notice must provide a general description sufficient to identify the person or the particular class or group to which the person belongs.[14]

Before 1970, Rule 30(b)(1) enabled litigants to schedule the depositions by describing categories of witnesses whom they

---

10. *T & W Funding Co. XII v. Pennant Rent-A-Car Midwest, Inc.*, 210 F.R.D. 730, 735 (D. Kan. 2002).
11. *QBE Ins. Corp. v. Jorda Enterprises, Inc.*, 277 F.R.D. 676, 688 (S.D. Fla. 2012).
12. *Id.*
13. *Id.* (citing *PPM Fin., Inc. v. Norandal USA, Inc.*, 392 F.3d 889, 894 (7th Cir. 2004)).
14. Fed. R. Civ. P. 30(b)(1).

believed would have the information they needed. They would describe the category as "the person with most knowledge." The problem was that those people would serially deny knowing facts that the organization clearly knew, or they would know only a fraction of what the whole organization did. This obstructive technique became known as *bandying*. Rule 30(b)(6) was created in large part to eliminate bandying. By requiring the organization to gather the information requested in the matters of examination, countless depositions could be eliminated. *The person-with-most-knowledge* description is a historical artifact that is no longer necessary.

With the advent of Rule 30(b)(6)'s deposition by *issue designation*, Rule 30(b)(1)'s deposition by *witness designation* took on a narrower function. Now, you designate a witness by category if you need to establish that a *particular* witness, who you know by description but not name, had (or did not have) particular information you need for the litigation. When using a 30(b)(1) deposition, the critical issue is not what the *organization* knew, but what that *witness* knew (or did not know). If your objective is to get substantive information from the organization, Rule 30(b)(6) is now the vehicle to gather that evidence.

Example: ACME Trucking

Recall our example in chapter 3, "Details of Rule 30(b)(6)," involving a commercial truck owned by ACME Trucking Co. You tried to learn whether ACME Trucking conducted a background check of Sam Bachelor, the driver of that commercial truck. To get that information, you took the ACME safety director's deposition, in which he said he didn't remember any results of the investigation. However, by using a 30(b)(6) deposition of ACME Trucking Co., requesting that ACME describe the company hiring protocols and the results of any background check of the involved driver, you now require the company to gather all the information and provide it to you at the deposition. "I don't know" is no longer an option for the company.

In *QBE v. Jorda*, the court identified the practical difficulties of trying to implement a person-with-most-knowledge standard:

> It might be difficult to determine which witness is the "most" knowledgeable on any given topic. And permitting a requesting party to insist on the production of the most knowledgeable witness could lead to time-wasting disputes over the comparative level of the witness's knowledge. For example, if the rule authorized a demand for the most knowledgeable witness, then the requesting party could presumably obtain sanctions if the witness produced had the *second* most amount of knowledge. This result is impractical, inefficient, and problematic, but it would be required by a procedure authorizing a demand for the "most" knowledgeable witness.[15]

Moreover, because the institutional knowledge is spread throughout the organization, the person with most knowledge may know as little as 10 or 20 percent of the information needed; clearly such a designation would be inadequate to fulfill the discovery needs.

Authority to Bind

When a party responds to a 30(b)(6) deposition notice, it must either designate one or more of its officers, directors, or managing agents to testify on its behalf, or designate another person who consents to speak for the organization.[16] The designated person must have the authority to speak on the organization's behalf about the matters of examination listed in the notice of deposition.

---

15. *QBE Ins. Corp. v. Jorda Enterprises, Inc.*, 277 F.R.D. 676, 688–689 (S.D. Fla. 2012).
16. Fed. R. Civ. P. 30(b)(6).

If the responding party designates an officer, director, or managing agent, that person by definition has the authority to bind the organization.[17] At times, an organization might choose, for any number of reasons, to designate someone other than its officers, directors, or managing agents for a deposition. It cannot, however, order someone, even an employee, to provide a binding testimony on its behalf. The consent requirement under Rule 30(b)(6) permits an employee or agent who has an independent or conflicting interest in the litigation to refuse to testify on behalf of the organization. Therefore, at the beginning of the deposition, if the witness isn't an officer, director, or managing agent, you need to establish that the person *consents* to bind the organization.

Technique: Establish If Witness Has Authority to Testify

When building the record, use questions like these to establish whether the designated witness has the authority to bind the organization:

Q: Are you currently an officer or director of Big Box Stores?

Q: Which office do you hold?

If the answer is no, then establish whether the witness is a managing agent:

Q: Are you a managing agent for Big Box Stores?

Q: Please describe the functions, responsibilities, and duties of your job.

Q: Do you have the power to exercise judgment and discretion in your job?

Q: Please describe.

---

17. *Cadent Ltd. v. 3M Unitek Corp.*, 232 F.R.D. 625, 628 (C.D. Cal. 2005).

If the answer is yes to any of the positions (officer, director, or managing agent), then the witness will have the authority to bind the organization.[18] If the witness is not an officer, director, or managing agent of the organization, then establish whether the witness has the authority to testify on behalf of the organization and whether the witness consents to do so:

Q: Has Big Box Stores designated you to testify on its behalf regarding any of the matters of examination in Exhibit 1, the 30(b)(6) Notice of Deposition?

Q: Do you have full authority to speak on behalf of Big Box Stores?

Q: Who designated you to testify?

Q: What is her role in Big Box Stores?

Q: What authority does she have to designate you to testify?

Q: Are you aware that the answers you give to my questions will be binding upon Big Box Stores?

Q: Do you agree to have your answers to my questions be binding upon Big Box Stores?

Multiple Designated Witnesses

If necessary, the responding party may designate multiple people to respond to all the matters of examination.[19] When there are multiple witnesses, each is allowed the seven-hour duration limit to testify.[20]

---

18. *Id.*
19. *QBE Ins. Corp. v. Jorda Enterprises, Inc.*, 277 F.R.D. 676, 688 (S.D. Fla. 2012) (citing *Ecclesiastes 9:10–11–12, Inc.*, 497 F.3d at 1147; *Marker v. Union Fidelity Life Insurance*, 125 F.R.D. 121, 127 (M.D.N.C. 1989)); *Alexander v. F.B.I.*, 186 F.R.D. 137, 142 (D.D.C. 1998)).
20. Fed. R. Civ. P. 30 advisory committee's note, Sub. (d)(2) (2000 Amendment) ("For purposes of this durational limit, the deposition of each person designated under Fed. R. Civ. P. 30(b)(6) should be considered a separate deposition."); *Canal Barge Co. v. Commonwealth Edison Co.*, 2001 WL 817853, *3 (N.D. Ill. 2001); *Sabre v. First Dominion Capital*, LLC, 51 Fed. R. Serv. 3d 1405 (S.D.N.Y. 2001).

Technique: Identify Witnesses with an Interrogatory

If you anticipate multiple witnesses in response to one notice, you might want to know their identities in advance to organize your deposition questions and thus streamline the process. You can use interrogatories to learn about these deponents. Rule 33(a)(1) limits you to twenty-five interrogatories, including discrete subparts,[21] and Rule 33(b)(2) allows your opponent thirty days to respond to the interrogatory. Therefore, you can use a witness interrogatory when there is no risk of using up your allotted number of questions and when there is sufficient time between the service and the deposition for the adversary to respond.

Following is a sample portion of an interrogatory asking about specific witnesses.

> **WITNESSES:** For each item categorized in the Plaintiff's notice of video-recorded deposition, pursuant to Fed. R. Civ. P. 30(b)(6) (see attached copy of deposition notice), identify the full name, employer, and job description of each person who will be designated to testify on behalf of the Defendant.

Duty to Prepare

As we've learned in previous chapters, Rule 30(b)(6) states that "[t]he persons designated must testify about information known or reasonably available to the organization."[22] Because the organization is a legal fiction, it appears vicariously through its witnesses.[23]

---

21. Fed. R. Civ. P 33(a)(1).
22. Fed. R. Civ. P. 30(b)(6).
23. *QBE Ins. Corp. v. Jorda Enterprises, Inc.*, 277 F.R.D. 676, 688 (S.D. Fla. 2012) (citing *United States v. Taylor*, 166 F.R.D. 356, 361 (M.D.N.C. 1996)).

Rule 30(b)(6) witnesses speak for the organization—they present the organization's position on the matters in your 30(b)(6) deposition notice. The responding party must prepare its witnesses to provide the organization's knowledge and positions, not only about facts, but also about the organization's subjective beliefs, opinions, interpretation of documents, and interpretation of events.[24]

The responding party is not permitted to undermine Rule 30(b)(6) by asserting that no witness is available who personally has direct knowledge concerning the areas of inquiry.[25] In fact, the witness does not need to have *any* personal knowledge of the matter in issue.[26]

> [T]he Rule makes plain its preference that a party not subvert the beneficial purposes of the Rule by simply incanting that no witness is available who personally has direct knowledge concerning all of the areas of inquiry.[27]

The responding party's duty to prepare a Rule 30(b)(6) witness "goes beyond matters personally known to the designee or to matters in which the designated witness was personally

---

24. *Lapenna v. Upjohn Co.*, 110 F.R.D. 15, 20 (E.D. Pa. 1986); *see also*, *Alexander v. F.B.I.*, 186 F.R.D. 148 (D.D.C. 1999); *Mitsui & Co. (U.S.A.)*, 93 F.R.D. at 66–67; Donald E. Frechette, "Beware of Fed. R. Civ. P. 30(b)(6) Deposition," *For the Defense* 38 (2000); *Wilson Land Corp. v. Smith Barney, Inc.*, 2001 WL 1745241 (E.D. N.C.); *United States v. Taylor*, 166 F.R.D. 356, 360 (M.D.N.C. 1996) aff'd, 166 F.R.D. 367 (M.D.N.C. 1996); *Calzaturficio S.C.A.R.P.A. s.p.a. v. Fabiano Shoe Co.*, 201 F.R.D. 33, 37 (D. Mass. 2001).
25. *United States v. Taylor*, 166 F.R.D. 356, 362 (M.D.N.C. 1996), aff'd, 166 F.R.D. 367 (M.D.N.C. 1996); *Prokosch v. Catalina Lighting, Inc.*, 193 F.R.D. 633, 638 (D. Minn. 2000); *Pham v. Hartford Fire Ins. Co.*, 193 F.R.D. 659, 663 (D. Colo. 2000).
26. *QBE Ins. Corp. v. Jorda Enterprises, Inc.*, 277 F.R.D. 676, 691 (S.D. Fla. 2012); *Federal Civil Rules Handbook*, 2012 Ed. at 838.
27. *Prokosch v. Catalina Lighting, Inc.*, 193 F.R.D. 633, 638 (D. Minn. 2000).

involved."[28] The testimony of a Rule 30(b)(6) witness represents the *collective knowledge of the organization*, not the specific witness's knowledge.

Regardless of whether the people whom the responding party designates have any personal knowledge of the matters in the deposition notice, the responding party must prepare its witnesses to provide non-evasive, complete, and binding answers for the organization.[29] The organization has the following duty:

> [T]o make a conscientious, good-faith effort to designate knowledgeable persons for Rule 30(b)(6) depositions and to prepare them to fully and unevasively answer questions about the designated subject matter.[30]

In other words, a responding party is expected to create an appropriate witness or witnesses to testify about all information that the organization knows.[31]

---

28. *QBE Ins. Corp. v. Jorda Enterprises, Inc.*, 277 F.R.D. 676, 689 (S.D. Fla. 2012) (citing *Wilson v. Lakner*, 228 F.R.D. 524 (D. Md. 2005)).
29. *Calzaturficio S.C.A.R.P.A. s.p.a. v. Fabiano Shoe Co.*, 201 F.R.D. 33, 36 (D. Mass. 2001); *Buycks-Roberson v. Citibank Fed. Sav. Bank*, 162 F.R.D. 338, 343 (N.D. Ill. 1995).
30. *Great Am. Ins. Co. of New York v. Vegas Const. Co.*, 251 F.R.D. 534, 539 (D. Nev. 2008) (citing *Starlight International, Inc. v. Herlihy*, 186 F.R.D. 626, 639 (D. Kan. 1999); *Dravo Corp. v. Liberty Mut. Ins. Co.*, 164 F.R.D. 70, 75 (D. Neb. 1995); *In re Vitamins Antitrust Litig.*, 216 F.R.D. 168, 172 (D.D.C. 2003); *see also, Mitsui & Co. (U.S.A.) v. Puerto Rico Water Res. Auth.*, 93 F.R.D. 62, 67 (D.P.R. 1981); Fed. R. Civ. P. 30(b)(6).
31. Fed. R. Civ. P. 30(b)(6) advisory committee's note, Sub. (b)(6) (1970 Amendment); *QBE Ins. Corp. v. Jorda Enterprises, Inc.*, 277 F.R.D. 676, 689 (S.D. Fla. 2012) (citing *Wilson v. Lakner*, 228 F.R.D. 524, 528 (D. Md. 2005)).

All Information Known or Reasonably Available

After you have notified the organization about the *reasonably particular* areas of inquiry, the organization must prepare its witness.

> [T]he corporation [entity] then must not only produce such number of persons as will satisfy the request, but more importantly, prepare them so that they may give complete, knowledgeable, and binding answers on behalf of the corporation.[32]

When preparing for a 30(b)(6) deposition, the Rule requires organizations to review all information known or reasonably available to them regarding the matters of examination.[33] The responding organization must ensure that its witness is prepared to provide all information known or reasonably available in the organization's control.[34] Courts recognize that the duty was created to prevent *trial by ambush*. Without this duty, the responding party could conduct a deceptive and incomplete review for the deposition, followed by a vigorous preparation for trial, and undermine the purpose of the rule.[35] This would totally defeat the purpose of the discovery process.[36]

---

32. *Prokosch v. Catalina Lighting, Inc.*, 193 F.R.D. 633, 638 (D. Minn. 2000) (citing *Marker v. Union Fidelity Life Ins. Co.*, 125 F.R.D. 121, 126 (M.D.N.C.1989)).
33. *See Calzaturficio S.C.A.R.P.A. s.p.a. v. Fabiano Shoe Co.*, 201 F.R.D. 33, 36 (D. Mass. 2001).
34. Fed. R. Civ. P. 30(b)(6); *Martin Cnty. Coal Corp. v. Universal Underwriters Ins. Servs.*, Inc., 2011 WL 836859, *3 (E.D. Ky. 2011) (quoting *Taylor*, 166 F.R.D. at 362); Sabre, 51 Fed. R. Serv. 3d 1405, citing 8A Charles A. Wright, Arthur R. Miller, Richard L. Marcus, *Fed. Prac. & Proc. Civ.* § 2103).
35. *Calzaturficio S.C.A.R.P.A. s.p.a. v. Fabiano Shoe Co.*, 201 F.R.D. 33, 38 (D. Mass. 2001); *Wilson v. Lakner*, 228 F.R.D. 524, 530 (D. Md. 2005); *United States v. Taylor*, 166 F.R.D. 356, 363 (M.D.N.C.), aff'd, 166 F.R.D. 367 (M.D.N.C. 1996) (ensuring responding parties cannot conduct a half-hearted inquiry before the deposition but a thorough and vigorous one before the trial).
36. *Starlight Int'l Inc. v. Herlihy*, 186 F.R.D. 626, 638 (D. Kan. 1999).

The responding party has the responsibility to prepare its Rule 30(b)(6) witness "to the extent the matters are reasonably available, whether from documents, past employees, or other sources."[37] When a responding party prepares a witness, it must account for known or available materials, including the following:

- Fact witness testimony
- Exhibits
- Documents
- Employees' files
- Interviews of former employees or others with knowledge[38]

Ultimately, the responding party is "obligated to produce one or more Rule 30(b)(6) witnesses who are thoroughly educated about the noticed deposition topics with respect to any and all facts known to it *or its counsel*."[39]

Witnesses

The responding party's duty includes questioning employees, agents, and others "who conceivably, but in realistic terms, may have information which may lead to or furnish the necessary and appropriate response" to the particular matters of examination.[40]

---

37. *Calzaturficio S.C.A.R.P.A. s.p.a. v. Fabiano Shoe Co.*, 201 F.R.D. 33, 37 (D. Mass. 2001).
38. *United States v. Taylor*, 166 F.R.D. 356, 362 (M.D.N.C. 1996), aff'd, 166 F.R.D. 367 (M.D.N.C. 1996); *Great Am. Ins. Co. of New York v. Vegas Const. Co.*, 251 F.R.D. 534, 540 (D. Nev. 2008); *Federal Civil Rules Handbook*, at 838; *Wilson v. Lakner*, 228 F.R.D. 524, 529 (D. Md. 2005) (preparation required from myriad sources).
39. *Taylor v. Shaw*, 2007 WL 710186 (D. Nev. March 7, 2007) (citing *Int'l Ass'n of Machinists & Aerospace Workers v. Werner-Masuda*, 390 F. Supp.2d 479, 487 (D. Md. 2005) (citing *In re Vitamins Antitrust Litig.*, 216 F.R.D. 168, 173 (D.D.C. 2003)).
40. *Moore's Federal Practice*, ¶ 36.11[5][d]; *Henry v. Champlain Enterprises, Inc.*, 212 F.R.D. 73, 78 (N.D.N.Y. 2003).

The organization must interview its employees to discover the relevant matters of examination. If the organization does not have *current employees* with enough knowledge to respond to the matters in the 30(b)(6) deposition notice, it is the organization's responsibility to train someone.

> Thus, Defendant is not relieved of its obligation even though no current employee may have sufficient knowledge to provide the requested information. In such a case, "the party is obligated to 'prepare [one or more witnesses] so that they may give complete, knowledgeable, and binding answers on behalf of the corporation.'"[41]

The inquiry may require a responding party to seek information from nonparties with whom there exists a relationship, but not from strangers.[42] For example, an organization may need to seek information from its accounting firm, but is not required to seek information from another company that it does not do business with. The key to fulfilling the duty is to ensure that the search for information is "reasonable" and is directed with "due diligence."[43] Thus, a responding party can be required to seek information from the following:

- Subsidiaries
- Parent companies

---

41. *Fowler v. State Farm Mut. Auto. Ins. Co.*, 2008 WL 4907865, *4 (D. Haw. 2008). See also, *Canal Barge Co. v. Commonwealth Edison Co.*, No. 98 C 0509, 2001 WL 817853, at *3 (N.D. Ill. July 19, 2001); *Ierardi v. Lorillard, Inc.*, 1991 WL 158911, *1 (E.D. Pa. 1991) (citing *Marker v. Union Fidelity Life Ins. Co.*, 125 F.R.D. 121, 126 (M.D.N.C. 1989)).
42. *Concerned Citizens of Belle Haven v. Belle Haven Club*, 223 F.R.D. 39, 44 (D. Conn. 2004).
43. *Id.*

- Contractual partners
- Original parties to subrogated claims
- Affiliates
- Partnerships
- Joint ventures
- Other departments within the organization[44]

The responding party does not, however, have a duty to inquire into the knowledge of an unrelated organization where the party does not have legal control of the information.[45] If the responding party researches the extent of its own organizational knowledge, that meets the duty to prepare. If the organization states, however, that it has no knowledge as to facts or cannot take a position as to the matters in inquiry, then the court will not allow the organization to assert facts or contrary positions later. If the responding party does not disclose the existing evidence at the deposition, then the court will not allow the responding party to later try to use the undisclosed evidence to ambush the requesting party. For example, the responding party cannot use undisclosed evidence in summary judgment motions, through an expert witness, or otherwise at trial.[46]

---

44. *United States v. Taylor*, 166 F.R.D. 356, 361 (M.D.N.C. 1996); *QBE Ins. Corp.*, 277 F.R.D. at 688; *Twentieth Century Fox Film Corp. v. Marvel Enterprises, Inc.*, 2002 WL 1835439, *3 (S.D.N.Y. 2002); *King v. Pratt & Whitney, a Div. of United Technologies Corp.*, 161 F.R.D. 475, 476 (S.D. Fla. 1995), aff'd sub nom. *King v. Pratt & Whitney*, 213 F.3d 646 (11th Cir. 2000), and aff'd sub nom. *King v. Pratt & Whitney*, 213 F.3d 647 (11th Cir. 2000).
45. *Covington v. Semones*, 2007 WL 1052460, *2 (W.D. Va. 2007).
46. For more information, *see* chapter 15, "Binding Effect," and chapter 17, "Using 30(b)(6) Testimony at Trial."

Example: ACME Trucking Personnel File for Driver

For example, in our case concerning the employee records of the driver for ACME Trucking Co., ACME Trucking states that it is unable to locate the driver's personnel file. It says the company has no records, or the records are lost, and so on. ACME's position on the driver is now established because of its 30(b)(6) response: the company doesn't know anything about its driver's work history. ACME is not allowed to later find the information about the driver and present documents at trial showing the driver was a model employee and repeatedly won safety awards. Their position at trial is established at the 30(b)(6) deposition.

Documents and Electronically Stored Information (ESI)

To prepare for the Rule 30(b)(6) deposition, the responding party must review all available documents and ESI that may contain responsive information. The documents and ESI that a witness must review to prepare include those in the company's own records. In addition, the witness must review all those documents that the organization has a legal right, authority, or practical ability to obtain. Even if the documents/ESI are a nonparty's possession or otherwise are not in the responding party's physical possession, the responding party must locate them and the witness must review them.[47]

A responding party is not allowed to narrowly construe *available* to mean information contained in documents that it physically controls or information that current employees hold. *Known information* includes *all* the facts the party has in its actual control, as well as information that it is actively using, reviewing, or gathering for the purposes of the litigation. What

---

47. *Starlight Int'l Inc. v. Herlihy*, 186 F.R.D. 626, 635 (D. Kan. 1999).

is reasonably available extends beyond mere physical possession or legal ownership. Federal courts have consistently held that *control* is defined as "the legal right, authority, or ability to obtain upon demand documents in the possession of another."[48]

The responding party's duty is to provide responsive, complete information on all the matters of examination. If after a thorough investigation, the responding party (and its witness) legitimately lacks the ability to answer relevant questions on listed topics, and the organization cannot better prepare that witness or obtain an adequate substitute, "then the 'we-don't-know' response can be binding on the corporation and prohibit it from offering evidence at trial on those points."[49] Phrased differently, the lack-of-knowledge answer is itself an answer, which will bind the corporation at trial.[50]

Technique: Establish Whether the Witness Is Prepared

It is important to establish whether or not the responding party prepared its designated witness to provide all information that the organization knew or reasonably had available. The organization must fully prepare the witness. Therefore, you should ask three critical questions to establish that the organization complied with this rule:

1) Did the organization gather all information known or reasonably available to it?

2) Where was that information, and how did the organization gather it?

3) Did the organization educate its designated witness with all the information it gathered?

---

48. *Prokosch v. Catalina Lighting, Inc.*, 193 F.R.D. 633, 638 (D. Minn. 2000).
49. *QBE Ins. Corp. v. Jorda Enterprises, Inc.*, 277 F.R.D. 676, 690 (S.D. Fla. 2012).
50. *Id.*; *see also, Great Am. Ins. Co. of New York v. Vegas Const. Co.*, 251 F.R.D. 534, 539 (D. Nev. 2008).

Preparation

Using the following outline, substitute the name of your deponent organization for ACME Trucking, and you will be ready to establish your record of the preparation that the organization conducted.

Q: What has ACME Trucking done to gather all the knowledge, known or reasonably available to ACME Trucking, with respect to matters of examination listed in the 30(b)(6) deposition notice that is Exhibit # _____?

Q: How was that information communicated to you?

Q: What was said?

Q: By whom?

Q: What was your role in gathering all the knowledge, known or reasonably available to ACME Trucking, with respect to [matter of inquiry 1]?

Q: Did anyone from ACME Trucking help prepare you for this testimony?

Q: Who?

Q: Anyone else?

Q: Which topics?

Q: What is your experience working with [matter of inquiry 1]?

Q: Who are all the people with knowledge about [matter of inquiry 1]?

Q: Are there any other people who have knowledge about [matter of inquiry 1]?

Q: List the names.

Q: Anyone else?

Q: Does anyone outside of your organization have information about [matter of inquiry 1]?

Q: Who?

Q: Has ACME Trucking talked to any of these people to ensure that 100 percent of the information available to ACME Trucking has been gathered about [matter of inquiry 1]?

Q: Have you talked to any of these people to ensure you have 100 percent of the information known to ACME Trucking about [matter of inquiry 1]?

If the answer is no, ask:

Q: What did they tell you?

If the answer is yes, ask:

Q: Why not?

Q: Are there any documents that contain information about [matter of inquiry 1]?

Q: What documents?

Q: Anything else?

Q: Has ACME Trucking gathered and reviewed those documents to ensure that 100 percent of the information available to ACME Trucking has been gathered about [matter of inquiry 1]?

Q: Who reviewed the documents?

Q: What did they learn?

Q: How was that communicated to you?

Q: Have you reviewed that information?

If the answer is no, ask:

Q: Why not?

Q: Is there any electronically stored information that contains information about [matter of inquiry 1]?

Duty to Prepare   283

Q: What?

Q: Anything else?

Q: Has ACME Trucking gathered and reviewed that electronic information to ensure that 100 percent of the information available to ACME Trucking has been gathered about [matter of inquiry 1]?

Q: Who reviewed the information?

Q: What did they learn?

Q: How was that communicated to you?

Q: Have you reviewed that information?

If the answer is no, ask:

Q: Why not?

Q: What has ACME Trucking done to make sure *you* have all the knowledge, known or reasonably available to ACME Trucking, with respect to [matter of inquiry 1]?

Q: How much time did you spend preparing to respond to the matters of examination listed in the 30(b)(6) deposition notice that is Exhibit #_____?

Q: Are you fully prepared to provide all information, known or reasonably available to ACME Trucking, with respect to the matters of examination listed in the 30(b)(6) deposition notice that is Exhibit #_____?

Q: Are you fully prepared to provide the position of ACME Trucking with respect to those matters of examination listed in the 30(b)(6) deposition notice that is Exhibit #_____?

Privilege Waiver

Facts that a corporation communicated to its attorney are not protected by the attorney–client privilege.[51] When a corporation produces an employee to testify about corporate knowledge in response to a Rule 30(b)(6) notice, the employee must provide responsive underlying factual information, even though such information was transmitted through a firm's corporate lawyers.[52] The corporation's duty to prepare a witness to provide knowledgeable answers reasonably available to the corporation includes factual information the witness learned through or from the corporation's counsel.[53] Even when the preparation process uses documents or communication with counsel that may be subject to attorney–client privilege under Rule 26(b)(5), the facts and other information contained are not privileged.[54] In addition, "clients cannot refuse to disclose facts which their attorneys conveyed to them and which the attorneys obtained from independent sources."[55]

If an organization designates an attorney, the designation can constitute a waiver of the attorney–client privilege and work product doctrines with regard to the factual matters for which

---

51. *Upjohn Co. v. United States*, 449 U.S. 383, 395–96, 101 S.Ct. 677, 66 L.Ed.2d 584 (1981).
52. *Sprint Communications Co., L.P. v. Theglobe.com, Inc.*, 236 F.R.D. 524, 529 (D. Kan. 2006) (citing *Security Ins. Co. of Hartford v. Trustmark Ins. Co.*, 218 F.R.D. 29, 34 (D. Conn. 2003)); *Great Am. Ins. Co. v. Vegas Constr. Co.*, 251 F.R.D. 534, 542 (D. Nev. 2008).
53. *Great American Ins. Co. v. Vegas Constr. Co.*, 251 F.R.D. 534, 542 (D. Nev. 2008).
54. *Sec. Ins. Co. of Hartford v. Trustmark Ins. Co.*, 218 F.R.D. 29, 33 (D. Conn. 2003) (citing *In re Six Grand Jury Witnesses*, 979 F.2d. 939, 945 (2d Cir. 1992)); *Upjohn Co. v. United States*, 449 U.S. 383, 395–96 (1981); see also, *Sprint Communications Co., L.P. v. Theglobe.com, Inc.*, 236 F.R.D. 524, 527 (D. Kan. 2006).
55. *Great Am. Ins. Co. v. Vegas Const. Co.*, 251 F.R.D. 534, 541 (D. Nev. 2008) (citing *Hickman v. Taylor*, 329 U.S. 495, 508, 67 S.Ct. 385, 91 L. Ed. 451 (1947)).

the designation was made.[56] This is because the privilege does not extend to facts, but only to communications themselves. If the organization had designated a non-attorney, that witness would have had to be prepared with those same facts whether or not the facts had been communicated between the attorney and client. The same responsibility extends to in-house counsel who consent to testify for the organization.

The mere fact that the counsel for the responding party might prepare a witness or witnesses for a 30(b)(6) deposition does not create an attorney–client privilege regarding the facts that the attorney and the witness might discuss in the case.[57] In *Wilson v. Lakner,* the court cautioned the following:

> Counsel may wish to exercise caution in preparing the witness or witnesses with privileged documents—otherwise the privilege may be waived as to those documents.[58]

Further, the work product doctrine provides no shield to the responding party based on the counsel's investigation: Although the actual investigation is protected, the deponent must be able to respond to the matters of examination, and preparation requires following the same investigative ground that the counsel used. The responding party's most efficient preparation—to review the counsel's compilations—requires caution. Privilege is not a valid reason not to produce a knowledgeable witness, but reviewing privileged documents waives any privilege objection with regard to the facts within them.[59]

---

56. *Upjohn Co. v. United States,* 449 U.S. 383, 395–396, 101 S. Ct. 677, 685, 66 L. Ed. 2d 584 (1981); *State ex rel. United Hosp. Ctr., Inc. v. Bedell,* 199 W. Va. 316, 333, 484 S.E.2d 199, 216 (1997).
57. *Wilson v. Lakner,* 228 F.R.D. 524, 529 (D. Md. 2005).
58. *Id.*
59. *Id.*; *see also, Sprint Communications Co., L.P. v. Theglobe.com, Inc.,* 236 F.R.D. 524, 529 (D. Kan. 2006).

Technique: Identify Information Sources

Identifying all *sources* of information (not just the information itself, but how the witness got it) is important when you are evaluating whether or not a witness does in fact possess all information known or reasonably available to the organization. If an attorney for the responding organization is the source of information for the witness, you need to determine whether that attorney has all information known to the organization. Attorneys for organizations do not have personal knowledge of institutional information. Therefore, understanding where and how the responding party gathered the information is important. Because facts and positions divulged to the witness in preparation for the 30(b)(6) deposition are not privileged, you must establish a record that the inquiry is specifically for facts, positions, and sources of information.

Q: Do you understand that your testimony today must represent all information, known or reasonably available to Big Box Stores, regarding the matters of examination listed in the 30(b)(6) deposition notice that is Exhibit #____?

Q: How did Big Box Stores prepare you to provide all information, known or reasonably available to Big Box Stores, regarding the matters of examination listed in the 30(b)(6) deposition notice that is Exhibit #____?

Q: What are all the sources of factual information that were available to Big Box Stores when gathering all of the information necessary to respond questions about the matters of examination listed in the 30(b)(6) deposition notice that is Exhibit #____?

Q: Please list all people who provided all the factual information, known or reasonably available to Big Box Stores, with respect to matters of examination listed in the 30(b)(6) deposition notice that is Exhibit #____

Q: What are the facts each person provided to you to respond to the matters of examination listed in the 30(b)(6) deposition notice that is Exhibit #____?

Q: What facts in response to the matters of examination listed in the 30(b)(6) deposition notice that is Exhibit #____ were provided to you by Big Box Stores' attorney?

Q: Did he tell you where he learned those facts?

Q: What was the source of that factual information?

Q: How do you know those facts represent all the information, known or reasonably available to Big Box Stores, with respect to matters of examination listed in the 30(b)(6) deposition notice that is Exhibit #____?

Q: What is the position of Big Box Stores in response to the matters of examination listed in the 30(b)(6) deposition notice that is Exhibit #____?

Duty to Substitute a New Witness

If the witness isn't prepared, the responding party has to provide someone else. If it becomes apparent during the deposition that the responding party has produced a witness who is not sufficiently prepared to testify on all of the matters, the responding party has a duty to substitute additional witnesses to fully respond to the discovery request.[60] The responding party must make the substitution on its own—without a motion to compel—in a timely manner.[61] The duty to substitute is a necessary requirement if the responding party fails to comply with their duty to prepare. Even when the responding party thought in good faith that its witness would satisfy the deposition notice, it still has a duty to substitute another person once parties realize the deficiency of its Rule 30(b)(6) witness.[62]

Rule 30(b)(6) requires complete disclosure, which the responding party is not allowed to subvert by producing an insufficient and unprepared witness. When initial witnesses fail to have

---

60. *QBE Ins. Corp. v. Jorda Enterprises, Inc.*, 277 F.R.D. 676, 690 (S.D. Fla. 2012)(citing *Alexander*, 186 F.R.D. at 142; *Marker v. Union Fid. Life Ins. Co.*, 125 F.R.D. 121, 127 (M.D.N.C. 1989)).
61. *Id.*
62. *Marker v. Union Fid. Life Ins. Co.*, 125 F.R.D. 121, 126 (M.D.N.C. 1989).

responsive answers on all matters in the notice, the court will grant you a motion to compel additional deponents.[63]

If the responding party provides an inadequately prepared witness, then Rule 37 permits a motion for sanctions. This means that the responding party pays the costs for the next deposition.[64] If your opponent prepares badly and then attempts to remedy the situation by providing another witness, your opponent's lack of preparation has still disrupted the proceedings. The mere fact that the requesting party later has an opportunity to depose a witness again does not cure the initial inadequacy of the witness.[65] The responding party's improper designation prevented the requesting party from obtaining adequate answers to its inquiries and required a second trip to complete the deposition. Because the responding party didn't prepare its witness properly, the responding party can be sanctioned:

> [I]nadequate preparation of a Rule 30(b)(6) designee can be sanctioned based on the lack of good faith, prejudice to the opposing side, and disruption of the proceedings.[66]

Therefore, the requesting party should seek sanctions of fees and costs.

---

63. *United Technologies Motor Sys., Inc. v. Borg-Warner Auto., Inc.*, 1998 WL 1796257, at *2 (E.D. Mich. 1998).
64. *QBE Ins. Corp. v. Jorda Enterprises, Inc.*, 277 F.R.D. 676, 699 (S.D. Fla. 2012); *Marker v. Union Fid. Life Ins. Co.*, 125 F.R.D. 121, 126–127 (M.D. N.C. 1989).
65. *Starlight Int'l Inc. v. Herlihy*, 186 F.R.D. 626, 640 (D. Kan. 1999)(citing *United States v. Taylor*, 166 F.R.D. 356, 363 (M.D.N.C. 1996), aff'd, 166 F.R.D. 367 (M.D.N.C. 1996)).
66. *United States v. Taylor*, 166 F.R.D. 356, 363 (M.D.N.C. 1996), aff'd, 166 F.R.D. 367 (M.D.N.C. 1996).

Technique: Establishing a Record of Inadequate Preparation

Once you establish on the record that the witness is not prepared or is inappropriate to respond to the matters identified in the 30(b)(6) notice, it is important to make a record of who may have the information you need and what their availability is. Then, on the record, request a commitment for substitution.

Q: Are you prepared to tell us everything that Big Box Stores knows or has available to it with respect to the matters of examination listed in the 30(b)(6) deposition notice that is Exhibit #____?

Q: Who would have that information?

Q: Where are they today?

Q: Counsel, since we are all here today, I am requesting that we take a short break so Big Box Stores can substitute a witness who can provide all information known to Big Box Stores in response to the matters of examination listed in the 30(b)(6) deposition notice that is Exhibit #____.

Q: If the counsel refuses, you can demand a substitute at a later date:

Q: At this time we will recess the deposition until we can depose a fully prepared witness. Counsel, when can Big Box Stores provide a substitute witness to complete this 30(b)(6) deposition?

Q: Let's set the calendar date now.

If the counsel refuses to set a date, arrange to reconvene:

Q: Please let me know this week when we can reconvene so we can keep this case moving.

By asking for a substitute witness on the record, you leave no question that you are attempting to work professionally with your adversary to establish a time to reconvene. If your adversary evades efforts to schedule a substitute deposition, you will have started a record establishing your attempts to "meet and confer" to resolve the problem.

Summary

- The responding party has a duty to designate an officer, director, managing agent, or other person who consents to bind the organization.

- The responding party's designated witness is not necessarily the person with the most, or with personal, knowledge.

- The responding party can produce multiple witnesses.

- The responding party must prepare its witnesses to provide all institutional information that is known or reasonably available to the organization.

- Reasonably available information means information that the responding party has the legal right to obtain.

- If the responding party produces a witness who is insufficiently prepared, the responding party has a duty to substitute an appropriate witness.

12

Scope of Inquiry

Limits, like fear, are often just an illusion.

—Michael Jordan

Introduction	293
Limiting the Scope Is Not Allowed	293
Scope of Inquiry Objections	298
Instructions Not to Answer	299
Summary	300

Introduction

While taking a 30(b)(6) witness's testimony, you may encounter objections claiming that you are asking questions that go beyond the scope of what you had requested the organization to prepare for in your 30(b)(6) notice. This objection could be your adversary's attempt to derail your line of questions. Or it may be that you *are* actually asking questions that are beyond what you asked your opponent to prepare for. Either way, you *can* ask questions that go beyond the matters you described in the notice. The rule is that you can ask questions as broadly as you would question any other deponent. Think of it this way: The other party must *prepare* for what is in the 30(b)(6) notice. But you are not limited to asking questions that are in that notice. You can go beyond the notice.

Limiting the Scope Is Not Allowed

The seminal case involving the scope of Rule 30(b)(6) deposition testimony is *King v. Pratt & Whitney, a Div. of United Technologies Corp.*[1] In *King*, the court was asked to rule on this issue: whether a deponent produced under a Rule 30(b)(6) notice may only be questioned regarding issues described in the notice, or may be questioned as broadly as any other deponent.

The court in *King* ruled as follows:

> Rule 30(b)(6) cannot be used to limit what is asked of a designated witness at a deposition. Rather, the Rule simply defines a corporation's obligations regarding whom they are obligated to produce for

---

1. *King v. Pratt & Whitney, a Div. of United Technologies Corp.*, 161 F.R.D. 475, 475 (S.D. Fla. 1995) aff'd sub nom. *King v. Pratt & Whitney*, 213 F.3d 646 (11th Cir. 2000) and aff'd sub nom. *King v. Pratt & Whitney*, 213 F.3d 647 (11th Cir. 2000).

such a deposition and what that witness is obligated to be able to answer.[2]

Because there is no specific limitation in Rule 30(b)(6) as to what you can ask at a deposition, the general deposition standards set forth in Rule 26 are controlling.[3]

Recognizing that Rule 30(b)(6) was designed to streamline the discovery of potentially relevant information, the court set forth a pragmatic analysis that has become the overwhelming majority rule.[4] In *King*, the court stated the following:

> Rule 30(b)(6) should not be read to confer some special privilege on a corporate deponent responding to this type of notice. Clearly, Plaintiff could simply re-notice a deponent under the regular notice provisions and ask him the same questions that were objected to.[5]

In *Detoy v. City & Cnty. of San Francisco*, the court found that postponing the 30(b)(6) deposition and demanding that the

---

2. *King v. Pratt & Whitney, a Div. of United Technologies Corp.*, 161 F.R.D. 475, 476 (S.D. Fla. 1995).
3. *Id.*
4. *Detoy v. City & Cnty. of San Francisco*, 196 F.R.D. 362, 366 (N.D. Cal. 2000); *New World Network Ltd. v. M/V NORWEGIAN SEA*, No. 05-22916 CIV, 2007 WL 1068124, at *3 (S.D. Fla. Apr. 6, 2007); *U.S. E.E.O.C. v. Caesars Entm't, Inc.*, 237 F.R.D. 428, 432 (D. Nev. 2006); *Bracco Diagnostics Inc. v. Amersham Health Inc.*, No. CIV.A. 03-6025 SRC, 2005 WL 6714281, at *2 (D. N.J. Nov. 7, 2005); *Edison Corp. v. Secaucus Town*, 17 N.J. Tax 178, 182 (1998); *Whiting v. Hogan*, No. 12-CV-08039-PHX-GMS, 2013 WL 1047012, at *2 (D. Ariz. Mar. 14, 2013); *Alsabur v. Autozone, Inc.*, No. 13-CV-01689-KAW, 2014 WL 2772486, at *2 (N.D. Cal. June 18, 2014); *Norman v. State Farm Fire & Cas. Co.*, No. 13-CV-01643-PAB-CBS, 2014 WL 6478046, at *6 (D. Colo. Nov. 19, 2014); *Crawford v. George & Lynch, Inc.*, 19 F. Supp.3d 546, 554 (D. Del. 2013); *F.D.I.C. v. Brudnicki*, No. 5:12-CV-00398-RS-GRJ, 2013 WL 5814494, at *1 (N.D. Fla. Oct. 29, 2013).
5. *King v. Pratt & Whitney, a Div. of United Technologies Corp.*, 161 F.R.D. 475, 476 (S.D. Fla. 1995).

notice be resent for the witness to appear on her own behalf—as a 30(b)(1) deponent—seemed artificial and wasteful of both the parties' resources and the witness's time. Presumably, if the witness is capable of testifying on behalf of the organization, the witness is also capable of testifying as an individual, at the same deposition.[6]

The underlying policy for Rule 30(b)(6) was not to provide greater notice or protections to corporate deponents, but rather to ensure the right person was present at the deposition.[7] The rule is not meant to limit the questions, but to specify the questions within the broad parameters of the discovery rules.[8] The description of the scope of the deposition in the notice sets forth the *minimum* about which the witness must be prepared to testify, not the maximum.[9]

Detoy recognized that limiting the scope of a 30(b)(6) deposition to what is in the deposition subpoena would frustrate Rule 26(b)(1).[10]

> [T]he scope of the deposition of the 30(b)(6) designee is determined solely by relevance under Rule 26, that is, that the evidence sought may lead to the discovery of admissible evidence.[11]

---

6. *Detoy v. City & County of San Francisco*, 196 F.R.D 362, 367 (N.D. Cal. 2000).
7. *King v. Pratt & Whitney, a Div. of United Technologies Corp.*, 161 F.R.D. 475, 476 (S.D. Fla.1995).
8. *Id.*
9. *Detoy v. City & County of San Francisco*, 196 F.R.D 362, 366 (N.D. Cal. 2000), citing *King v. Pratt & Whitney, a Div. of United Technologies Corp.*, 161 F.R.D. 475 (S.D. Fla.1995).
10. *Detoy v. City & County of San Francisco*, 196 F.R.D 362, 366 (N.D. Cal. 2000).
11. *K.S. ex rel. Isserlis v. Ambassador Programs, Inc.*, 2010 WL 1568391 *2 (E.D. Wash. April 14, 2010), citing *Detoy v. City and County of San Francisco*, 196 F.R.D. 362, 367 (N.D. Ca. 2000); *see also, U.S. E.E.O. V. v. Caesars Entertainment, Inc.*, 237 F.R.D. 428, 432 (D. Nev. 2006).

The court in *Detoy* went on to state that any attempt to limit the inquiry to the subject matter specified in the notice:

> . . . forecloses the deposing party from two of the most significant benefits of the deposition as a tool in the discovery process: (1) the ability to explore previously undisclosed areas of a case that are revealed by a deponent during deposition questioning; and (2) the ability to observe a deponent's response to an unexpected question.[12]

King rejected *Paparelli v. Prudential Ins. Co. of America*, which was the first case to consider the scope of 30(b)(6) inquiry and now is the minority position.[13] In *Paparelli*, the court ruled that the examining party should confine the examination of a 30(b)(6) corporate designated witness to matters stated with reasonable particularity in the deposition notice.[14] However, the court went on to rule that consistent with Rule 30(c), "evidence objected to *shall be taken* subject to objections."[15] Even under *Paparelli*, the witness must answer the questions posed. In *Paparelli*, the court stated, "Only the Court, not counsel, can order that a deposition be limited or that certain questions not be answered."[16] *Paparelli* is now the clear minority position.

---

12. *Detoy v. City & Cnty. of San Francisco*, 196 F.R.D. 362, 366 (N.D. Cal. 2000).
13. *Paparelli v. Prudential Ins. Co. of America*, 108 F.R.D. 727 (D. Mass 1985).
14. *Id.*
15. *Id.* at 730.
16. *Id.* at 731.

Technique: Elevator Door Case

This was a products liability injury case involving an elevator door that opened before the elevator car came to a full stop. The matters of examination in this case were as follows:

Matters of Examination

(a) The manner and system of keeping, maintaining, and indexing the records maintained by Elevator Doors Inc. in which the documents described in the attached order of the court were contained.

(b) The details of any search conducted by Elevator Doors Inc. in an endeavor to comply with the attached order.

At the deposition, the counsel for the plaintiff, in addition to asking questions clearly within the scope of the subject matter in the notice, also attempted to question the witness about a product letter. This letter, which the plaintiff's counsel had obtained independently from other litigation against Elevator Doors Inc., documented specific problems about the doors opening early. One of Elevator Doors Inc.'s parts suppliers wrote the letter to notify its customers of a faulty part.

The counsel for Elevator Doors Inc. objected to questions about this letter, saying it was "beyond the scope," and instructed the witness not to answer the questions. Rather than argue in a deposition, the plaintiff's counsel built a record of this instruction to the witness, to use later in a motion to compel and in a brief.

Q: What is the basis of your instruction not to answer?

A: Outside the scope.

Q: Is there any other basis for not answering?

A: No.

Scope of Inquiry Objections

Following are ideas and case law you can use if you are faced with scope of inquiry objections at a deposition. If an attorney defending a Rule 30(b)(6) deposition has objections to questions as being outside the scope of the 30(b)(6) designation, he should state the objection on the record. However, the witness should still answer the question, to the best of her ability.[17] Because the organization has a duty to prepare the witness only for the matters specified, only questions that elicit testimony *within* the scope of preparing for the 30(b)(6) notice are binding upon the organization.[18] Objections that state "beyond the scope" preserve the argument that the testimony goes to the witness's knowledge only, not the organization's. If it is a valid objection, those answers will not bind the organization, but the witness still must answer your questions.[19] The trial court will ultimately determine whether or not the testimony was actually within the scope of the 30(b)(6) deposition notice. If questions are ruled to be beyond the scope of the 30(b)(6) notice, the answers to that line of inquiry will convert to individual 30(b)(1) testimony. Before trial, the counsel for the responding party may request jury instructions that such answers were merely the answers or opinions of individual fact witnesses, not the organization's admissions.[20]

---

17. *Detoy v. City & Cnty. of San Francisco*, 196 F.R.D. 362, 367 (N.D. Cal. 2000).
18. *King v. Pratt & Whitney, a Div. of United Technologies Corp.*, 161 F.R.D. 475, 476 (S.D. Fla. 1995) aff'd sub nom. *King v. Pratt & Whitney*, 213 F.3d 646 (11th Cir. 2000) and aff'd sub nom. *King v. Pratt & Whitney*, 213 F.3d 647 (11th Cir. 2000).
19. *Dravo Corp. v. Liberty Mut. Ins. Co.*, 164 F.R.D. 70, 74 (D. Neb. 1995).
20. *Detoy v. City & Cnty. of San Francisco*, 196 F.R.D. 362, 367 (N.D. Cal. 2000), citing generally, Rodger L. Wilson and Steve C. Posner, "Specialty Law Column: Questions Beyond the Scope: Defending Against the Fed. R. Civ. P. 30(b)(6) Sneak Attack," *The Colorado Lawyer* 26, no. 7 (1997): 87, 90.

Instructions Not to Answer

A defending lawyer in a 30(b)(6) deposition *can* state that a question is beyond the scope, but they *cannot* instruct a witness not to answer. If a defending lawyer believes the question goes beyond what the organization was required to prepare for, then "beyond the scope" is the appropriate objection to make during a 30(b)(6) deposition. However, it is improper for attorneys defending 30(b)(6) depositions to instruct a witness *not to answer* because of the scope of inquiry. The only bases for instruction not to answer are set forth in Rule 30(d)(1):

> [T]o preserve a privilege, to enforce a limitation on evidence directed by the court, or to present a motion under paragraph (3), that the deposition is being conducted in bad faith or in such a way as unreasonably to annoy, embarrass, or oppress the deponent or a party.[21]

Anything else is improper and sanctionable. In *Batts v. County of Santa Clara*, the court emphasized that there is no gray zone when it comes to instructions not to answer:

> Whatever lack of clarity may exist in the law with respect to the proper scope of a Rule 30(b)(6) deposition, no such lack of clarity exists with respect to the limited circumstances in which counsel may instruct a witness not to answer a question. Thus, regardless of County Counsel's arguably understandable confusion regarding the propriety of Plaintiff's counsel's questioning, County Counsel's instruction to the witness not to answer was clearly improper.[22]

---

21. *Detoy v. City & Cnty. of San Francisco*, 196 F.R.D. 362, 367 (N.D. Cal. 2000).
22. *Batts v. County of Santa Clara*, 2010 WL 545847, *2 (N.D. Cal. Feb.11, 2010).

Technique: Make a Record of Instructions Not to Answer

If your opponent instructs a witness not to answer, it is important that you make a record of the basis for that instruction. There are only two permissible bases for instructing the witness not to answer a question. One is privilege, two is to enforce a limitation by the court. Therefore, if you want to bring a motion for sanctions against the obstructing attorney, you have to establish a record as to why the attorney instructed the witness not to answer.[23]

RESPONDING COUNSEL: Objection. I'm instructing the witness not to answer.

REQUESTING COUNSEL: What is the basis of that instruction, please?

RESPONDING COUNSEL: It's beyond the scope of the notice.

REQUESTING COUNSEL: Is there any other basis?

RESPONDING COUNSEL: No.

You now have the record to bring a motion to compel answers to this line of questioning and to request the court to sanction your adversary for not complying with the case law.

SUMMARY

- Rule 30(b)(6) questions are not limited to the scope of the deposition notice.

- Beyond-the-scope objections merely limit the binding effect of the testimony.

- Instructions not to answer are limited to preservation of privilege.

---

23. *See* chapter 14, "Motions to Compel and Sanctions," for more information on this topic.

13

Deposition Obstruction

The Rules squarely preclude this tactic that was mastered by deposition bullies, masquerading as members of the bar.[1]

—Hon. Edwin G. Torres

Introduction	303
Obstructive Deposition Tactics Are Prohibited	305
The *Hall* Standards	307
Conferring with Witnesses during Depositions	309
Objections	314
Type and Manner of Objections	314
Speaking Objections	315
Instructing Witness to Answer "If You Know"	317
Attorney's Lack of Understanding	319

---

1. *New World Network Ltd. v. M/V Norwegian Sea*, No. 05-22916 CIV, 2007 WL 1068124, at *4 (S.D. Fla. Apr. 6, 2007).

Reinterpreting or Rephrasing
the Examiner's Questions 319
Speculation 320
Asked and Answered 320
Relevance. 321
Improper Foundation 322
Overbroad. 322
Form 323
Vague. 325
Numerous "Proper" Objections 326
Instructions Not to Answer 328

SANCTIONS 329
CONCLUSION 334
SUMMARY 335

Introduction

Courts expect attorneys to operate on the honor system. The courts intend for attorneys to conduct discovery with minimal judicial control.[2] Unfortunately, as a result of the minimal oversight, discovery—a process intended to facilitate the free flow of information between parties—is now too often mired in obstructionism. Specifically, deposition obstruction is now a common occurrence in state and federal courts throughout the entire country.

Many lawyers have learned about deposition conduct in the trench. They have seen other lawyers misbehave. They have not had the opportunity to study deposition conduct law and therefore have come to believe that obstruction is what lawyers are supposed to do to protect their clients. When defending depositions, they use delay tactics, objections, comments, and threats to interfere with the opposing counsel's inquiries.

Those lawyers, known as *Rambo litigators*, mistakenly claim it is their ethical duty to use all means to zealously represent their clients. However, we must read the Rules of Professional Responsibility as a whole. Specifically, we must read our ethical duty to zealously advocate on behalf of a client in conjunction with Rule 3.4, "Fairness to Opposing Party and Counsel," which states the following:

> A lawyer shall not . . . unlawfully obstruct another party's access to evidence or unlawfully alter, destroy, or conceal a document or other material having potential evidentiary value.[3]

Lawfulness is not governed by the criminal code. Instead, lawfulness is the adherence to rules and laws that govern our judicial

---

2. Cassie B. Hanson, "When Does Zealous Advocacy Become Obstruction?," *Office of Law. Prof'l Resp.*, Minn. Law (Apr. 7, 2008).
3. Model Rules of Prof'l Conduct R. 3.4(a).

system. Failure to comply with the Rules of Civil Procedure is an unlawful obstruction of access to material having potential evidentiary value.

Examples of obstruction are as many as there are lawyers who have taken a single deposition. The simplest requests, such as, "Please tell us what happened," may result in senseless objections:

- Lack of foundation.

- Vague.

- You are being unfair because you need to let him look at the documents you have in your hand before he can answer accurately.

The opposing lawyer may follow the objection with, "You may answer if you know." State and federal courts throughout the country universally prohibit such objections. Yet they continue.

Commentators have identified the courts' reluctance to impose sanctions under Rule 37 as one of the factors that has encouraged some litigators to use evasive and dilatory behavior in response to discovery requests.[4] As a result, obstructive deposition conduct has become the natural product of that unchecked behavior. Girard and Espinosa describe the role of the judiciary in enabling the growing problem of litigation obstruction:

> [L]itigators and trial lawyers do not deserve all the blame for obstructionist discovery conduct because judges so often ignore this conduct, and by doing so we reinforce—even incentivize—obstructionist tactics. . . . Unless judges impose serious adverse

---

4. *Sec. Nat. Bank of Sioux City, Iowa v. Abbott Labs.*, 299 F.R.D. 595, 597 n.7 (N.D. Iowa 2014), rev'd on other grounds, 800 F.3d 936 (8th Cir. 2015), citing Daniel C. Girard & Todd I. Espinosa, "Limiting Evasive Discovery: A Proposal for Three Cost-Saving Amendments to the Federal Rules," *Denv. U. L. Rev.* 87 (2010): 473, 483.

consequences, like court-imposed sanctions, litigators' conditional reflexes will persist. The point of court-imposed sanctions is to stop reinforcing winning through obstruction.[5]

The court's ability to stop obstructive conduct is most clearly seen following the South Carolina Supreme Court's decision in the case of *In re Anonymous Member of S. Carolina Bar*.[6] In that case, the South Carolina Supreme Court held that supervising attorneys are responsible for the discovery abuses by attorneys they supervise (including speaking objections, instructions not to answer, and objections that are no more than an attempt to coach a witness).[7] *In re Anonymous Member of S. Carolina Bar* stopped virtually all deposition obstruction in South Carolina, overnight.

We are all responsible for following the Rules of Civil Procedure and the Rules of Professional Conduct. The following pages provide those legal standards, as well as the techniques to expose the obstruction. As in any aspect of litigation, there will be some judges who simply don't want to enforce the rules. However, if you build a solid record that exposes serious obstruction and you have acted professionally, you will greatly enhance your chances of prevailing with the motions set forth in this chapter.

OBSTRUCTIVE DEPOSITION TACTICS ARE PROHIBITED

Attorneys should not engage in any conduct during a deposition that judicial officers would not allow in their presence.[8] In the

---

5. Daniel C. Girard & Todd I. Espinosa, "Limiting Evasive Discovery: A Proposal for Three Cost-Saving Amendments to the Federal Rules," *Denv. U. L. Rev.* 87 (2010): 473, 483.
6. *In re Anonymous Member of S. Carolina Bar*, 346 S.C. 177, 552 S.E.2d 10 (2001).
7. *Id.*
8. Fed. R. Civ. P. 30(d) advisory committee's note (1993 Amendment).

landmark case, *Hall v. Clifton Precision*,[9] the court evaluated and listed what was to be considered appropriate deposition conduct:

> The underlying purpose of a deposition is to find out what a witness saw, heard, or did—what the witness thinks. A deposition is meant to be a question-and-answer conversation between the deposing lawyer and the witness. There is no proper need for the witness's own lawyer to act as an intermediary, interpreting questions, deciding which questions the witness should answer, and helping the witness to formulate the answers. The witness comes to the deposition to testify, not to indulge in a parody of Charlie McCarthy, with lawyers coaching or bending the witness's words to mold a legally convenient record. It is the witness—not the lawyer—who is the witness.[10]

The court went on to explain that:

> depositions are to be limited to what they were and are intended to be: question-and-answer sessions between a lawyer and a witness aimed at uncovering the facts in a lawsuit. When a deposition becomes something other than that because of strategic interruptions, suggestions, statements, and arguments of counsel, it not only becomes unnecessarily long, but it ceases to serve the purpose of the Federal Rules of Civil Procedure: to find and fix the truth.[11]

---

9. *Hall v. Clifton Precision, a Div. of Litton Sys., Inc.*, 150 F.R.D. 525 (E.D. Pa. 1993).
10. *Id.* at 528.
11. *Id.* at 531.

The *Hall* Standards

Courts throughout the country have recognized the standards of deposition conduct established in *Hall*.[12] In sum, they provide as follows:

1. A witness may seek clarification, definition, or explanation of words, questions, or documents only from the deposing counsel, not from the counsel for the witness.

2. Defending counsel can make no objections except those that would be waived if not made under Fed. R. Civ. P. 32(d)(3)(B) and those necessary to assert a privilege, to enforce a limitation on evidence directed by the court,

---

12. *Miller v. Waseca Med. Ctr.*, 205 F.R.D. 537, 539 (D. Minn. 2002); *Armstrong v. Hussmann Corp.*, 163 F.R.D. 299, 303–05 (E.D. Mo. 1995); *In re ML-Lee Acquisition Fund II, L.P. & ML-Lee Acquisition Fund (Ret. Accounts) II, L.P. Sec. Litig.*, 848 F. Supp. 527, 567 (D. Del. 1994); *Bucher v. Richardson Hosp. Auth.*, 160 F.R.D. 88, 94 (N.D. Tex. 1994); *Holland v. Fisher*, No. 92-3900, 1994 WL 878780, at *6 (Mass. Super. Dec. 21, 1994); *Van Pilsum v. Iowa State Univ. of Sci. & Tech.*, 152 F.R.D. 179, 180–81 (S.D. Iowa 1993); *Johnson v. Wayne Manor Apartments*, 152 F.R.D. 56, 58–59 (E.D. Pa. 1993); *Damaj v. Farmers Ins. Co.*, 164 F.R.D. 559, 560 (N.D. Okla. 1995); *Acri v. Golden Triangle Mgmt. Acceptance Co.*, No. 9312188, 142 Pitt. Legal J. 225 (Pa. Ct. 1994); *Acri v. Golden Triangle Mgmt. Acceptance Co.*, No. G.D. 93-12188, 142 Pitt. Legal J. 225, 226 (Ct. Com. P1. Alleghany County 1994); *Paramount Commc'ns Inc. v. QVC Network, Inc.*, 637 A.2d 34, 55 (Del. Super. Ct. 1994); *Dominick v. Troscoso*, No. 942395B, 1996 WL 408769 (Mass. Super. Ct. July 17, 1996); *Burrows v. Redbud Cmty. Hosp. Dist.*, 187 F.R.D. 606, 614 (N.D. Cal. 1998); *Quantachrome Corp. v. Micromeritics Instrument Corp.*, 189 F.R.D. 697, 699–702 (S.D. Fla. 1999); *Collins v. Int'l Dairy Queen, Inc.*, No. 94954MACWDO, 1998 WL 293314 at *1 (M.D. Ga. June 4, 1998); *Chapsky v. Baxter V. Mueller Div., Baxter Healthcare Corp.*, No. 93c6524, 1994 WL 327348 at *1 (N.D. Ill. July 6, 1994); *Sinclair v. Kmart Corp.*, No. 951170JTM, 1996 WL 748038 at *7 (D. Kan. Dec. 9, 1996); *Boyd v. Univ. of Md. Med. Sys.*, 173 F.R.D. 143, 144–47 (D. Md. 1997); *Metayer v. PFL Life Ins. Co.*, No. 98177PC, 1999 WL 33117063 at *2 (D. Me. 1999); *Phinney v. Paulshock*, 181 F.R.D. 185, 205–07 (D.N.H. 1998); *Mruz v. Caring, Inc.*, 107 F. Supp. 2d 596, 605–07 (D.N.J. 2000); *Prudential Ins. Co. of Am. v. Nelson*, 11 F. Supp. 2d 572, 581–82 (D.N.J. 1998); *Teletel, Inc. v. Tel-Tel U.S. Corp.*, No. 99Civ4811(LLS), 2000 WL 1335872 at *2 (S.D.N.Y. Sept. 15, 2000).

or to present a Fed. R. Civ. P. 30(d) motion to terminate a bad-faith deposition. Therefore, any other objections need not and shall not be made during the course of a deposition.

3. Defending counsel may not instruct a witness not to answer a question, unless it is to preserve a privilege or to comply with a court-directed limitation on evidence.

4. Defending counsel shall not make any objections or statements that might suggest an answer to a witness.

5. Defending counsel and their witness-clients shall not engage in private, off-the-record conferences during depositions or during breaks or recesses, except for the purpose of deciding whether to assert a privilege.

6. Witness–defending counsel conferences are a proper subject for inquiry by deposing counsel, who may inquire whether there has been any witness coaching and, if so, what.

7. Defending counsel who confer with their clients must disclose that fact on the record and disclose the purpose and outcome of the conference.

8. The deposing counsel should provide the defending counsel with a copy of all documents shown to the witness during the deposition, and may do so either before the deposition begins or contemporaneously with the showing of each document. The witness and the witness's counsel do not have the right to discuss documents privately before the witness answers questions about them.

9. Depositions shall otherwise be conducted in compliance with this opinion which accompanies this order.[13]

---

13. *Hall*, 150 F.R.D. at 531–32.

Courts around the country have universally accepted these standards except for the prohibition against any form of attorney–client communication once the deposition has started.

Conferring with Witnesses during Depositions

There is no dispute that witness coaching during the deposition is universally prohibited. Depositions are to proceed in the same manner as the examination and cross-examination of witnesses at trial.[14] The United States Supreme Court has clearly defined the role of counsel during the client's testimony:

> When a defendant becomes a witness, he has no constitutional right to consult with his lawyer while he is testifying. He has an absolute right to such consultation before he begins to testify, but neither he nor his lawyer has a right to have the testimony interrupted in order to give him the benefit of counsel's advice.[15]

During a civil trial, a witness's attorney does not sit beside the witness stand telling the witness what to say or not to say. Simply because the fact finder is not present in the deposition room does not open the door to such behavior.[16] The questioner is entitled to the witness's candid answers, not merely the witness repeating words that the opposing counsel places in the witness's ear.[17]

---

14. Fed. R. Civ. P. 30(c)(1).
15. *Perry v. Leeke*, 488 U.S. 272, 281 (1989).
16. *Hall*, 150 F.R.D. at 528.
17. Harold Baer, Jr. and Robert C. Meade, "The Conduct and Misconduct of the Deposition," *APR N.Y. St. B.J.* 64 (Mar./Apr. 1992): 16; Steven J. Helmers, "Depositions: Objections, Instructions and Sanctions," *S.D. L. Rev.* 33 (1987–1988): 272.

The time for a lawyer and client to prepare for a deposition is *before* the deposition, not *during* it. Once the deposition begins, the preparation period is over, and the witness is on his own.[18]

> A deponent and the deponent's attorney have no right to confer during a deposition in a civil proceeding, except for the purpose of determining whether a privilege shall be asserted.[19]

Attorneys are absolutely prohibited from communicating with their clients during the active questioning at a deposition, except to protect a privilege. However, there is a split in authority as to whether an attorney may confer with the client during breaks. In *Hall* standards 5 through 7, the court expressly held "that conferences between witness and lawyer are prohibited both during the deposition and during recesses."[20] The court explained the following:

> Recess conferences are not covered by the attorney–client privilege, at least as to what is said by the lawyer to the witness. Therefore, any such conferences are fair game for inquiry by the deposing attorney to ascertain whether there has been any coaching and, if so, what.[21]

---

18. *In re Alexander Grant & Co. Litig.*, 110 F.R.D. 545, 547 (S.D. Fla. 1986); *Nutmeg Ins. Co. v. Atwell, Vogel & Sterling A Div. of Equifax Servs., Inc.*, 120 F.R.D. 504 (W.D. La. 1988); *Smith v. Logansport Cmty. Sch. Corp.*, 139 F.R.D. 637 (N.D. Ind. 1991); and *Hall*, 150 F.R.D. at 528.
19. *United States v. Philip Morris Inc.*, 212 F.R.D. 418, 420 (D.D.C. 2002); *see also, e.g., Hall*, 150 F.R.D. at 529; *Morales v. Zondo, Inc.*, 204 F.R.D. 50 (S.D.N.Y. 2001); Moore et al., *Moore's Federal Practice*, ¶ 30.42[2] (3d ed., Matthew Bender 1997).
20. *Hall*, 150 F.R.D. at 529.
21. *Id.* at 532, n. 7.

A conference is permissible if its purpose is to determine whether to assert a privilege.

> However, when such a conference occurs, the conferring attorney should place on the record the fact that the conference occurred, the subject of the conference, and the decision reached as to whether to assert a privilege.[22]

With today's advancements in communication through technology, the defending attorney's means of conferring with the deponent have also evolved. In *Ngai v. Old Navy*, the defending attorney and deponent "exchanged numerous text messages both before and during the telephonic deposition."[23] The court found the following:

> [I]t appears that some of the instructions counsel gave to the deponent were intended to influence the fact-finding goal of the deposition process and such conduct would be a proper subject of examination.[24]

The court ruled those text messages were "not protected by the attorney–client privilege."[25] *Ngai*, following *Hall v. Clifton*, ruled that when there has been a communication between an attorney and client during a deposition or deposition break, the deposing attorney is allowed to question the deponent about the contents of the discussion to determine if any witness-coaching occurred.[26]

---

22. *Plaisted v. Geisinger Med. Ctr.*, 210 F.R.D. 527, 535 (M.D. Pa. 2002), citing *Hall*, 150 F.R.D. at 529–30.
23. *Ngai v. Old Navy*, No.CIV.A. 07-5653KSHPS, 2009 WL 2391282, at *1 (D.N.J. July 31, 2009).
24. *Id.* at *4 (citing *Hall*, 150 F.R.D. at 528).
25. *Id.* at *1.
26. *Id.* at *1 (citing *Plaisted v. Geisinger Medical Center*, 210 F.R.D. 527, 533 (M.D. Pa. 2002)).

Therefore, in *Ngai*, the court ordered the defendant to produce the text messages exchanged between the time the deposition began and when it concluded.[27]

There is a minority view, in the case of *In re Stratosphere Corp. Sec. Litigation*, that allows defending attorneys to confer with their clients during breaks, only if the defending attorneys *did not request* the breaks.[28]

> This Court will not preclude an attorney, during a recess that he or she did not request, from making sure that his or her client did not misunderstand or misinterpret questions or documents, or attempt to help rehabilitate the client by fulfilling an attorney's ethical duty to prepare a witness.[29]

No one can interrupt between a question and an answer. Nor is it appropriate to request a recess in the middle of a line of questions. However, if the examiner takes a break, *Stratosphere* jurisdictions allow communications between attorneys and their clients.

If a witness makes substantive changes to their testimony after the break, there is little authority on the extent of inquiry the court will permit to establish the basis for that change. Arguably the same principles that apply to the Sham Affidavit Rule[30] would also apply to inquiring about the factual basis for changing the testimony. The witness should be required to testify about the basis of her changed testimony at the reconvened deposition because "[w]hen a party affirmatively relies on privileged information, then the information is automatically placed into issue and any privilege that would otherwise attach is impliedly waived."[31]

---

27. *Id.* at *6.
28. *In re Stratosphere Corp. Sec. Litig.*, 182 F.R.D. 614, 621 (D. Nev. 1998).
29. *Id.*; see also *Odone v. Croda Int'l PLC.*, 170 F.R.D. 66, 68–69 (D.D.C. 1997).
30. *See* chapter 16, "Changing the Testimony."
31. *QBE Ins. Corp. v. Jorda Enters., Inc.*, 286 F.R.D. 661, 664 (S.D. Fla. 2012).

Technique: Building a Record of Discussions during Breaks

Regardless of whether your jurisdiction follows *Hall* or *Stratosphere*, you need to be sure that the jury understands that any changes to the testimony were attorney driven. You can do this by exposing the communication immediately following the break, with or without (depending on the jurisdiction) inquiring into the substance:

Q: Are you ready to proceed with questions?

Q: Did you have an opportunity to meet with your lawyer during the break?

Q: Is there anything you want to change?

Q: If so, what do you want to change?

In *Stratosphere* jurisdictions, if a change in testimony occurs, the jury will assume the defending attorney directed it. Cuisimano and Wenner's[32] research in "Overcoming Jury Bias" identified jurors' distrust of information that they believe lawyers have manipulated. In *Hall* jurisdictions, you can make additional inquiries about what the attorney and defendant discussed.

Q: How long did you talk?

Q: Tell us about that conversation.

Q: What did you discuss?

Q: What else?

Q: Did your lawyer show you any documents?

If the answer is yes, ask:

Q: What are they?

Q: Why are you changing your answer?

Q: Why didn't you tell us that when I asked you the questions the first time?

---

32. Greg Cusimano and David Wenner, "Overcoming Jury Bias" (paper and lecture, meeting of the National College of Advocacy, Mariott Mountain Shadow Resort, Phoenix, AZ, February 12–16, 2003).

Q: What did your lawyer say to cause you to change your answer?

Q: Why didn't you have that information the first time you were providing testimony to the jury?

Objections

The remainder of this chapter is a comprehensive list of improper objections and prohibited conduct. The following sections provides the relevant case law you can use in your brief for sanctions to enforce professional deposition conduct that does not impede your access to information. If you are faced with obstructive deposition conduct, remember that it is your job to build a clear record of the opposing counsel's conduct, so you can document their behavior in your brief.

Type and Manner of Objections

Rules 30(c)(2) and 32(d) govern objections in depositions.[33] Most objections are improper at depositions because they can be a thinly veiled mask of witness coaching. The rules preserve those objections, so they should be made at trial, not at the deposition. The exceptions—those objections that should be made at deposition—are those objections to errors or irregularities that can be corrected at the deposition.

- **Substantive objections** such as hearsay, relevance, competency, or materiality, are *preserved* by Rule 32(d)(3)(A) and are therefore unnecessary at the deposition.[34] For example, if you make the request, "Please tell me what you heard," and the opposing attorney objects, saying you are calling for hearsay, that is an improper objection *at the deposition*.

---

33. Fed. R. Civ. P. 30(c)(2), 32(d).
34. Fed. R. Civ. P. 32(d)(3)(A).

The objection is preserved, and the opposing attorney should raise it at the time of trial if you try to introduce the statement as evidence.

- **Error objections** such as those you can correct on the record, such as the form of the question or the sufficiency of the oath, are waived under Rule 32(d)(3)(B)(i) if the opposing counsel does not make them at the time of the deposition. Therefore, courts require attorneys to object to these types of situations at the deposition. On the following pages, I will develop what constitutes a proper form objection.

Allowing counsel to raise most objections later at trial permits the preliminary examination to proceed without constant interruptions.[35] The purpose of the various rules is to prevent interference with the orderly flow of the deposition. Using excessive objections to obstruct meaningful elicitation of testimony is prohibited.[36] Because lawyers can use objections as a tool for disruption, *objections that are not required to be made at the deposition are inappropriate.*[37]

Speaking Objections

When the responding counsel makes an objection, Rule 30(c)(2) requires as follows: "An objection must be stated concisely in a non-argumentative and non-suggestive manner."[38] Objections that suggest answers to questions are commonly called *speaking objections.*[39] Speaking objections occur when the defending attorney actually engages in coaching the witness. Through comments

---

35. Fed. R. Civ. P. 30(c) advisory committee note (1993 Amendments).
36. *See In re, Stratosphere Corp. Sec. Litig.*, 182 F.R.D. 614, 619 (D. Nev. 1998), citing *Am. Directory Serv. Agency, Inc. v. Beam*, 131 F.R.D. 15, 18–19 (D.D.C. 1990).
37. Herr & Haydock, *Civil Rules Annotated* § 30.22, at 107 (3d ed., West Group 1998).
38. Fed. R. Civ. P. 30(c)(2).
39. *Cincinnati Ins. Co. v. Serrano*, No. 11-2075-JAR, 2012 WL 28071, at *1 (D. Kan. Jan. 5, 2012).

contained in the objection, the attorney directs the witness's attention to what the right or "correct answer should be."[40] Speaking objections are prohibited. The court also considers interruptions and question clarifications by the defending counsel improper.[41]

The Federal bar counsel for the Second Circuit reported the following:

> Virtually every active litigator has encountered the situation where, while purporting to voice an objection to a question, the defending attorney is actually engaged in coaching the witness, attempting in the course of articulating the objection to direct the witness's attention to what the "right" or "correct" answer should be.[42]

Witness coaching during a deposition is prohibited.[43] The prohibition includes subtle forms of coaching, as well as blatant instructions.

Sadly, witness coaching works. You can see it when a witness adopts the opposing lawyer's coaching objection. For example, the defending attorney objects, stating, "The question is vague." The witness then parrots a request to clarify the question.[44] The

---

40. *Applied Telematics, Inc. v. Sprint Corp.*, No. 94-CV-4603, 1995 WL 79237 (E.D. Pa. Feb. 22, 1995) (citing the Federal Bar Council Comm. on Second Circuit Courts, A Report on the Conduct of Depositions, 131 F.R.D. 613, 617 (1990) (quoted by Virginia E. Hench, "Mandatory Disclosure and Equal Access to Justice: The 1993 Federal Discovery Rules Amendments and the Just, Speedy and Inexpensive Determination of Every Action," *Temp. L. Rev.* 67 (1994): 179, 218 n.182).
41. *Unique Concepts, Inc. v. Brown*, 115 F.R.D. 292, 293 (S.D.N.Y. 1987) (Attorney's constant interruptions throughout the deposition, his silencing of the witness, and obstructive demands for explanations from the examiner rendered the deposition worthless and an exercise in futility).
42. A Report on the Conduct of Depositions, 131 F.R.D. 613 (2nd Cir. 1990).
43. *Hall v. Clifton Precision, a Div. of Litton Sys., Inc.*, 150 F.R.D. 525 (E.D. Pa. 1993).
44. See *Cordova v. United States*, No. CIV.05 563 JB/LFG, 2006 WL 4109659, at *3 (D.N.M. July 30, 2006) (awarding sanctions based on a lawyer's deposition coaching because "it became impossible to know if [a witness's] answers

court prohibits objections that prompt witnesses to request that the examiner clarify otherwise clear questions.[45] Despite the Federal Rules' prohibition on witness coaching, there continue to be attorneys who prompt witnesses in numerous subtle (and not so subtle) ways.

As with all other forms of improper behavior during a deposition, your job while taking the deposition is to build a record of your opponent's conduct.

Instructing Witness to Answer "If You Know"

The tactic of frequently concluding objections by telling the witness, "You can answer if you know," or something similar, is prohibited coaching. After receiving this instruction, a witness will often claim to be unable to answer the question. Courts have described the tactic as impermissible, "raw, unmitigated" witness coaching.

> When a lawyer tells a witness to answer "if you know," it not-so-subtly suggests that the witness may not know the answer, inviting the witness to dodge or qualify an otherwise clear question. For this reason, ". . . instructions to a witness that they may answer a question 'if they know' or 'if they understand the question' are raw, unmitigated coaching, and are never appropriate."[46]

"If you know," not so subtly suggests that the witness may not know the answer, inviting the witness to dodge or qualify an

---

emanated from her own line of reasoning or whether she adopted [the] lawyer's reasoning from listening to his objections").
45. *Sec. Nat. Bank of Sioux City, Iowa v. Abbott Labs.*, 299 F.R.D. 595, 604 (N.D. Iowa 2014), rev'd on other grounds, 800 F.3d 936 (8th Cir. 2015).
46. *Sec. Nat. Bank of Sioux City, Iowa v. Abbott Labs.*, 299 F.R.D. at 607 (quoting *Cincinnati Ins. Co.*, 2012 WL 28071 at *5, and citing *Specht v. Google, Inc.*, 268 F.R.D. 596, 599 (N.D. Ill. 2010) and *Oleson v. Kmart Corp.*, 175 F.R.D. 560, 567 (D. Kan. 1997)).

otherwise clear question.[47] The if-you-know technique is sanctionable misconduct.[48]

> **Technique: Dealing with Clarification Questions**
>
> Only the witness knows whether she understands a question. The witness has a duty to request clarification if needed. Rather than giving the witness a laundry list of deposition rules, as the questioner, you want the witness to commit at the beginning of the deposition that *she* will ask *you* for clarification when necessary. For example:
>
> Q: Will you tell me if you don't understand my question?
>
> Q: Will you tell me if you find my question to be confusing?
>
> Q: Will you tell me if I have assumed an incorrect fact in a question?
>
> Q: Will you tell me if you don't know the answer to a question?
>
> Q: Do you understand these simple deposition rules?
>
> Q: Will you need to be reminded to follow these rules?
>
> If the witness testifies that she recognizes the need to notify you if she doesn't understand a question, or if there is an incorrectly assumed fact in the question, then you will have a record establishing that the witness understood her duty.

It is the witness's responsibility to ask for clarifications. If the defending counsel feels that an answer shows failure to understand a question, they may remedy the problem on cross-examination.[49] They are not allowed to coach the witness while they are being examined.

---

47. *Sec. Nat. Bank of Sioux City, Iowa v. Abbott Labs.*, 299 F.R.D. 595, 607 (N.D. Iowa 2014), rev'd on other grounds, 800 F.3d 936 (8th Cir. 2015).
48. *Cincinnati Ins. Co.*, 2012 WL 28071, at *5.
49. *Cincinnati Ins. Co.*, 2012 WL 28071, at *5, *see also Hall*, 150 F.R.D. at 528–29.

Attorney's Lack of Understanding

A lawyer's claim that he doesn't understand a question is not a proper reason to disrupt the deposition.[50]

> Lawyers may not object simply because they find a question to be vague, nor may they assume that the witness will not understand the question. The witness—not the lawyer—gets to decide whether he or she understands a particular question.[51]

If the deponent lacks knowledge or understanding, then the *deponent* should say so, not seek understanding or direction about how to answer the question from her attorney. The interrogating counsel has the right to the deponent's answers, not an attorney's answers.[52]

Reinterpreting or Rephrasing the Examiner's Questions

If the defending attorney reinterprets or rephrases your questions, that is prohibited witness coaching. This strategy gives the witness additional information to consider in answering a question. It allows the defending attorney to answer the question first with the witness then adopting that answer, or even gives the attorney the chance to audibly disagree with the witness's answer. When the attorney acts as an intermediary, it is no longer a question-and-answer session between the examiner and the witness.[53]

---

50. *Applied Telematics, Inc. v. Sprint Corp.*, No. 94-CV-4603, 1995 WL 79237 (E.D. Pa. Feb. 22, 1995), citing *Hall*, 150 F.R.D. at 530 n.10.
51. *Cincinnati Ins. Co.*, 2012 WL 28071 at , *5, and *Hall*, 150 F.R.D. at 528–29, and Peter M. Panken & Mirande Valbrune, "Enforcing the Prohibitions Against Coaching Deposition Witnesses," *Prac. Litig.*, (Sept. 2006): 15, 16.
52. *In re Stratosphere Corp. Sec. Litig.*, 182 F.R.D. 614, 621 (D. Nev. 1998).
53. *Hall*, 150 F.R.D. at 528; *Alexander v. F.B.I.*, 186 F.R.D. 21, 52–53 (D.D.C. 1998).

Speculation

An objection that a question calls for speculation is a foundation objection and not a form objection. It also tends to coach witnesses to respond that they do not know the answer. Under Rule 32 the objection is preserved and is therefore unnecessary and improper.[54]

Asked and Answered

Complexity, confusion, and ambiguity can be fatal to the plaintiff—the party with the burden of proof.[55] If questions are loaded with ambiguity, jurors will find that the plaintiff has not met the burden of proof, and you will have a defense verdict. Because creating ambiguity is a well-known defense strategy, it is critical to create a clear record.[56] If you use the techniques discussed at length in *Advanced Depositions Strategy and Practice*,[57] then as the examining attorney, you may require the witness to answer questions through your cross-examinations. Don't let the witness sidestep questions—get the answer to the question you're asking, not the one they want to answer. These techniques include:

- Pressing the witness with cross-examination.
- Clarifying answers.
- Insuring the witness has answered the question you actually asked.
- Breaking down long answers into a shorter question-and-answer format so you will be able to use those tight responses for impeachment in the future.

---

54. *Cincinnati Ins. Co. v. Serrano*, 2012 WL 28071, at *4.
55. Rick Friedman & Patrick Malone, *Rules of the Road: A Plaintiff Lawyer's Guide to Proving Liability*, 2nd ed. (Portland, OR: Trial Guides, 2010), 1.
56. *See* Rick Friedman & Patrick Malone, *Rules of the Road: A Plaintiff Lawyer's Guide to Proving Liability*, 2nd ed. (Portland, OR: Trial Guides, 2010).
57. Phillip H. Miller & Paul J. Scoptur, *Advanced Depositions Strategy and Practice* (Portland, OR: Trial Guides 2013).

As the inquiring attorney, you are working to develop a clear record. However, unscrupulous lawyers will try to prevent you from developing that clear record by interfering with the orderly flow of the deposition.[58] Here are some examples:

- I think he has already answered the question.
- It's repetitious.
- The question has already been asked.
- It's already been asked and answered.

These are not objections. They are inappropriate, prohibited interruptions to the flow of the deposition.[59]

Relevance

Courts have firmly prohibited objections based on relevance. [60]

> [D]iscovery may be used to elicit information that will lead to relevant evidence; each question and answer need not be one that could be one that would itself be proper at trial.[61]

While the Federal Rules of Evidence prohibit introducing certain types of evidence, these rules govern what you can introduce as evidence at trial, not at the discovery stage.[62]

---

58. *See In re Stratosphere Corp. Sec. Litig.*, 182 F.R.D. at 616–19, citing *Am. Directory Serv. Agency, Inc. v. Beam*, 131 F.R.D. 15, 18–19 (D.D.C. 1990).
59. *Armstrong v. Hussmann Corp.* 163 F.R.D. 299, 301–02 (E.D. Mo. 1995).
60. *See Furniture World, Inc. v. D.A.V. Thrift Stores, Inc.*, 168 F.R.D. 61 (D.N.M. 1996); *Nat'l Microsales Corp. v. Chase Manhattan Bank, N.A.*, 761 F. Supp. 304, 307 (S.D.N.Y. 1991); *Gall v. St. Elizabeth Med. Ctr.*, 130 F.R.D. 85, 87 (S.D. Ohio 1990); *Perrignon v. Bergen Brunswig Corp.*, 77 F.R.D. 455, 461 (N.D. Cal. 1978).
61. *Redwood v. Dobson*, 476 F.3d 462, 469 (7th Cir. 2007).
62. *See Herchenroeder v. Johns Hopkins Univ. Applied Physics Lab.*, 171 F.R.D. 179, 180 (D. Md. 1997); *Shapiro v. Freeman*, 38 F.R.D. 308, 311 (S.D.N.Y. 1965).

> [Rule 26(b) is] widely recognized as a discovery rule which is liberal in scope and interpretation, extending to those matters which are relevant and reasonably calculated to lead to the discovery of admissible evidence.[63]

Objections to the scope of the discovery are not appropriate at depositions. If there are legitimate concerns as to whether the discovery can lead to admissible evidence, those objections must be raised in a motion for protective order. There is no basis for objections as to relevance.

Improper Foundation

An objection to *improper foundation* is a relevance objection. Therefore, like other objections about relevance, it is improper.[64] A witness's response to a specific question might not seem to have adequate foundation at the deposition. However, this does not mean you can't later make a foundation at trial, through evidence outside of the deposition, and use the witness's response to your question as evidence.[65]

Overbroad

An objection that a question is "overbroad" is not an evidentiary objection, but is an objection that the question, in part, exceeds the scope of discovery under Rule 26(b).[66] This is not an objection that goes to the *form* of the inquiry. Rather, "objection, overbroad" is only appropriate as the prerequisite to bringing a motion to terminate or limit the deposition.

---

63. *Hofer v. Mack Trucks, Inc.*, 981 F.2d 377, 380 (8th Cir. 1992) (citing *Kramer v. Boeing Co.*, 126 F.R.D. 690, 692 (D. Minn. 1989) (and cases cited therein)).
64. *Cincinnati Ins. Co. v. Serrano*, 2012 WL 28071, at *4.
65. *Id.*
66. *Id.*

Form

Rule 32(d)(3) provides that unless your opponent makes certain objections during a deposition, the ability to make those objections will be waived at trial. Specifically, the court will waive an objection to an error or irregularity at an oral examination if one of the following takes place:

(i) it relates to the manner of taking the deposition, the form of a question or answer, the oath or affirmation, a party's conduct, or other matters that might have been corrected at that time; and

(ii) it is not timely made during the deposition.[67]

The advisory committee notes clarify the types of objections that must be stated on a deposition record:

> While objections may, under the revised rule, be made during a deposition, they ordinarily should be limited to those that under Rule 32(d)(3) might be waived if not made at that time, i.e., objections on grounds that might be immediately obviated, removed, or cured, such as to the form of a question or the responsiveness of an answer.[68]

Therefore, it is only necessary to object at a deposition when the *form* of the question (not the *nature* of the question) is objectionable and when an objection would provide an opportunity to correct the form.[69] Thus, the objecting party should wait until trial (or just before trial) to make the objection, when and if you

---

67. Fed. R. Civ. P. 32(d)(3).
68. Fed. R. Civ. P. 30(d) advisory committee's note (1993 Amendment).
69. Schwarzer et al., *Federal Civil Procedure Before Trial* § 11:493, at 11–99 (The Rutter Group 2005).

offer the deposition testimony evidence.[70] If you don't offer the particular piece of evidence at trial, your opponent would have no need to object to it. To the extent that your opponent makes objections, the courts will treat deposition objections differently from trial objections—the testimony continues subject to the objections, and the objections are preserved for trial.[71]

There are two lines of cases that deal with what the objecting attorney should say when objecting to form: stating "objection as to form" only, and giving a brief statement about the objection.

Stating "Objection as to Form" Only

Some courts explicitly require lawyers to state nothing more than "objection as to form" during depositions.[72] This phrase is sufficient to let you know the grounds for the objection and to allow you to revise the question if necessary.[73] Any further explanation is inappropriate. The objector, your opponent, should only give explanation or clarification if you ask them to.[74] If you ask the objector to state a reason for the form objection, then a simple explanation is appropriate.[75] Unless you request clarification, your opponent does not need to give any further explanation. Any additional comment will have the effect of suggesting to the witness how to answer the pending question.

---

70. *In re Stratosphere Corp. Sec. Litig.*, 182 F.R.D. 614, 618 (D. Nev. 1998).
71. Fed. R. Civ. P. 30(c)(2); *W. R. Grace & Co. v. Pullman Inc.*, 74 F.R.D. 80, 83–84 (W.D. Okla. 1977); *Drew v. Int'l Bhd. of Sulphite & Paper Mill Workers*, 37 F.R.D. 446, 449–50 (D.D.C 1965).
72. *See Offshore Marine Contractors, Inc. v. Palm Energy Offshore*, L.L.C., No. CIV.A. 10–4151, 2013 WL 1412197, at *4 (E.D. La. Apr. 8, 2013).
73. *See* Wright et al., *Federal Practice and Procedure*, Civil 2d § 2156, at 206 (2d ed., West 1994); *In re St. Jude Med., Inc.*, No. 1396, 2002 WL 1050311, at *5 (D. Minn. May 24, 2002) ("Objecting counsel shall say simply the word 'objection', and no more, to preserve all objections as to form.").
74. *Quantachrome Corp. v. Micrometrics Inst. Corp.*, 189 F.R.D 697, n. 4 (S.D. Fla. 1999).
75. *Turner v. Glock, Inc.*, No. CIV.A. 1:02CV825, 2004 WL 5511620, at *1 (E.D. Tex. Mar. 29, 2004).

Once counsel representing any party states "objection" after a question, then all parties have preserved all possible objections to the form of the question unless the objector states a particular ground or grounds of objection, in which case that ground or those grounds alone are preserved.[76]

Giving a Brief Statement about Objection

An alternative line of cases calls for the objecting attorney to give a brief statement identifying the basis for the form objection, without suggesting how the witness should answer the question.[77] These courts reason that unspecified form objections do nothing to alert the examiner to a question's alleged defect, and therefore do not allow the examiner to immediately cure the objection. This line of cases has been the subject of criticism because any explanation of the defect has a very significant risk of coaching the witness.

Vague

An objection that a question is "vague" is considered a speaking objection disguised as a form objection.[78] Using the term "objection, vague" expresses a concern that the witness may not understand the question, which in turn coaches the witness to hedge the answer.[79] If the witness does not understand a question, it is the witness's duty to request clarification. Courts have ruled "objection, vague" as a prohibited speaking objection.[80]

---

76. *In re St. Jude Med., Inc.*, No. 1396, 2002 WL 1050311, at *5 (D. Minn. May 24, 2002).
77. *Mayor & City Council of Baltimore v. Theiss*, 354 Md. 234, 729 A.2d 965, 976 (1999); *Sec. Nat. Bank of Sioux City, Iowa v. Abbott Labs.*, 299 F.R.D. 595, 603 (N.D. Iowa 2014), rev'd on other grounds, 800 F.3d 936 (8th Cir. 2015).
78. *Cincinnati Ins. Co. v. Serrano*, 2012 WL 28071, at *5.
79. *Id.*
80. *Id.* at *4; *Applied Telematics, Inc. v. Sprint Corp.*, No. CIV.A. 94-CV-4603, 1995 WL 79237 (E.D. Pa. Feb. 22, 1995), citing *Hall*, 150 F.R.D. at 530 n.10.

Numerous "Proper" Objections

The advisory committee notes explain that "the making of an excessive number of unnecessary objections may itself constitute sanctionable conduct."[81] "Protection" can become a cover for obstruction.[82] A defending attorney's "vague" and "form" objections, and variations thereof, frustrate the free flow of the depositions, and therefore courts have held them as sanctionable.[83] "[E]xcessive and unnecessary interruptions are an independent reason to impose sanctions."[84]

When proper form objections transcend into witness coaching, they are impermissible and sanctionable. In *Security National Bank*, the court described the process as the "tag-team match" performed by the deponent and the defending attorney:

> Immediately after most of these "form" objections, the witness gave the seemingly Pavlovian response, "Rephrase." At times, the transcript feels like a tag-team match, with counsel and witness delivering the one-two punch of "objection"—"rephrase."[85]

---

81. Fed. R. Civ. P. 30(d) advisory committee's note (1993 Amendment); *see also Morales v. Zondo, Inc.*, 204 F.R.D. 50, 54–57 (S.D.N.Y. 2001) (example of sanctionable interference with a deposition through pervasive objections).
82. William Fortune et al., *Modern Litigation and Professional Responsibility Handbook: The Limits of Zealous Advocacy* § 6.7.4, at 264 and n. 267 (Aspen Law & Business 1996).
83. *Phillips v. Manufacturers Hanover Trust Co.*, No. 92 CIV. 8527(KTD), 1994 WL 116078 (S.D.N.Y. Mar. 29, 1994).
84. Fed. R. Civ. P. 30(d)(2), advisory committee's note (1993 Amendment).
85. *Sec. Nat. Bank of Sioux City, Iowa v. Abbott Labs.*, 299 F.R.D. 595, 603 (N.D. Iowa 2014), rev'd on other grounds, 800 F.3d 936 (8th Cir. 2015).

Technique: Building the Record of Obstructive Objections

Whenever your opponent makes any objection other than form, make a simple statement on the record, requesting that there not be speaking objections:

REQUESTING COUNSEL: Please do not make suggestive comments in the presence of the witness.

Do not engage in a repartee with the adversary! No matter how enlightened you think you sound, it will read poorly. Always use the word *please*. Remain professional. You serve no purpose by attempting to instruct your adversary on the most fundamental Rules of Civil Procedure. Simply and politely keep repeating, "Please do not make suggestive comments in the presence of the witness." Then insist on the answer and continue with the questioning. When the next speaking objection recurs, repeat the process.

Immediately calling the court is seldom successful in stopping abusive conduct. Without a sufficient record, the court will not understand the gravity of the problem. The court will be frustrated with your call. The court will make a ruling on your question's propriety, rather than the propriety of your opponent's conduct. Then the problem will occur again, and the cycle of delay will continue. Remember the doctrine of litigation jujitsu. Turn your opponents' obstructions back on them. Build a long record of repeated obstructions in the face of your polite requests to stop. The worse they act, the worse they will look. If you give them enough rope, they will hang themselves. Once you make the record, you will have the ammunition to bring a successful motion for sanctions.

Instructions Not to Answer

There are only three grounds on which your opponent can instruct the witness not to answer. Rule 30(c)(2) specifies that an attorney may instruct a deponent not to answer only when necessary to:

- Preserve a privilege.
- Enforce a limitation ordered by the court.
- Present a motion under Rule 30(d)(3).[86]

Instructing a witness not to answer a question for any other reason is sanctionable.[87]

If your opponent believes that your inquiry is harassing the witness, he or she is not allowed to tell the witness not to answer. Rather, Rule 30(d)(3)(A) states as follows:

> At any time during a deposition, the deponent or a party may move to terminate or limit it on the ground that it is being conducted in bad faith or in a manner that unreasonably annoys, embarrasses, or oppresses the deponent or party.[88]

In *Redwood v. Dobson*, the Seventh Circuit ruled that an attorney's instructions to a witness not to answer deposition questions that "neither shielded a privilege nor supplied time to apply for a protective order were unprofessional and violated the Federal Rules of Civil Procedure as well as the ethical rules that govern

---

86. Fed. R. Civ. P. 30(c)(2).
87. *Ralston Purina Co. v. McFarland*, 550 F.2d 967, 973 (4th Cir. 1977); *Detoy v. City & Cnty. of San Francisco*, 196 F.R.D. 362, 365–66 (N.D. Cal. 2000); *Boyd v. Univ. of Md. Med. Sys.*, 173 F.R.D. 143, 144–47 (D. Md. 1997); *Int'l Union of Elec., Radio & Mach. Workers AFL-CIO v. Westinghouse Elec. Corp.*, 91 F.R.D. 277, 279–80 (D.D.C. 1981); *Preyer v. U.S. Lines, Inc.*, 64 F.R.D. 430, 431 (E.D. Pa. 1973).
88. Fed. R. Civ. P. 30(d)(3)(A).

legal practice."[89] In addition, the court went on to say, "Counsel for the witness may halt the deposition and apply for a protective order . . . but must not instruct the witness to remain silent."[90]

Chief Judge Easterbrook clearly stated the policies underlying the rule:

> Mutual enmity does not excuse the breakdown of decorum. It is precisely when animosity runs high that playing by the rules is vital. Rules of legal procedure are designed to defuse, or at least channel into set forms, the heated feelings that accompany much litigation. Because depositions take place in law offices rather than courtrooms, adherence to professional standards is vital, for the judge has no direct means of control.[91]

Technique: Stopping an Abusive Deposition

If the questioning in a deposition becomes abusive, the defending lawyer has the obligation to make a record of it and then recess the deposition in order to move for a protective order.

DEFENDING LAWYER: Objection, harassing the witness. At this point we are calling for a recess for the purpose of making a motion for protective order.

SANCTIONS

Rule 30(d)(2) provides for sanctions when there has been deposition misconduct. Rule 30(d)(2) states the following:

> The court may impose an appropriate sanction— including the reasonable expenses and attorney's

---

89. *Redwood v. Dobson*, 476 F.3d 462, 469 (7th Cir. 2007).
90. *Id.* at 467–68.
91. *Id.* at 469–70.

fees incurred by any party—on a person who impedes, delays, or frustrates the fair examination of the deponent.[92]

When you're using Rule 30(d)(2) to ask the court for sanctions, the rule doesn't define what is appropriate. Typically, you must request a remedy from the court. The court will then determine if that remedy is appropriate. However, courts also have the power to create their own sanctions in response to abusive behavior.[93] "[T]he inherent power of a court can be invoked even if procedural rules exist which sanction the same conduct."[94]

When a judge decides to sanction a party under Rule 30(d)(2), the judge does not have to find that a party acted in bad faith.[95] If the judge decides that your opponent's continued comments, clarifications, and objections are getting in the way of you fairly examining the witness, then the judge can impose sanctions, no matter what your opponent's intent was.[96]

Sanctions are supposed to not only reimburse a litigant for unnecessary costs, but more importantly preserve the integrity of the judicial process. The Federal Rules specifically acknowledge that one of the functions of discovery sanctions should be deterrence.[97] The United States Supreme Court stated the following:

---

92. Fed. R. Civ. P. 30(d)(2).
93. *Sec. Nat. Bank of Sioux City, Iowa v. Abbott Labs.*, 299 F.R.D. 595, 599 (N.D. Iowa. 2014) (citing *Chambers v. NASCO, Inc.*, 501 U.S. 32, 44–45, 111 S. Ct. 2123, 115 L. Ed. 2d 27 (1991) and *Roadway Exp., Inc. v. Piper*, 447 U.S. 752, 765, 100 S. Ct. 2455, 65 L. Ed. 2d 488 (1980)), rev'd on other grounds, 800 F.3d 936 (8th Cir. 2015).
94. *Sec. Nat. Bank of Sioux City, Iowa v. Abbot Labs.*, 299 F.R.D. at 599 (citing *Chambers*, 501 U.S., 4927 (1991)), rev'd on other grounds, 800 F.3d 936 (8th Cir. 2015).
95. *GMAC Bank v. HTFC Corp.*, 248 F.R.D. 182, 196 (E.D. Pa. 2008).
96. Fed. R. Civ. P. 30(d)(2).
97. *See* Fed. R. Civ. P. 26, advisory committee's note (1983 Amendment).

> Sanctions to deter discovery abuse would be more effective if they were diligently applied not merely to penalize those whose conduct may be deemed to warrant such a sanction, but to deter those who might be tempted to such conduct in the absence of such a deterrent.[98]

Those sanctions can range from admonishment to awarding costs and attorney's fees to striking pleadings or, in extreme cases, litigation-ending sanctions. The court also has the inherent power to craft such sanctions as deemed appropriate for the situation. In *Sec. Nat. Bank of Sioux City, Iowa v. Abbott Laboratories*, the court crafted an "out of the box" sanction to deter future misconduct:

> While monetary sanctions are certainly warranted for Counsel's witness coaching and excessive interruptions, a more outside-the-box sanction may better serve the goal of changing improper tactics that modern litigators are trained to use. Counsel must write and produce a training video in which Counsel, or another partner in Counsel's firm, appears and explains the holding and rationale of this opinion, and provides specific steps lawyers must take to comply with its rationale in future depositions in any federal and state court. . . . The lawyers who must receive this notice and access include each lawyer at Counsel's firm—including its branch offices worldwide—who engages in federal or state litigation or who works in any practice group in which at least two of the lawyers have filed

---

98. *Nat'l Hockey League v. Metro. Hockey Club, Inc.*, 427 U.S. 639, 643, 96 S. Ct. 2778, 49 L. Ed. 2d 747 (1976).

an appearance in any state or federal case in the United States.[99]

While recognizing the prohibition of disruptive deposition conduct, the Eighth Circuit vacated the trial court's unusual sanction, stating that the offending attorney was not given adequate notice of the unusual nature of the sanction the court was considering.[100] Further, the offending conduct occurred two years earlier without complaint from the opposing counsel or inquiry by the magistrate judge.[101] In its opinion, the court explained, sanctions should be imposed "within a time frame that has a nexus to the behavior sought to be deterred."[102] The court of appeals determined the following:

> [W]ithout deciding that there was sanctionable conduct here, defense counsel has already suffered inevitable financial and personal costs, and any additional sanction proceeding so long after the disputed conduct would not usefully serve the deterrent purpose of Rule 30(d)(2).

There is no dispute that disruptive and suggestive conduct by the defending counsel at depositions is prohibited. However, in order to prevent the practice, the rule of *Sec. Nat. Bank* requires you to call the conduct to the court's attention. If that conduct continues in violation of the court order, the *Sec. Nat. Bank*'s "out of the box" sanction is not necessarily prohibited if the offending attorney had adequate notice of the sanction being considered.

---

99. *Sec. Nat. Bank of Sioux City, Iowa v. Abbott Labs.*, 299 F.R.D. 595, 597 (N.D. Iowa 2014), rev'd on other grounds, 800 F.3d 936 (8th Cir. 2015).
100. *Sec. Nat. Bank of Sioux City, Iowa v. Abbott Labs.*, 2015 WL 5042248, *8 (8th Cir. 2015).
101. *Id.* at *6.
102. *Sec. Nat. Bank of Sioux City, Iowa v. Abbott Labs.*, 2015 800 F.3d 936 (8th Cir. 2015) (citing *Thomas v. Capital Sec. Servs., Inc.*, 836 F.2d 866, 881 (5th Cir. 1988)).

Technique: Documenting Deposition Obstruction

Once you have established a record of serious deposition obstruction in the face of polite professional requests to stop, you are now in a position to bring a motion to compel the discovery that was obstructed and for sanctions. The most persuasive opening paragraph of the brief in support of sanctions for deposition misconduct starts as follows:

> The Plaintiff, [name] requests Rule 37 sanctions for the deposition misconduct of the Defendant's counsel and an order compelling discovery. Throughout the deposition, the Defendant's counsel repeatedly engaged in disruptive and improper conduct in violation of the Rules of Civil Procedure, including the following:
>
> - 320 interjections
> - 31 instructions not to answer
> - 97 objections
> - 10 interjections based on the counsel's own failure to understand a question
>
> The Plaintiffs' counsel repeatedly asked the Defendants' counsel to please refrain from making speaking objections. The Defendants' counsel nonetheless continued to disrupt the deposition.
>
> In addition, the Defendant failed to properly prepare its Rule 30(b)(6) designee to respond to three of the seven matters of examination designated in the deposition notice and improperly limited

```
            the scope of the inquiry in violation of
            the rule of King v. Pratt & Whitney.
```

At this point in the brief, you can use the authority contained in this chapter to provide the legal support for the specific violations that occurred during the deposition. Attach to the memorandum each page where your opponent makes an obstructing comment, highlight every comment, and color-code the highlighting to correspond with the categories of impermissible conduct set forth in the opening paragraph of your brief. As the judge reads the transcript, your repeated, polite requests to refrain will be apparent. The highlighted pages will be more persuasive than any argument that you can make. You have revealed your opponent's obstructionist conduct. If it is truly obstructive, the court will not tolerate it.

Conclusion

The purpose of any deposition is to obtain and record the witness's clear, truthful answers to questions that address matters within the scope of discovery. Attorneys should both protect their clients' interests and maintain the judicial process's integrity. Certainly there are times, although technically inconsistent with the rules, when comments and actions of the attorneys participating in the deposition can be helpful to the expeditious completion of the discovery process. However, if you complain that the conduct is obstructing the deposition, your opponent must follow the rules.[103]

---

103. *See Cincinnati Ins. Co. v. Serrano*, 2012 WL 28071, at *6 (D. Kan. Jan. 5, 2012).

Summary

- Deposition obstruction is prohibited.
- Substantive objections are preserved.
- Objections at depositions are inappropriate unless the counsel is required to assert them at that time.
- Objections to form must be made to preserve the record.
- Excessive permissible objections can be sanctionable.
- Speaking objections are prohibited.
- All witness coaching is prohibited.
- There can never be an attorney–client conference between question and answer unless it is to preserve a privilege.
- Attorney–client conferences on breaks may constitute a waiver of privilege depending on the jurisdiction.
- Deposition obstruction is sanctionable.

14

Motions to Compel and Sanctions

Pursue one great decisive aim with force and determination.

—Carl von Clausewitz

Introduction. 339

Motion to Compel Facts 339

Motion to Exclude Different Testimony 339

Failure to Provide a Witness 340

Delay Tactics. 342

Appearance with Inadequate or
    Unprepared Testimony 343

Duty to Confer. 347

Expenses for Compelled Depositions 349

Failure to Comply with an Order
    for Disclosure: Subsequent Sanctions..........352
Summary......................................355

Introduction

Despite the undisputed duties to designate and prepare witnesses to respond to 30(b)(6) deposition notices, you will no doubt continue to have adversaries who provide unprepared witnesses or who refuse to participate in discovery. The rules and the case law give you the tools to compel answers regarding the information you are looking for and to call for sanctions for failing to comply. This chapter will provide you with the legal authority and techniques for building the best record when your adversary refuses to attend or provides a 30(b)(6) witness who is unprepared to answer the matters of examination you gave them.

Motion to Compel Facts

Rule 37 provides the procedure for compelling your opponents to disclose information and for locking down your opponents' positions when they refuse to give you information.[1] Rule 37(a)(3)(A) provides the following:

> **To Compel Disclosure.** If a party fails to make a disclosure required by Rule 26(a), any other party may move to compel disclosure and for appropriate sanctions.

Motion to Exclude Different Testimony

There are times when disclosure of additional information is the remedy you desire. However, if you are using the 30(b)(6) deposition to establish a party's *position*, then your goal is to ensure that your opponent does not change their position at a later date. In that case, Rule 37(c)(1) provides for the sanction that excludes contrary evidence that the opponent should have provided at the deposition.

---

1. Fed. R. Civ. P. 37.

If a party fails to provide information or identify a witness as required by Rule 26(a) or (e), the party is not allowed to use that information or witness to supply evidence on a motion, at a hearing, or at a trial, unless the failure was substantially justified or is harmless.[2]

Failure to Provide a Witness

There is no question that a responding party is required to provide a prepared witness. As discussed in chapter 10, "Duty to Attend," the responding party or its counsel does not have the authority to simply refuse to attend a deposition because it finds the 30(b)(6) deposition notice objectionable.[3] The responding party must either appear or bring a timely motion for protective order. If a responding party objects to the 30(b)(6) deposition, Rule 37 and the advisory committee comments make it clear that the objecting party must seek a protective order before the scheduled deposition.[4] Failing to move for a protective order *before* the deposition results in a waiver of any objections to the deposition.[5]

Failure to appear at the 30(b)(6) deposition is sanctionable under Rule 37(d)(1)(A)(i).[6]

---

2. Fed. R. Civ. P. 37(c)(1).
3. *See* chapter 10, "Duty to Attend."
4. Fed. R. Civ. P. 37 advisory committee's note, sub. (d) (1970 Amendment); *Ecclesiastes 9:10-11-12, Inc. v. LMC Holding Co.*, 497 F.3d 1135, 1147-48 (10th Cir. 2007).
5. *QBE Ins. Corp. v. Jorda Enterprises, Inc.*, 277 F.R.D. 676, 682 (S.D. Fla. 2012).
6. Fed. R. Civ. P. 37(d)(1)(A)(i); *see* Chapter 10, "Duty to Attend."

Motion; Grounds for Sanctions. The court where the action is pending may, on motion, order sanctions if:

> (i) a party or a party's officer, director, or managing agent—or a person designated under Rule 30(b)(6) or 31(a)(4)—fails, after being served with proper notice, to appear for that person's deposition[.][7]

Technique: Letter to Opponent about Refusing to Attend

If your opponent outright refuses to attend the deposition, make a communications record (email or correspondence) letting your opponent know that the deposition will proceed as scheduled, and then make a record of your opponent's non-attendance at the scheduled deposition. In that way, you are establishing a clear record that you made a reasonable effort to resolve the dispute. For example:

> Dear Tony,
>
> This follows our conversation of January 27 regarding the 30(b)(6) deposition scheduled for February 17. You have indicated that you object to the deposition and are refusing to attend. With all due respect, it is not the prerogative of counsel to determine whether to participate in discovery. Under Fed. R. Civ. P. 37(d)(2), your objection to the deposition is not a basis for refusing to designate a deponent. I want to work with you, under the framework of the Rules of Civil Procedure, to advance the discovery in an efficient fashion. However, I cannot agree to canceling a deposition simply because you object. It is my intention to be at the deposition as scheduled. At that time I will make a record of your witness's absence. It is my hope that you will reconsider your position. I look forward to seeing you on February 17. Thank you for your attention.
>
> Sincerely,
>
> Mark Kosieradzki

---

7. Fed. R. Civ. P. 37(d)(1)(A)(i).

Delay Tactics

Delay tactics are commonplace in litigation. Your opponent might claim that the counsel or the designated witness is unavailable to attend the deposition for months on end. Such delays place the requesting party at a tactical disadvantage. The court in *Hall v. Clifton Precision* recognized the following:

> Depositions serve another purpose as well: the memorialization, the freezing, of a witness's testimony at an early stage of the proceedings, before that witness's recollection of the events at issue either has faded or has been altered by intervening events, other discovery, or the helpful suggestions of lawyers.[8]

In order to eliminate potential allegations that you were uncooperative with establishing the date of the deposition, it is best to make a clear written record (through email or letter) stating that if there is a conflict with the date, a reasonable alternative date can be arranged. However, until an alternative date is agreed upon, the deposition will continue as scheduled.

Technique: Letter to Opponent about Deposition Schedule

Dear Tony,

This follows our conversation of January 27 regarding the 30(b)(6) deposition scheduled for February 17. You have indicated that you have a scheduling conflict with the deposition scheduled for February 17. I am of course willing to work with you to find an alternative date within a reasonable time frame. However, given the need to sequence the discovery, I cannot postpone this deposition more than 45 days. I can be available

---

8. *Hall v. Clifton Precision*, 150 F.R.D. 525, 528 (E.D. Pa. 1993).

on February 9, 10, 13, 16, 17, 18, 23, 25, or 27, or March 2, 3, 4, 5, 6, 10, 12, 16, or 17. Please let me know immediately which of those days works for you. However, until such time as we have an agreed on an alternative date, the 30(b)(6) deposition will remain as scheduled. I look forward to hearing from you soon.

Sincerely,

Mark Kosieradzki

By making multiple alternative dates available, it is clear that you are making professional accommodations. However, if the objecting counsel is claiming an unreasonable delay to participate in discovery, then it will be that attorney's obligation to explain to the court, during the motion for a protective order, why he or she accepted representation without having the time to work on the case. Rule 1.3 of the Model Rules of Professional Conduct states "a lawyer shall act with reasonable diligence and promptness in representing a client." The comments to this rule state, "A lawyer's work load must be controlled so that each matter can be handled competently."[9]

Appearance with Inadequate or Unprepared Testimony

As I explained in chapter 10, "Duty to Attend," the responding party must provide a fully prepared witness for testimony. Rule 37(a)(4) treats an incomplete answer as a failure to respond:

> **Evasive or Incomplete Disclosure, Answer, or Response.** For purposes of this subdivision (a), an evasive or incomplete disclosure, answer, or response must be treated as a failure to disclose, answer, or respond.[10]

---

9. Comment to *Model Rules of Professional Conduct* 1.3.
10. Fed. R. Civ. P. 37(a)(4); *See also Great Am. Ins. Co. v. Vegas Constr. Co.*, 251 F.R.D. 534, 543 (D. Nev. 2008); *Resolution Trust Corp. v. Southern Union*, 985

In *Great Am. Ins. Co. v. Vegas Constr. Co.*, the court explained that, when a designated witness for a Rule 30(b)(6) deposition fails to provide useful information, he "is no more present for deposition than would be a deponent who physically appears for the deposition but sleeps through it."[11]

> [If the designated witness] is not knowledgeable about relevant facts, and the principal has failed to designate an available, knowledgeable, and readily identifiable witness, then the appearance is, for all practical purposes, no appearance at all.[12]

The responding party must correct the failure by providing a properly prepared witness, without further motion practice.[13] This is known as the *duty to substitute*.[14] If the party refuses to substitute, then a motion to compel disclosure, using Rule 37(a)(1), and a motion for sanctions is necessary.[15] As in the case of refusal to appear, if it is clear that the party inadequately prepared its witness, then refusing to substitute is the same as refusing to appear, subject to sanctions under Rule 37(d)(1)(A)(i).[16]

F.2d 196, 197 (5th Cir. 1993).
11. *Great Am. Ins. Co. v. Vegas Constr. Co.*, 251 F.R.D. 534, 542 (D. Nev. 2008) (citing *Black Horse*, 228 F.3d 300, 304 (3d Cir. 2000)).
12. *Great Am. Ins. Co. v. Vegas Constr. Co.*, 251 F.R.D. 534, 542 (D. Nev. 2008) (citing *Resolution Trust Corp. v. Southern Union Co., Inc.*, 985 F.2d 196, 197 (5th Cir. 1993)).
13. *Buycks-Roberson v. Citibank Federal Sav. Bank*, 162 F.R.D. 338, 343 (1995); In *Resolution Trust Corp. v. S. Union Co.*, 985 F.2d 196, 197 (5th Cir. 1993).
14. *See* chapter 10, "Duty to Attend."
15. *Peshlakai v. Ruiz*, 2014 WL 459650 (D. N.M. Jan. 9, 2014) (reprimanding a plaintiff for merely serving another notice rather than filing a motion to compel).
16. Fed. R. Civ. P. 37(d)(1)(A)(i); *see* chapter 10, "Duty to Attend."

Technique: Building a Record of an Unprepared Witness

The key to successful motion practice is having a solid record for the court. Therefore, the record should clearly establish that the witness is unprepared to respond to the matter of inquiry set forth in the 30(b)(6) notice of deposition.

Q: Let's move on to Matter of Inquiry #7 contained in Exhibit 5, Notice of 30(b)(6) Deposition: the policies and procedures for ensuring that residents at St. Sebastian Nursing Home received all prescribed medications in accordance with physician orders. Do you see that in Exhibit 5?

A: Yes.

Q: Please share with all of us the policies and procedures for ensuring that residents at St. Sebastian Nursing Home received all prescribed medications in accordance with physician orders.

A: I can tell you how I do it.

Q: What did St. Sebastian Nursing Home do to prepare you to provide all information, known or reasonably available to St. Sebastian Nursing Home, regarding the policies and procedures for ensuring that residents at St. Sebastian Nursing Home received all prescribed medications in accordance with physician orders?

A: I can only tell you what I know.

Q: Was anything done to provide you with all information, known or reasonably available to St. Sebastian Nursing Home, regarding the policies and procedures for ensuring that residents at St. Sebastian Nursing Home received all prescribed medications in accordance with physician orders?

A: No.

Q: Are there other people at St. Sebastian Nursing Home that have information regarding the policies and procedures for ensuring that residents at St. Sebastian Nursing Home received all prescribed medications in accordance with physician orders?

A: Yes.

Q: Have you spoken with them?

A: No.

Q: Has anyone spoken with them?

A: I don't know.

Q: Has anyone shared with you what policies and procedures are used?

A: No.

Q: Do you have information, one way or the other, as to whether everyone uses the same procedure you use?

A: I don't know.

Q: Is there a policy or procedure at St. Sebastian Nursing Home for ensuring the accurate delivery of prescribed medications consistent with physician orders?

A: I'm sure there is.

Q: What is it?

A: I'm not sure.

Q: Who would know?

A: The Director of Nursing, Sally DeCartes.

Mr. Kosieradzki: At this time we are requesting that St. Sebastian Nursing Home substitute a witness to provide the complete answer to Matter of Inquiry #7: the policies and procedures for ensuring that residents at St. Sebastian Nursing Home received all prescribed medications in accordance with physician orders.

It is important to note that the request was to substitute a *separate witness*, as opposed to a demand for testimony from Sally DeCartes. Although Sally DeCartes is a logical source for the information, in a 30(b)(6) deposition, the responding party has the exclusive right to choose who the witness will be.[17] The responding organization can either substitute a witness of its choosing or be faced with

---

17. *See* chapter 3, "Details of Rule 30(b)(6)."

a motion to compel, with possible sanctions, because the designated witness is not prepared to provide all information known or reasonably available to St. Sebastian Nursing Home. Whereas, if you request Sally DeCartes specifically, you will be taking her deposition as an individual under Rule 30(b)(1), not the organization's deposition under 30(b)(6). If Ms. DeCartes has not prepared for a 30(b)(1), there is no consequence to the organization if she cannot provide the requested information.

Duty to Confer

Rule 37 requires parties to make a good-faith effort to resolve discovery disputes before pursuing a motion to compel. Rule 37(a)(1) provides the following:

> **Motion for an Order Compelling Disclosure or Discovery.** On notice to other parties and all affected persons, a party may move for an order compelling disclosure or discovery. The motion must include a certification that the movant has in good faith conferred or attempted to confer with the person or party failing to make disclosure or discovery in an effort to obtain it without court action.[18]

Under Rule 37(a)(1), the party seeking a motion to compel is required to first voice its discovery concerns explicitly to the opposing counsel to attempt to resolve the dispute.[19] If parties cannot resolve the dispute, the party seeking the motion to compel must certify that both parties were unable to resolve the dispute, despite a good-faith effort to do so.

When professionals work together within the Rules of Civil Procedure and the case law interpreting those rules, they can resolve

---

18. Fed. R. Civ. P. 37(a)(1).
19. *Id.*

most discovery disputes. Sometimes disputes require a judge to interpret the rules or the request; however, those instances should be few and far between. Unfortunately, some litigators continue to delay, obstruct, or use spurious objections as a weapon to pressure their adversaries into trading away legitimate requests for discovery in order to avoid the necessity of a motion. Although such conduct is prohibited, it does exist.

Technique: Ask Your Opponent to Provide Legal Authority

Regardless of whether the discovery conference is with the professional or the unscrupulous lawyer, the best practice is to keep a record of all communications to ensure there is no misunderstanding of any conversations that occurred. Those emails or letters should accurately represent what occurred and focus any dispute on legitimate legal issues. When trying to resolve the dispute, always request that your adversaries provide the legal authority for their positions. If your adversary provides authority for the first time in the motion papers or hearing, the documented request is evidence that the attorney did not act in good faith during the meet-and-confer conferences.

> Dear Tony,
>
> Thank you for taking the time to talk to me this afternoon about our concerns to your objections to our Rule 30(b)(2), Rule 30(b)(6), and Rule 34 document deposition. I was pleased that we were able resolve seven of our eight disagreements. You continue to object to the production of the human resources files of your client's discharged employees, Dominique Cantrell and Sally Lou Fabio. I directed you to the case of *Cardenas v. The Prudential Insurance Company*, 2003 WL 244640, at 2 (D. Minn.), wherein the court ordered the disclosure of the personnel files. These files are relevant because they may contain work history, evaluations, disciplinary actions, incident investigations, intra-company disputes, staffing complaints, applications, resignation letters, licensing information, and continuing education classes, among other documents that may lead to information

regarding the conduct of the employees who were responsible for the care at this nursing home. If you have any contrary authority that you plan to provide to the court, please provide that authority to me at this time so we can continue to work at resolving this issue. If you do not have any legal authority, please confirm the basis of your objection. Thank you for your attention.

Sincerely,

Mark Kosieradzki

Expenses for Compelled Depositions

If the court grants your motion to compel, Rule 37(a)(5)(A) requires an order for payment of expenses and attorney fees, from either the disobedient party, its counsel, or both, incurred as a result of the failure to comply with the 30(b))(6), unless the failure to comply is justified or the award would be unjust.[20] The rule provides the following:

> The court must, after giving an opportunity to be heard, require the party . . . whose conduct necessitated the motion, the party or attorney advising that conduct, or both to pay the movant's reasonable expenses incurred in making the motion, including attorney's fees.[21]
>
> i) Unless the movant did not confer in good faith prior;
>
> ii) Unless the opposing party's refusal to permit discovery was justified;

---

20. Fed. R. Civ. P. 37(b)(2)(C).
21. Fed. R. Civ. P. 37(a)(5)(A).

iii) Unless circumstances make the award unjust.[22]

Rule 37(a)(5)(A) presumes that the disobedient party will pay the expenses of the motion. However, the Rule also provides that the disobedient party can avoid expenses if it shows that its failure to comply was justified or that special circumstances make an award of expenses unjust.[23]

Technique: Expenses and Fees

When the requesting party seeks an award of fees and expenses, the court will evaluate if the responding party's failure to provide a fully prepared witness was justified. Was it a mistake or an intentional obstruction? Was there a *colorable* legal argument—it at least has some basis? In order to provide the court with a record on which to base its decision, the 30(b)(6) witness can resolve these questions. If a witness is not prepared, then the responding party's failure to prepare them is sanctionable conduct. However, you need a record to prove this. You need the 30(b)(6) witness to show they could have been prepared but they weren't.

Q: What has St. Sebastian Nursing Home done to gather all the knowledge, known or reasonably available to St. Sebastian Nursing Home, with respect to medication distribution procedures?

Q: How was that information conveyed to you?

Q: What was your role in gathering all the knowledge, known or reasonably available to St. Sebastian Nursing Home, with respect to medication distribution procedures?

Q: What is your experience working with medication distribution procedures?

Q: Who are all the people with knowledge of the medication distribution procedures?

Q: Did you talk to them?

Q: Did anyone talk to them?

---

22. Fed. R. Civ. P. 37(a)(5)(A)(i–iii).
23. Fed. R. Civ. P. 37 advisory committee's note (1970 Amendment).

If the answer was no, ask:

Q: Why not?

Q: Who were all the people involved in gathering the information regarding medication distribution procedures?

Q: Are there documents that contain information regarding medication distribution procedures?

Q: Did anyone look at those documents?

If the answer was no, ask:

Q: Why not?

Q: What has St. Sebastian Nursing Home done to make sure you have all the knowledge, known or reasonably available to St. Sebastian Nursing Home, with respect to the medication distribution procedures?

Q: How much time did you spend preparing to respond to the medication distribution procedures?

If the court finds witness is unprepared and the responding party expended little or no effort preparing the witness on the matter of examination, then the responding party cannot argue that its failure was substantially justified. In that situation, file the fee petition for the motion to compel as soon as possible after the court grants grants the motion to compel.[24]

If there is an order compelling additional discovery, the court, as a part of the sanction, may order that the costs for the subsequent deposition be shifted to the party whose conduct made the motion to compel necessary, and that the time and location be made convenient to the party that had to make the motion.

---

24. *Carolina Cas. Ins. Co. v. Elliott*, 2010 WL 5089988 (E.D. Wisc. Dec. 7, 2010).

Failure to Comply with an Order for Disclosure: Subsequent Sanctions

Once the court has granted a motion to compel disclosure of information, the court will sanction any further failure to meet the requirements of the rules more severely. In discussing the trial court's discretion to issue sanctions, the United States Supreme Court noted that "[a] primary aspect of that discretion is the ability to fashion an appropriate sanction for conduct which abuses the judicial process."[25] Rule 37(b)(2)(A) specifically calls for severe sanctions for a party's failure to comply with a court order that required 30(b)(6) testimony:

> *If a party or a party's officer, director, or managing agent—or a witness designated under Rule 30(b)(6) or 31(a)(4)—fails to obey an order to provide or permit discovery, including an order under Rule 26(f), 35, or 37(a), the court where the action is pending may issue further just orders.*[26]

Those sanctions may include the following:

- Adverse inferences
- Prohibiting claims or defenses
- Striking pleadings
- Staying proceedings until obeyed
- Dismissing the action
- Default judgment
- Contempt of court[27]

---

25. *Chambers v. NASCO, Inc.*, 501 U.S. 32, 44–45, 111 S. Ct. 2123, 2133, 115 L. Ed. 2d 27 (1991).
26. Fed. R. Civ. P. 37(b)(2)(A), (emphasis added).
27. Fed. R. Civ. P. 37(b)(2)(A)(i–vii).

Depending on the stage of the litigation and on how egregious the responding party's position is, the sanctions can range from requiring a simple witness substitution to imposing costs to ending the litigation.

In addition to excluding evidence, the court may also award monetary sanctions. Failing to adequately prepare a witness for a 30(b)(6) deposition has been found to be sanctionable conduct for the attorney, as well as for the organization.[28] The court can impose monetary sanctions pursuant to Federal Rule of Civil Procedure 37(b)(2)(C) and 28 U.S.C. § 1927.[29] Title 28 U.S.C. § 1927 permits sanctions when an attorney's conduct, "viewed objectively, manifests either intentional or reckless disregard of the attorney's duties to the court."[30] The court can also sanction an attorney for a client's continued noncompliance with discovery. In *Aviva Sports, Inc. v. Fingerhut Direct Marketing, Inc.*, the court said the counsel could not stick its head in the sand and cower behind a client's disobedient conduct.[31]

Courts have also determined that selective preparation is sanctionable conduct. In *Sciarretta v. Lincoln Nat. Ins. Co.*, the court

---

28. *See Aviva Sports, Inc., v. Fingerhut Direct Marketing, Inc.*, 2013 WL 3833065, at *6 (D. Minn. July 23, 2013) ("[The attorney] shall be jointly and severally liable for Aviva's reasonable costs and attorneys' fees incurred in connection with the failed depositions and in bringing the motion for sanctions."); *see also Lee v. First Lenders Ins. Servs., Inc.*, 236 F.3d 443, 445 (8th Cir. 2001); *Malautea v. Suzuki Motor Co., Ltd.*, 987 F.2d 1536, 1544 (11th Cir. 1993) ("[§ 1927] allows district courts to assess attorney's fees against litigants, counsel, and law firms who willfully abuse the judicial process by conduct tantamount to bad faith.").
29. *Aviva Sports, Inc., v. Fingerhut Direct Marketing, Inc.*, 2013 WL 3833065 at *6 (D. Minn. July 23, 2013).
30. *Clark v. United Parcel Serv., Inc.*, 460 F.3d 1004, 1011 (8th Cir. 2006) (quoting *Tenkku v. Normandy Bank*, 348 F.3d 737, 743 (8th Cir. 2003).
31. *Aviva Sports, Inc. v. Fingerhut Direct Marketing, Inc.*, 2013 WL 3833065 at *6 (D. Minn. July 23, 2013); *see Devaney v. Cont'l Am. Ins. Co.*, 989 F.2d 1154, 1161–62 (11th Cir. 1993) (explaining that Rule 37 does not require that in order for sanctions to be imposed upon the attorney, the attorney must have instigated the relevant misconduct).

found that preparing a witness with only a self-serving half of the story was an act of bad faith.[32] In *Sciarretta*, the court sanctioned the responding organization $850,000 for failing to properly prepare its 30(b)(6) witness.[33]

Sanctions play a critical role in maintaining the integrity of our judicial system. The United States Supreme Court, recognizing the importance of compliance with the rules, stated the following:

> [S]anctions must be applied diligently both "to penalize those whose conduct may be deemed to warrant such a sanction, [and] to deter those who might be tempted to such conduct in the absence of such a deterrent."[34]

Recognizing the importance of compliance with the federal rules, the court in *Pioneer Drive LLC v. Nissan Diesel America, Inc.*, ordered the defendant to serve and file the following with the court:

> [A] statement providing (a) who it designated for each matter listed in the Notice, and (b) that each designee is capable of testifying on behalf of the Defendant and that failure to do so will be treated as contempt of court. The statement must be (c) signed by each designee and Defendant's counsel and indicate that they understand what is expected of them as evidenced in the 30(b)(6) Notice and this Order.[35]

---

32. *Sciarretta v. Lincoln Nat. Life Ins. Co.*, 778 F.3d 1205, 1213 (11th Cir. 2015).
33. *Sciarretta v. Lincoln Nat. Life Ins. Co.*, 778 F.3d 1205, 1213-14 (11th Cir. 2015).
34. *Comiskey v. JFTJ Corp.*, 989 F.2d 1007, 1012 (8th Cir. 1993) (citing *National Hockey League v. Metropolitan Hockey Club*, 427 U.S. 639, 643, 96 S.Ct. 2778, 2781, 49 L.Ed.2d 747 (1976)).
35. *Pioneer Drive LLC v. Nissan Diesel America, Inc.*, 262 F.R.D. 552, 561 (D. Mt. 2009).

The *Pioneer Drive* court warned that the defendant's failure to comply with the court's order would not be tolerated:

> Failure to provide knowledgeable designees who can answer on behalf of Defendant shall be treated as contempt of court pursuant to Fed. R. Civ. P. 37(b), and in such a circumstance Defendant's designee(s) and counsel may be jailed until the matters are testified to properly.[36]

Summary

- The responding party cannot refuse to designate a 30(b)(6) deponent.

- The responding party waives objections if it does not file for a protective order before the deposition date.

- The responding party's failure to appear at a deposition is sanctionable.

- An unprepared witness is the same as an absent witness.

- The court must award expenses to the requesting party in a motion to compel unless the responding party's position was justifiable.

- The responding party's failure to comply with an order to provide 30(b)(6) testimony could result in litigation-ending sanctions.

- Attorneys can be assessed monetary sanctions for their client's misconduct.

---

36. *Pioneer Drive LLC v. Nissan Diesel America, Inc.*, 262 F.R.D. 552, 560–561 (D. Mt. 2009).

15

Binding Effect

If you want a happy ending, that depends, of course, on where you stop your story.

—Orson Welles

Introduction 359
The Witness Does Not Have Information 363
    Unprepared Witnesses 364
    Unavailable Information: Natural Binding Effect 365
    Good-Faith Discovery of New Information 366
Summary 370

Introduction

An organization appears vicariously through its 30(b)(6) witness.[1] Courts have well established that the 30(b)(6) witness's testimony will bind the organization. What that means is not as clear. This chapter will explain the evolving history of the *binding-effect* doctrine. This includes the differing judicial interpretations and the underlying policies, which will help you build a record to maximize your ability to hold the organization to its testimony.

At the outset, understand that the rule itself is silent as to whether the testimony is binding. Rather, the doctrine of binding effect arose from judicial interpretations of Rule 30(b)(6). In *Marker v. Union Fidelity Life Ins.*, the court stated the following:

> The corporation then must not only produce such number of persons as will satisfy the request, but more importantly, prepare them so that they may give complete, knowledgeable, and *binding* answers on behalf of the corporation.[2]

However, some courts pushed back, holding that the Rule 30(b)(6) witness's testimony was not tantamount to a *judicial admission*. *Judicial admission* means that the judge has admitted the evidence for this case and that the admission can't be changed.[3]

---

1. *United States v. Taylor*, 166 F.R.D. 356, 361 (M.D.N.C. 1996) (citing *Resolution Trust Corp. v. Southern Union Co.*, 985 F.2d 196, 197 (5th Cir. 1993)).
2. *Marker v. Union Fidelity Life Ins.*, 125 F. R. D. 121, 126 (M.D.N.C. 1989) (emphasis added).
3. *State Farm Mut. Auto. Ins. Co. v. Worthington*, 405 F.2d 683, 686 (8th Cir. 1968) citing Wigmore, *Evidence* § 2588 (3rd ed. 1940). ("[C]ases hold that judicial admissions are binding for the purpose of the case in which the admissions are made including appeals. This does not make the same judicial admissions conclusive and binding in separate and subsequent cases. The purpose of a judicial admission is that it acts as a substitute for evidence in that it does away with the need for evidence in regard to the subject matter of the judicial admission.")

Rather, just as in the deposition of individuals, the testimony was only a statement of the corporate person, which, if altered, could be explained and explored through cross-examination.[4]

As time went on, it became apparent that such an interpretation of the rule was squarely at odds with the underlying policy of preparation and disclosure that led to the creation of Rule 30(b)(6). Under these early interpretations, responding parties would simply not provide information during the 30(b)(6) depositions and later attempt to add or change testimony.

In *Rainey v. American Forest and Paper Ass'n, Inc.*, the court recognized the evasive game that lawyers were playing. *Rainey* held that the objectives of preparation and information disclosure contained in the Advisory Committee comments to Rule 30(b)(6) were to guide the operation of Rule 30(b)(6):

> Foremost among those purposes, according to the Advisory Committee notes, is to curb the "bandying" by which officers or managing agents of a corporation are deposed in turn but each disclaims knowledge of facts that are clearly known to persons in the organization and thereby to it.[5]

Rainey reiterated the long-established policy that the "rule aims to prevent a corporate defendant from thwarting inquiries during discovery, then staging an ambush during a later phase of the case."[6]

---

4. *United States v. Taylor*, 166 F.R.D. 356, 362–63, n. 6 (M.D.N.C. 1996) (citing *W.R. Grace & Co. v. Viskase Corporation*, No. 90C5383, 1991 WL 211647 (N.D. Ill. Oct. 15, 1991)).
5. *Rainey v. American Forest and Paper Ass'n, Inc.*, 26 F. Supp.2d 82, 95 (D.C. 1998).
6. *Rainey v. American Forest and Paper Ass'n, Inc.*, 26 F. Supp.2d 82, 95 (D.C. 1998) (citing *Ierardi v. Lorillard, Inc.*, 1991 WL 158911, at *3 (E.D. Pa. Aug. 13, 1991)).

The court in *United States v. Taylor* said it would be unfair to allow the "sandbagging" of an opponent by allowing an organization to conduct "a half-hearted inquiry before the deposition but a thorough and vigorous one before the trial."[7] Under *Rainey*, while the testimony is not a judicial admission, the responding organization cannot alter its testimony without establishing that the information was not available at the time of deposition.[8]

In practice, application of the binding-effect rule arises when:

1. A witness does not have the information to respond appropriately to the matters of examination at the time of the deposition.

2. The organization attempts to change its witness's testimony after the deposition.[9]

Because 30(b)(6) witness testimony is not a judicial admission, courts have taken differing approaches in dealing with changing testimony. Under the *Taylor* line of cases, the organization is subject to impeachment.[10] By contrast, under the *Rainey* line of cases, while the testimony is not a judicial admission, an organization cannot alter it unless the organization establishes that it didn't have the information at the time of deposition.[11]

Technique: Convert Positions to Requests for Admission

If you want to flesh out whether your adversary is going to try to change their testimony, you can convert the responding party's ultimate positions and factual assertions that they made during

---

7. *United States v. Taylor*, 166 F.R.D. 356, 362 (M.D.N.C. 1996).
8. *Rainey*, 26 F. Supp.2d at 95.
9. *See* chapter 16, "Changing the Testimony."
10. *United States v. Taylor*, 166 F.R.D. 356, 361 (M.D.N.C. 1996).
11. *Rainey v. American Forest and Paper Ass'n, Inc.*, 26 F. Supp. 2d 82, 95 (D.D.C. 1998).

the 30(b)(6) testimony to requests for admissions using Rule 36. This rule provides the following:

> A party may serve on any other party a written request to admit, for purposes of the pending action only, the truth of any matters within the scope of Rule 26(b)(1) relating to: (A) facts, the application of law to fact, or opinions about either.[12]

If the responding party does not unconditionally admit those facts and positions, you can make a motion to determine the sufficiency of the answers under Rule 36(a)(6). The rule states the following:[13]

> **Motion Regarding the Sufficiency of an Answer or Objection.** The requesting party may move to determine the sufficiency of an answer or objection. Unless the court finds an objection justified, it must order that an answer be served. On finding that an answer does not comply with this rule, the court may order either that the matter is admitted or that an amended answer be served.[14]

If the responding party does not admit its facts and positions unconditionally, it will have to justify its position to the court and explain why the information it provided at the 30(b)(6) deposition was not accurate or was incomplete. If the responding party cannot justify its failure to admit the information provided in the 30(b)(6) deposition, it can be subject to sanctions under Rule 37(c)(2). This rule provides the following:

> **Failure to Admit.** If a party fails to admit what is requested under Rule 36 and if the requesting party later proves a document to be genuine or the matter true, the requesting party may move that the party who failed to admit pay the reasonable expenses, including attorney's fees, incurred in making that proof.[15]

---

12. Fed. R. Civ. P. 36(a)(1).
13. Fed. R. Civ. P. 36(a)(6).
14. Fed. R. Civ. P. 36(a)(6).
15. Fed. R. Civ. P. 37(c)(2).

> If the responding party does justify its failure to admit, it will simultaneously have to explain why it didn't provide accurate answers in the 30(b)(6) deposition. As I discussed in chapter 14, "Motions to Compel and Sanctions," the organization is subject to sanctions under Rule 37(a)(4), for failing to provide complete answers.[16]

The Witness Does Not Have Information

In *QBE Ins. Corp. v. Jorda Enterprises, Inc.*, the court squarely addressed the consequences of failing to provide information when responding to a 30(b)(6) deposition notice.[17] *QBE* discussed the difference between *unavailable information* and an *unprepared witness*. If the deponent provides an ambiguous answer or says, "I don't know," to questions on topics that were clearly spelled out in the deposition notice, then the witness is either unprepared or the information is unavailable to the organization. In either case, unless the responding party legitimately did not have the information, the responding party should not be able to offer an answer at trial that it was not able to provide at the deposition.[18] If the organization does not have knowledge on a topic, it is bound to that lack of information.[19] If the organization had access to the information, it is not fair to allow the organization to effectively change its answer by introducing new evidence before the court later.[20]

---

16. Fed. R. Civ. P. 37(a)(4).
17. *QBE Ins. Corp. v. Jorda Enterprises, Inc.*, 277 F.R.D. 676 (S.D. Fla. 2012).
18. *Id.* at 681; *see also*, *United States v. Taylor*, 166 F.R.D. 356, 362 (M.D. N.C. 1996).
19. *QBE Ins. Corp. v. Jorda Enterprises, Inc.*, 277 F.R.D. 676, 685 (S.D. Fla. 2012).
20. *Ierardi v. Lorillard, Inc.*, 1991 WL 158911, at *3 (E.D. Pa. 1991).

Example: ACME Trucking Co.

In our ACME Trucking case, you gave ACME Trucking a 30(b)(6) notice asking the company to be prepared to answer questions about the maintenance history on a particular truck and about ACME's maintenance policies in general. At the 30(b)(6) deposition, the designated witness repeatedly stated that he did not have any maintenance documentation on the particular truck and that the documents had been lost in a computer malfunction. This testimony at a 30(b)(6) deposition binds ACME Trucking to that answer: the maintenance records are lost. ACME Trucking cannot later introduce maintenance records for this truck at trial except if they can show that it was impossible to access the information at the time of the deposition. If they do this, they have to explain why it was impossible to access. If they can't explain why, then they are bound by their earlier testimony and can't introduce the evidence.

Unprepared Witnesses

If the 30(b)(6) notice clearly identifies the matters the organization must prepare for and the organization fails to prepare its witness, the integrity of the judicial process demands that the organization *not* be allowed to circumvent the rule and provide information at a later date. A party's failure to prepare for the 30(b)(6) deposition is sanctionable under Rule 37(d)(1)(A).[21] The organization's lack of preparation constitutes nonappearance under the rules, which the court can sanction.[22]

---

21. Fed. R. Civ. P. 37 (d)(1)(A) Failure to Attend Deposition, Serve Answers to Interrogatories, or Respond to a Request for Document Inspection. The entity's lack of preparation constitutes nonappearance under the rules. Fed. R. Civ. P. 37 advisory committee's note, sub. (d) (1970 Amendment); *Resolution Trust Corp. v. Southern Union Co.*, 985 F.2d 196, 197 (5th Cir. 1993); *Great Am. Ins. Co. v. Vegas Constr. Co.*, 251 F.R.D. 534, 542 (D. Nev. 2008); *Buycks-Roberson v. Citibank Federal Sav. Bank*, 162 F.R.D. 338, 343 (N.D. Ill. 1995); *Dravo Corp. v. Liberty Mut. Ins. Co.*, 164 F.R.D. 70, 75 (D. Neb. 1995).
22. Fed. R. Civ. P. 37 (d)(1)(A) Failure to Attend Deposition, Serve Answers to Interrogatories, or Respond to a Request for Document Inspection. Fed. R. Civ. P. 37 advisory committee's note, sub. (d) (1970 Amendment); *Resolution Trust*

One sanction is excluding the evidence.[23] Thus, a motion for sanctions can affirmatively bind entities and prevent your adversaries from changing their stories. This result is based on the principle that a party "cannot meet its discovery obligations by sticking its head in the sand and refusing to look for the answer and then saying it does not know the answer."[24] The conclusion that a lack-of-knowledge response at the 30(b)(6) deposition binds the corporation at trial is, for all practical purposes, a variation on the rule and philosophy against trial by ambush.[25]

Unavailable Information: Natural Binding Effect

When the organization does not have knowledge on a topic, it is bound to that lack of information.[26] The rule 30(b)(6) imposes a duty to provide testimony on matters known or reasonably available to the corporation.[27] The organization has:

> a duty to make a conscientious, good-faith effort to designate knowledgeable persons for Rule 30(b)(6) depositions and to prepare them to fully and non-evasively answer questions about the designated subject matter.[28]

Corp. v. Southern Union Co., 985 F.2d 196, 197 (5th Cir. 1993); *Great Am. Ins. Co. v. Vegas Constr. Co.*, 251 F.R.D. 534, 542 (D. Nev. 2008); *Buycks-Roberson v. Citibank Federal Sav. Bank*, 162 F.R.D. 338, 343 (N.D. Ill. 1995);
23. Fed. R. Civ. P. 37(b)(2)(A)(i–vii).
24. *In re Ind. Serv. Orgs. Antitrust Litig.*, 168 F.R.D. 651, 653 (D. Kan. 1996).
25. *Calzaturficio S.C.A.R.P.A. s.p.a. v. Fabiano Shoe Co., Inc.*, 201 F.R.D. 33, 38 (D. Mass. 2001).
26. *QBE Ins. Corp. v. Jorda Enterprises, Inc.*, 277 F.R.D. 676, 681 (S.D. Fla. 2012).
27. *See* chapter 11, "Duty to Prepare."
28. Fed. R. Civ. P. 30(b)(6); *Great Am. Ins. Co.*, 251 F.R.D. 534, 539 (D. Nev. 2008) (citing *Starlight International, Inc. v. Herlihy*, 186 F.R.D. 626, 639 (D. Kan. 1999); *Dravo Corp. v. Liberty Mut. Ins. Co.*, 164 F.R.D. 70, 75 (D. Neb. 1995); *In re: Vitamins Antitrust Litigation*, 216 F.R.D. 168, 172 (D. D.C. 2003); *see also Mitsui & Co. (U.S.A.) v. Puerto Rico Water Res. Auth.*, 93 F.R.D. 62, 67 (D.P.R. 1981).

If the organization conducts a complete and diligent search to prepare for the 30(b)(6) deposition and is unable to find the information, then its obligation to prepare is complete.[29] However, the natural consequence for not providing information at the deposition is to prevent offering the unanswered questions from the deposition as evidence at trial.[30]

Good-Faith Discovery of New Information

Fairness dictates that the organization *should* be able to amend its position with additional testimony when it genuinely finds new information in the discovery process, *and* when it didn't know the information at the time of the 30(b)(6) deposition.[31] In those cases, the responding party seeking to offer the information has to explain why it didn't know this information earlier or why the information was unavailable.[32] Unless the organization can prove that it didn't know the information earlier or that the information was inaccessible, an organization cannot later give new or different allegations that it could have made at the time of the 30(b)(6) deposition.[33] This approach maintains the integrity of the judicial process by giving the rule a meaningful effect and simultaneously allowing the organization acting in good faith to offer evidence that is disclosed responsibly.

---

29. *QBE Ins. Corp. v. Jorda Enterprises, Inc.*, 277 F.R.D. 676, 696 (S.D. Fla. 2012).
30. *Id.* at 676, 681.
31. *Rainey v. American Forest & Paper Ass'n., Inc.*, 26 F. Supp.2d 82, 94 (D.D.C. 1998).
32. *Id.* at 82, 95.
33. *Id.* at 82, 94 (citing *Ierardi v. Lorillard, Inc.*, 1991 WL 158911, at *3 (E.D. Pa. Aug.13, 1991); *United States v. Taylor*, 166 F.R.D. 356, 361 (M.D.N.C. 1996), aff'd *United States v. Taylor*, 166 F.R.D. 367 (M.D.N.C. 1996)).

Technique: New Evidence

In attempting to evade the responsibilities of 30(b)(6), responding parties will commonly "discover" new evidence or witnesses after the 30(b)(6) deposition. You will undoubtedly engage in a dispute as to whether or not the responding party had the evidence available at the time of the deposition. You need to make a record of how the responding party prepared its information, so the court can evaluate whether the responding party had the evidence at the time of the deposition. If the responding party had the opportunity to gather the information and failed to do so, the court should bar the responding party's changed position. Establishing the lack of preparation is a three-step process:

1. Identify all sources of information, including witnesses, documents, and electronically stored evidence.

2. Prove the organization's ability to contact the witnesses and review the documents and electronically stored evidence.

3. Demonstrate the organization's failure to investigate and adequately prepare for the testimony.

Questions about Search for Evidence

Following are some sample questions you can use to identify how an organization prepared (or didn't prepare) for a 30(b)(6) deposition.

Q: Are you aware that the testimony you provide today must represent all information, known or reasonably available to ACME Trucking Co., with respect to the matters of examination listed in the 30(b)(6) deposition notice that is Exhibit #____?

Q: What are all of the sources of information reasonably available to ACME Trucking Co. with respect to the matters of examination listed in the 30(b)(6) deposition notice that is Exhibit #____?

Q: Who are the persons who have information with respect to the matters of examination listed in the 30(b)(6) deposition notice that is Exhibit #____?

Q: Anyone else?

Q: Who else?

Q: Is that everyone?

Q: Did you, or anyone from ACME Trucking Co., talk to them about the matters of examination listed in the 30(b)(6) deposition notice that is Exhibit #____?

If the answer was no, ask:

Q: Why not?

If the answer was yes, ask:

Q: What did they tell you?

Q: Has every person within ACME Trucking Co., in regard to the matters of examination listed in the 30(b)(6) deposition notice that is Exhibit #____, been contacted to gather that information?

Q: Is there anyone outside of ACME Trucking Co. who could have information with respect to the matters of examination listed in the 30(b)(6) deposition notice that is Exhibit #____?

Q: Who?

Q: Anyone else?

Q: Who else?

Q: Is that everyone?

Q: Did you, or anyone from ACME Trucking Co., talk to them about the matters of examination listed in the 30(b)(6) deposition notice that is Exhibit #____?

If the answer was no, ask:

Q: Why not?

If the answer was yes, ask:

Q: What did they tell you?

Q: Is there anyone else, anywhere in the world, who could have information to respond to the matters of examination listed in the 30(b)(6) deposition notice that is Exhibit #____?

Binding Effect 369

Q: Did you, or anyone from ACME Trucking Co., talk to them about the matters of examination listed in the 30(b)(6) deposition notice that is Exhibit #____?

If the answer was no, ask:

Q: Why not?

If the answer was yes, ask:

Q: What did they tell you?

Q: Have all people who could have information to respond to the matters of examination listed in the 30(b)(6) deposition notice that is Exhibit #____ been interviewed to gather available information?

If the answer was no, ask:

Q: Why not?

Q: What are all the documents that could have information to respond to the matters of examination listed in the 30(b)(6) deposition notice that is Exhibit #____?

Q: Are there any others?

Q: What others?

Q: Have you listed all the documents that could have information to respond to the matters of examination listed in the 30(b)(6) deposition notice that is Exhibit #____?

Q: Are there any other documents outside of ACME Trucking Co. that could have information to respond to the matters of examination listed in the 30(b)(6) deposition notice that is Exhibit #____?

Q: Have all documents that could have information to respond to the matters of examination listed in the 30(b)(6) deposition notice that is Exhibit #____ been gathered and reviewed to provide us with all available information?

Q: Who conducted that search?

Q: Has ACME Trucking Co. gathered and reviewed all sources of electronically stored information that could have information to respond to the matters of examination listed in the 30(b)(6) deposition notice that is Exhibit #____?

Q: Who conducted that search?

Q: Has everything possible been done to investigate and gather all information, known and reasonably available to ACME Trucking Co., to respond fully and completely to the matters of examination listed in the 30(b)(6) deposition notice that is Exhibit #____?

Q: To ensure that the court and jury have all the information to respond to the matters of examination listed in the 30(b)(6) deposition notice that is Exhibit #____, what else could have been done to gather information?

Q: Has everything possible been done to gather all information, known or reasonably available to ACME Trucking Co., to respond fully and completely to the matters of examination listed in the 30(b)(6) deposition notice that is Exhibit #____?

With a detailed record of the preparation process, you can either establish that there was no additional information available or that the witness was unprepared.

Summary

- Rule 30(b)(6) testimony binds the designating organization.
- Rule 30(b)(6) testimony is considered an evidentiary admission.
- Failure to prepare for a Rule 30(b)(6) deposition can result in the court excluding responsive evidence.
- Attorneys may be subject to monetary sanctions for failure to prepare their clients for the 30(b)(6) deposition.
- If a party cannot provide responsive evidence at the deposition, then the court can exclude any evidence the party finds before trial. This is a natural consequence.

- If the responding party discovers new evidence, it may be allowed to introduce that new evidence.
- The new evidence must have been genuinely unavailable at the time of deposition to be admissible.

16

Changing the Testimony

A deposition is not a take-home examination.[1]
—The Hon. F. A. Little

Introduction.	375
Sham Affidavit Rule	375
Deposition Errata Sheet Changes	376
First Procedural Requirement: List of Changes and Reasons.	377
Second Procedural Requirement: Within Thirty Days	378
Three Schools of Permissible Change	380
Strict Rule: Clerical Errors Only	380
Moderate Rule: Explainable Substantive Changes.	381
Liberal Rule: Contradictions and Substantive Alterations.	385

---

1. *Greenway v. Int'l Paper Co.*, 144 F.R.D. 322, 325 (W.D. La. 1992).

Inquiring into the Basis for
    the Errata Sheet Change 386
Summary 389

Introduction

It is undisputed that 30(b)(6) testimony binds the organization. Nonetheless, organizations continue to change their witnesses' testimonies—in errata sheets to their depositions, with affidavits in response to motions for summary judgment, or at trial. How the courts handle those attempts to change the testimony varies by jurisdiction and by the stage of the litigation.

Sham Affidavit Rule

Historically, parties responding to a summary judgment motion tried to create a factual dispute by filing affidavits with information that conflicted with the deposition testimony. This is called a *sham fact issue*. When those affidavits attempted to create a sham fact issue in response to summary judgment motions, the courts refused to consider the contradictory testimony.[2] The *sham affidavit rule* emerged to prohibit self-serving affidavits that were "purposeful rewrites, tailored to manufacture an issue of material fact" to defeat summary judgment.[3]

---

2. *Franks v. Nimmo*, 796 F.2d 1230, 1237 (10th Cir. 1986) citing *Foster v. Arcata Associates, Inc.*, 772 F.2d 1453, 1462 (9th Cir. 1985), *cert. denied*, 475 U.S. 1048, 106 S.Ct. 1267, 89 L.Ed.2d 576 (1986); *Biechele v. Cedar Point, Inc.*, 747 F.2d 209, 215 (6th Cir.1984); *Van T. Junkins & Associates, Inc. v. U.S. Industries, Inc.*, 736 F.2d 656, 657–58 (11th Cir. 1984); *Camfield Tires, Inc. v. Michelin Tire Corp.*, 719 F.2d 1361, 1364 (8th Cir. 1983); *Perma Research & Development Co. v. Singer Co.*, 410 F.2d 572, 578 (2d Cir. 1969).
3. *Devon Energy Corp. v. Westacott*, No. CIV.A. H-09-1689, 2011 WL 1157334, at *5 (S.D. Tex. Mar. 24, 2011); *see Hambleton Bros. Lumber Co. v. Balkin Enterprises.*, 397 F.3d 1217, 1225 (9th Cir. 2005); *EBC, Inc. v. Clark Building Sys., Inc.*, 618 F.3d 253, 268 (3d Cir. 2010).

When evaluating whether or not affidavits create sham factual disputes, the court will consider the following:

- Whether the *affiant* (the person who signed the affidavit) was cross-examined during his or her earlier testimony.
- Whether the affiant had access to the pertinent evidence at the time of the earlier testimony.
- Whether the affidavit was based on newly discovered evidence.
- Whether the earlier testimony reflects confusion that the affidavit attempts to explain.[4]

If it is a sham affidavit, the court will disregard it.

Deposition Errata Sheet Changes

Similar to the sham affidavits filed in response to summary judgments, some organizations also attempt to change their witness's 30(b)(6) testimony by submitting errata sheets after the deposition that materially alter the witness's testimony.

Although Rule 30(e)(1) allows a deponent to make changes in "form or substance" to the deposition transcript, how courts interpret that rule is not as straightforward as many lawyers think. The rule has specific requirements, and the courts have limited what changes parties can make.

The purpose of the rule is to correct substantive errors.[5] The language of Rule 30 specifies two explicit requirements:

- The errata sheet must list the reasons for the change.
- The change must be made within thirty days.

---

4. *Franks v. Nimmo*, 796 F.2d 1230, 1237 (10th Cir. 1986); *see Camfield Tires, Inc. v. Michelin Tire Corp.*, 719 F.2d 1361, 1364–65 (8th Cir. 1983); *Perma Research & Development Co. v. Singer Co.*, 410 F.2d 572, 578 (2d Cir. 1969).
5. *Garcia v. Pueblo Country Club*, 299 F.3d 1233, 1242 (10th Cir. 2002).

Rule 30(e)(1) states as follows:

> On request by the deponent or a party before the deposition is completed, the deponent must be allowed thirty days after being notified by the officer that the transcript or recording is available in which:
>
> (A) to review the transcript or recording; and
>
> (B) if there are changes in form or substance, to sign a statement listing the changes and the reasons for making them.[6]

First Procedural Requirement: List of Changes and Reasons

The first procedural requirement of the 30(e)(1)(B) errata rule is to require the deponent to "sign a statement listing the changes and reasons for making them." If the deponent does not provide sufficient reasons for a change, then the deponent has violated the rule, and that procedural defect alone renders the errata sheet improper.[7] The mere statement of some reason does not alone satisfy the rule. The reasons the deponent gives for the changes cannot be conclusory—the deponent must explain why they are changing the testimony and he was unable to state them during the deposition.[8] For example, courts have disregarded errata changes to "correct the record" as procedurally defective.[9]

Every change must have a reason.[10] If the party or the deponent attempting to change a deposition transcript fails to state the

---

6. Fed. R. Civ. P. 30(e)(1).
7. *EBC, Inc. v. Clark Bldg. Sys., Inc.*, 618 F.3d 253, 266 (3d Cir. 2010); *E.I. Du Pont de Nemours and Co. v. Kolon Ind., Inc.*, 277 F.R.D. 286, 295 (E.D. Vir. 2011); *Wyeth v. Lupin Ltd.*, 252 F.R.D. 295, 296 (D. Md. 2008).
8. *Harden v. Wicomico Cty*, 263 F.R.D. 304, 307 (D. Md. 2009).
9. *Candy Craft Creations, LLC v. Gartner*, 2015 WL 1541507, *11 (S.D. Ga. 2015).
10. *EBC, Inc. v. Clark Bldg. Sys., Inc.*, 618 F.3d 253, 266 (3d Cir. 2010) (citing *Duff v. Lobdell–Emery Mfg. Co.*, 926 F. Supp. 799, 804 (N.D. Ind. 1996)).

reasons for the changes, the reviewing court may strike the errata sheet.[11] Courts require that each change must have a specific reason that explains the nature of, and the need to make, the change.[12]

Second Procedural Requirement: Within Thirty Days

The second procedural requirement rule states that deponents have thirty days after the court reporter has notified them to review the deposition transcript. During that time, they can sign a statement listing any changes to the transcript *and* the reasons for those changes.[13] The Rule 30(e) thirty-day clock begins to run when the court reporter notifies the party that the transcript is available for review, *not* when the party or deponent physically receives the transcript from the court reporter.[14] If the deponent received notice via e-mail that the transcript was available, then Rule 6 allows three additional days because service was by electronic means.[15]

If the deponent is an organization being deposed under Rule 30(b)(6), that organization may designate multiple witnesses to respond. The testimony that the witnesses give at 30(b)(6) depositions represents the organization's knowledge, not the individual deponents' knowledge. Because the organization is the deponent, as opposed to the individual witnesses, the

---

11. *EBC, Inc. v. Clark Bldg. Sys., Inc.*, 618 F.3d 253, 266 (3d Cir. 2010).
12. *E.I. Du Pont de Nemours and Co. v. Kolon Ind., Inc.*, 277 F.R.D. 286, 295 (E.D. Vir. 2011) (citing *Lugtig v. Thomas*, 89 F.R.D. 639, 641 (N.D. Ill. 1981) ("after each change, the deponent must state the specific reason for that particular change")).
13. *EBC v. Clark Bldg. Systems, Inc.*, 618 F.3d 253, 266 (3rd Cir. 2010) (citing *Holland v. Cedar Creek Mining, Inc.*, 198 F.R.D. 651, 653 (S.D.W.Va. 2001)).
14. *EBC, Inc. v. Clark Bldg. Sys., Inc.*, 618 F.3d 253, 266 (3d Cir. 2010) (citing *Hambleton Bros. Lumber Co. v. Balkin Enters., Inc.*, 397 F.3d 1217, 1224 (9th Cir. 2005)).
15. Fed. R. Civ. P. 6; *see also*, *Beal v. Wyndham Vacation Resorts, Inc.*, 956 F. Supp. 962, 965 (W.D. Wis. 2013).

courts treat all witnesses as a single deposition.[16] Therefore, the thirty-day deadline for filing corrections starts to run at the end of the final witness's testimony.[17]

Corrections to previous errata submissions must also fall within this thirty-day window. A deponent cannot submit a defective errata sheet to satisfy the time requirement, and then submit a corrected sheet after the thirty-day time limit.[18] Courts will consider the delay as a waiver of the deponent's right to object to an alleged error.[19]

If parties or deponents fail to return the deposition with properly executed changes within thirty days, this constitutes a waiver of their right to examine and read the transcript.[20] Although it is within the discretion of the court, "most courts will insist on strict adherence to the technical requirements of Rule 30(e)."[21] Failure to provide the reasons for the change and failure to sign the errata sheet within the thirty-day limit results in a waiver of that right under the rule.

---

16. *In re Weatherford Intern, Securities Litigation*, 2013 WL 4505259, *3 (S.D. N.Y. 2013).
17. *Id.*
18. *E.I. du Pont de Nemours & Co. v. Kolon Indus., Inc.*, 277 F.R.D. 286, 296 (E.D. Va. 2011).
19. *Id.* (citing *Calloway v. Marvel Entm't Group, div. of Cadence Indus. Corp.*, 110 F.R.D. 45, 52 (S.D.N.Y. 1986)).
20. *E.I. du Pont de Nemours & Co. v. Kolon Indus., Inc.*, 277 F.R.D. 286, 296 (E.D. Va. 2011) (citing *Soto v. McLean*, Nos. 7:96CV134BR2, 7:96CV135BR2, 1998 WL 1110688, at *2. (E.D.N.C. 1998) (quoting *Qatar Nat'l Navigation & Transp. Co. v. Citibank*, N.A., No. 89-CIV-464, 1996 WL 601540, at *1 (S.D. N.Y. Oct. 18, 1996) (quoting *Calloway v. Marvel Entm't Group*, 110 F.R.D. 45, 52 (S.D.N.Y. 1986))); see *Blackthorne v. Posner*, 883 F. Supp. 1443, 1454 (D. Or. 1995).
21. *EBC v. Clark Bldg. Systems, Inc.*, 618 F.3d 253, 265 (3rd Cir. 2010); *Hambleton Bros. Lumber Co. v. Balkin Enters.*, 397 F.3d 1217, 1224 (9th Cir. 2005); *E.I. du Pont de Nemours and Co. v. Kolon Indus., Inc.*, 277 F.R.D. 286, 296 (E.D. Vir. 2011); *Workman v. Chinchinian*, 807 F. Supp. 634, 644–45 (E.D. Wash. 1992); *Calloway v. Marvel Entm't Group, div. of Cadence Indus. Corp.*, 110 F.R.D. 45, 52 (S.D.N.Y. 1986).

Three Schools of Permissible Change

The courts universally accept that Rule 30(e) permits transcript corrections. For example, if the reporter recorded the answer as yes, but the deponent actually said no, that correction is a substantive change, which all courts permit under the plain text of the rule. The crucial question, however, is whether there are any limits to the types of substantive changes that a deponent may make to a transcript. Courts are divided about the leeway they should give deponents under Rule 30(e) to alter the substance of prior testimony.

There are three schools evaluating the extent of *permissible* changes to depositions with an errata sheet under Rule 30(e)(1)(B):

- Strict rule: clerical errors only.
- Moderate rule: explainable substantive changes.
- Liberal rule: contradictions and substantive alterations.

Strict Rule: Clerical Errors Only

Courts that adhere to a strict interpretation of Rule 30(e) limit errata sheet changes to typographic and transcription errors. Should the reporter make a substantive error (for example, he reported yes, but the deponent said no) or a formal error (for example, he reported the name to be Lawrence Smith, but the proper name is Laurence Smith) then corrections from the deponent would be in order.[22] Any changes beyond that are prohibited. These courts rely on the principle that they cannot interpret Rule 30 to allow a witness to alter testimony under oath. In *Greenway v. Int'l Paper Co.*, the court explained its interpretation:

> The Rule cannot be interpreted to allow one to alter what was said under oath. If that were the case, one

---

22. *Greenway v. Int'l Paper Co.*, 144 F.R.D. 322, 325 (W.D. La. 1992).

could merely answer the questions with no thought at all, then return home and plan artful responses. Depositions differ from interrogatories in that regard. *A deposition is not a take-home examination.*[23]

Moderate Rule: Explainable Substantive Changes

The majority of circuit courts have elected to balance protection from discovery misconduct with potentially legitimate substantive changes (such as an honest mistake or misstatement), by applying the analysis used in the sham affidavit rule to Rule 30(e) corrections.[24] In addition to clerical error changes, the moderate rule also permits substantive changes if there is a "satisfactory explanation."[25]

Although some substantive changes are allowed, the moderate approach does not allow wholesale revisions of the sworn testimony. In *E.I. du Pont de Nemours & Co. v. Kolon Indus., Inc.*, the court observed that it makes no sense to allow deponents to

---

23. *Greenway v. Int'l Paper Co.*, 144 F.R.D. 322, 325 (W.D. La. 1992); *Garcia v. Pueblo Country Club*, 299 F.3d 1233, 1242, n. 5 (10th Cir. 2002); *see also*, *Tuttle v. Tyco Elecs. Installation Servs., Inc.*, No. 2:06-cv-581, 2008 WL 343178, at *4 (S.D. Ohio Feb.7, 2008); *Trout v. FirstEnergy Generation Corp.*, 339 F. App'x 560, 565 (6th Cir. 2009).
24. *Devon Energy Corp. v. Westacott*, 2011 WL 1157334, at *4 (S.D. Tex. Mar. 24, 2011) (citing *Reilly v. TXU Corp.*, 230 F.R.D. 486, 490 (N.D. Tex. 2005)); However, the Circuits differ as to the extent they allow the alterations of the prior testimony which defeats the errata sheet *Burns v. Bd. of Cnty. Comm'rs*, 330 F.3d 1275, 1282 (10th Cir. 2003) ("We see no reason to treat Rule 30(e) corrections differently than affidavits, and we hold that [the plaintiff's] attempt to amend his deposition testimony must be evaluated under [the sham affidavit doctrine]."); *Thorn v. Sundstrand Aerospace Corp.*, 207 F.3d 383, 389 (7th Cir. 2000) (finding that Rule 30(e) changes that contradict the original deposition testimony should be dealt with the same way as subsequent affidavits that contradict a witness's earlier deposition); *E.I. du Pont de Nemours & Co. v. Kolon Indus., Inc.*, 277 F.R.D. 286, 297 (E.D. Va. 2011); *Rios v. Bigler*, 847 F. Supp. 1538, 1546-47 (D. Kan. 1994).
25. *See, e.g.*, *Wyeth v. Lupin Ltd.*, 252 F.R.D. 295, 296 (D. Md. 2008); *Holland v. Cedar Creek Min., Inc.*, 198 F.R.D. 651, 653 (S.D.W.Va. 2001).

change sworn testimony merely because after the deposition they wish that they had said something else.[26] "Indeed, to adopt such an approach would be to set at naught the efficacy of the deposition process."[27]

The *E.I. du Pont* court recognized that parties could not use the Rule 30(e) errata process to revise their testimony after a deposition in order to enhance their case.[28] Allowing such a process would undermine the purpose of depositions under the federal rule.[29] Citing *Hall v. Clifton Precision*, the court in *E.I. du Pont*, stated the following:

> The purpose of a deposition is to memorialize testimony or to obtain information that can be used at trial or that eliminates the pursuit of issues or that inform decisions as to the future course of the litigation. One of the main purposes of the discovery rules, and the deposition rules in particular, is to elicit the facts before the trial and to memorialize witness testimony before the recollection of events fade or "it has been altered by . . . helpful suggestions of lawyers." *Hall v. Clifton Precision*, 150 F.R.D. 525, 528 (E.D. Pa. 1993). Those purposes are disserved by allowing deponents to "answer questions [at a deposition] with no thought at all" and later to craft answers that better serve the deponent's cause. Indeed, to allow such conduct makes a mockery of the serious and important role that depositions play in the litigation process.[30]

---

26. *E.I. du Pont de Nemours & Co. v. Kolon Indus., Inc.*, 277 F.R.D. 286, 297 (E.D. Va. 2011).
27. *Id.*
28. *Id.*
29. *Id.*
30. *Id.* (citing *Hall v. Clifton Precision*, 150 F.R.D. 525, 528 (E.D. Pa.1993)).

By applying the sham affidavit rule to errata sheet analysis, the courts strictly limit the witnesses' errata changes. A change of substance that actually contradicts the transcript is impermissible unless the party plausibly shows that the change corrects an error in transcription, such as dropping a "not."[31] The courts endorsing the moderate interpretation of Rule 30(e)(1)(B) hold that the purpose of an errata sheet is "to *correct alleged inaccuracies* in what the deponent *said* at his deposition, not to modify what he wishes that he had said."[32]

In *Wyeth v. Lupin Ltd.*, the court refused to allow altering the testimony of the 30(b)(6) with an errata sheet.[33] In granting the motion to strike the errata sheet, the court stated that the changes "represent lawyerly fixing of potentially problematic testimony . . ."[34] The court found the following:

> The errata sheet "clarifications" in this case are akin to a student who takes her in-class examination home, but submits new answers only after realizing a month later that the import of her original answers could possibly result in a failing grade.[35]

The court explained,

> To allow these types of corrections would undermine the Rule 30(b)(6) deposition. An interpretation of liberal—indeed unlimited—amendments and

---

31. *Thorn v. Sundstrand Aerospace Corp.*, 207 F.3d 383, 389 (7th Cir. 2000).
32. *Crowe v. Marchand*, 2006 U.S. Dist. LEXIS 98142, 2006 WL 5230014, at *1 (D.R.I. 2006); *Burns v. Bd. of County Com'rs.*, 330 F.3d 1275, 1282 (10th Cir. 2003).
33. *Wyeth v. Lupin Ltd.*, 252 F.R.D. 295 (D. Md. 2008).
34. *Id.* at 295, 297; *see, e.g.*, *Eckert v. Kemper Fin. Servs., Inc.*, 1998 WL 699656, at *5 (N.D. Ill. Sept. 30, 1998) (precluding "wholesale changes to previous sworn testimony" that was, in fact, a "damaging [party] admission").
35. *Wyeth v. Lupin Ltd.*, 252 F.R.D. 295, 297 (D. Md. 2008).

corrections would discourage the careful preparation of 30(b)(6) witnesses. Rather than advancing the pursuit of truth in discovery, a policy of liberal "amendments" and "corrections" would encourage and intensify lawyer word-smithing and parsing.[36]

The sham affidavit rule approach pragmatically reinforces the importance of the 30(b)(6) deposition's binding effect. The rule holds that a party may not, without "satisfactory explanation," create an issue of fact by submitting an affidavit that conflicts with previous sworn testimony simply to avoid summary judgment.[37]

The testimony of a Rule 30(b)(6) witness differs from that of a 30(b)(1) individual deponent. Whereas the 30(b)(1) deponent has no duty to prepare, the designating organization must fully prepare its 30(b)(6) witness to provide all information known or reasonably available to the organization. Therefore, when evaluating whether there is in fact a "satisfactory explanation" for the revised testimony, the court must evaluate whether the organization has satisfied its duty to prepare.[38]

Consistent with *Rainey v. American Forest and Paper Ass'n, Inc.*, the responding party must prove why the supposed new information was not available at the time of the deposition.[39] The satisfactory-explanation test maintains the integrity of the judicial process by requiring organizations to comply with its preparation and disclosure requirements established in Rule 30(b)(6).

---

36. *Id.*
37. 131 A.L.R. Fed. 403 (1996); *see, e.g., Abreu-Guzman v. Ford*, 241 F.3d 69, 74 (1st Cir. 2001); *Margo v. Weiss*, 213 F.3d 55, 60 (2d Cir. 2000); *Peck v. Bridgeport Machines, Inc.*, 237 F.3d 614, 619 (6th Cir. 2001); *Addisu v. Fred Meyer, Inc.*, 198 F.3d 1130, 1142 (9th Cir. 2000); *Franks v. Nimmo*, 796 F.2d 1230 (10th Cir. 1986).
38. *See* chapter 11, "Duty to Prepare."
39. *Rainey v. American Forest and Paper Ass'n, Inc.*, 26 F. Supp.2d 82, 95 (D.D.C. 1998).

> The cure for this violation should not be simply to give the plaintiff a chance to depose [that witness]. If such were the remedy, corporate parties would have every incentive to "bandy" or attempt "trial by ambush," as the only downside to their strategy would be that their adversary might eventually procure access to their theretofore-concealed witness. This incentive structure would eviscerate the force of Rule 30(b)(6), and would delay litigation, heighten suspicions, and obfuscate the discovery process. Rule 30(b)(6) was designed to prevent such consequences, and in order to adhere to its terms, it is improper to consider the [new witness's] affidavit for purposes of plaintiff's motion for summary judgment.[40]

If the responding party gives a satisfactory explanation for its change in testimony, the court has the discretion to allow the amendment to the deposition. However, if the court does not find the responding party's explanation satisfactory, the court will not condone the catch-me-if-you-can approach to litigation.

Liberal Rule: Contradictions and Substantive Alterations

The minority position, explicitly adopted by the Second Circuit, permits the responding party to submit broad changes in an errata sheet, to both form and substance of the deposition.[41] Under this

---

40. *Id.* at 82, 96.
41. *Podell v. Citicorp Diners Club, Inc.*, 112 F.3d 98, 103 (2d Cir. 1997); *see also*, *Eicken v. USAA Fed. Savings Bank*, 498 F. Supp.2d 954, 961–62 (S.D. Tex. 2007) (permitting changes to deposition testimony even when the majority of the 45 changes reversed the original answers); *EEOC v. J.H. Walker, Inc.*, 2007 WL 172626, at *10–13 (S.D. Tex. Jan. 18, 2007); *Medina v. Horseshoe Entm't*, 2006 WL 2038057, at *4 (W.D. La. July 19, 2006); *Agrizap, Inc. v. Woodstream Corp.*, 232 F.R.D. 491, 493, n. 2 (E.D. Pa. 2006); *Reilly v. TXU Corp.*, 230 F.R.D. 486,

approach, the court treats both the fact and extent of the changes as subjects for impeachment that may affect a witness's credibility.[42] The changed version does not replace the original testimony, which remains part of the record on which the witness may be examined and impeached.[43]

Procedurally, Rule 30 requires that the responding party make changes within thirty days of notification that the transcript is available *and* provide the reasons for making the changes.[44] If the responding party files the changes within thirty days, but leaves out the reasons for the change, this is a procedural defect that will defeat the errata sheet submission.[45] This is a liberal rule, but don't get overconfident, because the courts strictly enforce the rule—a defect will negate it.

Inquiring into the Basis for the Errata Sheet Change

If the responding party has submitted substantive changes in the errata sheet, the requesting party can reopen the deposition and ask additional questions about the responding party's altered

---

490 (N.D. Tex. 2005); *see also, Foutz v. Town of Vinton*, 211 F.R.D. 293, 295 (W.D. Va. 2002); *DeLoach v. Philip Morris Cos.*, 206 F.R.D. 568, 572–73 (M.D.N.C. 2002); *Elwell v. Conair, Inc.*, 145 F. Supp. 2d 79, 86–87 (D. Me. 2001); *Holland v. Cedar Creek Mining, Inc.*, 198 F.R.D. 651, 653 (S.D.W.Va. 2001); *Titanium Metals, Corp. v. Elkem Mgmt., Inc.*, 191 F.R.D. 468, 472 (W.D. Pa. 1998); *U.S. ex rel. Burch v. Piqua Eng'g, Inc.*, 152 F.R.D. 565, 566–67 (S.D. Ohio 1993); *Sanford v. CBS, Inc.*, 594 F. Supp. 713, 714–15 (N.D. Ill. 1984); *Lugtig v. Thomas*, 89 F.R.D. 639, 641–42 (N.D. Ill. 1981); *Allen & Co. v. Occidental Petroleum Corp.*, 49 F.R.D. 337, 340 (S.D.N.Y. 1970); *Colin v. Thompson*, 16 F.R.D. 194, 195 (W.D. Mo. 1954); *De Seversky v. Republic Aviation Corp.*, 2 F.R.D. 113, 115 (E.D.N.Y. 1941).
42. *Lugtig v. Thomas*, 89 F.R.D. 639, 642 (N.D. Ill.1981).
43. *Podell v. Citicorp Diners Club, Inc.*, 112 F.3d 98, 103 (2d Cir. 1997); *E.E.O.C. v. Skanska USA Bldg., Inc.*, 278 F.R.D. 407, 410 (W.D. Tenn. 2012).
44. *See, e.g., Duff v. Lobdell-Emery Mfg. Co.*, 926 F. Supp. 799, 803–04 (N.D. Ind. 1996).
45. *Wyeth v. Lupin Ltd.*, 252 F.R.D. 295, 296 (D. Md. 2008) (citing *Duff v. Lobdell-Emery Mfg. Co.*, 926 F. Supp. 799, 803–04 (N.D. Ind. 1996)).

testimony.[46] Courts that permit substantive changes to deposition testimony with errata sheets use a materiality test to determine if the deposition may be reopened to inquire into the basis for the change.[47] If the court decides that the change from the errata sheet is material, the court will allow a new deposition.

Most courts permit parties to ask questions about the basis for changes to testimony regardless of "whether such changes originate with the attorney or the deponent."[48] Deponents must testify at the reconvened deposition as to why they changed their testimony. The courts have explained the following:

> [W]hen a party affirmatively relies on privileged information, then the information is automatically placed into issue and any privilege that would otherwise attach is impliedly waived.[49]

Technique: Asking about Testimony Changes

If the court allows a 30(b)(6) deposition to be reconvened because the responding party gave material alterations to its previous testimony in an errata sheet, you should make a record about the *reasons* for the change, before you go into detail about the actual changes.

Q: You testified on January 16, 2015, correct?

Q: You testified that you would provide all information known or reasonably available to Big Box Stores about the matters in the deposition notice, correct?

---

46. *See Podell v. Citicorp Diners Club*, 112 F.3d 98, 103 (2d Cir.1997); *E.I. du Pont de Nemours & Co. v. Kolon Indus., Inc.*, 277 F.R.D. 286, 296 (E.D. Va. 2011); *Lugtig*, 89 F.R.D. at 641; *see also Foutz v. Town of Vinton, Virginia*, 211 F.R.D. 293, 295 (W.D. Va. 2002).
47. *Tingley Sys., Inc. v. CSC Consulting, Inc.*, 152 F. Supp. 2d 95, 121 (D. Mass. 2001); *Luhman v. Dalkon Shield Claimants Trust*, 1994 WL 542048 (D. Kan. Oct. 3, 1994).
48. *Tingley Sys., Inc. v. CSC Consulting, Inc.*, 152 F. Supp.2d 95, 121 (D. Mass. 2001).
49. *QBE Ins. Corp. v. Jorda Enters., Inc.*, 286 F.R.D. 661, 664 (S.D. Fla. 2012).

Q: Did you mean it?

Q: Did you tell the truth?

Q: You told us that the Big Box Stores handpicked you to provide the information for the jury. Isn't that true?

Q: In fact, you told us at the deposition that the lawyer sitting next to you today prepared you to provide all information, known or reasonably available to Big Box Stores, when you testified before, correct?

Q: You even told us that you knew that you had to give the most complete and honest answers possible because the information was going to be presented to the jury, correct?

Q: Then you testified, correct?

Q: After it was all finished, we went home thinking it was over, right?

Q: Then you changed the testimony you gave under oath, right?

Q: Why?

Q: You told us you knew this was for the benefit of the jury, right?

Q: Why didn't you tell the jury that information when you were testifying under oath the first time?

Q: Why wasn't that information available to you before?

Q: Who provided this new information to you?

Q: Who did you talk to about changing your testimony under oath?

Q: What did he say?

Q: Why didn't you talk to him before the first time you testified?

Q: Did you speak to Big Box Stores' lawyer about changing your testimony?

Q: What did he say?

Q: What facts did he provide to you?

Q: Did you ask why that information wasn't provided to you before you testified the first time?

Q: What did he say?

Q: What else?

If you create a record showing that the organization did not properly prepare the witness, you make it more difficult for the organization to base its changed position on an unavailability of necessary evidence. The organization's failure to fully investigate during its preparation for the 30(b)(6) deposition does not constitute newly discovered evidence. Rather, it indicates lack of preparation, which is sanctionable conduct.

Summary

- A responding party cannot use a sham affidavit to create a factual dispute.
- Rule 30 allows for errata changes to depositions.
- A responding party must sign errata changes within thirty days of when it receives notice that the transcript is available.
- A responding party must explain its reasons for errata changes.
- Courts differ on what changes they permit.
- Some courts allow changes only to typographic and transcription errors.
- Some courts allow corrections to inaccuracies of testimony if they do not contradict the testimony and if there is a sufficient explanation as to why the change is necessary.
- Some courts allow any changes subject to impeachment.
- If an errata change is material, the requesting party can reconvene the deposition.

- You can reconvene the deposition and ask the witness about his reasons for change.
- If the 30(b)(6) witness changes his testimony based on conversation with a lawyer or by viewing privileged documents, any privilege, including attorney–client privilege, is waived.

17

Using 30(b)(6) Testimony at Trial

It ain't over till it's over.

—Yogi Berra

Introduction.................................393	
The 30(b)(6) Witness Testifies	
Vicariously for the Organization..............394	
Using a Party 30(b)(6) Deposition at Trial.........396	
Using 30(b)(6) Depositions from Other Cases......398	
Compelling Live Testimony	
from the 30(b)(6) Witness at Trial 400	
Using Nonparty 30(b)(6) Witness	
Depositions at Trial.........................402	
Attempts to Change the Story at Trial..............404	
Organization Disavows the	
30(b)(6) Witness at Trial....................405	
Organization Brings a Different Witness to Trial....406	

Organization's Experts Can't
Contradict 30(b)(6) Testimony................407

MOTION *IN LIMINE* 408

SUMMARY 410

Introduction

Throughout this book, I have discussed the rules for taking 30(b)(6) depositions and the techniques to ensure that you are able to discover information or lock down positions from organizations. Once you have mastered the techniques and you have that killer 30(b)(6) deposition transcript in your hand, the final step is to present the information you captured in the 30(b)(6) deposition to the jury.

Because 30(b)(6) witnesses are prepared to testify about information that the organization gathered from multiple sources throughout the organization, their testimony is often based on hearsay. As a result, there is a tension between the policies underlying open economical discovery using Rule 30(b)(6) and the Rules of Evidence requiring witnesses to testify based only on their personal knowledge. This chapter will explain how the courts have resolved this tension in favor of the full disclosure of 30(b)(6) witness testimony to the jury. The organization is testifying through the 30(b)(6) witness. The witness provides the organization's personal knowledge.

The chapter will also explain the different rules for reading 30(b)(6) deposition into evidence or for playing the video to the jury. The rules that you need to follow differ, depending on if the 30(b)(6) witness is a party or nonparty. In addition, if instead of presenting the deposition to the jury, you decide to subpoena a 30(b)(6) witness to testify at trial, there are again different subpoena rules that you must follow, depending on whether the 30(b)(6) witness is a party or a nonparty. This chapter will explain those differences.

Often, in an effort to circumvent the binding effect of the testimony,[1] organizations will attempt to change the deposition story by using other witnesses or using expert testimony that disregards the organization's 30(b)(6) admissions. In order to be

---

1. *See* chapter 15, "Binding Effect."

armed for that type of ambush, this chapter will provide the cases you need to support your ability to cross-examine those witnesses with the organization's 30(b)(6) transcript.

The 30(b)(6) Witness Testifies Vicariously for the Organization

When introducing the deposition testimony of a nonparty 30(b)(6) witness, there is an inherent tension between the Federal Rules of Evidence and Rule 30(b)(6). The Rules of Evidence call for witnesses with personal knowledge to introduce the evidence. Whereas, Rule 30(b)(6) requires that an organization prepare a designated witness to provide all knowledge known to all people within that organization.

The policies underlying the American system of jurisprudence contemplate the mutual disgorgement of facts by the parties to enable a jury to make a balanced and informed decision. Depositions are the vehicle to gather that information. However, because it is impossible to take testimony from an organization, the testimony you collect under Rule 30(b)(6) must be obtained from people that the organization selects to speak on its behalf.[2] Therefore, the selected 30(b)(6) witness does not give personal opinions, but rather represents the organization's position on the topics.[3] When the organization provides the designated witness, it authorizes and prepares that witness to speak on its behalf. The organization prepares that witness with all facts, subjective beliefs, and opinions within the areas covered by the deposition notice.[4] Conceptually, the organization is the equivalent of a single person who is the confluence of the knowledge of many people.

---

2. *See* 8A Wright, Miller & Marcus, *Federal Practice and Procedure* § 2103, at 36–37 (2nd ed. 1994).
3. *Brazos River authority v. GE Ionics, Inc.*, 469 F.3d 416, 433 (5th Cir. 2006) (citing *U.S. v. Taylor*, 166 F.R.D. 356, 361 (M.D.N.C. 1996).
4. *Brazos River Authority v. GE Ionics, Inc.*, 469 F.3d 416, 433 (5th Cir. 2006).

Courts have resolved the tension between Rule 30(b)(6) and the evidentiary personal knowledge requirement by explaining that a 30(b)(6) witness "testifies 'vicariously,' for the corporation, as to its knowledge and perceptions."[5] Consistent with the purposes underlying the rule, a 30(b)(6) witness may "testify not only to matters within his personal knowledge but also to matters known or reasonably available to the organization."[6] In *Sara Lee Corp. v. Kraft Foods Inc.*, the court recognized the importance of the policies that led to the creation of Rule 30(b)(6):

> When it comes to using Rule 30(b)(6) depositions at trial, strictly imposing the personal knowledge requirement would only recreate the problems that Rule 30(b)(6) was created to solve.[7]

A 30(b)(6) witness's trial testimony is not limited to facts. Similar to the 30(b)(6) deposition, the trial testimony must also provide the organization's opinions and positions.[8] At trial, the 30(b)(6) witness may embrace opinions that go to ultimate fact.[9] Rule 704(a) provides that testimony "in the form of an opinion or inference otherwise admissible is not objectionable because it embraces an ultimate issue to be decided by the trier of fact."[10]

---

5. *Sara Lee Corp. v. Kraft Foods Inc.*, 276 F.R.D. 500, 503 (N.D. Ill. 2011) (citing *Brazos River Auth. v. GE Ionics, Inc.*, 469 F.3d 416, 434 (5th Cir. 2006)).
6. *Sara Lee Corp. v. Kraft Foods Inc.*, 276 F.R.D. 500, 503 (N.D. Ill. 2011) (citing *PPM Finance, Inc. v. Norandal USA, Inc.*, 392 F.3d 889, 894–95 (7th Cir. 2004).
7. *Sara Lee Corp. v. Kraft Foods Inc.*, 276 F.R.D. 500, 503 (N.D. Ill. 2011).
8. *See Brazos River Authority v. GE Ionics, Inc.*, 469 F.3d 416, 435 (5th Cir. 2006); *United States v. Taylor*, 166 F.R.D. 356, 361 (M.D.N.C. 1996).
9. *Brazos River Authority v. GE Ionics, Inc.*, 469 F.3d 416, 435 (5th Cir. 2006).
10. *Id.*; Fed. R. E. 704 (Opinion on an Ultimate Issue (a) In General — Not Automatically Objectionable. An opinion is not objectionable just because it embraces an ultimate issue.)

Using a Party 30(b)(6) Deposition at Trial

Rule 32(a)(3) expressly allows you to use an adverse party's 30(b)(6) witness deposition at trial for any purpose. The rule states the following:

> **Deposition of Party, Agent, or Designee.** An adverse party may use for any purpose the deposition of a party or anyone who, when deposed, was the party's officer, director, managing agent, or designee under Rule 30(b)(6) or 31(a)(4).[11]

Using Rule 32(a)(3), you may introduce the 30(b)(6) deposition of an adverse party as part of your substantive proof. Because it is the testimony of a party, it is unnecessary to establish the adversary's availability to testify at trial.[12] You can use the deposition regardless of whether the specific witness who gave the testimony is available or not.

On the other hand, as a general rule, an organization cannot introduce the deposition testimony of its own 30(b)(6) witness at trial. Rule 32(a)(3) allows only an *adverse party* to use the 30(b)(6) deposition for any purpose. However, if the 30(b)(6) witness is not available, there is an exception to that general principle. Rule 32(a)(4)(c) states the following:

> (4) **Unavailable Witness.** A party may use for any purpose the deposition of a witness, *whether or not a party*, if the court finds:

> (C) that the witness cannot attend or testify because of age, illness, infirmity, or imprisonment;

---

11. Fed. R. Civ. P. 32(a)(3).
12. *King & King Enters. v. Champlin Petroleum Co.*, 657 F.2d 1147, 1163–64 (10th Cir. 1981); *see also Coughlin v. Capitol Cement Co.*, 571 F.2d 290, 308 (5th Cir. 1978) (citing *Fey v. Walston & Co., Inc.*, 493 F.2d 1036, 1046 (7th Cir. 1974); *Community Counseling Service, Inc. v. Reilly*, 317 F.2d 239, 243 (4th Cir. 1963); 4 *Moore's Federal Practice* P 26.29, at 1653 (2d ed. 1968)).

(D) that the party offering the deposition could not procure the witness's attendance by subpoena; or

(E) on motion and notice, that exceptional circumstances make it desirable—in the interest of justice and with due regard to the importance of live testimony in open court—to permit the deposition to be used.[13]

Although the organization's 30(b)(6) witness may fall within one of these categories, such as age, illness, infirmity, or imprisonment, that alone does not allow the organization to introduce its own 30(b)(6) deposition as evidence. Before the organization can introduce the deposition into evidence, it still must show that the witness is *unable* to testify.[14]

Example: Inverness Investments

You represent a client who was defrauded by Inverness Investments. You can prove your case with the 30(b)(6) witness's testimony. Because it was a seven-hour deposition, you choose to play selected relevant excerpts of the video to the jury.

Your adversary representing Inverness Investments, however, wants to play other portions of the deposition that she believes are beneficial. You have made the tactical decision that you want to be able to cross-examine Inverness Investments' 30(b)(6) witness with documents you discovered after you took his deposition. You can object to your adversary using portions of the 30(b)(6) testimony, insisting that the witness is available to testify. Therefore, the Inverness Investments 30(b)(6) witness will be required to appear, and you will be able to cross-examine him with this newly discovered information, unless the organization can show that the witness is unavailable.

---

13. Fed. R. Civ. P. 32(a)(4)(c).
14. See *Delgado v. Pawtucket Police Dept.*, 668 F.3d 42, 49 (1st Cir. 2012), (Witness's imprisonment did not alone justify admission of his deposition testimony in lieu of live testimony without establishing that his imprisonment prevented him from testifying in person).

Using 30(b)(6) Depositions from Other Cases

An organization may have provided 30(b)(6) witnesses to testify in depositions in other similar lawsuits. Rather than reinventing the wheel by retaking their depositions to get the same information, you may want to use the testimony from those prior cases in your lawsuit. However, before you do, you need to understand the case law so that when the organizations' lawyers object to your use of those transcripts from other cases, you are prepared to respond.

In *Runge v. Stanley Fastening Sys., L.P.*, the court explained the circumstances in which a 30(b)(6) deposition taken in a previous lawsuit could be used in subsequent lawsuits against the same party:

> The general rule is that "depositions taken in a prior action are admissible in a subsequent action if there is substantial identity of issues and parties in the two actions." 10A Fed. Proc., L.Ed. § 26:521.

In order to use a deposition from a previous lawsuit, you don't have to have 100 percent of the same parties from the previous deposition. The real test is that at the time the other testimony was given, was the subject matter of the deposition sufficiently close to this trial so that the cross-examination would have fairly dealt with the same issues?

> Significantly, "total identity of parties . . . is not required," *Id.*, and the "same party" rule has "been construed liberally in light of the twin goals of fairness and efficiency." *Phillip M. Adams & Associates, LLC v. Winbond Electronics Corp.* 2010 WL 3655869, at *1 (D. Utah Sept. 14, 2010) (quoting *Hub v. Sun Valley Co.* 682 F.2d 776, 778 (9th Cir. 1982)). Thus, courts interpreting this rule "recognize that the real test should be whether the former

testimony was given upon such an issue that the party-opponent in that case had the same interest and motive in his cross-examination that the present opponent now has." *Id.* (citing Wright, Miller & Marcus, Federal Practice and Procedure § 2150). As such, "many cases have held that a deposition can be offered against one who was a party to the former suit even though the party now using the deposition was not." Wright, Miller & Marcus, Federal Practice and Procedure § 2150 (emphasis added; collecting cases, including *Ikerd v. Lapworth* 435 F.2d 197 (7th Cir. 1970)).[15]

Therefore, you can use the 30(b)(6) testimony from the prior lawsuits if the issues in those lawsuits are close enough to the issues in your case.

Example: *Runge v. Stanley Fastening Sys., L.P.*

Andrew Runge suffered a tragic injury when his father's pneumatic nail gun accidently tripped and shot a nail into his heart. As a result of the accident, Andrew suffered brain injuries that left him functionally blind and cognitively impaired. His family sued Stanley Fastening Systems, L.P., in a products liability lawsuit alleging that the nail gun was unreasonably dangerous and defectively designed. In order to bolster their claim that the nail gun was defective and unreasonably dangerous, they wanted to use depositions that were taken in previous products liability lawsuits involving Stanley nail guns. Stanley opposed using those transcripts at trial. The court found that the prior lawsuits were sufficiently similar, and therefore the court allowed the testimony from prior lawsuits at Andrew's trial.[16]

---

15. *Runge v. Stanley Fastening Sys., L.P.*, No. 4:09-CV-00130-TWP, 2011 WL 6755161, at 3 (S.D. Ind. Dec. 23, 2011).
16. *Id.*

Compelling Live Testimony from the 30(b)(6) Witness at Trial

In the discovery phase of the litigation, Rule 30(b)(6) requires the organization to designate and prepare witnesses to testify at a deposition on its behalf. However, Rule 30(b)(6) applies to the deposition and is silent about the trial. Rule 45, on the other hand, does provide a procedure for compelling a person to testify at trial. The courts have reconciled these two rules by finding that the organization is a party that appears vicariously through its 30(b)(6) witnesses.[17] Thereby, the organization must designate a person to appear on its behalf at trial as well.

Consistent with the policies underlying Rule 30(b)(6), courts have enforced trial subpoenas that compel an organization's representative to attend (rather than a specifically identified person).[18] Similar to a Rule 30(b)(6) notice, the trial subpoena identifies the matters of inquiry for which the responding organization must prepare and produce a witness.[19]

Serving Subpoenas on Party Organizations

The one-hundred-mile geographic limitations for federal subpoenas does not apply to the subpoena of organizations' representatives.[20] Rule 45(c)(3)(A) excludes parties and their officers from

---

17. *Sara Lee Corp. v. Kraft Foods Inc.*, 276 F.R.D. 500, 503 (N.D. Ill. 2011) (citing *Brazos River Auth. v. GE Ionics, Inc.*, 469 F.3d 416, 434 (5th Cir. 2006)).
18. *Conyers v. Balboa Ins. Co.*, No. 8:12-CV-30-T-33EAJ, 2013 WL 2450108, at *1 (M.D. Fla. June 5, 2013); *see also, Aristocrat Leisure Ltd. v. Deutsche Bank Trust Co. Americas*, 262 F.R.D. 293, 303 (S.D.N.Y. 2009); *Williams v. Asplundh Tree Expert Co.*, No. 3:05CV479J33MCR, 2006 WL 2598758, at *2 (M.D. Fla. Sept. 11, 2006).
19. *Conyers v. Balboa Ins. Co.*, No. 8:12-CV-30-T-33EAJ, 2013 WL 2450108, at *1 (M.D. Fla. June 5, 2013); *see also, Aristocrat Leisure Ltd. v. Deutsche Bank Trust Co. Americas*, 262 F.R.D. 293, 303 (S.D.N.Y. 2009); *Williams v. Asplundh Tree Expert Co.*, No. 3:05CV479J33MCR, 2006 WL 2598758, at *2 (M.D. Fla. Sept. 11, 2006).
20. Fed. R. Civ. P. 45.

the one-hundred-mile geographic limitations for the service of a subpoena. Specifically, Rule 45(c)(3)(A)(ii) provides the following:

> On timely motion, the court by which a subpoena was issued shall quash or modify the subpoena if it requires a person who is *not a party or an officer of a party* to travel to a place more than one hundred miles from the place where that person resides, is employed, or regularly transacts business in person, except that, subject to the provisions of clause (c)(3)(B)(iii) of this rule, such a person may in order to attend trial be commanded to travel from any such place within the state in which the trial is held.[21]

The plain, unambiguous language of Rule 45(b)(2), imposing a one-hundred-mile subpoena rule, is expressly limited by Rule 45(c)(3)(A)(ii). Rule 45(c)(3)(A)(ii) mandates that a district court quash a subpoena if it requires "a person who is *not a party* or *an officer of a party*" to travel more than one hundred miles from his or her residence or place of employment.[22] As a result, a majority of courts found that because Rule 45(c)(3)(A)(ii) is limited to nonparties and officers of nonparties, then the *inverse* of that is that parties and officers of parties *can* be subpoenaed. The courts have created the inference that because Rule 45(c)(3)(A)(ii) is silent on parties, then Rule 45(b)(2) authorizes the court to subpoena an officer or high-level employees of an organization party to attend a trial beyond the one-hundred-mile limit.[23]

---

21. Fed. R. Civ. P. 45(c)(3)(A)(ii). (Emphasis added.)
22. *In re Vioxx Products Liab. Litig.*, 438 F. Supp. 2d 664, 667 (E.D. La. 2006).
23. *In re Vioxx Products Liab. Litig.*, 438 F. Supp. 2d 664, 667 (E.D. La. 2006); see also, *Williams v. Asplundh Tree Expert Co.*, No. 3:05CV479J33MCR, 2006 WL 2598758, at *2 (M.D. Fla. Sept. 11, 2006); *Ferrell v. IBP, Inc.*, 2000 WL 34032907, *1 (N.D. Iowa 2000); *In re Methyl Tertiary Butyl Ether ("MTBE") Prods. Liab. Litig.*, MDL No. 1358, 2009 WL 1840882, at *1 (S.D.N.Y. June 24, 2009); *Younis v. Am. Univ. in Cairo*, 30 F. Supp.2d 390, 395, n. 44 (S.D.

When you subpoena organizational representatives of a party to testify at trial, they are clearly testifying on behalf of the organization, rather than in an individual capacity.[24] The court considers the organizational representative to be a party, regardless of whether or not the representative is an officer of the organization. Therefore, the organization should produce the representative even if the representative resides outside the one-hundred-mile limit.[25]

When you are issuing a subpoena of a party organization, which requires the organization to designate a witness to testify on its behalf, it is the organization that will choose the witness. Therefore, the organization can select a witness within or outside of the one-hundred-mile limit. It would not be fair to allow the organization to evade the subpoena requirement by claiming that their designee is outside the one-hundred-mile limit. Therefore, even if the party organization's designated witness is outside the one-hundred-mile limit, the party is required to produce that designated witness at trial.[26]

Using Nonparty 30(b)(6) Witness Depositions at Trial

A deposition of a nonparty 30(b)(6) witness is a statement made outside of trial. Therefore, by definition, it is hearsay.[27] The nonparty 30(b)(6) deposition cannot be considered as admissible under Federal Rule of Evidence 801(d)(2), because the Rule applies only to party opponents. Further, because the deposition is of a nonparty witness, it not admissible under Rule 32(a)(3), which is limited to parties.[28]

N.Y.1998); *In re Ames Dep't Stores, Inc.*, No. 01–42217, 2004 WL 1661983, at *1 (Bankr.S.D. N.Y. June 25, 2009); *Am. Fed'n of Gov't Employees, Local 922 v. Ashcroft*, 354 F. Supp.2d 909, 915 (E.D. Ark. 2003); *Aristocrat Leisure Ltd. v. Deutsche Bank Trust Co. Americas*, 262 F.R.D. 293, 302 (S.D.N.Y. 2009).
24. *Williams v. Asplundh Tree Expert Co.*, No. 3:05CV479J33MCR, 2006 WL 2598758, at *2 (M.D. Fla. Sept. 11, 2006).
25. *Id.* at *3.
26. *Aristocrat Leisure Ltd. v. Deutsche Bank Trust Co. Americas*, 262 F.R.D. 293, 303 (S.D.N.Y. 2009).
27. Fed. R. E. 801(c).
28. *Stearns v. Paccar, Inc.*, 1993 WL 17084, *4 (10th Cir. 1993); Fed. R. E. 801(d)(2).

In order to introduce the testimony of a nonparty 30(b)(6) witness, you need to establish that the testimony is admissible under a separate rule. Rule 32(a) establishes the conditions that must be present before you can introduce nonparty 30(b)(6) deposition testimony. The nonparty 30(b)(6) deposition testimony is admissible if you establish that the *person*[29] who was the nonparty's 30(b)(6) witness is unavailable under one of the five conditions in Rule 32(a)(4). This rule provides the following:

> **Unavailable Witness.** A party may use for any purpose the deposition of a witness, whether or not a party, if the court finds:
>
> (A) that the witness is dead;
>
> (B) that the witness is more than one hundred miles from the place of hearing or trial or is outside the United States, unless it appears that the witness's absence was procured by the party offering the deposition;
>
> (C) that the witness cannot attend or testify because of age, illness, infirmity, or imprisonment;
>
> (D) that the party offering the deposition could not procure the witness's attendance by subpoena; or
>
> (E) on motion and notice, that exceptional circumstances make it desirable—in the interest of justice and with due regard to the importance of live testimony in open court—to permit the deposition to be used.[30]

---

29. *See* chapter 3, "Details of Rule 30(b)(6)."
30. Fed. R. Civ. P. 32(a)(4).

If the person whom the organization had previously designated in response to a nonparty 30(b)(6) deposition is within the subpoena range of the court, that person will be required to testify rather than introducing the testimony transcript. That witness may testify as the organization's representative. In *Sara Lee*, the court ruled that the 30(b)(6) witness of a nonparty, who was subpoenaed to testify at trial, could testify outside of his or her personal knowledge about matters of the corporation's "collective knowledge or subjective belief."[31] Such topics include matters about which the corporation's official position is relevant, such as corporate policies and procedures, or the corporation's opinion about whether a business partner complied with the terms of a contract.[32]

Attempts to Change the Story at Trial

Trial by ambush is the greatest prejudice that a party could experience.[33] The very purpose of discovery is "to avoid 'trial by ambush.'"[34] Rule 30(b)(6) was created to enable litigants involving institutional adversaries to identify facts and positions before trial. Nevertheless, organizations often attempt to change their testimony in the following ways:

---

31. *Sara Lee Corp. v. Kraft Foods Inc.*, 276 F.R.D. 500, 503 (N.D. Ill. 2011).
32. *Id.*
33. *See, e.g., Hickman v. Taylor*, 329 U.S. 495, 507, 67 S. Ct. 385, 392, 91 L. Ed. 451 (1947) ("Mutual knowledge of all the relevant facts gathered by both parties is essential to proper litigation. To that end, either party may compel the other to disgorge whatever facts he has in his possession. The deposition-discovery procedure simply advances the stage at which the disclosure can be compelled from the time of trial to the period preceding it, thus reducing the possibility of surprise"); *Reed v. Binder*, 165 F.R.D. 424, 431 (D.N.J. 1996) ("The failure to comply with the disclosure requirements of the Rule frustrates the purpose of the Rules—the elimination of unfair surprise and the conservation of resources.").
34. *Ierardi v. Lorillard, Inc.*, No. CIV. A. 90-7049, 1991 WL 158911, at *3 (E.D. Pa. Aug. 13, 1991) (citing *Federal Deposit Ins. Corp. v. Butcher*, 116 F.R.D. 196, 201 (E.D. Tenn. 1986)).

1. The organization disavows the 30(b)(6) witness and claim that he no longer binds the organization.

2. The organization brings a different witness to trial than the one who testified in the 30(b)(6) deposition, who tells a different story at trial. They attempt to say "the original 30(b)(6) designee was wrong."

3. They have the experts tell a different story than the 30(b)(6) witness did.

The policy reasons underlying the binding effect of the 30(b)(6) testimony is a philosophy to prevent trial by ambush.[35]

Organization Disavows the 30(b)(6) Witness at Trial

If an organization presents a witness at trial who was formerly a 30(b)(6) witness in a deposition, the organization can't disavow that witness's status as a representative of the organization. That witness can be cross-examined with his earlier testimony, and the organization is bound by it.

In *Brazos River Authority v. GE Ionics, Inc.*, the Fifth Circuit Court of Appeals ruled that when a witness, who previously testified in a deposition under Rule 30(b)(6) is made available at trial, he can be cross-examined about the same matters, within the organization's knowledge, that he testified about at the deposition.[36] The organization cannot make the witness available at trial and then object to matters that the witness testified about at the 30(b)(6) deposition on grounds that the witness had only institutional knowledge of the issues, not personal knowledge.[37] When a witness who was a 30(b)(6) witness is testifying at trial, the *Sara Lee*

---

35. *QBE v. Jorda*, 277 F.R.D. 676, 690 (S.D. Fla. 2012) (citing *Calzaturficio S.C.A.R.P.A. s.p.a. v. Fabiano Shoe Co., Inc.*, 201 F.R.D. 33, 38 (D. Mass. 2001); *Wilson v. Lakner*, 228 F.R.D. 524, 531 (D. Md. 2005); *United States v. Taylor*, 166 F.R.D. 356, 363 (M.D.N.C. 1996)).
36. *Brazos River Authority v. GE Ionics, Inc.*, 469 F.3d 416, 434 (5th Cir. 2006).
37. *Id.*

and *Brazos* courts made it clear that attorneys could cross-examine that witness based on the prior 30(b)(6) testimony.[38]

Example: Cedar Gardens Homes

Cedar Gardens Homes is being sued because a resident died in their care due to negligence from understaffing. Sally Carpenter, the director of nursing, was designated by Cedar Gardens Homes to testify in a 30(b)(6) deposition. As the 30(b)(6) witness, she stated the corporation's policy was to follow the federal nursing home regulations for staffing. She went on to testify that because of budget constraints, they often did not have enough staff to provide for patient care.

Cedar Gardens Homes wants to call Sally Carpenter at trial to say that all care was properly given to this patient. However, Cedar Gardens also claims Sally Carpenter doesn't have personal knowledge as to whether or not there was enough staff on the shifts when the resident didn't get care. They tried to disavow her status as a corporate representative and object to her testimony as to understaffing.

Cedar Gardens Homes wants her to testify about the care that was given to this patient, but they want to prevent her from testifying about the corporation's positions regarding staffing. Cedar Gardens is attempting to claim that at the 30(b)(6) deposition, she was the corporation, but at trial, they are offering her testimony as an individual and not as the voice of the corporation. They claim that she doesn't have personal knowledge of the days at issue and therefore can't testify.

Organization Brings a Different Witness to Trial

If the organization chooses to use a different witness who has been strategically insulated from the 30(b)(6) testimony, that act simply denies the accuracy of the 30(b)(6) deposition testimony. This presents a tension between Rule 30(b)(6) and evidentiary Rule 613. The witness at trial is not the person who made the

---

38. *Sara Lee Corp. v. Kraft Foods Inc.*, 276 F.R.D. 500 (N.D. Ill. 2011); *Brazos River Authority v. GE Ionics, Inc.*, 469 F.3d 416 (5th Cir. 2006).

prior inconsistent statement at the deposition. Consistent with the principle that the 30(b)(6) witness was testifying vicariously on behalf of the organization, in *Wilson v. Lakner*, the court stated that *any* witness who contradicted the 30(b)(6) witness's sworn testimony could be cross-examined with the 30(b)(6) deposition. The court could order the witness to testify about why the opposing counsel was not apprised of the amendments to the testimony prior to trial.[39]

Example: Cedar Gardens Homes

Cedar Gardens Homes attempts to call the staffing director, Betty Wilkins, who testifies that the nursing home was never understaffed. Using the rule from *Wilson v. Lakner*, you can cross-examine Betty Wilkins about the corporation's position—that the facility was understaffed—as Sally Carpenter expressed in her 30(b)(6). The court could order Betty Wilkins to testify about why the opposing counsel was never notified that the corporation's position about staffing levels changed.

Organization's Experts Can't Contradict 30(b)(6) Testimony

A party should not be allowed to attempt to circumvent the policies underlying Rule 30(b)(6). They should not introduce testimony at trial that rejects their own previous 30(b)(6) deposition testimony of positions and facts. Courts have granted motions *in limine* to exclude expert testimony that contradicts 30(b)(6) testimony.[40] Expert testimony is governed by Fed. R. E. 702, which states that expert witness testimony is admissible only if

---

39. *Wilson v. Lakner*, 228 F.R.D. 524, 530 (D. Md. 2005)
40. *Great Am. Ins. Co. of NY v. Summit Exterior Works, LLC*, No. 3:10 CV 1669 JGM, 2012 WL 459885, at *8 (D. Conn. Feb. 13, 2012) (granting motion *in limine* to exclude expert testimony that contradicts 30(b)(6) factual testimony).

(a) the expert's scientific, technical, or other specialized knowledge will help the trier of fact to understand the evidence or to determine a fact in issue;

(b) the testimony is based upon sufficient facts or data;

(c) the testimony is the product of reliable principles and methods; and

(d) the expert has reliably applied the principles and methods to the facts of the case.[41]

The expert's opinion must be based on sufficient facts or data. If the court deems that the facts or data are established by virtue of the 30(b)(6) testimony, then the expert has no foundation to speculate that the facts are other than what has been established.

Example: Cedar Gardens Homes

Because the Cedar Gardens Homes admitted in Sally Carpenter's 30(b)(6) deposition that the facility was understaffed, they are bound by that. They cannot call a staffing expert to testify that Sally Carpenter's 30(b)(6) testimony was wrong.

Motion in Limine

Courts that enforce Rule 30(b)(6) disclosure prevent trial testimony that is inconsistent or that contradicts the 30(b)(6) witness's testimony. The doctrine of *judicial estoppel* is a procedural fairness mechanism that prevents parties from taking different positions in litigation to benefit them at that time. Judicial estoppel prevents a party from asserting a position, benefitting from that position, and then, when it becomes more convenient or

---

41. Fed. R. Evid. 702.

profitable, retreating from that position later in the litigation.[42] Since estoppel is an equitable doctrine, courts have discretion to invoke it as the judge deems appropriate.[43]

An alternative to a motion for outright prevention is a motion *in limine* to require an *in camera* hearing if the organization plans to diverge from its 30(b)(6) testimony. When possible, courts should determine preliminary questions concerning whether the evidence is admissible prior to trial.[44] The Federal Rules of Evidence and the Federal Rules of Civil Procedure and the interpretative rulings from the Supreme Court all encourage parties to use pretrial motions, such as motions *in limine*, "to narrow the issues and minimize disruptions at trial."[45] Heard in advance of trial, the motion asks a trial court to instruct another party, the party's counsel, or other witnesses not to mention certain facts or opinions without further permission from the court.[46] Motions *in limine* serve a gatekeeping function that permits the trial judge to eliminate evidentiary submissions that would be inadmissible.[47] Motions *in limine* are a vehicle to enforce the policies of Rule 30(b)(6), reduce the risk of trial by ambush, and ensure the parties respect the integrity of the judicial process by enforcing compliance with the Rules of Civil Procedure.

---

42. *Johnson v. Parker Tractor & Implement Co., Inc.*, 132 So.3d 1032, 1037 (Miss. 2014).
43. *In re Gray*, 519 B.R. 767, 774 (B.A.P. 8th Cir. 2014) reh'g denied, No. 14-6027, 2014 WL 7477715 (B.A.P. 8th Cir. Dec. 31, 2014); *Peralta v. Vasquez*, 467 F.3d 98, 105 (2d Cir. 2006); *In re Residential Capital*, LLC, 519 B.R. 890, 906 (Bankr. S.D.N.Y. 2014); *Johnson v. Parker Tractor & Implement Co., Inc.*, 132 So.3d 1032, 1037 (Miss. 2014).
44. Fed. R. E. 104(a); *Dow Corning Corp. v. Weather Shield Mfg., Inc.*, 09-10429, 2011 WL 4506167, at *2 (E.D. Mich. Sept. 29, 2011).
45. *United States v. Brawner*, 173 F.3d 966, 970 (6th Cir. 1999).
46. *See Lapasinskas v. Quick*, 17 Mich.App. 733, 737, n. 1, 170 N.W.2d 318 (1969).
47. *Dow Corning Corp. v. Weather Shield Mfg., Inc.*, 2011 WL 4506167, at *2 (E.D. Mich. Sept. 29, 2011); *Command Cinema Corp. v. VCA Labs, Inc.*, 464 F. Supp.2d 191 (S.D.N.Y. 2006); *Noble v. Sheahan*, 116 F. Supp. 2d 966, 969 (N.D. Ill. 2000); *see also*, *Luce v. United States*, 469 U.S. 38, 41, n.4 (1984).

By requiring the *in camera* review, the court is able to evaluate (pursuant to *Rainey v. American Forest and Paper Ass'n, Inc.*)[48] whether the evidence was available at the time of the deposition.[49] Equally important, the *in camera* process reduces the risk of trial by ambush because the organization is placed on notice that the court will not tolerate attempts to "slip it in."

Example: Cedar Gardens Homes

Rather than simply cross-examining Sally Carpenter, the Cedar Gardens Homes 30(b)(6) witness, an alternative would be to ask the court to enforce the binding effect of 30(b)(6) to preserve the integrity of the judicial process. The motion *in limine* should be to preemptively exclude the testimony of the staffing director Betty Wilkins and the testimony of the staffing expert.

Summary

- A 30(b)(6) witness who receives a subpoena to testify at trial can testify outside of his personal knowledge about matters of the organization's "collective knowledge or subjective belief."

- An adverse party may use a party's 30(b)(6) deposition *for any purpose*.

- An organization cannot introduce the deposition testimony of its own witness at trial without showing witness unavailability.

---

48. *Rainey v. American Forest and Paper Ass'n, Inc.*, 26 F. Supp.2d 82 (D.D.C. 1998).
49. *See* chapter 16, "Changing the Testimony."

- In order to introduce the deposition testimony of a *non-party* 30(b)(6) witness, it is necessary to establish that the individual witness is unavailable under Rule 32(a)(4).

- When a witness who previously testified as a Rule 30(b)(6) witness is made available at trial, he can be cross-examined about matters within the organization.

Epilogue

If strength were all, tiger would not fear scorpion.

—Charlie Chan

Trials are supposed to be about the truth. They're about making a better society by applying the rule of law and holding wrongdoers accountable. We didn't go to law school to learn how to weasel out of the truth. We went to law school to make the world a better place. The problem is that somewhere along the way, many lawyers decided that the rule of law is what you can get away with, a *catch me if you can*. Rule 30(b)(6) was developed to try to get the focus back on finding the truth without a game of cat-and-mouse. Despite its extraordinary power, it's the most underused and misunderstood rule in our arsenals.

    I join trial teams throughout the country to work with their 30(b)(6) projects. I've lectured in thirty-four states. It seems that wherever I go, people say, "Mark, your presentation is all fine and dandy, but our judges never enforce those rules." Despite opposition, I say, try it! If you follow the techniques that I've developed, and if you give the court a well-researched case with a factual record to support your position, then what we have found is that nine times out of ten, they will go with you. I get emails and letters from lawyers throughout the country saying, "I can't believe it! This stuff really works! I feel strong. I can stand up to these giants."

They relate back to me the Charlie Chan adage that I always share with them. "If strength were all, tiger would not fear scorpion." You can do it. Go out there, use the rules, and find the truth.

—MRK

Appendix A

Rule 30(b)(6) in All Fifty States

State courts have either established rules for depositions by issue designation that are substantially similar to Federal Rule 30(b)(6), or have developed procedures that accomplish the same goals sought by the federal courts. When the state rule is based on its federal counterpart, those states often look to federal authority for guidance in interpreting their state rule. This appendix provides a quick reference to the individual states' deposition by designation rules and the states' case law discussing the use of federal precedent when interpreting the respective rules.

Alabama

Ala. R. Civ. P. 30(b)(6) is virtually identical to Fed. R. Civ. P. 30(b)(6). The Alabama rule states:

> A party may in the party's notice and in a subpoena name as the deponent a public or private corporation or a partnership or association or governmental agency and describe with reasonable particularity the matters on which examination is requested. In that event, the organization so named shall designate one or more officers, directors, or managing agents, or other persons who consent to testify on its behalf, and may set forth, for each person

designated, the matters on which the person will testify. A subpoena shall advise a nonparty organization of its duty to make such a designation. The persons so designated shall testify as to matters known or reasonably available to the organization. This subdivision (b)(6) does not preclude taking a deposition by any other procedure authorized in these rules.[1]

The Alabama Supreme Court has held that, "[b]ecause the Alabama and Federal rules are virtually *verbatim*, 'a presumption arises that cases construing the Federal Rules are authority for construction of the Alabama Rules.'"[2]

Alaska

Alaska R. Civ. P. 30(b)(6) is virtually identical to Fed. R. Civ. P. 30(b)(6). The Alaska rule states:

> A party may in the party's notice and in a subpoena name as the deponent a public or private corporation or a partnership or association or governmental agency and describe with reasonable particularity the matters on which examination is requested. In that event, the organization so named shall designate one or more officers, directors, or managing agents, or other persons who consent to testify on its behalf, and may set forth, for each person designated, the matters on which the person will testify. A subpoena shall advise a nonparty organization of its duty to make such a designation. The persons so designated shall testify as to matters known or

---

1. Ala. R. Civ. P. 30(b)(6).
2. *Smith v. Wilcox Cty. Board of Educ.*, 365 So. 2d 659, 661 (Ala. 1978).

reasonably available to the organization. This subparagraph (b)(6) does not preclude taking a deposition by any other procedure authorized in these rules.[3]

The Alaska Supreme Court has held that " . . . in interpreting our civil rules we have often looked to identical federal counterparts for guidance."[4]

Arizona

Ariz. R. Civ. P. 30(b)(6) is substantially similar to Fed. R. Civ. P. 30(b)(6). The body of the Arizona rule is virtually identical, except the Arizona rule omits "and in a subpoena," which refers to depositions of nonparty organizations. The rule states:

> A party may in the party's notice name as the deponent a public or private corporation or a partnership or association or governmental agency and designate with reasonable particularity the matters on which examination is requested. The organization so named shall designate one or more officers, directors, or managing agents, or other persons who consent to testify on its behalf, and may set forth, for each person designated, the matters on which that person will testify. The persons so designated shall testify as to matters known or reasonably available to the organization. This subdivision (b)(6) does not preclude taking a deposition by any other procedure authorized in these rules.[5]

---

3. Alaska R. Civ. P. 30(b)(6).
4. *Brown v. Lange*, 21 P.3d 822, 825 (Alaska 2001).
5. Ariz. R. Civ. P. 30(b)(6).

The Arizona Supreme Court has held that, "[b]ecause Arizona has substantially adopted the Federal Rules of Civil Procedure, we give great weight to the federal interpretations of the rules."[6]

Arkansas

Ark. R. Civ. P. 30(b)(6) is virtually identical to Fed. R. Civ. P. 30(b)(6). The Arkansas rule states:

> A party may in his notice and in the subpoena name as the deponent a public or private corporation or a partnership or association or governmental agency and describe with reasonable particularity the matters on which examination is requested. In that event, the organization so named shall designate one or more officers, directors, or managing agents, or other persons who consent to testify on its behalf, and may set forth, for each person designated, the matters on which he will testify. A subpoena shall advise a nonparty organization of its duty to make such a designation. The persons so designated shall testify as to matters known or reasonably available to the organization. This subdivision (b)(6) does not preclude taking a deposition by any other procedure authorized by these rules.[7]

The Arkansas Supreme Court has held that, "[b]ased upon the similarities of our rules with the Federal Rules of Civil Procedure, we consider the interpretation of these rules by federal courts to be of a significant precedential value."[8]

---

6. *Edwards v. Young*, 486 P.2d 181, 182 (Ariz. 1971).
7. Ark. R. Civ. P. 30(b)(6).
8. *City of Fort Smith v. Carter*, 216 S.W.3d 594, 598 (Ark. 2005).

California

Although California has a rule for taking depositions of organizations, it differs substantially from Fed. R. Civ. P. 30(b)(6). Cal. Code Civ. P. § 2025.230 states:

> If the *deponent named is not a natural person*, the deposition notice shall describe with reasonable particularity the matters on which examination is requested. In that event, *the deponent shall designate* and produce at the deposition those of its officers, directors, managing agents, employees, or agents who are most qualified *to testify on its behalf* as to those matters to the extent of any *information known or reasonably available to the deponent.*[9]

Like the Federal Rule, California focuses on seeking specific information rather than identifying a specific deponent: "[t]he deposition notice shall describe with reasonable particularity the matters on which examination is requested." However, unlike the Federal Rule, which requires the organization to designate witnesses to provide all information "known or reasonably available to the organization," the California Rule requires the organization to designate people or agents who are "most qualified to testify on its behalf as to those matters to the extent of any information known or reasonably available to the *deponent*."

The California Court of appeals has clarified, "But a person most knowledgeable is not limited to testifying on personal knowledge in a deposition. Instead, he may testify to the extent of information 'reasonably available to the deponent.'"[10] While limited state case law exists on the mechanics of Cal. Code Civ. P.

---

9. Cal. Code Civ. P. § 2025.230. [Emphasis added.]
10. *Serratos v. Countrywide Home Loans*, No. 2D CIVIL B236996, 2013 WL 6271926, at *5 (Cal. Ct. App. Dec. 4, 2013).

§ 2025.230, the plain language of the rule as well as case law suggest that *deponent* in the California rule is parallel to *organization* in the Federal rule. Therefore, under the rule, the deponent organization is also required to prepare its designee. In *Maldonado v. Superior Court*, the California Court of Appeals explained that, "Under the current law, '[i]f the subject matter of the questioning is clearly stated, the burden is on the entity, not the examiner, to produce the right witnesses. And, if the particular officer or employee designated lacks personal knowledge of all the information sought, he or she is supposed to find out from those who do!'"[11] Further, with respect to producing documents at a § 2025.230 document deposition, the California Court of Appeals held that, "When a request for documents is made, however, the witness or someone in authority is expected to make an inquiry of everyone who might be holding responsive documents or everyone who knows where such documents might be held."[12] Thus, the operative effect of this rule is aligned with Fed. R. Civ. P. 30(b)(6).

Colorado

Colo. R. Civ. P. 30(b)(6) is substantially similar to Fed. R. Civ. P. 30(b)(6). The body of the Colorado rule is virtually identical, except the Colorado rule omits "and in a subpoena," which refers to depositions of a nonparty organization. The rule states:

> A party may in his notice name as the deponent a public or private corporation or a partnership or association or governmental agency and designate with reasonable particularity the matters on which examination is requested. The organization

---

11. *Maldonado v. Superior Court*, 94 Cal. App. 4th 1390, 1395–96 (2002) (citing Weil & Brown, Cal. Practice Guide: Civil Procedure Before Trial ¶ 8:475, (The Rutter Group 2001)).
12. *Maldonado v. Superior Court*, 94 Cal. App. 4th 1390, 1396 (2002).

so named shall designate one or more officers, directors, or managing agents, or other persons who consent to testify on its behalf, and may set forth, for each person designated, the matters on which he will testify. The persons so designated shall testify as to matters known or reasonably available to the organization. This subsection (b)(6) does not preclude taking a deposition by any other procedure authorized in these rules.[13]

The Colorado Supreme Court has held that, "[b]ecause the Colorado Rules of Civil Procedure are patterned on the federal rules, we may also look to the federal rules and decisions for guidance."[14]

In *D.R. Horton, Inc. v. D & L Landscaping, LLC.*, the Colorado Court of Appeals stated, "There is a paucity of Colorado law interpreting C.R.C.P. 30(b)(6) and its use. However, the rule has been interpreted in federal courts and other state courts. Because the federal rule is identical to Colorado's rule, federal cases interpreting the rule are highly persuasive."[15]

Connecticut

Conn. Prac. Book § 13–27(h) is substantially similar to Fed. R. Civ. P. 30(b)(6). The body of the Connecticut rule is virtually identical, except the Connecticut rule adds the naming of "a state officer in an action arising out of the officer's performance of employment" to the rule.

---

13. Colo. R. Civ. P. 30(b)(6).
14. *Garrigan v. Bowen*, 243 P.3d 231, 235 (Colo. 2010).
15. *D.R. Horton, Inc. v. D & L Landscaping, LLC*, 215 P.3d 1163 (Colo. App. 2008) citing *Leaffer v. Zarlengo*, 44 P.3d 1072, 1080–81 (Colo. 2002); *Akin v. Four Corners Encampment*, 179 P.3d 139, 146 (Colo. App. 2007).

> A party may in the notice and in the subpoena name as the deponent a public or private corporation or a partnership or an association or a governmental agency or *a state officer in an action arising out of the officer's performance of employment* and designate with reasonable particularity the matters on which examination is requested. The organization or state officer so named shall designate one or more officers, directors, or managing agents, or other persons who consent to testify on its behalf, and may set forth, for each person designated, the matters on which the person will testify. The persons so designated shall testify as to matters known or reasonably available to the organization. This subsection does not preclude the taking of a deposition by any other procedure authorized by the rules of practice.[16]

The Connecticut Supreme Court has not yet provided a general rule allowing for the use of federal case law to interpret the state's rules of civil procedure. When interpretive issues involving civil procedure arise, however, the court has applied federal case law about specific rules, including Fed R. Civ. P. 23,[17] Fed R. Civ. P. 32(a)(2),[18] and Fed R. Civ. P. 56,[19] to construe the state's corresponding rules of civil procedure.

The general applicability of federal case law to the Connecticut rules has been provided by the Appellate Court of Connecticut, which has held that, "[w]here a state rule is similar to a federal rule, we review the federal case law to assist our interpretation of our rule."[20]

---

16. Conn. Prac. Book § 13–27(h). [Emphasis added.]
17. *Collins v. Anthem Health Plans, Inc.*, 836 A.2d 1124, 1135 (Conn. 2003).
18. *Gateway Co. v. DiNoia*, 654 A.2d 342, 350 (Conn. 1995).
19. *Mac's Car City, Inc. v. Am. Nat. Bank*, 532 A.2d 1302, 1304 (Conn. 1987).
20. *Pelarinos v. Henderson*, 643 A.2d 894, 897 (Conn. 1994).

With respect to Fed. R. Civ. P. 30(b)(6), specifically, the Superior Court of Connecticut has, in an unpublished opinion, expressly held that, "[d]ue to the absence of Connecticut authority construing Conn. Prac. Book § 13–27(h) or its predecessor, § 244(g), the Court should look to Fed. R. Civ. P. 30(b)(6) for guidance, which contains a similar provision addressing designee depositions."[21]

Delaware

Del. Super. Ct. Civ. R. P. 30(b)(6) is substantially similar to Fed. R. Civ. P. 30(b)(6). The body of the Delaware rule is virtually identical, except the Delaware rule omits "and in a subpoena," which refers to depositions of a nonparty organization. The rule states:

> A party may in the party's notice name as the deponent a public or private corporation or a partnership or association or governmental agency and describe with reasonable particularity the matters on which examination is requested. The organization so named shall designate one or more officers, directors, or managing agents, or other persons who consent to testify on its behalf, and may set forth, for each person designated, the matters on which the person will testify. The persons so designated shall testify as to matters known or reasonably available to the organization. This subdivision (b)(6) does not preclude taking a deposition by any other procedure authorized in these Rules.[22]

---

21. *DDG Properties Co. v. Konover Cont. Corp.*, No. X03CV990501534S, WL 1513928 (Conn. Super. Ct. 2000).
22. Del. Super. Ct. Civ. R. P. 30(b)(6).

Relying on previous authority, the Delaware Supreme Court has instructed the following:

> Decisions interpreting the Federal Rules of Civil Procedure are usually of great persuasive weight in the construction of parallel Delaware rules; however, such decisions are not actually binding upon Delaware courts.[23]

Florida

Fla. R. Civ. P. 1.310(b)(6) is substantially similar to Fed. R. Civ. P. 30(b)(6). The body of the Florida rule is virtually identical, except the Florida rule omits "and in a subpoena," which refers to depositions of a nonparty organization.

> In the notice a party may name as the deponent a public or private corporation, a partnership or association, or a governmental agency, and designate with reasonable particularity the matters on which examination is requested. The organization so named shall designate one or more officers, directors, or managing agents, or other persons who consent to do so, to testify on its behalf and may state the matters on which each person designated will testify. The persons so designated shall testify about matters known or reasonably available to the organization. This subdivision does not preclude taking a deposition by any other procedure authorized in these rules.[24]

---

23. *Cede & Co. v. Technicolor, Inc.*, 542 A.2d 1182, 1191 (Del. 1988) (internal citations omitted)
24. Fla. R. Civ. P. 1.310(b)(6).

Furthermore, the Florida Supreme Court has provided an instruction that state courts may look to federal case law for guidance when interpreting the state's rules, holding that, "[a]lthough the Federal Rules of Civil Procedure and the Florida Rules of Civil Procedure differ in some respects, 'the objective in promulgating the Florida rules has been to harmonize our rules with the federal rules' . . . Thus, we look to the federal rules and decisions for guidance in interpreting Florida's civil procedure rules."[25]

With respect to Fla. R. Civ. P. 1.310(b)(6), the District Court of Appeals has stated that the Florida rule was borrowed from Fed. R. Civ. P. 30(b)(6). The Court used the body of federal authority from throughout the country to describe the obligations and effect of the testimony under the Fla. R. Civ. P. 1.310(b)(6).[26]

Georgia

Ga. Code Ann. § 9–11–30(b)(6) is substantially similar to Fed. R. Civ. P. 30(b)(6). The body of the Georgia rule is virtually identical, except the Georgia rule omits "and in a subpoena," which refers to depositions of a nonparty organization. The rule states:

> A party may, in his or her notice, name as the deponent a public or private corporation or a partnership or association or a governmental agency and designate with reasonable particularity the matters on which examination is requested. The organization so named shall designate one or more officers, directors, or managing agents, or other persons who consent to testify on its behalf, and may set forth, for each person designated, the matters on which he

---

25. *Gleneagle Ship Management Co. v. Leondakos*, 602 So. 2d 1282, 1283–84 (Fla. 1992) (internal citations omitted).
26. *Carriage Hills Condominium, Inc. v. JBH Roofing & Constructors, Inc.*, 109 So.3d 329 (Dist. Ct. App. Fla., 4th Dist. 2013).

or she will testify. The persons so designated shall testify as to matters known or reasonably available to the organization. This paragraph does not preclude taking a deposition by any other procedure authorized in this chapter.[27]

The Georgia Supreme Court has not yet provided a general rule allowing for the use of federal case law to interpret the state's rules of civil procedure. When interpretive issues involving civil procedure arise, however, the court has applied federal case law about specific rules, including Fed. R. Civ. P. 9(c), [28] Fed. R. Civ. P. 16,[29] and Fed. R. Civ. P. 25(c),[30] to construe the state's corresponding rules of civil procedure.

Furthermore, the Court of Appeals of Georgia has provided guidance on this issue, holding that " . . . the Georgia Civil Procedure Act was taken from the Federal Rules of Civil Procedure, and 'with slight immaterial variations, its sections are substantially identical to corresponding rules. Because of this similarity, it is proper that we give consideration and great weight to constructions placed on the Federal Rules by the federal courts.'"[31]

Hawaii

Haw. R. Civ. P. 30(b)(6) is virtually identical to Fed. R. Civ. P. 30(b)(6). The Hawaii rule states:

A party may in the party's notice and in a subpoena name as the deponent a public or private corporation or a partnership or association or governmental

---

27. Ga. Code Ann. § 9-11-30(b)(6).
28. *McDonough Const. Co. v. McLendon Elec. Co.*, 250 S.E.2d 424, 429 (Ga. 1978).
29. *Ambler v. Archer*, 196 S.E.2d 858, 862 (Ga. 1973).
30. *Nat'l City Mortgage Co. v. Tidwell*, 749 S.E.2d 730, 732 (Ga. 2013).
31. *Bicknell v. CBT Factors Corp.*, 321 S.E.2d 383, 385 (Ga. App. 1984).

> agency and describe with reasonable particularity the matters on which examination is requested. In that event, the organization so named shall designate one or more officers, directors, or managing agents, or other persons who consent to testify on its behalf, and may set forth, for each person designated, the matters on which the person will testify. A subpoena shall advise a nonparty organization of its duty to make such a designation. The persons so designated shall testify as to matters known or reasonably available to the organization. This subdivision (b)(6) does not preclude taking a deposition by any other procedure authorized in these rules.[32]

The Supreme Court of Hawaii has held that, "[w]here we have patterned a rule of procedure after an equivalent rule within the FRCP, interpretations of the rule 'by the federal courts are deemed to be highly persuasive in the reasoning of this court.'"[33]

IDAHO

Idaho. R. Civ. P. 30(b)(6) is virtually identical to Fed. R. Civ. P. 30(b)(6). The Idaho rule states:

> A party may in the party's notice and in a subpoena name as the deponent a public or private corporation or a partnership or association or governmental agency and describe with reasonable particularity the matters on which examination is requested. In that event, the organization so named shall designate one or more officers, directors, or managing

---

32. Haw. R. Civ. P. 30(b)(6).
33. *Kawamata Farms, Inc. v. United Agri Products*, 948 P.2d 1055, 1092–93 (Haw. 1997) (internal citations omitted).

agents, or other persons who consent to testify on its behalf, and may set forth, for each person designated, the matters on which the person will testify. A subpoena shall advise a nonparty organization of its duty to make such a designation. The persons so designated shall testify as to matters known or reasonably available to the organization. This subdivision (b)(6) of this rule does not preclude taking a deposition by any other procedure authorized in these rules.[34]

Speaking to the interpretation of the state's rules, the Idaho Supreme Court has commented that " . . . part of the reason for adopting the Federal Rules of Civil Procedure in Idaho, and interpreting our own rules adopted from the federal courts as uniformly as possible with the federal cases, was to establish a uniform practice and procedure in both the federal and state courts in the State of Idaho."[35]

Illinois

Ill. Sup. Ct. R. 206(a)(1) is virtually identical to Fed. R. Civ. P. 30(b)(6). The final sentence of the Federal counterpart rule, "this paragraph does not preclude a deposition by any other procedure allowed by these rules," does not have a correlation in the Illinois state rule. Additionally, the Illinois rule adds the provision that an organization may be deposed "if required." The rule states:

> A party may in the notice and in a subpoena, *if required*, name as the deponent a public or private corporation or a partnership or association or governmental agency and describe with reasonable

---

34. Idaho. R. Civ. P. 30(b)(6).
35. *Chacon v. Sperry Corp.*, 723 P.2d 814, 819 (Idaho 1986).

particularity the matters on which examination is requested. In that event, the organization so named shall designate one or more officers, directors, or managing agents, or other persons to testify on its behalf, and may set forth, for each person designated, the matters on which that person will testify. The subpoena shall advise a nonparty organization of its duty to make such a designation. The persons so designated shall testify as to matters known or reasonably available to the organization.[36]

The Illinois Supreme Court has not yet provided a general rule allowing for the use of federal case law to interpret the state's rules of civil procedure. When interpretive issues involving civil procedure arise, however, the court has applied federal case law about specific rules, including Fed. R. Civ. P. 23,[37] and Fed. R. Civ. P. 36,[38] to construe the state's corresponding rules of civil procedure.

Indiana

Ind. R. Trial P. 30(b)(6) is substantially similar to Fed. R. Civ. P. 30(b)(6). The body of the Indiana rule is virtually identical, except the Indiana rule omits "and in a subpoena," which refers to depositions of a nonparty organization. The rule states:

> A party may in his notice name as the deponent an organization, including without limitation a governmental organization, or a partnership and designate with reasonable particularity the matters on which examination is requested. The organization so named shall designate one or more officers, directors, or

---

36. Ill. Sup. Ct. R. 206(a)(1). [Emphasis added.]
37. *Mashal v. City of Chicago*, 981 N.E.2d 951, 959 (Ill. 2012).
38. *P.R.S. Int'l, Inc. v. Shred Pax Corp.*, 703 N.E.2d 71, 77 (Ill. 1998).

managing agents, executive officers, or other persons duly authorized and consenting to testify on its behalf. The persons so designated shall testify as to matters known or available to the organization. This subdivision (B)(6) does not preclude taking a deposition by any other procedure authorized in these rules.[39]

The Indiana Supreme Court has not yet provided a general rule allowing for the use of federal case law to interpret the state's rules of civil procedure. When interpretive issues involving civil procedure arise, however, the court has applied federal case law about specific rules, including Fed. R. Civ. P. 23,[40] Fed. R. Civ. P. 41(a)(2),[41] and Fed. R. Civ. P. 60(b),[42] to construe the state's corresponding rules of civil procedure.

The applicability of federal case law to the Indiana rules has been provided by the Court of Appeals of Indiana in a sweeping holding that states as follows: "In the absence of state law, we look to federal decisions for guidance in interpreting our rules of procedure which are similar to the Federal Rules of Civil Procedure."[43]

Iowa

Iowa R. Civ. P. 1.707(5) is virtually identical to Fed. R. Civ. P. 30(b)(6). The Iowa rule states:

A notice or subpoena may name as the deponent a public or private corporation or a partnership or association or governmental agency and describe

---

39. Ind. R. Trial P. 30(b)(6).
40. *Associated Med. Networks, Ltd. v. Lewis*, 824 N.E.2d 679, 685 (Ind. 2005).
41. *Highland Realty, Inc. v. Indianapolis Airport Auth.*, 563 N.E.2d 1271, 1273 (Ind. 1990).
42. *Soft Water Utilities, Inc. v. Le Fevre*, 301 N.E.2d 745, 747 (Ind. 1973).
43. *Jackson v. Russell*, 491 N.E.2d 1017, 1018 (Ind. Ct. App. 1986).

with reasonable particularity the matters on which examination is requested. In that event, the organization so named shall designate one or more officers, directors, or managing agents, or other persons who consent to testify on its behalf, and may set forth, for each person designated, the matters on which the witness will testify. A subpoena shall advise a nonparty organization of its duty to make such a designation. The persons so designated shall testify as to matters known or reasonably available to the organization. This rule does not preclude taking a deposition by any other procedure authorized in the rules in this chapter.[44]

The Iowa Supreme Court has not yet provided a general rule allowing for the use of federal case law to interpret the state's rules of civil procedure. When interpretive issues involving civil procedure arise, however, the court has applied federal case law about specific rules, including Fed. R. Civ. P. 11,[45] Fed. R. Civ. P. 13,[46] Fed. R. Civ. P. 26(b),[47] and Fed. R. Civ. P. 56,[48] to construe the state's corresponding rules of civil procedure.

The Court of Appeals of Iowa has previously expressed that, "[i]n federal court, corporate designee depositions are governed by Federal Rule of Civil Procedure 30(b)(6). The counterpart in our state law is Iowa Rule of Civil Procedure 1.707(5)."[49]

---

44. Iowa R. Civ. P. 1.707(5).
45. *Barnhill v. Iowa Dist. Court for Polk Cty.*, 765 N.W.2d 267, 273 (Iowa 2009), as corrected (May 14, 2009).
46. *Harrington v. Polk Cty. Fed. Sav. & Loan Ass'n of Des Moines*, 196 N.W.2d 543, 545 (Iowa 1972).
47. *Wells Dairy, Inc. v. Am. Indus. Refrigeration, Inc.*, 690 N.W.2d 38 (Iowa 2004).
48. *Brody v. Ruby*, 267 N.W.2d 902, 904 (Iowa 1978).
49. *Am. Bank & Trust Co. v. Leyden*, 842 N.W.2d 679 (Iowa Ct. App. 2013).

Kansas

Kan. Stat. Ann. § 60–230 is virtually identical to Fed. R. Civ. P. 30(b)(6). The Kansas rule states:

> In its notice or subpoena, a party may name as the deponent a public or private corporation, a partnership, an association, a governmental agency, or other entity and must describe with reasonable particularity the matters for examination. The named organization must then designate one or more officers, directors, or managing agents, or designate other persons who consent to testify on its behalf; and it may set out the matters on which the person designated will testify. A subpoena must advise a nonparty organization of its duty to make this designation. The persons designated must testify about information known or reasonably available to the organization. This subsection does not preclude a deposition by any other procedure allowed by the rules of civil procedure.[50]

The Kansas Supreme Court has not yet provided a general rule allowing for the use of federal case law to interpret the state's rules of civil procedure. When interpretive issues involving civil procedure arise, however, the court has applied federal case law about specific rules, including Fed. R. Civ. P. 12,[51] Fed. R. Civ. P. 23,[52] Fed. R. Civ. P. 24(a)(2),[53] Fed. R. Civ. P. 54(b),[54]

---

50. Kan. Stat. Ann. § 60–230.
51. *Aeroflex Wichita, Inc. v. Filardo*, 275 P.3d 869, 875–76 (Kan. 2012).
52. *Newton v. Hornblower, Inc.*, 582 P.2d 1136, 1141 (Kan. 1978).
53. *Ternes v. Galichia*, 305 P.3d 617, 620 (Kan. 2013).
54. *Dennis v. Se. Kansas Gas Co.*, 610 P.2d 627, 632 (Kan. 1980).

Fed. R. Civ. P. 55(b),[55] Fed. R. Civ. P. 60(b),[56] to construe the state's corresponding rules of civil procedure.

Kentucky

Ky. R. Civ. P. 30.02(6) is virtually identical to Fed. R. Civ. P. 30(b)(6). The Kentucky rule states:

> A party may in his notice and in a subpoena name as the deponent a public or private corporation or a partnership or association or governmental agency and describe with reasonable particularity the matters on which examination is requested. In that event, the organization so named shall designate one or more officers, directors, or managing agents, or other persons who consent to testify on its behalf, and may set forth, for each person designated, the matters on which he will testify. A subpoena shall advise a nonparty organization of its duty to make such a designation. The persons so designated shall testify as to matters known or reasonably available to the organization. This paragraph (6) does not preclude taking a deposition by any other procedure authorized in these rules.[57]

The Kentucky Supreme Court has not yet provided a general rule allowing for the use of federal case law to interpret the state's rules of civil procedure. When interpretive issues involving civil procedure arise, however, the court has applied federal case law about specific rules, including Fed. R. Civ. P. 24,[58]

---

55. *Montez v. Tonkawa Vill. Apartments*, 523 P.2d 351, 354 (Kan. 1974).
56. *Id.*
57. Ky. R. Civ. P. 30.02(6).
58. *Pearman v. Schlaak*, 575 S.W.2d 462, 464 (Ky. 1978).

Fed. R. Civ. P. 26(b),[59] Fed. R. Civ. P. 35(a),[60] Fed. R. Civ. P. 54(b),[61] to construe the state's corresponding rules of civil procedure.

Louisiana

La. Code Civ. P. art. 1442 is substantially similar to Fed. R. Civ. P. 30(b)(6). The body of the rule is virtually identical, except the Louisiana rule omits "and in a subpoena," which refers to depositions of a nonparty organization. The rule states:

> A party may in his notice name as the deponent a public or private corporation or a partnership or association or governmental agency and designate with reasonable particularity the matters on which examination is requested. The organization so named shall designate one or more officers, directors, or managing agents, or other persons who consent to testify on its behalf, and may set forth, for each person designated, the matters on which he will testify. The persons so designated shall testify as to matters known or reasonably available to the organization. This Article does not preclude taking a deposition by any other procedure authorized in this Chapter.[62]

The Supreme Court of Louisiana has held the following: "Since we obtained these discovery rules from the federal rules, we may

---

59. *O'Connell v. Cowan*, 332 S.W.3d 34, 40 (Ky. 2010), *reh'g granted, opinion modified* (Dec. 16, 2010).
60. *Perry v. Com., ex rel. Kessinger*, 652 S.W.2d 655, 658 (Ky. 1983).
61. *Watson v. Best Fin. Servs., Inc.*, 245 S.W.3d 722, 725 (Ky. 2008).
62. La. Code Civ. P. art. 1442.

look for guidance from the federal decisions which have interpreted identical provisions."[63]

The Court of Appeal of Louisiana, Third Circuit, in an unpublished opinion, has held that "La. Code Civ. P. art. 1442 is patterned after Rule 30(b)(6) of the Federal Rules of Civil Procedure."[64]

MAINE

Me. R. Civ. P. 30(b)(6) is virtually identical to Fed. R. Civ. P. 30(b)(6). The Maine rule states:

> A party may in the party's notice and in a subpoena name as the deponent a public or private corporation or a partnership or association or governmental agency and designate with reasonable particularity the matters on which examination is requested. In that event, the organization so named shall designate one or more officers, directors, or managing agents, or other persons who consent to testify on its behalf, and may set forth, for each person designated, the matters on which the person will testify. A subpoena shall advise a nonparty organization of its duty to make such a designation. The persons so designated shall testify as to matters known or reasonably available to the organization. This subdivision (b)(6) does not preclude taking a deposition by any other procedure authorized in these rules.[65]

The Supreme Judicial Court of Maine has not yet provided a general rule allowing for the use of federal case law to interpret the

---

63. *Madison v. Travelers Ins. Co.*, 308 So. 2d 784, 786 (La. 1975).
64. *Kopnicky v. Citgo Petroleum Corp.*, 2007-01483 (La. App. 3d Cir. 2007).
65. Me. R. Civ. P. 30(b)(6).

state's rules of civil procedure. When interpretive issues involving civil procedure arise, however, the court has applied federal case law about specific rules, including Fed. R. Civ. P.17(a),[66] to construe the state's corresponding rule of civil procedure.

MARYLAND

Md. Rule 2-412(d) is virtually identical to Fed. R. Civ. P. 30(b)(6). The final sentence of the federal counterpart rule, "this paragraph does not preclude a deposition by any other procedure allowed by these rules," however, does not have a correlation in the Maryland state rule. The rule states:

> A party may in a notice and subpoena name as the deponent a public or private corporation or a partnership or association or governmental agency and describe with reasonable particularity the matters on which examination is requested. The organization so named shall designate one or more officers, directors, managing agents, or other persons who will testify on its behalf regarding the matters described and may set forth the matters on which each person designated will testify. A subpoena shall advise a nonparty organization of its duty to make such a designation. The persons so designated shall testify as to matters known or reasonably available to the organization.[67]

The Maryland Court of Appeals has not yet provided a general rule allowing for the use of federal case law to interpret the state's rules of civil procedure. When interpretive issues involving civil procedure arise, however, the court has applied federal case law about

---

66. *Tisdale v. Rawson*, 822 A.2d 1136, 1141 (Me. 2003).
67. Md. Rule 2-412(d).

specific rules, including Fed. R. Civ. P. 23,[68] Fed. R. Civ. P. 24,[69] Fed. R. Civ. P. 36,[70] and Fed. R. Civ. P. 54(b),[71] to construe the state's corresponding rules of civil procedure.

Massachusetts

Mass. R. Civ. P. 30(b)(6) is virtually identical to Fed. R. Civ. P. 30(b)(6). The Massachusetts rule states:

> A party may in his notice and in a subpoena name as the deponent a public or private corporation or a partnership or association or governmental agency and describe with reasonable particularity the matters on which examination is requested. The organization so named shall designate one or more officers, directors, or managing agents, or other persons who consent to testify on its behalf, and may set forth, for each person designated, the matters on which he will testify. A subpoena shall advise a nonparty organization of its duty to make such a designation. The persons so designated shall testify as to matters known or reasonably available to the organization. This subdivision (b)(6) does not preclude taking a deposition by any other procedure authorized in these rules.[72]

The Massachusetts Supreme Judicial Court has held as follows: "We look to Federal decisions interpreting the Federal Rules of Civil Procedure for guidance."[73]

---

68. *Philip Morris Inc. v. Angeletti*, 752 A.2d 200, 219 (Md. 2000).
69. *Duckworth v. Deane*, 903 A.2d 883, 891 (Md. 2006).
70. *Murnan v. Joseph J. Hock, Inc.*, 335 A.2d 104, 106 (Md. 1975).
71. *Planning Bd. of Howard Cty. v. Mortimer*, 530 A.2d 1237, 1239–40 (Md. 1987).
72. Mass. R. Civ. P. 30(b)(6).
73. *Cronin v. Strayer*, 467 N.E.2d 143,149 (Mass. 1984).

Michigan

Mich. Ct. R. 2.306(b)(5) is virtually identical to Fed. R. Civ. P. 30(b)(6). The Michigan rule states:

> In a notice and subpoena, a party may name as the deponent a public or private corporation, partnership, association, or governmental agency and describe with reasonable particularity the matters on which examination is requested. The organization named must designate one or more officers, directors, or managing agents, or other persons, who consent to testify on its behalf, and may set forth, for each person designated, the matters on which the person will testify. A subpoena must advise a nonparty organization of its duty to make the designation. The persons designated shall testify to matters known or reasonably available to the organization. This subrule does not preclude taking a deposition by another procedure authorized in these rules.[74]

The Michigan Supreme Court has held, in reference to the Rules of Civil Procedure, as follows: "Because of the similarity of the state and Federal provisions, we deem it proper to look to the Federal courts for guidance."[75]

Minnesota

Minn. R. Civ. P. 30.02(f) is virtually identical to Fed. R. Civ. P. 30(b)(6). The Minnesota rule states:

---

74. Mich. Ct. R. 2.306(b)(5).
75. *D'Agostini v. City of Roseville*, 240 N.W.2d 252, 253 (Mich. 1976).

> A party may in the party's notice and in a subpoena name as the deponent a public or private corporation or a partnership, association, or governmental agency and describe with reasonable particularity the matters on which examination is requested. In that event, the organization so named shall designate one or more officers, directors, or managing agents, or other persons who consent to testify on its behalf, and may set forth, for each person designated, the matters on which the person will testify. A subpoena shall advise a nonparty organization of its duty to make such a designation. The persons so designated shall testify as to matters known or reasonably available to the organization. This provision does not preclude taking a deposition by any other procedure authorized in these rules.[76]

The Minnesota Supreme Court has held that, "[w]here the language of the Federal Rules of Civil Procedure is similar to language in the Minnesota civil procedure rules, federal cases on the issue are instructive."[77]

Mississippi

Miss. R. Civ. P. 30(b)(6) is virtually identical to Fed. R. Civ. P. 30(b)(6). The Mississippi rule states:

> A party may in his notice and in a subpoena name as the deponent a public or private corporation or a partnership or association or governmental agency and describe with reasonable particularity the matters on which examination is requested. In that

---

76. Minn. R. Civ. P. 30.02(f).
77. *T.A. Schifsky & Sons, Inc. v. Bahr Const., LLC,* 773 N.W.2d 783 (Minn. 2009).

event, the organization so named shall designate one or more officers, directors, or managing agents, or other persons who consent to testify on its behalf, and may set forth, for each person designated, the matters on which he will testify. A subpoena shall advise a nonparty organization of its duty to make such a designation. The persons so designated shall testify as to matters known or reasonably available to the organization. This subsection (b)(6) does not preclude taking a deposition by any other procedure authorized in these rules.[78]

The Mississippi Supreme Court has held that, "[i]n construing our rules, we look for guidance to the federal cases since the MRCP were patterned after the Federal Rules of Procedure."[79]

Missouri

Mo. R. Civ. P. 57.03(b)(4) is virtually identical to Fed. R. Civ. P. 30(b)(6). The rule states:

A party may in the notice and in a subpoena name as the deponent a public or private corporation or a partnership or association or governmental agency and describe with reasonable particularity the matters on which examination is requested. In that event, the organization so named shall designate one or more officers, directors, or managing agents, or other persons who consent to testify on its behalf and may set forth, for each person designated, the matters on which the person will testify. A subpoena shall advise a nonparty organization of its duty to

---

78. Miss. R. Civ. P. 30(b)(6).
79. *Bourn v. Tomlinson Interest, Inc.*, 456 So. 2d 747, 749 (Miss. 1984).

make such a designation. The persons so designated shall testify as to matters known or reasonably available to the organization. This Rule 57.03(b)(4) does not preclude taking a deposition by any other procedure authorized in these rules.[80]

The Supreme Court of Missouri, *en banc*, has declared that Rule 57.03(b)(4) is "Missouri's counterpart to Rule 30(b)(6) of the Federal Rules of Civil Procedure."[81] In *State ex rel. Plank v. Koehr*, the court analyzes the Missouri rule, using federal case law.

Montana

Mont. R. Civ. P. 30(b)(6) is virtually identical to Fed. R. Civ. P. 30(b)(6). The Montana rule states:

> In its notice or subpoena, a party may name as the deponent a public or private corporation, a partnership, an association, or a governmental agency and must describe with reasonable particularity the matters for examination. The named organization must then designate one or more officers, directors, or managing agents, or designate other persons who consent to testify on its behalf; and it may set out the matters on which each person designated will testify. A subpoena must advise a nonparty organization of its duty to make this designation. The persons designated must testify about information known or reasonably available to the organization. This paragraph (6) does not preclude a deposition by any other procedure allowed by these rules.[82]

---

80. Mo. R. Civ. P. 57.03(b)(4).
81. *State ex rel. Plank v. Koehr*, 831 S.W.2d 926, 928 (Mo. 1992).
82. Mo. R. Civ. P. 57.03(b)(4).

The Montana Supreme Court has held that "[t]hese provisions are identical to and modeled upon Rule 30(e) of the Federal Rules of Civil Procedure, which confers federal court interpretations of the federal rule persuasive authority."[83] Although a different subsection of Mont R. Civ. P. 30, this holding applies to state rules involving depositions.

Nebraska

Neb. R. Sup. Ct. § 6–330(b)(6) is virtually identical to Fed. R. Civ. P. 30(b)(6). The Nebraska rule states:

> A party may in his or her notice and in a subpoena name as the deponent a public or private corporation or a partnership or association or governmental agency and describe with reasonable particularity the matters on which examination is requested. In that event, the organization so named shall designate one or more officers, directors, or managing agents, or other persons who consent to testify on its behalf, and may set forth, for each person designated, the matters on which he or she will testify. A subpoena shall advise a nonparty organization of its duty to make such a designation. The persons so designated shall testify as to matters known or reasonably available to the organization. This subdivision (b)(6) does not preclude taking a deposition by any other procedure authorized in these rules.[84]

The Nebraska Supreme Court has held that "[i]nasmuch as the Nebraska Rules of Discovery are generally and substantially patterned after the corresponding discovery rules in the Federal Rules

---

83. *Albert v. Hastetter*, 48 P.3d 749, 757 (Mont. 2002).
84. Neb. R. Sup. Ct. § 6–330(b)(6).

of Civil Procedure, Nebraska courts will look to federal decisions interpreting corresponding federal rules for guidance in construing similar Nebraska rules."[85]

Nevada

Nev. R. Civ. P. 30(b)(6) is virtually identical to Fed. R. Civ. P. 30(b)(6). The rule states:

> A party may in the party's notice and in a subpoena name as the deponent a public or private corporation or a partnership or association or governmental agency and describe with reasonable particularity the matters on which examination is requested. In that event, the organization so named shall designate one or more officers, directors, or managing agents, or other persons who consent to testify on its behalf, and may set forth, for each person designated, the matters on which the person will testify. A subpoena shall advise a nonparty organization of its duty to make such a designation. The persons so designated shall testify as to matters known or reasonably available to the organization. This subdivision (b)(6) does not preclude taking a deposition by any other procedure authorized in these rules.

The Supreme Court of Nevada has held that "[f]ederal cases interpreting the Federal Rules of Civil Procedure 'are strong persuasive authority, because the Nevada Rules of Civil Procedure are based in large part upon their federal counterparts.'"[86]

---

85. *Gernstein v. Lake*, 610 N.W.2d 714, 716 (Neb. 2000).
86. *Executive Mgmt., Ltd. v. Ticor Title Ins. Co.*, 38 P.3d 872, 876 (Nev. 2002) (internal citations omitted).

New Hampshire

N.H. R. Super. Ct. 26(m) is virtually identical to Fed. R. Civ. P. 30(b)(6). The rule states:

> In its notice or subpoena, a party may name as the deponent a public or private corporation, a partnership, an association, a governmental agency, or other entity and must describe with reasonable particularity the matters for examination. The named organization must then designate one or more officers, directors, or managing agents, or designate other persons who consent to testify on its behalf; and it may set out the matters on which each person designated will testify. A subpoena must advise a nonparty organization of its duty to make this designation. The persons designated must testify about information known or reasonably available to the organization. This paragraph (m) does not preclude a deposition by any other procedure allowed by these rules.[87]

The New Hampshire Supreme Court has not addressed the role of federal decisions on the Federal Rules of Civil Procedure when interpreting their corresponding rules. The comments to N.H. R. Super. Ct. 26(m), however, expressly provide that "[t]he jurisprudence used by the federal courts interpreting cognate Federal Rule of Civil Procedure 30(b)(6) should be used as a guide in the interpretation of Rule 26(m)."[88]

---

87. N.H. R. Super. Ct. 26(m).
88. N.H. R. Super. Ct. 26(m) cmt.

New Jersey

N.J. Ct. R. 4:14–2(c) is substantially similar to Fed. R. Civ. P. 30(b)(6). The body of the New Jersey rule is virtually identical, except the New Jersey rule omits "and in a subpoena," which refers to depositions of a nonparty organization. Additionally, the final sentence of the federal counterpart rule, "this paragraph does not preclude a deposition by any other procedure allowed by these rules," does not have a correlation in the New Jersey state rule. The rule states:

> A party may in the notice name as the deponent a public or private corporation or a partnership or association or governmental agency and designate with reasonable particularity the matters on which examination is requested. The organization so named shall designate one or more officers, directors, or managing agents, or other persons who consent to testify on its behalf, and may set forth for each person designated the matters on which testimony will be given. The persons so designated shall testify as to matters known or reasonably available to the organization.[89]

The Supreme Court of New Jersey has held that, "[s]ince our court rules are based on the Federal Rules of Civil Procedure, it is appropriate to turn to federal case law for guidance."[90] Furthermore, the Tax Court of New Jersey has expressed as follows: "There are, however, decisions by United States District Courts concerning the relationship between Fed.R. Civ.P. 30(b)(6) and Fed.R. Civ.P. 26(b)(1), which rules are, in substance, identical to R. 4:14–2(c) and R. 4:10–2(a), respectively."[91]

---

89. N.J. Ct. R. 4:14–2(c).
90. *Freeman c. Lincoln Beach Motel*, 442 A.2d 650, 651 (N.J. Law Div. 1981).
91. *Edison Corp. v. Secaucus Town*, 17 N.J. Tax 178, 181 (1998).

New Mexico

N.M. Sup. Ct. R. 1-030(b)(6) is virtually identical to Fed. R. Civ. P. 30(b)(6). The New Mexico rule states:

> A party may, in the party's notice and in a subpoena, name as the deponent a public or private corporation or a partnership or association or governmental agency and describe with reasonable particularity the matters on which examination is requested. In that event, the organization so named shall designate one or more officers, directors, or managing agents, or other persons who consent to testify on its behalf, and may set forth, for each person designated, the matters on which the person will testify. A subpoena shall advise a nonparty organization of its duty to make such a designation. The persons so designated shall testify as to matters known or reasonably available to the organization. This subparagraph does not preclude taking a deposition by any other procedure authorized in these rules.[92]

The New Mexico Supreme Court has held that, "[w]hen our state court rules closely track the language of their federal counterparts, we have determined that federal construction of the federal rules is persuasive authority for the construction of New Mexico rules."[93]

---

92. N.M. Sup. Ct. R. 1-030(b)(6).
93. *Albuquerque Redi-Mix, Inc. v. Scottsdale Ins. Co.*, 168 P.3d 99, 102 (N.M. 2007).

New York

New York is the only state where the Rules of Civil Procedure governing the courts of general jurisdiction do not have a rule for taking depositions of organizations by issue designation. Article 31 of the N.Y. Civ. Prac. Law & R. governs depositions in civil settings. There are no provisions within Article 31 that are analogous to Fed. R. Civ. P. 30(b)(6).

N.Y. Civ. Prac. Law & R. 3106(d) is the only deposition rule which addresses deposing members of organizations. The rule approximates Federal Rule 30(b)(1), which provides for the requesting party to identify the desired witness by "description or title." The rule permits the organization to choose whom they wish to tender as a witness, without imposing any obligation to ensure the witness has knowledge on the relevant deposition topics. There are no provisions for designating "matters of examination." The New York rule states:

> Designation of deponent. A party desiring to take the deposition of a particular officer, director, member, or employee of a person shall include in the notice or subpoena served upon such person the identity, description, or title of such individual. Such person shall produce the individual so designated unless they shall have, no later than ten days prior to the scheduled deposition, notified the requesting party that another individual would instead be produced and the identity, description, or title of such individual is specified. If timely notification has been so given, such other individual shall instead be produced.[94]

In New York, the rules governing depositions of organizations, however, are developing. On December 1, 2015, the Commercial

---

94. N.Y. Civ. Prac. Law & R. 3106(d).

Division of the New York state courts adopted a rule, which is substantially equivalent to Federal Rule 30(b)(6).[95] The Commercial Division is restricted to commercial cases with minimum monetary thresholds, as defined in Comp. Codes R. & Regs. tit. 22, § 202.70(a) and § 202.70(b) and § 202.70(c). The 2015 rule does not apply to the courts of general jurisdiction.

The 2015 rule, N.Y. Comp. Codes R. & Regs. tit. 22, § 202.70(g), Rule 11-f, is generally patterned on Fed. R. Civ. P. 30(b)(6). Like its federal counterpart, it provides for depositions of entities by issue designation, which the counsel can serve on a party, or by subpoena on a nonparty, to provide information known or reasonably available to the organization. The New York Commercial Courts rule is more expansive than the federal in that it also provides for individual designations (like N.Y. Civ. Prac. Law & R. 3106(d)) by including a provision that expressly governs deposition notices and subpoenas that identify particular employees. It also codifies the federal common law by stating that the "testimony given pursuant to this Rule shall be usable against the entity."

N.Y. Comp. Codes R. & Regs. tit. 22, § 202.70(g), Rule 11-f ("Depositions of Entities; Identification of Matters"), states:

> (a) A notice or subpoena may name as a deponent a corporation, business trust, estate, trust, partnership, limited liability company, association, joint venture, public corporation, government, or governmental subdivision, agency or instrumentality, or any other legal or commercial entity.
>
> (b) Notices and subpoenas directed to an entity may enumerate the matters upon which the person is to be examined, and if so enumerated, the matters must be described with reasonable particularity.

---

95. Connors, Practice Commentary, *McKinney's Cons. Laws of N.Y.*, 2015 Update, N.Y. Civ. Prac. Law & R. 3106.

(c) If the notice or subpoena to an entity does not identify a particular officer, director, member, or employee of the entity, but elects to set forth the matters for examination as contemplated in section (b) of this Rule, then no later than ten days prior to the scheduled deposition:

> (1) the named entity must designate one or more officers, directors, members, or employees, or other individual(s) who consent to testify on its behalf;
>
> (2) such designation must include the identity, description, or title of such individual(s); and
>
> (3) if the named entity designates more than one individual, it must set out the matters on which each individual will testify.

(d) If the notice or subpoena to an entity does identify a particular officer, director, member, or employee of the entity, but elects to set forth the matters for examination as contemplated in section (b) of this Rule, then:

> (1) pursuant to CPLR 3106(d), the named entity shall produce the individual so designated unless it shall have, no later than ten days prior to the scheduled deposition, notified the requesting party that another individual would instead be produced and the identity, description, or title of such individual is specified. If timely notification has been so given, such other individual shall instead be produced;

(2) pursuant to CPLR 3106(d), a notice or subpoena that names a particular officer, director, member, or employee of the entity shall include in the notice or subpoena served upon such entity the identity, description, or title of such individual; and

(3) if the named entity, pursuant to subsection (d)(1) of this Rule, cross-designates more than one individual, it must set out the matters on which each individual will testify.

(e) A subpoena must advise a nonparty entity of its duty to make the designations discussed in this Rule.

(f) The individual(s) designated must testify about information known or reasonably available to the entity.

(g) Deposition testimony given pursuant to this Rule shall be usable against the entity on whose behalf the testimony is given to the same extent provided in CPLR 3117(2) and the applicable rules of evidence.

(h) This Rule does not preclude a deposition by any other procedure allowed by the CPLR.[96]

There are no appellate decisions that expressly hold that the Commercial Court should look to federal authority for guidance in interpreting N.Y. Comp. Codes R. & Regs. tit. 22, § 202.70(g), Rule 11-f. However, the 2012 Report and Recommendations to the Chief Judge of the State of New York, regarding procedures in the Commercial Division, made various recommendations to

---

96. N.Y. Comp. Codes R. & Regs. tit. 22, § 202.70(g), Rule 11-f ("Depositions of Entities; Identification of Matters").

"harmonize" the procedures of the state and federal courts.[97] In view of the apparent similarity between the state and federal rules, it is reasonable to surmise that the New York courts will be looking to the federal decisions for guidance.

North Carolina

N.C. R. Civ. P. 30(b)(6) is substantially similar to its Fed. R. Civ. P. 30(b)(6). However, the North Carolina rule contains a clarifying sentence regarding requirements for subpoenaing parties.

> A party may in his notice and in a subpoena name as the deponent a public or private corporation or a partnership or association or governmental agency and describe with reasonable particularity the matters on which examination is requested. In that event, the organization so named shall designate one or more officers, directors, or managing agents, or other persons who consent to testify on its behalf, and may set forth, for each person designated, the matters on which he will testify. A subpoena shall advise a nonparty organization of its duty to make such a designation. *It shall not be necessary to serve a subpoena on an organization which is a party, but the notice, served on a party without an accompanying subpoena shall clearly advise such of its duty to make the required designation.* The persons so designated shall testify as to matters known or reasonably available to the organization. This subsection (b)(6) does not preclude taking a

---

97. Report and Recommendations to the Chief Judge of the State of New York, The Chief Judge's Task Force on Commercial Litigation in the 21st Century, June 2012 at 16.

deposition by any other procedure authorized in these rules.[98]

The North Carolina Supreme Court has held that, "[b]ecause the Federal Rules of Civil Procedure are the source of the North Carolina Rules of Civil Procedure, this Court has said that we will look to decisions under the federal rules 'for enlightenment and guidance as we develop 'the philosophy of the new rules.'"[99]

NORTH DAKOTA

N.D. R. Civ. P. 30(b)(6) is virtually identical to Fed. R. Civ. P. 30(b)(6). The North Dakota rule states:

> In its notice or subpoena, a party may name as the deponent a public or private corporation, a partnership, an association, a governmental agency, or other entity and must describe with reasonable particularity the matters for examination. The named organization must then designate one or more officers, directors, or managing agents, or designate other persons who consent to testify on its behalf; and it may set out the matters on which each person designated will testify. A subpoena must advise a nonparty organization of its duty to make this designation. The persons designated must testify about information known or reasonably available to the organization. This paragraph (6) does not preclude a deposition by any other procedure allowed by these rules.[100]

---

98. N.C. R. Civ. P. 30(b)(6). [Emphasis added.]
99. *Goins v. Puleo*, 512 S.E.2d 748, 752 (N.C. 1999).
100. N.D. R. Civ. P. 30(b)(6).

The North Dakota Supreme Court has held this standard: "Our Rules of Civil Procedure were derived from the Federal Rules of Civil Procedure and any construction and interpretation given to the federal rules is entitled to appreciable weight by this Court in interpreting and construing our rules."[101]

Ohio

Ohio R. Civ. P. 30(b)(5) is substantially similar to Fed. R. Civ. P. 30(b)(6). The body of the Ohio rule is virtually identical, except the Ohio rule omits "and in a subpoena," which refers to depositions of a nonparty organization. Additionally, the Ohio rule adds the word "proper" to describe the organization's designated deponent. Thus, a deponent organization has the duty of providing the "proper" deponent under the rule.

> A party, in the party's notice, may name as the deponent a public or private corporation, a partnership, or an association and designate with reasonable particularity the matters on which examination is requested. The organization so named shall choose one or more of its *proper* employees, officers, agents, or other persons duly authorized to testify on its behalf. The persons so designated shall testify as to matters known or available to the organization. Division (b)(5) does not preclude taking a deposition by any other procedure authorized in these rules.[102]

The Ohio Supreme Court has held that, "[b]ecause the Ohio Rules of Civil Procedure are modeled after the Federal Rules of Civil

---

101. *Larson v. Unlimited Bus. Exch. of N. Dakota, Inc.*, 330 N.W.2d 518, 520 (N.D. 1983).
102. Ohio R. Civ. P. 30(b)(5). [Emphasis added.]

Procedure, federal law interpreting the federal rule is appropriate and persuasive authority in interpreting a similar Ohio rule."[103]

Oklahoma

Okla. Stat. Ann. tit. 12 § 3230(c)(5) is virtually identical to Fed. R. Civ. P. 30(b)(6). The Oklahoma rule differs from the federal rule in that it requires the deponent party to deliver the designation of persons to testify and the subject of the testimony to the other party. The final sentence of the federal counterpart rule, "this paragraph does not preclude a deposition by any other procedure allowed by these rules," does not have a correlation in the Oklahoma state rule. The rule states:

> A party may in the notice and in a subpoena name as the deponent a public or private corporation or a partnership or association or governmental agency and describe with reasonable particularity the matters on which examination is requested. In that event, the organization so named shall designate one or more officers, directors, or managing agents, or other persons who consent to testify on its behalf, and may set forth, for each person designated, the matters on which that person will testify. *Such designation of persons to testify and the subject of the testimony shall be delivered to the other party or parties prior to or at the commencement of the taking of the deposition of the organization.* A subpoena shall advise a nonparty organization of its duty to make such a designation. The persons so designated shall testify as to matters known or reasonably available to the organization.[104]

---

103. *Felix v. Ganley Chevrolet, Inc.*, 49 N.E.3d 1224, 1230 (Ohio 2015).
104. Okla. Stat. Ann. tit. 12 § 3230(c)(5). [Emphasis added.]

The Supreme Court of Oklahoma has previously instructed that courts may compare discovery rules to their federal counterparts, holding as follows: "We may look to discovery procedures in the federal rules when construing similar language in the Oklahoma Discovery Code."[105] In this case, the court has expressly provided that rule Okla. Stat. Ann. tit. 12 § 3230(c)(5) is the counterpart of Fed. R. Civ. P. 30(b)(6).

OREGON

Or. R. Civ. P. 39(c)(6) is substantially similar to Fed. R. Civ. P. 30(b)(6). The Oregon rule differs in that it requires a deponent organization to provide the names of designated individuals no fewer than three days before the scheduled deposition. The rule states:

> A party may in the notice and in a subpoena name as the deponent a public or private corporation or a partnership or association or governmental agency and describe with reasonable particularity the matters on which examination is requested. *In that event, the organization so named shall provide notice of no fewer than three (3) days before the scheduled deposition, absent good cause or agreement of the parties and the deponent, designating the name(s) of one or more officers, directors, managing agents, or other persons* who consent to testify on its behalf and setting forth, for each person designated, the matters on which such person will testify. A subpoena shall advise a nonparty organization of its duty to make such a designation. The persons so designated shall testify as to matters known or reasonably available to the organization. This subsection does not preclude

---

105. *Crest Infiniti, II, LP v. Swinton*, 174 P.3d 996, 999 (Okla. 2007).

taking a deposition by any other procedure authorized in these rules.[106]

The Oregon Supreme Court has not yet provided a general rule allowing for the use of federal case law to interpret the state's rules of civil procedure. When interpretive issues involving civil procedure arise, however, the court has applied federal case law about specific rules, including Fed. R. Civ. P. 42(a), (b),[107] Fed. R. Civ. P. 54(b),[108] and Fed. R. Civ. P. 56,[109] to construe the state's corresponding rules of civil procedure.

Pennsylvania

Pa. R. Civ. P. 4007.1(e) is substantially similar to Fed. R. Civ. P. 30(b)(6). The Pennsylvania rule adds that a party must describe with reasonable particularity "the materials to be produced." The comments to the rule state that "[s]ubdivision (e) is adapted, almost verbatim, from Fed. R. Civ. P. 30(b)(6)."[110] The rule states:

> A party may in the notice and in a subpoena, if issued, name as the deponent a public or private corporation or a partnership or association or governmental agency and describe with reasonable particularity the matters to be inquired into *and the materials to be produced*. In that event, the organization so named shall serve a designation of one or more officers, directors, or managing agents, or other persons who consent to testify on its behalf, and may set forth, for each person designated the

---

106. Or. R. Civ. P. 39(c)(6). [Emphasis added.]
107. *Vander Veer v. Toyota Motor Distributors, Inc.*, 577 P.2d 1343, 1349 (Or. 1978).
108. *State ex rel. Zidell v. Jones*, 720 P.2d 350, 356 (Or. 1986).
109. *Taylor v. Baker*, 566 P.2d 884, 886 (Or. 1977).
110. Pa. R. Civ. P. 4007.1.

matters on which each person will testify. A subpoena shall advise a nonparty organization of its duty to make such a designation. The person or persons so designated shall testify as to matters known or reasonably available to the organization. This subdivision (e) does not preclude taking a deposition by any other procedure authorized in these rules.[111]

The Pennsylvania Supreme Court has not yet provided a general rule allowing for the use of federal case law to interpret the state's rules of civil procedure. When interpretive issues involving civil procedure arise, however, the court has applied federal case law about specific rules, including Fed. R. Civ. P. 56(c),[112] to construe the state's corresponding rule of civil procedure.

Rhode Island

R.I. Ct. R. 30(b)(6) is virtually identical to Fed. R. Civ. P. 30(b)(6). The Rhode Island rule states:

> A party may in the witness's notice or in a subpoena name as the deponent a public, private, or governmental organization and describe with reasonable particularity the matters on which examination is requested. In that event, the organization so named shall serve and file, prior to the deposition, a written designation which identifies one or more officers, directors, or managing agents, or other persons who consent to testify on its behalf, and shall set forth, for each person designated the matters on which the person will testify. A subpoena shall advise a

---

111. Pa. R. Civ. P. 4007.1(e). [Emphasis added.]
112. *Allen v. Carr*, 233 A.2d 227, 228 (Pa. 1967).

nonparty organization of its duty to make such a designation. The person so designated shall testify as to matters known or reasonably available to the organization. This subdivision (b)(6) does not preclude taking a deposition by any other procedure authorized in these rules.[113]

The Rhode Island Supreme Court has held the following: "This Court has stated that where the Federal rule and our state rule are substantially similar, we will look to the Federal courts for guidance or interpretation of our own rule."[114]

South Carolina

S.C. R. Civ. P. 30(b)(6) is virtually identical to Fed. R. Civ. P. 30(b)(6). The South Carolina rule states:

> A party may in his notice and in a subpoena name as the deponent a public or private corporation or a partnership or association or governmental agency and describe with reasonable particularity the matters on which examination is requested. In that event, the organization so named shall designate one or more officers, directors, or managing agents, or other persons who consent to testify on its behalf, and may set forth, for each person designated, the matters on which he will testify. A subpoena shall advise a nonparty organization of its duty to make such a designation. The persons so designated shall testify as to matters known or reasonably available to the organization. This

---

113. R.I. Ct. R. 30(b)(6).
114. *Heal v. Heal*, 762 A.2d 463, 466–67 (R.I. 2000).

subdivision (b)(6) does not preclude taking a deposition by any other procedure authorized in these rules.[115]

The Supreme Court of South Carolina has held the following: "Since our Rules of Procedure are based on the Federal Rules, where there is no South Carolina law, we look to the construction placed on the Federal Rules of Civil Procedure."[116]

South Dakota

S.D. Codified Laws § 15-6-30(b) is virtually identical to Fed. R. Civ. P. 30(b)(6). The South Dakota rule states:

> A party may in the notice and in a subpoena name as the deponent a public or private corporation or a partnership or association or governmental agency and describe with reasonable particularity the matters on which examination is requested. In that event, the organization so named shall designate one or more officers, directors, or managing agents, or other persons who consent to testify on its behalf, and may set forth, for each person designated, the matters on which the person will testify. A subpoena shall advise a nonparty organization of its duty to make such a designation. The persons so designated shall testify as to matters known or reasonably available to the organization. This subdivision does not preclude taking a deposition by any other procedure authorized in these rules.[117]

---

115. S.C. R. Civ. P. 30(b)(6).
116. *Gardner v. Newsome Chevrolet-Buick, Inc.*, 304 S.C. 328, 330, 404 S.E.2d 200, 201 (1991).
117. S.D. Codified Laws § 15-6-30(b).

The South Dakota Supreme Court has held as follows: "South Dakota has generally adopted the Federal Rules of Civil Procedure . . . Though federal interpretations of federal civil and appellate procedural rules are not binding on us in an interpretation of like rules in our State's courts, it is appropriate to 'turn to the federal court decisions for guidance in their application and interpretation.'"[118]

TENNESSEE

Tenn. R. Civ. P. 30.02(6) is virtually identical to Fed. R. Civ. P. 30(b)(6). The Tennessee rule states:

> A party may in the party's notice and in a subpoena name as the deponent a public or private corporation or a partnership or association or governmental agency and describe with reasonable particularity the matters on which examination is requested. In that event, the organization so named shall designate one or more officers, directors, or managing agents, or other persons who consent to testify on its behalf, and may set forth, for each person designated, the matters on which the person will testify. A subpoena shall advise a nonparty organization of its duty to make such a designation. The persons so designated shall testify as to matters known or reasonably available to the organization. This subdivision (6) does not preclude taking a deposition by any other procedure authorized in these rules.[119]

The Tennessee Supreme Court has held that " . . . when interpreting our own rules of civil procedure, we consult and are guided

---

118. *Sander v. Geib, Elston, Frost Professional Ass'n*, 506 N.W.2d 107, 122 (S.D. 1993) (internal citation omitted).
119. Tenn. R. Civ. P. 30.02(6).

by the interpretation that has been applied to comparable federal rules of procedure."[120]

Texas

Tex. R. Civ. P. 199.2(b)(1) is substantially similar to Fed. R. Civ. P. 30(b)(6). The body of the Texas rule is virtually identical, except Texas rule omits "and in a subpoena," which refers to depositions of a nonparty organization. The Texas rule also requires that the deponent organization designate a deponent in "a reasonable time before the deposition." The rule states:

> The notice must state the name of the witness, which may be either an individual or a public or private corporation, partnership, association, governmental agency, or other organization. If an organization is named as the witness, the notice must describe with reasonable particularity the matters on which examination is requested. In response, the organization named in the notice must—*a reasonable time before the deposition*—designate one or more individuals to testify on its behalf and set forth, for each individual designated, the matters on which the individual will testify. Each individual designated must testify as to matters that are known or reasonably available to the organization. This subdivision does not preclude taking a deposition by any other procedure authorized by these rules.[121]

The Texas Supreme Court has held that " . . . when interpreting our own rules of civil procedure, we consult and are guided by the

---

120. *Turner v. Turner*, 473 S.W.3d 257, 268 (Tenn. 2015).
121. Tex. R. Civ. P. 199.2(b)(1). [Emphasis added.]

interpretation that has been applied to comparable federal rules of procedure."[122]

Utah

Utah R. Civ. P. 30(b)(6) is virtually identical to Fed. R. Civ. P. 30(b)(6). The final sentence of the federal counterpart rule, "this paragraph does not preclude a deposition by any other procedure allowed by these rules," does not have a correlation in the Utah state rule. The rule states:

> A party may name as the witness a corporation, a partnership, an association, or a governmental agency, describe with reasonable particularity the matters on which questioning is requested, and direct the organization to designate one or more officers, directors, managing agents, or other persons to testify on its behalf. The organization shall state, for each person designated, the matters on which the person will testify. A subpoena shall advise a nonparty organization of its duty to make such a designation. The person so designated shall testify as to matters known or reasonably available to the organization.[123]

The Utah Supreme Court has held the following: "We may also rely on interpretations of similar federal rules by federal courts to assist our own interpretation."[124]

---

122. *Sw. Ref. Co. v. Bernal*, 22 S.W.3d 425, 433 (Tex. 2000).
123. Utah R. Civ. P. 30(b)(6).
124. *Robinson v. Taylor*, 356 P.3d 1230, 1234 (Utah 2015).

Vermont

Vt. R. Civ. P. 30(b)(6) is substantially similar to Fed. R. Civ. P. 30(b)(6). The body of the Vermont rule is virtually identical, except the Vermont rule omits "and in a subpoena," which refers to depositions of a nonparty organization. The rule states:

> A party may in the party's notice name as the deponent a public or private corporation or a partnership or association or governmental agency and designate with reasonable particularity the matters on which examination is requested. The organization so named shall designate one or more officers, directors, or managing agents, or other persons who consent to testify on its behalf, and may set forth, for each person designated, the matters on which the person will testify. The persons so designated shall testify as to matters known or reasonably available to the organization. This paragraph (b)(6) does not preclude taking a deposition by any other procedure authorized in these rules.[125]

The Vermont Supreme Court has held that its " . . . interpretation of Vermont Rules of Civil Procedure is often guided by federal precedent on identical federal rules."[126]

Virginia

Va. Sup. Ct. R. 4:5(b)(6) is substantially similar to Fed. R. Civ. P. 30(b)(6). The body of the Virginia rule is virtually identical, except the Virginia rule omits "and in a subpoena," which refers to depositions of a nonparty organization. The rule states:

---

125. Vt. R. Civ. P. 30(b)(6).
126. *Follo v. Florindo*, 970 A.2d 1230, 1237 (Vt. 2009).

> A party may in his notice name as the deponent a public or private corporation or a partnership or association or governmental agency and designate with reasonable particularity the matters on which examination is requested. The organization so named shall designate one or more officers, directors, or managing agents, or other persons who consent to testify on its behalf, and may set forth, for each person designated, the matters on which he will testify. The persons so designated shall testify as to matters known or reasonably available to the organization. This subdivision (b)(6) does not preclude taking a deposition by any other procedure authorized in these Rules.[127]

The Supreme Court of Virginia has not yet provided a general rule allowing for the use of federal case law to interpret the state's rules of civil procedure. When interpretive issues involving civil procedure arise, however, the court has applied federal case law about specific rules, including Fed. R. Civ. P. 37,[128] to construe the state's corresponding rules of civil procedure.

Additionally, the Circuit Court of Virginia, Fairfax County, has previously held that "Rules 4:5, 4:7, and 4:12 are closely modeled after the Federal Rules of Civil Procedure ('FRCP'). *See*, Fed. R. Civ. P. 30, 32, and 37. Where, such as here, the Virginia Supreme Court has not addressed a particular discovery issue, federal case law interpreting the FRCP may be instructive."[129]

---

127. Va. Sup. Ct. R. 4:5(b)(6).
128. *Brown v. Black*, 534 S.E.2d 727, 729-30 (Va. 2000).
129. *The Staples Corp. v. Washington Hall Corp.*, 44 Va. Cir. 372 (1998).

Washington

Wash. Super. Ct. Civ. R. 30(b)(6) is virtually identical to Fed. R. Civ. P. 30(b)(6). The Washington rule states:

> A party may in a notice and in a subpoena name as the deponent a public or private corporation or a partnership or association or governmental agency and designate with reasonable particularity the matters on which examination is requested. In that event, the organization so named shall designate one or more officers, directors, or managing agents, or other persons who consent to testify on its behalf, and may set forth, for each person designated, the matters known on which the deponent will testify. A subpoena shall advise a nonparty organization of its duty to make such a designation. The persons so designated shall testify as to the matters known or reasonably available to the organization. This subsection (b)(6) does not preclude taking a deposition by any other procedure authorized in these rules.[130]

The Washington State Supreme Court has held that, "[w]here a state rule parallels a federal rule, analysis of the federal rule may be looked to for guidance, though such analysis will be followed only if the reasoning is found to be persuasive."[131] Additionally, the Court of Appeals of Washington, Division 3, has used federal authority when interpreting Rule 30(b)(6).[132]

---

130. Wash. Super. Ct. Civ. R. 30(b)(6).
131. *Beal for Martinez v. City of Seattle*, 954 P.2d 237, 241 (Wash. 1998).
132. *Dalton v. State*, 137 Wash. App. 1033 (2007).

WEST VIRGINIA

W. Va. R. Civ. P. 30(b)(7) is virtually identical to Fed. R. Civ. P. 30(b)(6). The West Virginia rule states:

> A party may in a notice and in a subpoena name as the deponent a public or private corporation or a partnership or association or governmental agency and describe with reasonable particularity the matters on which examination is requested. In that event, the organization so named shall designate one or more officers, directors, or managing agents, or other persons who consent to testify on its behalf, and may set forth, for each person designated, the matters on which the person will testify. A subpoena shall advise a nonparty organization of its duty to make such a designation. The persons so designated shall testify as to matters known or reasonably available to the organization. This subdivision does not preclude taking a deposition by any other procedure authorized in these rules.[133]

The West Virginia Supreme Court of Appeals has held the following: "Because the West Virginia Rules of Civil Procedure are patterned after the Federal Rules of Civil Procedure, we often refer to interpretations of the Federal Rules when discussing our own rules."[134]

WISCONSIN

Wis. Stat. Ann. § 804.05(2)(e) is substantially similar to Fed. R. Civ. P. 30(b)(6). The body of the Wisconsin rule is virtually

---

133. W. Va. R. Civ. P. 30(b)(7).
134. *Keplinger v. Virginia Elec. & Power Co.*, 537 S.E.2d 632, 641 (W. Va. 2000).

identical, except the Wisconsin rule omits "and in a subpoena," which refers to depositions of a nonparty organization. Different from the parallel federal rule, the state rule also incorporates the naming of "a state officer in an action arising out of the officer's performance of employment." The rule states:

> A party may in the notice name as the deponent a public or private corporation or a limited liability company or a partnership or an association or a governmental agency *or a state officer in an action arising out of the officer's performance of employment* and designate with reasonable particularity the matters on which examination is requested. The organization or state officer so named shall designate one or more officers, directors, or managing agents, or other persons who consent to testify on its behalf, and may set forth, for each person designated, the matters on which the person will testify. The persons so designated shall testify as to matters known or reasonably available to the organization. This paragraph does not preclude taking a deposition by any other procedure authorized by statute or rule.[135]

The Wisconsin Supreme Court has instructed the bench and bar as follows: "When 'a state rule mirrors the federal rule, we consider federal cases interpreting the rule to be persuasive authority.'"[136]

Wyoming

Wyo. R. Civ. P. 30(b)(6) is virtually identical to Fed. R. Civ. P. 30(b)(6). The rule states:

---

135. Wis. Stat. Ann. § 804.05(2)(e). [Emphasis added.]
136. *Luckett v. Bodner*, 769 N.W.2d 504, 511 (Wis. 2009).

A party may in the party's notice and in a subpoena name as the deponent a public or private corporation or a partnership or association or governmental agency and describe with reasonable particularity the matters on which examination is requested. The organization so named shall designate one or more officers, directors, or managing agents, or other persons who consent to testify on its behalf, and may set forth, for each person designated, the matters on which the person will testify. A subpoena shall advise a nonparty organization of its duty to make such a designation. The persons so designated shall testify as to matters known or reasonably available to the organization. This subdivision (b)(6) does not preclude taking a deposition by any other procedure authorized in these rules.[137]

The Wyoming Supreme Court has held the following: "We consider federal authority interpreting procedural rules highly persuasive when our rules are sufficiently similar or identical."[138]

---

137. Wyo. R. Civ. P. 30(b)(6).
138. *CSC Grp. Holdings, LLC v. Automation & Elecs., Inc.*, 638 P.3d 302, 308 (Wyo. 2016).

Appendix B

Sample 30(b)(6) Notice

In chapter 3, "Details of Rule 30(b)(6)," we learned that the Rule 30(b)(6) deposition notice could not identify a specific person to testify. Rather, the notice must be directed to the organization. The notice asks the organization to do the following:

- Fully prepare officers, directors, managing agents, or other people who consent to testify on behalf of the organization
- Provide all information known or reasonably available to the organization
- Fully respond to the matters of examination you have identified in your notice

You can use the federal 30(b)(6) notice in this appendix in any federal action and you can be adapt it to work in a lawsuit in state court by substituting the individual state rule and state caption style. Once you have adapted the template notice to your jurisdiction, substitute [Designator] with the name of the organization that you are deposing. Then insert the matters of examination that you have crafted, consistent with the principles discussed in chapter 7, "Crafting the 30(b)(6) Notice."

30(b)(6)

UNITED STATES DISTRICT COURT

DISTRICT OF [STATE]

[PLAINTIFF],	COURT FILE NO.:
Plaintiff,	PLAINTIFF'S NOTICE OF DEPOSITION OF [DESIGATOR],
vs.	PURSUANT TO FED. R. CIV. P. 30(b)(6)
[DEFENDANT],	[Discovery Set #___]
Defendant.	

TO: [DESIGNATOR] AND ITS ATTORNEY:

PLEASE TAKE NOTICE, that pursuant to Fed. R. Civ. P. 30(b)(6), the stenographic video deposition of [Designator], will be taken before a qualified Notary Public at [Address], in [City], [State], on [Date] at [Time], and thereafter by adjournment until the same shall be completed.

Pursuant to Fed. R. Civ. P. 30(b)(6), [Designator], is required to designate and fully prepare one or more officers, directors, managing agents or other persons who consent to testify on behalf of [Designator], and whom [Designator], will fully prepare to testify regarding all information that is known or reasonably available to [Designator]'s organization regarding the following designated matters:

MATTERS OF EXAMINATION

1.)

2.)

3.)

[Law Firm Name]

Dated: [Date]   _____

[Attorney]
[Street Address]
[Phone]
Attorney for [Plaintiff]

Appendix C

Document Deposition Notice

In chapter 8, "Document Depositions," we learned that Rule 30(b)(6) could be coupled with Rule 30(b)(2) and Rule 34 to create a deposition notice and a deposition to determine if the production of requested documents is complete. The Rule 30(b)(6), Rule 30(b)(2), and Rule 34 document deposition is the tool to ensure that your opponent has produced a complete set of records in response to your request (or initial disclosures). If the produced records are incomplete or if your opponent makes spurious objections, this deposition is the tool you can use to build a record that identifies missing records and creates a factual record upon which the court can base its rulings.

You can use the Rule 30(b)(6), Rule 30(b)(2), and Rule 34 document deposition notice in this appendix in any federal action, or you can adapt it to work in your lawsuit in state court by substituting the individual state rule and state caption style. Once you adapt the template notice to your jurisdiction, substitute the word [Designator] with the name of the organization you are deposing. Then insert the schedule of documents.

UNITED STATES DISTRICT COURT

DISTRICT OF [STATE]

[PLAINTIFF],	COURT FILE NO.:
Plaintiff,	PLAINTIFF'S NOTICE OF DEPOSITION OF [DESIGATOR],
vs.	PURSUANT TO FED. R. CIV. P. 30(b)(6)
[DEFENDANT],	[Discovery Set #__]
Defendant.	

TO: [DESIGNATOR] AND ITS ATTORNEYS:

PLEASE TAKE NOTICE that, pursuant to Fed. R. Civ. P. 30(b)(6), 30(b)(2) and 34, the stenographic video-recorded deposition of [Designator] will be taken before a qualified Notary Public at [location], [street address], on [date] at [time], and thereafter by adjournment until the same shall be completed.

Pursuant to Fed. R. Civ. P. 30(b)(6), [Designator] is required to designate and fully prepare one or more officers, directors, managing agents or other persons who consent to testify on behalf of [Designator], and whom [Designator] will fully prepare to testify regarding all information that is known or reasonably available to [Designator]'s organization regarding the following designated matters:

1. The existence of the documents and/or electronically stored data requested below pursuant to Fed. R. Civ. P. 34.

2. The systems, process and purpose for the creation, duplication and/or storage of the documents and/or electronically stored data requested below pursuant to Fed. R. Civ. P. 34.

3. Any and all document and/or electronically stored data retention/destruction policies that relate to any of the documents requested below pursuant to Fed. R. Civ. P. 34.

4. The location of the documents and/or electronically stored data requested below pursuant to Fed. R. Civ. P. 34.

5. The organization, indexing and/or filing of the documents and/or electronically stored data requested below pursuant to Fed. R. Civ. P. 34.

6. The method of search for the documents and/or electronically stored data requested below pursuant to Fed. R. Civ. P. 34.

7. The completeness of the documents and/or electronically stored data produced pursuant to Fed. R. Civ. P. 34.

PLEASE TAKE NOTICE that, pursuant to Fed. R. Civ. P. 34, within 30 days [Designator] shall provide a written response, including any objections and/or claims of privilege, to Plaintiff's request for documents and tangible things identified in the following Schedule of Documents, which are in the possession, custody or control of [Designator] its attorneys or other representatives or agents.

PLEASE TAKE NOTICE that, pursuant to Fed. R. Civ. P. 30(b)(2), Plaintiff requests that [Designator] designee, responsive to this deposition notice, produce, at the time of the deposition, the documents identified in the schedule of documents contained in this deposition notice.

SCHEDULE OF DOCUMENTS

1.)

2.)

3.)

PLEASE TAKE NOTICE that this document requests is deemed continuing. Should you in the future discover any information relating to any of the above matters of inquiry, you are required to notify the Plaintiff's / Plaintiffs' counsel of this new or additional information by way of supplemental discovery responses, pursuant to Fed. R. Civ. P. 26(e). Objection will be made at trial to the use of information not properly disclosed in accordance with the Federal Rules of Civil Procedure.

Dated: [Date] _____

                              [Attorney]
                              [Attorney Firm Name]
                              [Attorney Street Address and Phone]

Appendix D

Rule 30(b)(6) Depositions for Email

In chapter 9, "Electronic Discovery," we learned that electronically stored information (ESI) often holds key evidence to your case. However, accessing that information requires that you learn the technological framework of the organization's computer systems relating to the specific data you want to discover. The advisory committee to the federal rules suggested that the parties learn about those systems through the Rule 26(f) discovery conference. In that discovery conference, the parties should be able to learn about the following:

- The various sources of information, within the responding party's control, that the responding party will search.

- Whether the responding party can reasonably access this information.

- The burden or cost the responding party will face in retrieving and reviewing the information.

The responding attorney, whose client controls information relating to the ESI, may be unable or unwilling to provide the information you need to craft relevant and proportional ESI requests. Rule 30(b)(6) ESI depositions are an effective tool that enables you to learn about the structure of the ESI.

There is no one-size-fits-all deposition 30(b)(6) notice, particularly when seeking e-discovery, because the factual circumstances will invariably lead to distinct ESI issues. The federal 30(b)(6) ESI deposition notice in this appendix has been crafted for the discovery of e-mail. You can use this notice in any federal action or adapt it for your lawsuit in state court by substituting the individual state rule and state caption style. Once you adapt the notice to your jurisdiction, substitute the word [Designator] with the name of the organization that you are deposing. As in all litigation, you need to modify the matters of examination to fit your case's needs.

UNITED STATES DISTRICT COURT

DISTRICT OF [STATE]

[PLAINTIFF],	COURT FILE NO.:
Plaintiff,	PLAINTIFF'S NOTICE OF DEPOSITION OF [DESIGATOR],
vs.	PURSUANT TO FED. R. CIV. P. 30(b)(6), 30(b)(2) and 34
[DEFENDANT],	[Discovery Set #___]
Defendant.	

TO: [DEFENDANT] AND ITS ATTORNEYS:

PLEASE TAKE NOTICE that, pursuant to Fed. R. Civ. P. 30(b)(6), 30(b)(2) and 34, the stenographic video-recorded deposition of [Designator] will be taken before a qualified Notary Public at [Address], in [City], [State], on [Date] at [Time], and thereafter by adjournment until the same shall be completed.

Pursuant to Fed. R. Civ. P. 30(b)(6), [Designator] is required to designate and fully prepare one or more officers, directors, managing agents, or other persons who consent to testify on behalf of [Designator], and whom [Designator] will fully prepare to testify regarding all information that is known or reasonably available to [Designator]'s organization regarding the following designated matters:

MATTERS OF EXAMINATION

1. Electronic Mail System (email):

   a. Describe the Electronic Mail System(s) that are, and have been, used by [Designator] from [date] to the present.

2. Email Location:

   a. Give the physical locations of email servers kept within the custody of [Designator].
   b. Explain whether the email system is hosted by a third party.

3. Configuration:

   a. Explain whether client/custodian systems are configured to store email locally.
   b. Describe how the email system is configured (i.e., is the system set to store all incoming and outgoing emails in a central location (IMAP) or only set to deliver messages to client devices (POP)).

c. Explain how centralized email databases, if applicable, use uniform file-naming conventions and specific file path locations for data storage.

4. Preservation, archive, disaster recovery:

 a. Describe all preservation, archive and disaster recovery systems used by [Designator] from [date] to the present.

 b. Give the location of email stored for preservation, archive and disaster recovery.

 c. Identify and describe all software used in preservation, archive and disaster recovery systems.

 d. Identify and describe backup and archival disk or tape inventories or schedules.

5. Security applications:

 a. Describe all security applications that log information pertaining to email transmissions.

 b. Explain how all centralized security applications and IT management software that log information pertaining to email transmissions are used.

 c. Explain where the ESI associated with the security application is stored.

d. Explain how and where are security application logs are stored.

e. Explain what types of security application logs are created by the security applications.

6. Account management and IT policies, procedures and protocols:

    a. Explain [Designator]'s electronic records management policies and procedures.

    b. Explain [Designator]'s retention and destruction policies used by [Designator] from [date] to the present.

7. Credentials:

    a. Give the identities of all current and former personnel who have or had access to network administration, backup, archiving, or other system operations from [date] to the present.

PLEASE TAKE NOTICE that, pursuant to Fed. R. Civ. P. 34, that within 30 days [Designator] shall provide a written response, including any objections and/or claims of privilege, to Plaintiff's request for documents and tangible things identified in the following Schedule of Documents, which are in the possession, custody or control of [Designator], its attorneys or other representatives or agents.

PLEASE TAKE NOTICE that, pursuant to Fed. R. Civ. P. 30(b)(2), Plaintiff requests that [Designator]'s designee, responsive to this deposition notice, produce, at the time of the deposition, the documents identified in the schedule of documents contained in this deposition notice.

SCHEDULE OF DOCUMENTS

1. Contracts with third-party email hosting service providers.

2. All written policies and enforcement procedures regarding ESI management.

3. All written policies and enforcement procedures regarding all centralized security applications and IT management software.

4. Any instructions, guidelines or policies issued to [Designator] are personnel concerning the use of electronic mail.

5. All data flow diagrams involving the email system.

PLEASE TAKE NOTICE that that the Rule 34 requests are deemed continuing. Should you in the future discover any information relating to any of the above matters of inquiry, you are required to notify the Plaintiff's counsel of this new or additional information by way of supplemental discovery responses, pursuant to Fed. R. Civ. P. 26(e). Objection will be made at trial to the use of information not properly disclosed in accordance with the Federal Rules of Civil Procedure.

Dated: [Date]　　　　　　　　_____

　　　　　　　　　　　　　[Law Firm]

　　　　　　　　　　　　　[Attorney]

　　　　　　　　　　　　　[Street Address]

　　　　　　　　　　　　　[Phone]

　　　　　　　　　　　　　Attorney for [Plaintiff]

Appendix E

CONTENTION 30(b)(6) DEPOSITION

In chapter 7, "Crafting the 30(b)(6) Notice," we learned that you can ask about the factual basis of *contentions*, *denials*, and *affirmative defenses* in your 30(b)(6) deposition.

You can use the federal 30(b)(6) deposition notice in this appendix in any federal action or adapt it to work in your lawsuit in state court by substituting the individual state rule and state caption style. Once you adapt the notice to your jurisdiction, substitute the word [Designator] with the name of the organization that you are deposing. Then insert the paragraph number of the affirmative defense and the actual language of that defense. As in all litigation, when crafting the matters of examination, use your professional judgment to comply with the needs of your case, consistent with the authority described in chapter 7. As discussed in chapter 7, contentions, denials, and affirmative defenses that are factually based are generally subject to 30(b)(6) questioning.

30(b)(6)

UNITED STATES DISTRICT COURT

DISTRICT OF [STATE]

[PLAINTIFF],	COURT FILE NO.:
Plaintiff,	PLAINTIFF'S NOTICE OF DEPOSITION OF [DESIGATOR],
vs.	PURSUANT TO FED. R. CIV. P. 30(b)(6)
[DEFENDANT],	[Discovery Set #___]
Defendant.	

TO: [DEFENDANT] AND ITS ATTORNEYS:

PLEASE TAKE NOTICE that, pursuant to Fed. R. Civ. P. 30(b)(6) the stenographic video-recorded deposition of [Designator] will be taken before a qualified Notary Public at [Address], in [City], [State], on [Date] at [Time], and thereafter by adjournment until the same shall be completed.

Pursuant to Fed. R. Civ. P. 30(b)(6), [Designator] is required to designate and fully prepare one or more officers, directors, managing agents or other persons who consent to testify on behalf of [Designator], and whom [Designator] will fully prepare to testify regarding all information that is known or reasonably available to [Designator]'s organization regarding the following designated matters:

MATTERS OF EXAMINATION

1. All facts and documents upon which you base your contention set forth in Paragraph [Affirmative Defense #] of your Answer to Plaintiff's Complaint asserting that: [Insert the verbatim language of the Affirmative Defense].

2. [Repeat for each Affirmative Defense]

3. [Repeat for each Affirmative Defense]

Dated: [Date] _____

[Law Firm]

[Attorney]

[Street Address]

[Phone]

Attorney for [Plaintiff]

Appendix F

Corporate Structure 30(b)(6) Deposition Notice

In chapter 7, "Crafting the 30(b)(6) Notice," we learned that facts and positions are appropriate areas for 30(b)(6) deposition questioning. In many lawsuits, the relationship between organizations, such as parent companies and subsidiaries, is important in developing direct participant liability of the various organizations, or for piercing the corporate veil. The deposition notice in this appendix provides the framework you can work with for discovering those relationships.

You can use the federal 30(b)(6) deposition notice in this appendix in any federal action or adapt it to work in your lawsuit in state court by substituting the individual state rule and state caption style. Once you have adapted the notice to your jurisdiction, substitute the word [Designator] with the name of the organization that you are deposing. Then insert the names of the various related entities that you are trying to learn about. As in all litigation, when crafting your matters of examination use your professional judgment to fulfill the needs of your case.

30(b)(6)

UNITED STATES DISTRICT COURT

DISTRICT OF [STATE]

[PLAINTIFF],	COURT FILE NO.:
Plaintiff,	PLAINTIFF'S NOTICE OF DEPOSITION OF [DESIGATOR],
vs.	PURSUANT TO FED. R. CIV. P. 30(b)(6)
[DEFENDANT],	
	[Discovery Set #___]
Defendant.	

TO: DEFENDANT AND ITS ATTORNEY :

PLEASE TAKE NOTICE that, pursuant to Fed. R. Civ. P. 30(b)(6) the stenographic video-recorded deposition of [Designator] will be taken before a qualified Notary Public at [Address], in [City], [State], on [Date] at [Time], and thereafter by adjournment until the same shall be completed.

Pursuant to Fed. R. Civ. P. 30(b)(6), [Designator] is required to designate and fully prepare one or more officers, directors, managing agents, or other persons who consent to testify on behalf of [Designator], and whom [Designator] will fully prepare to testify regarding all information that is known or reasonably available to [Designator]'s organization regarding the following designated matters:

MATTERS OF EXAMINATION

1. The business functions, day-to-day operations, and revenue-generating business activities of [Designator] in [Year] through the present time.

2. The organizational structure of including:

   a. [Designator]'s relationship to each of the following entities in [Year] and at the present time:

      1) [Related Entity]

      2) [Related Entity]

      3) [Related Entity]

   b. [Designator]'s role in the finances and business activities of each of the following entities in [Year] and at the present time:

      1) [Related Entity]

      2) [Related Entity]

      3) [Related Entity]

3. The identity, job title and responsibilities of all persons who directed and/or supervised the business functions, day-to-day operations, and revenue-generating business activities of [Designator] in [Year].

   a. For each person identified, which persons also directed and/or supervised any of the business functions, day-to-day operations, and revenue-generating business activities of any of the following companies at any time in [Year] or at the present time:

      1) [Related Entity]

      2) [Related Entity]

      3) [Related Entity]

4. The identity, job title and responsibilities of all persons with authority to establish policy and make planning level decisions for [Designator] in [Year] and at the present time.

   a. For each person identified, which persons also had authority to establish any policy and make planning level decisions for any of the following companies at any time in [Year] or at the present time:

1) [Related Entity]

2) [Related Entity]

3) [Related Entity]

5. The identity and role of every person who served as an executive officer for [Designator] at any time in [Year].

   a. For each officer identified, identify which officers also served as an executive officer for any of the following companies at any time in [Year]:

   1) [Related Entity]

   2) [Related Entity]

   3) [Related Entity]

6. The identity of each person or entity having an ownership interest in [Designator] of ten (10) percent or more at any time in [Year] or at the present time:

   a. For each person or entity identified, identify any ownership interest that person or entity also had in any of the following companies at any time in [Year] or at the present time:

1) [Related Entity]

2) [Related Entity]

3) [Related Entity]

7. The identity, including current or last known address of every member of the Board of Directors for [Designator] at any time in [Year].

   a. For each Board member identified, identify whether that Board member also served as an Board member for any of the following companies at any time in [Year]:

      1) [Related Entity]

      2) [Related Entity]

      3) [Related Entity]

Dated: [Date]   _____

                                  [Law Firm]

                                  [Attorney]

                                  [Street Address]

                                  [Phone]

                                  Attorney for [Plaintiff]

Index

A

ABA Model Rules of Professional Conduct
   on communication with employees 116–124
   on communication with former employees 123–126
   on involuntary representation 130–134
   on responsibilities during investigations 126–129
   Rule 1.3 343
   Rule 3.4 303
   Rule 4.1 126–127
   Rule 4.2 116–126, 130–132
   Rule 4.3 127–129
   Rule 7 132–133
abusive depositions 328–329
Advanced Depositions Strategy and Practice (Miller and Scoptur) 13, 20, 320
adverse parties 396
affiants 376
affirmative defenses (matters of examination) 154–160
Alabama, state service of process rules 52–53
Allen, Woody 245
alter ego test 122
Ameristar Jet Charter, Inc. v. Signal Composites, Inc. 69–70
Apex Doctrine 105–110
Aponte-Navedo v. Nalco Chem. Co. 218
archive systems (electronic discovery) 224
asked and answered objection 320–321
associations
   definition of 48–49

service of summons and complaints 50–51
Athridge v. Aetna 170
attorney-client privilege
   changing the testimony and 390
   establishing involuntary representation and 133
   establishing witness status and 97–99
   Hall standards 307–312
   objections to nonparty subpoenas and 46
   preparing witnesses for depositions and 158–159
   privilege waiver and 284–285
   recess conferences and 308, 310–311
   text messages and 311
authority to bind 269–271
Aviva Sports, Inc. v. Fingerhut Direct Marketing, Inc. 353

B

backup data (hidden information) 211
Baker, Howard 81
Ball, David 11
bandying 34, 268, 360, 385
Banks v. Office of the Senate Sergeant-At-Arms 110–111
Batts v. County of Santa Clara 299
Berra, Yogi 391
Bettinger, Carl 11
binding effect of testimony
   about 361–363
   blocking attempts to alter testimony and 14
   duty to designate and 269–271
   fact witness depositions and 254–255
   for individuals 73

497

for low-level employees 120
for officers, directors, or
 managing agents 9–10, 33,
 84–87, 100
testimony at trial and 393–394
unavailable information versus
 unprepared witness 363–370
witness does not have
 information 363–370
boilerplate objections
to deposition notices 247–248
to document requests 163–164,
 168–169, 169, 202
to electronic discovery 221–222
*Brazos River Authority v. GE Ionics,
 Inc.* 405–406
brief writing
for motion to compel 13
in response to motions 12
building a record
about 19
discussions during breaks
 313–314
establishing motive 24–26
establishing standards of conduct
 22–23
figuring out your case 11
goal of 20
locking down facts 20–21
neutralizing defenses 25–27
obstructive objections 327
setting up legal framework 19
suggested resources 11, 13, 20

C
*Cache La Poudre Feeds, LLC v. Land
 O'Lakes, Inc.* 175–176
California, state service of process
 rules 52–53
Calvin, Charlie 207
*Calzaturio S.C.A.R.P.A. S.P.A. v.
 Fabiano Shoe Co., Inc.* 172–173
Campbell v. Facebook, Inc. 236,
 238–239
*Cardenas v. The Prudential Insurance
 Company* 348
Chan, Charlie 1

changing testimony
about 14, 100, 375
attempting to change story at
 trial 404–408
attorney-client privilege and
 390
attribute 393–394
building a record of discussions
 during breaks 313–314
deposition errata sheet changes
 376–379
inquiring into basis for errata
 sheet changes 386–389
schools of permissible change
 380–386
Sham Affidavit Rule 312, 375–
 376, 381–384
clarification questions for witnesses
 318
Clausewitz, Carl von 337
comparative fault (legal defense) 25
contentions (matters of examination)
 154–160
control, defined 172–173
control-group employees 120–121
corporations, deposing. *See* deposing
 organizations
Cusimano, Greg 313
custody, defined 172–173

D
Dahl, Roald 113
data dumps, witnesses interpreting
 238–239
David Ball on Damages (Ball) 11
defects (legal defense) 25
defenses, neutralizing 25–27
delay tactics 342–343
deleted files (hidden information)
 212
denials of facts (matters of
 examination) 154–160
deposing organizations
about 7–10
binding effect of testimony
 9–10, 33, 84–87, 100,
 359–371

building a record 19–27
changing the testimony 375–390
crafting 30(b)(6) notices 137–160
deposing executives 101–111
deposing foreign organizations 55–56
deposing low-level employees 115–134
deposing noncorporate organizations 48–53
depcsing nonparties 32–33, 37–40
deposing officers, directors, and managing agents 33, 83–111
deposition obstruction 303–335
document depositions 47–48, 163–205
duty to attend 247–261
duty to prepare 36–37, 100, 265–290
electronic discovery 209–243
establishing depositions are necessary 102–110
identifying villain 24
in state courts 10
motions to compel and sanctions 339–355
naming individuals in depositions 36–37, 256
preparing for 19–27
Rule 30(b)(6) details 31–55
Rule 30(b)(6) logistics 59–79
scope of inquiry 293–300
steps of Rule 30(b)(6) 11–14
ten-deposition limit 9, 65, 68–69
using 30(b)(6) testimony at trial 393–411
deposition obstruction. *See* obstruction tactics (depositions)
depositions by issue designation. *See* Rule 30(b)(6)
designee depositions
individual versus 72–76
Rule 30(b)(6) on 86

Rule 31(a)(4) on 86
testifying at trial 396
destruction policies
document depositions on 191–193
electronic discovery on 230–231
Detoy v. City & Cnty. of San Francisco 294–296
directors of organizations
binding effect of testimony 9–10, 84–87, 100
duty to designate 266–272
location of depositions 87–88
rules governing testimony of former employees 93–100
testifying at trial 396
discovery conferences 214–217, 221, 348
"discovery on discovery" 177–179
discovery rule 260, 322
.doc format 213
document depositions
about 40, 163
defining possession, custody, and control 172–174
determining whom to depose 181–184
discovery about discovery is permissible 177–179
document production witness 165–166, 182–183
duty to prepare and 279–280
duty to supplement 203–204
foundation for document searches 184–201
getting complete responses to requests 165–166
Hall standards 307
interpretation of documents 151–152
interpretation of events 152–153
matters of inquiry for document searches 184–201
objections to document requests 166–172, 179–180, 202–203

objections to nonparty
  subpoenas 45–48
organizations cannot insist on
  alternate discovery 176–177
preempting improper objections
  202–203
problems with document
  requests 163–165
produced documents must be
  organized 174–175
producing documents on time
  180–181
solution to challenges with
  document requests 175–179
document production witnesses
  165–166, 182–183
document searches (matters of
  inquiry)
  1a. Is this the right witness?
    185–186
  1b. What documents exist?
    186–187
  1. Do the documents exist?
    185–187
  2a. Who knows how the
    documents are created?
    188–189
  2b. Where are the documents
    created? 189–190
  2c. Are the documents
    duplicated? 190–191
  2d. What is the purpose of the
    documents? 191
  2. What are the systems,
    processes, and purposes
    for creation, duplication,
    and storage of documents?
    187–191
  3. What are the document
    destruction and retention
    policies? 191–193
  4. Where are the documents
    located? 193–194
  5. How are the documents
    organized, indexed, and filed?
    194–195
  6a. How did the organization
    search for the document?
    196–200
  6b. Were there previous
    searches for these documents?
    197–198
  6c. How did you prepare? 198
  6. How did the organization
    search for the documents?
    196–200
  7. Is the document set complete?
    200–201
documents, interpretation of
  151–152
.docx format 213
due diligence 238, 277
dump-truck production of
  documents 174–175
duty to attend
  about 247–248
  duty to move for protective
    order 248–252, 255,
    328–329
  establishing an alternative date
    252
  failure to provide witness
    340–341
  grounds for sanctions 248, 251
  lacking in sufficient particularity
    256
  objections to 30(b)(6) notices
    255
  objection to 30(b)(6) method
    of discovery is without basis
    252–255
  overbroad or unduly
    burdensome 257–259
  specific people cannot be named
    as 30(b)(6) deponents 256
duty to confer 255, 347–349
duty to designate
  about 266–269
  authority to bind 269–271
  multiple designated witnesses
    271–272
duty to move for protective order
  248–252, 255, 328–329, 340

duty to prepare
   about 265–266, 272–274
   all information known or
      reasonably available 275–276
   appearance with inadequate
      or unprepared testimony
      343–347
   documents 279–280
   duty to designate 266–272
   duty to substitute a new witness
      287–289, 344
   electronically stored information
      279–280
   establishing preparation
      organization conducted
      281–283
   failure to provide witness
      340–341
   identifying information sources
      286–287
   privilege waiver 284–287
   Rule 30(b)(1) 36–37, 100, 384
   Rule 30(b)(6) 36–37, 100
   witnesses 272–279, 364–365
duty to substitute a new witness
   287–289, 344
duty to supplement (document set)
   203–204

E
Easterbrook, Frank 329
Ecclesiastes 9:10–11–12, Inc. v. LMC Holding Co. 255
eDiscovery & Digital Evidence treatise 217–218
E.I. du Pont de Nemours & Co. v. Kolon Indus., Inc. 381–382
Einstein, Albert 135
Electronic Communications Privacy Act 239
electronic discovery
   about 209
   discovery rules for tailoring
      requests 212–221
   duty to prepare 279–280
   email testimony 227–234

   identifying incomplete
      e-discovery 236–238
   internal database report
      capabilities 240
   overburdensome by design data
      recovery 235
   overcoming objections 221–226
   producing ESI 212–214
   proving spoliation of 241–242
   requiring witnesses to interpret
      data dumps 238–239
   tailoring requests 212–221
   technological framework
      210–212
email testimony questions
   on archive systems 228
   on creation and storage
      229–230
   on deletion and preservation
      230–231
   on email systems 228
   on format 229
   on retention policy 229
   on search difficulties 234
   on search parameters 232–234
   on search software 231–232
employees, low-level. *See* low-level employees
errata sheet changes
   about 376–377
   basis for 386–389
   list of changes and reasons
      requirement 377–378
   within thirty days requirement
      378–379
error objections 315
ESI (electronically stored information)
   about 209
   discovery rules for tailoring
      requests 212–221
   duty to prepare 279–280
   email testimony 227–234
   identifying incomplete
      e-discovery 236–238
   internal database report
      capabilities 240

overburdensome by design data recovery 235
overcoming objections 221–226
producing 212–214
proving spoliation of 241–242
requiring witnesses to interpret data dumps 238–239
tailoring requests 212–221
technological framework 210–212
Espinosa, Todd I. 304–305
events, interpretation of 152–154
Excel spreadsheets (Microsoft) 213
executives of organizations
alternatives to deposing 110–111
deposing 101–104
establishing depositions are necessary 104–110
ex parte communication
with former employees 123–126
with low-level employees 116–122
expenses and fees
expenses for compelled depositions 349–351
travel expenses 63
expert witness testimony 407–408

F
facts
contentions of 154–160
denials of 154–160
locking down in depositions 20–21
matters of examination 146–147, 154–160
F.D.I.C. v. Horn 242
Federal Judicial Center 175, 211, 217
Federal Practice and Procedure (Wright, Miller, and Marcus) 254, 399
Federal Rule of Civil Procedure entries. *See* entries beginning with Rule

Federal Rules of Evidence
on motions in limine 409
on personal knowledge requirements 394–395
prohibiting types of evidence 321
Rule 613 406–407
Rule 702 407–408
Rule 704(a) 395
Rule 801(d)(2) 86, 402
Feigenson, Neil 11
figuring out your case. *See* building a record
Fleetboston Robertson Stephens, Inc. v. Innovex, Inc. 125–126
foreign object after surgery case 146–147
foreign organizations, deposing 55–56
for if-you-know obstruction technique 317–318
formats (electronic discovery) 213, 229
former officers, directors, and managing agents of organizations, deposing 93–100
form objection 323–325
foundation for document search (matters of inquiry)
1a. Is this the right witness? 185–186
1b. What documents exist? 186–187
1. Do the documents exist? 185–187
2a. Who knows how the documents are created? 188–189
2b. Where are the documents created? 189–190
2c. Are the documents duplicated? 190–191
2d. What is the purpose of the documents? 191
2. What are the systems, processes, and purposes for creation, duplication,

and storage of documents? 187–191
3. What are the document destruction and retention policies? 191–193
4. Where are the documents located? 193–194
5. How are the documents organized, indexed, and filed? 194–195
6a. How did the organization search for the document? 196–200
6b. Were there previous searches for these documents? 197–198
6c. How did you prepare? 198
6. How did the organization search for the documents? 196–200
7. Is the document set complete? 200–201
about 184–185
Frank, Frederick 57
Friedman, Rick 11, 22
Frost, John 161

G
Girard, Daniel C. 304–305
Goldberg v. Raleigh Manufacturers 176
good-faith effort
discovery of new information 366–370
duty to confer 255, 347–349
duty to prepare 274, 287–288, 365
government entities, deposing 48, 54–55
Great Am. Ins. Co. v. Vegas Constr. Co. 344
Greenway v. Int'l Paper Co. 380

H
Hall standards 307–313
Hall v. Clifton Precision 306, 311, 342, 382

harassing witnesses 328–329
Hartford Fire Ins. Co. v. P & H Cattle Co. 143–145
hearsay rules 26, 86, 402
hidden information (ESI) 211–213
Hub v. Sun Valley Co. 398–399

I
Ideal Aerosmith, Inc. v. Acutronic USA, Inc. 237–238
if-you-know obstruction technique 317–318
Ikerd v. Lapworth 399
Illinois, on executive protection 106
immunity (legal defense) 25
impeachment 73, 87
improper foundation objection 322
in camera hearings 409–410
individuals
binding effect of testimony 73
deposing managing agents as 83
designee v. individual depositions 72–76
naming in depositions 36–37, 256
Rule 30(b)(1) on deposing 36–37, 69, 72–75, 347
serving 51
In re Anonymous Member of S. Carolina Bar 305
In re Stratosphere Corp. Sec. Litigation 312–313
institutional knowledge
document requests and 163
duty to attend and 258
duty to prepare and 265, 267, 269, 286–287
Rule 30(b)(6) depositions and 31
trial by ambush and 404–405
instructions not to answer 134, 299–300, 328–329
interpretation of documents (matters of examination) 151–152
interpretation of events (matters of examination) 152–154
interrogatories

depositions versus 381
    identifying witnesses with 272
involuntary representation 130–134
I/P Engine, Inc. v. AOL, Inc. 70
irrelevant claims
    in objections to document
        requests 164, 169
    in objections to notices 255,
        260–261

J
Johnson v. Big Lots Stores, Inc. 209
Johnson v. Cadillac Plastic Group Inc.
    121
Jordan, Michael 291
judicial admission 359
judicial estoppel 408–409
jurors
    beliefs about standards of
        conduct 22
    discounting self-serving evidence
        20
    engaging in the story 24–25
    evaluating liability 22, 24

K
Kerry, John 5
King v. Pratt & Whitney, a Div. of
    United Technologies Corp. 293–
    294, 296, 334
"know nothing" affidavits 104

L
Legal Blame (Feigenson) 11
legal framework
    setting up 19
    using to lock down facts 20–21
letters to opponents (techniques)
    deposition schedule 342–343
    establishing an alternative date
        252
    providing legal authority
        348–349
    refusing to attend deposition
        341
liability, jurors evaluating 22, 24
Lincoln, Abraham 17

Little, F. A. 373
location of depositions
    nonparty 42–45, 64
    officers, directors, and managing
        agents 87–88
    party 61–64
locking down
    facts in depositions 20–21
    opponent's position for trial
        13–14, 20–21
Loops LLC v. Phoenix Trading, Inc. 69
low-level employees
    about 115, 120–122
    communicating with 116–124
    communicating with former
        employees 123–126
    involuntary representation
        130–134
    responsibilities during
        investigation 126–129
    serving subpoenas 84–85

M
Malone, Patrick 11, 22
managing agents of organizations
    about 83–84
    binding effect of testimony
        9–10, 84–87, 100
    determining 85, 88–93
    duty to designate 266–272
    location of depositions 87–88
    rules governing testimony of
        former employees 93–100
    testifying at trial 396
Manual for Complex Litigation 175,
    211, 217
Marcus, Richard L. 254, 399
Marker v. Union Fidelity Life Ins. 359
Massachusetts, on "remember
    nothing" affidavits 103
matters of examination
    about 139, 145–146
    contentions, denials, and
        affirmative defense 154–160
    drafting 182–184
    facts 146–147, 154–160

interpretation of documents 151–152
interpretation of events 152–154
positions, subjective beliefs, and opinions 150–151
sources of information 147–150, 286–287
matters of inquiry (document searches)
  1a. Is this the right witness? 185–186
  1b. What documents exist? 186–187
  1. Do the documents exist? 185–187
  2a. Who knows how the documents are created? 188–189
  2b. Where are the documents created? 189–190
  2c. Are the documents duplicated? 190–191
  2d. What is the purpose of the documents? 191
  2. What are the systems, processes, and purposes for creation, duplication, and storage of documents? 187–191
  3. What are the document destruction and retention policies? 191–193
  4. Where are the documents located? 193–194
  5. How are the documents organized, indexed, and filed? 194–195
  6a. How did the organization search for the document? 196–200
  6b. Were there previous searches for these documents? 197–198
  6c. How did you prepare? 198
  6. How did the organization search for the documents? 196–200
  7. Is the document set complete? 200–201
McNearney v. Washington Dept. of Corrections 237
metadata (hidden information) 211
Microsoft Excel spreadsheets 213
Microsoft PowerPoint presentations 213
Microsoft Word documents 213
Miller, Arthur R. 254, 399
Miller, Phillip 13, 20, 320
Model Rules of Professional Conduct (ABA)
  on communication with employees 116–124
  on communication with former employees 123–126
  on involuntary representation 130–134
  on responsibilities during investigations 126–129
  Rule 1.3 343
  Rule 3.4 303
  Rule 4.1 126–127
  Rule 4.2 116–126, 130–132
  Rule 4.3 127–129
  Rule 7 132–133
motion *in limine* 407–410
motion regarding sufficiency of an answer or objection 362
motion to compel
  adversaries' sequence of depositions 60
  compelling disclosure 339
  duty to confer and 347–349
  expenses for compelled depositions 349–351
  writing briefs for 13
motion to exclude different testimony 339–340
motion to quash 45–47, 101–104
motive, establishing 24–26
multiple designated witnesses 271–272

multiple witnesses for single notice 65–68

N

naming individuals in depositions 36–37, 256
necessity of deposition 102–110
Network Tallahassee, Inc. v. Embarq Corp. 164, 170–171
neutralizing defenses 25–27
New York, on executive protection 107
Ngai v. Old Navy 311–312
no duty (legal defense) 25
noncorporate organizations, deposing 48–53
nonparty organizations
    document requests and 181
    location of depositions 42–45, 64
    objections to nonparty subpoenas 45–48
    serving subpoenas on 32–33, 37–41
    testifying at trial 394–395, 401–404
notices (deposition)
    about 32–33, 137
    crafting 11–12
    deciding on method of discovery 156–159, 252–255
    duty to appear 247–261
    issuing 35–36, 38
    matters of examination for 139, 145–157
    multiple notices 68–72
    multiple witnesses for single notice 65–68
    naming individuals in 36–37, 256
    objections to 247–248, 255
    painstaking specificity standard 137–142
    qualifiers in 142–145
    reasonable particularity standard 137–142, 256
    serving 12

O

objections as obstruction tactics
    about 314
    asked and answered 320–321
    attorney's lack of understanding 319
    building a record of 327
    excessive number of objections 326
    form of the question 323–325
    improper foundation 322
    instructing witness to answer "if you know" 317–318
    instructions not to answer 328–329
    overbroad 322
    reinterpreting or rephrasing the examiner's questions 319
    relevance 321–322
    scope of inquiry 293–300
    speaking objections 315–317, 325
    speculation 320
    type and manner of objections 314–315
    vague 325
objections to deposition notices. *See* duty to attend; *See* duty to prepare
objections to document requests
    about 166
    boilerplate language 163–164, 168–169, 169, 202
    examples of 164
    must respond within thirty days 166–167, 180
    preempting improper objections 179, 202–203
    stating objections with particularity 167
    "subject to and without waiving" phrase 170–172
    waiving all objections 168
    waiving untimely objections 167–168
objections to electronic discovery 221–226

objections to nonparty subpoenas
    about 45–48
    filing within fourteen-day
        window 46
    subpoenas for documents and
        testimony are separate 47
objections to scope of inquiry
    293–300
obstruction tactics (depositions)
    about 303–305
    appearance with inadequate
        or unprepared testimony
        343–347
    bandying 34, 268, 360, 385
    conferring with witnesses during
        depositions 309–314
    delay tactics 342–343
    documenting 333–334
    failure to comply with order for
        disclosure 352–356
    failure to provide witness
        340–341
    Hall standards 307–309
    improper objections and
        prohibited behavior 314–329
    prohibited nature of 305–309
    sanctions for deposition
        misconduct 329–333
    scope of inquiry and 293–300
officers of organizations
    binding effect of testimony
        9–10, 33, 84–87, 100
    duty to designate 266–272
    location of depositions 87–88
    rules governing testimony of
        former employees 93–100
    testifying at trial 396
opinions (matters of examination)
    150–151
oral examinations of witnesses
    254–255
organizations, deposing. *See* deposing
    organizations
overbroad claims
    in deposition obstruction 322
    in objections to document
        requests 164
    in objections to notices 142–
        145, 159, 255, 257–259
overburdensome claims
    in document depositions 194
    in electronic discovery 222,
        224, 234–235
    in objections to document
        requests 168
    in objection to notices 159,
        255, 257–259
"Overcoming Jury Bias" (Cusimano
    and Wenner) 313

P

painstaking specificity standard
    (notices) 137–142
*Paparelli v. Prudential Ins. Co. of
    America* 296
partnerships, service rule for 50–51
person represented by counsel,
    communication with 116–122
*Phillip M. Adams & Associates, LLC
    v. Winbond Electronics Corp.*
    398–399
*Pioneer Drive LLC v. Nissan Diesel
    America, Inc.* 78–79, 354–355
positions (matters of examination)
    150–151
possession, defined 172–173
PowerPoint presentations (Microsoft)
    213
.ppt format 213
.pptx format 213
preempting improper objections
    179, 202–203
preparing for 30(b)(6) depositions
    about 19
    establishing motive 24–26
    establishing standards of conduct
        22–23
    figuring out your case 11–14
    locking down facts 20–21
    neutralizing defenses 25–27
    setting up legal framework 19
    suggested resources 11, 13, 20
privilege waiver 284–287

Professional Conduct (ABA Model
    Rules)
  on communication with
      employees 116–124
  on communication with former
      employees 123–126
  on involuntary representation
      130–134
  on responsibilities during
      investigations 126–129
  Rule 1.3 343
  Rule 3.4 303
  Rule 4.1 126–127
  Rule 4.2 116–126, 130–132
  Rule 4.3 127–129
  Rule 7 132–133
protective order, duty to move for
    248–252, 255, 328–329, 340
.pst format 213
punch-in/punch-out time clock
    systems 148–149, 240
Pynchon, Thomas 263

Q
*QBE Ins. Corp. v. Jorda Enterprises,
    Inc.* 267, 269, 363
qualifiers in deposition notices
    142–145
*Quality Aero Technology v. Telemetric
    Elektronic* 68

R
*Rainey v. American Forest and Paper
    Ass'n, Inc.* 360–361, 384, 410
Rambo litigators 303
reasonable particularity standard
    crafting deposition notices 137–
      142, 256, 265
    duty to prepare 265, 275–276
recess conferences 308, 310–311
records custodian depositions 181
Redwood v. Dobson 328–329
reinterpreting examiner's questions
    319
relevance objection 321–322
relevant discovery 214, 260
"remember nothing" affidavits 104

rephrasing examiner's questions 319
residual data (hidden information)
    212
responsibilities of organizations
  duty to attend 247–261
  duty to prepare 265–290
  understanding 13–14
Restatement (Third) of Law
    Governing Lawyers 122
retention policies
  document depositions on
      191–193
  electronic discovery on 229
*Rice's Toyota World, Inc. v. Southeast
    Toyota Distributors, Inc.* 76–77
Roach, Hal, Sr. 29
Ruiz-Bueno v. Scott 177–178, 218,
    237
Rule 4 50–51
Rule 4(e) 51
Rule 4(h) 50
Rule 11 118
Rule 16(b) 215
Rule 26
  about 212
  on boilerplate objections 222
  on ESI retrieval costs 214–217
  executive protection and 105–
      106, 108–109
  on incomplete electronic
      discovery 236
  on organization's claims and
      defenses 154
Rule 26(a) 204, 339–340
Rule 26(a)(1) 215
Rule 26(a)(1)(B) 215
Rule 26(b) 260, 322
Rule 26(b)(1)
  on discovery on discovery 177
  on incomplete electronic
      discovery 236
  on relevant discovery 214, 260
  on requests for admission 362
  on sources of information
      147–148
Rule 26(b)(5) 284
Rule 26(c) 101, 249–250

Rule 26(c)(1) 105
Rule 26(c)(2) 61, 87–88
Rule 26(d) 59–60
Rule 26(e) 340
Rule 26(e)(1) 204
Rule 26(f) 215–217, 221, 352
Rule 26(f)(3)(C) 215
Rule 28(a) 79
Rule 28(c) 79
Rule 30 380–381, 386
Rule 30(a)(1) 61
Rule 30(a)(2)(A)(i) 9, 65, 68
Rule 30(a)(2)(A)(ii) 69
Rule 30(b)(1)
   binding effect of testimony 9–10, 33, 84–87, 100, 254–255
   deposing directors 93–100
   deposing individuals 36–37, 69, 72–75, 347
   deposing low-level employees 130
   deposing managing agents 84–100
   deposing officers 33, 93–100
   duty to prepare 36–37, 100, 384
   identifying management agents 88–93
   identifying witnesses by description 267–268
   records custodian depositions 181
   rules governing testimony of former employees 93–100
Rule 30(b)(2)
   about 40
   challenges accompanying document requests and 175–179
   duty to supplement and 203–204
   getting complete responses to document requests 164–166
   objections to document requests 166–172
   preempting improper objections 202–203
   producing documents on time 180–181
Rule 30(b)(3)(A) 76
Rule 30(b)(6)
   about 31, 59
   actual rule 32–33
   benefiting both sides 33–36
   binding-effect doctrine and 359–371
   building a record 20
   cannot name individuals 36–37, 256
   changing testimony and 375–379, 383–389
   crafting notices 137–160
   cut-to-the-chase policy 34
   deposing noncorporate organizations 48–53
   deposing nonparty organizations 32–33, 37–40
   deposing officers, directors, and managing agents 85–86, 100–101, 110–111
   deposition time limitations, calculations of 66–67, 75
   designee v. individual depositions 72–76
   discovery plan and 33
   document deposition goals 181–182
   document requests, challenges accompanying 175–179
   duty to attend 247–261
   duty to prepare 36–37, 100–101, 265–290
   duty to supplement and 203–204
   electronic discovery and 209, 217–242
   foundation concerning document search 184–201
   getting complete responses to document requests 164–166
   issuing subpoenas 41

location of nonparty depositions 42–45, 64
location of party depositions 61–64
matters of examination 182–184
motions to compel and sanctions 339–355
multiple notices 68–72
multiple witnesses for single notice 65–68
objections to document requests 166–172
objections to nonparty subpoenas 45–48
preempting improper objections 202–203
producing documents on time 180–181
scope of inquiry 293–300
sequence of depositions 59–60
step 1: figuring out your case 11
step 2: crafting 30(b)(6) notice 11–12
step 3: serving 30(b)(6) notice and starting maneuvering 12
step 4: taking the deposition 12–13
step 5: writing a brief 13
step 6: deposing again and locking down 13–14
step 7: blocking attempts to alter testimony 14
step 8: using 30(b)(6) testimony in summary judgments or trial 14
testimony at trial 393–410
video depositions 76–79
Rule 30(c)(2) 314–315, 328
Rule 30(d) 308
Rule 30(d)(1) 66–67, 299
Rule 30(d)(2) 329–332
Rule 30(d)(3) 328
Rule 30(d)(3)(A) 328
Rule 30(e) 378–382
Rule 30(e)(1) 376–377
Rule 30(e)(1)(B) 377, 383

Rule 31(a)(4) 86, 248, 341, 352
Rule 32(a) 33, 403
Rule 32(a)(3) 86–87, 396, 402
Rule 32(a)(4) 403
Rule 32(d) 314
Rule 32(d)(3) 323
Rule 32(d)(3)(A) 314
Rule 32(d)(3)(B) 307
Rule 32(d)(3)(B)(i) 315
Rule 33(b)(4) 167–168
Rule 34
   about 163
   challenges accompanying document requests and 175–179
   defining possession, custody, and control 172–174
   determining whom to depose 181–184
   duty to supplement and 203–204
   electronic discovery and 212–213
   getting complete responses to requests 164–166
   goals of document deposition 175–179
   objections to document requests 166–172
   organizing produced documents 174–175
   preempting improper objections 202–203
   problems with document requests 163–165
   producing documents on time 180–181
Rule 34(a)(1) 172–173
Rule 34(b)(1)(C) 213
Rule 34(b)(2)(A) 166–167
Rule 34(b)(2)(E) 212–214
Rule 34(b)(2)(E)(i) 174
Rule 35 352
Rule 36 362
Rule 36(a)(6) 362
Rule 37
   to compel disclosure 339

duty to attend 248, 340
duty to confer 347
duty to prepare 288, 340
sanctions for deposition misconduct and 304, 333–334
Rule 37(a) 352
Rule 37(a)(1) 344, 347
Rule 37(a)(3)(A) 339
Rule 37(a)(4) 343, 363
Rule 37(a)(5)(A) 349–350
Rule 37(b) 355
Rule 37(b)(2)(A) 352
Rule 37(b)(2)(C) 353
Rule 37(c)(1) 204, 339
Rule 37(c)(2) 362
Rule 37(d) 10, 251
Rule 37(d)(1)(A) 249, 364
Rule 37(d)(1)(A)(i) 248, 340, 344
Rule 37(d)(2) 248–250, 341
Rule 37(e) 241
Rule 45 88, 130
Rule 45(a)(1)(A)(iii) 181
Rule 45(a)(2) 41
Rule 45(b) 49–50
Rule 45(b)(2) 401
Rule 45(c) 42–44
Rule 45(c)(1)(a) 43–44
Rule 45(c)(1)(B)(ii) 44
Rule 45(c)(3)(A) 400–401
Rule 45(c)(3)(A)(ii) 401
Rule 45(c)(3)(B)(iii) 401
Rule 45(d)(2)(B) 46
Rule 45(d)(3) 43, 45
Rule 45(d)(3)(A)(ii) 43
Rules of the Road (Friedman and Malone) 11, 22
Runge v. Stanley Fastening Sys., L.P. 398–399

S

S2 Automation LLC v. Micron Technology, Inc. 178
sanctions
 for appearance with inadequate or unprepared testimony 343–347
 to compel disclosure 339
 for deposition misconduct 305–306, 329–333
 for excessive number of objections 326–327
 for failure to attend deposition 248, 251
 for failure to comply with order for disclosure 352–356
 for failure to designate witness 74, 266, 269
 for failure to disclose information and supplement disclosures 204
 for failure to prepare 200, 288, 364–365
 for failure to provide a witness 340–341
 grounds for 248, 251, 341
 for if-you-know technique 317–318
 for instructions not to answer 299–300, 328
 for involuntary representation 133
 for spoliation of ESI 241–242
Sara Lee Corp. v. Kraft Foods Inc. 395, 404–406
schedule, deposition 342–343
Scheindlin, Shira Ann 163
Sciarretta v. Lincoln Nat. Ins. Co. 353–354
scope of inquiry
 about 293
 instructions not to answer 299–300
 limiting is not allowed 294–297
 objections to 298
Scoptur, Paul 13, 20, 320
search software (electronic discovery) 231–234
Sec. Ins. Co. of Hartford v. Trustmark Ins. Co. 159
Sec. Nat. Bank of Sioux City, Iowa v. Abbott Labs 326, 331–332
sequence of depositions 59–60

service rule for subpoenas.
    See subpoenas
Sham Affidavit Rule 312, 375–376, 381–384
sham fact issue 375
sources of information (matters of examination) 147–150, 286–287
speaking objections 315–317, 325
speculation objection 320
Spieker v. Quest Cherokee, LLC 223
spoliation of electronic discovery 241–242
standards of conduct 22–23
Starbucks Corp. v. ADT Sec. Servs., Inc. 235
state courts
    deposing organizations in 10
    procedures for serving subpoenas 52–54
storage questions
    for document depositions 187–191
    for electronic discovery 229–230
subjective beliefs (matters of examination) 150–151
"subject to and without waiving" objection 170–172
subpoena duces tecum 40, 46–47
subpoenas
    about 32–33
    delivery of 50–51
    including requirements in 39–41
    issued by presiding court 41
    low-level employees 84–85
    objections to nonparty 45–48
    producing documents 40
    serving corporations, partnerships, or associations 50–51
    serving individuals 51
    serving nonparty organizations 32–33, 37–41
    serving party organizations 400–402

state service of process rules 52–54
testifying at trial and 393
substantive changes to testimony 381–386
substantive errors 381–382
substantive objections 314–315
summary judgments
    no factual basis for claims and 19
    sham fact issue and 375
    using 30(b)(6) testimony in 14
superseding cause (legal defense) 25
surveillance videos 140–142
system data (hidden information) 211

T
techniques
    asking about testimony changes 387–389
    asking opponent to provide legal authority 348–349
    building record of discussions during breaks 313–314
    building record of obstructive objections 327
    building record of unprepared witness 345–346
    convert positions to requests for admission 361–363
    dealing with clarification questions 318
    designing 30(b)(6) contention notice 155
    documenting deposition obstruction 333–334
    drafting matters of examination 182–183
    email retrieval 225–226
    establishing an alternative date 252
    establishing if witness has authority to testify 270–271
    establishing involuntary representation 133–134

establishing record of inadequate preparation 289
establishing that communication is voluntary 128–129
establishing whether the witness is prepared 280
establishing witness's status 96–99
expenses and fees 350–351
exploring punch-in/punch-out time clock systems 240
foreign object after surgery case 146–147
identifying information sources 286–287
identifying witnesses with an interrogatory 272
includes requirements in the subpoena 39
issuing a 30(b)(6) notice 35
letter to opponent about deposition schedule 342–343
letter to opponent about refusing to attend 341
looking for key pieces of information about documents in your list 184–185
making record of instructions not to answer 300
new evidence 367–370
stopping abusive depositions 329
technological framework (ESI)
 about 210
 hidden information 210–212
 principal sources of devices generating and storing ESI 210–211
Terra Inter., Inc. v. Mississippi Chemical Corp. 132
testimony at trial
 about 14, 393–394
 attempts to change the story at trial 404–408
 motion in limine and 407–410
 trial by ambush and 404–410

witnesses testifies vicariously for organization 394–404
testimony, changing. *See* changing testimony
text messages, attorney-client privilege and 311
30(b)(6) notices. *See* notices (deposition)
30(b)(6) subpoenas. *See* subpoenas
time clock systems 148–149, 240
time limitations for depositions, calculation of 66–67, 75
Torres, Edwin G. 301
transcript corrections, permissible changes
 about 380
 clerical errors only 380–381
 contradictions and substantive alterations 385–386
 explainable substantive changes 381–385
 liberal rule 385–386
 moderate rule 381–385
 strict rule 380–381
travel expenses 63
trial by ambush
 binding effect and 360, 365
 changing the testimony and 385
 duty to prepare and 275, 278
 testimony at trial and 394, 404–410
Twelve Heroes, One Voice (Bettinger) 11

U

unavailable information versus unprepared witnesses 365–370
unavailable witness 396, 403
United States Code - Title 28 353
United States Supreme Court 330–331
United States v. Taylor 150, 258, 361

V

vague objection 325
video depositions 76–79, 393

W

Washington, state service of process rules 53
Welles, Orson 357
Wenner, David 313
Westley v. Oclaro, Inc. 218–219
Wilson v. Lakner 158, 259, 285, 407
witnesses. *See also* matters of inquiry (document search)
   appearance with inadequate or unprepared testimony 343–347
   attempting to change story at trial 393–408
   binding effect of testimony 363–370
   conferring with, during depositions 309–314
   dealing with clarification questions 318
   designee v. individual depositions 72–76
   document production 165–166, 182–183
   do not have information 363–370
   duty to designate 266–272
   duty to prepare 265–266, 272–279, 364–365
   duty to substitute a new witness 287–289, 344
   establishing authority to testify 270–271
   establishing facts through adversaries' 20
   establishing preparedness of 280
   establishing record of inadequate preparation 289
   establishing status of 96–99
   failure to provide 340–341
   Hall standards 307–309
   harassing 328–329
   identifying as managing agents 88–93
   identifying by description 267–268
   identifying early in litigation 9
   identifying information sources 286–287
   identifying with interrogatory 272
   instructing to answer "if you know" 317–318
   instructions not to answer 134, 299–300, 328–329
   interpreting data dumps 238–239
   multiple designated witnesses 271–272
   multiple witnesses for single notice 65–68
   oral examinations of 254–255
   recess conferences and 308, 310–311
   scope of inquiry objections 293–300
   testifying at trial 393–408
   unavailable 396, 403
   unavailable information versus unprepared witness 363–370
Word documents (Microsoft) 213
work product
   crafting deposition notices 155
   facts not subject to protection 158, 285
   privilege waiver and 284–285
   waiving all objections 168
Wright, Charles Alan 254, 399
Wyeth v. Lupin Ltd. 383

X

.xls format 213
.xlsx format 213

Z

Zubulake v. UBS Warburg 163

About the Author

Mark Kosieradzki, of the Kosieradzki Smith law firm in Minneapolis, Minnesota, is recognized in Best Lawyers in America. The National Board of Trial Advocacy and the Minnesota State Bar Association certified Mark as a civil trial specialist, and he is a past president of both the Minnesota Association for Justice and the Minnesota Chapter of the American Board of Trial Advocates (ABOTA).

Mark has joined trial teams throughout the United States, assisting them with all aspects of the 30(b)(6) depositions in their cases. As a diplomat in the National College of Advocacy, Mark is recognized as one of the country's leading authorities on the use of 30(b)(6) depositions. He has lectured in thirty-four states and three countries. His experience covers a wide variety of wrongful death and catastrophic injury cases, including malpractice, construction injuries, nursing home abuse, interstate trucking accidents, and products liability.

Mark is the creator of the American Association for Justice's deposition DVD, *Deposing the Corporate Representative: 30(b)(6)*, and Trial Guides's *Using 30(b)(b) to Win Your Case*. Mark's work with 30(b)(6) depositions is also featured in Trial Guides's DVD series, *Rules of the Road: Roadmap to a Winning System*.

When Mark turned fifty, he had a midlife crisis and started playing the blues harmonica.